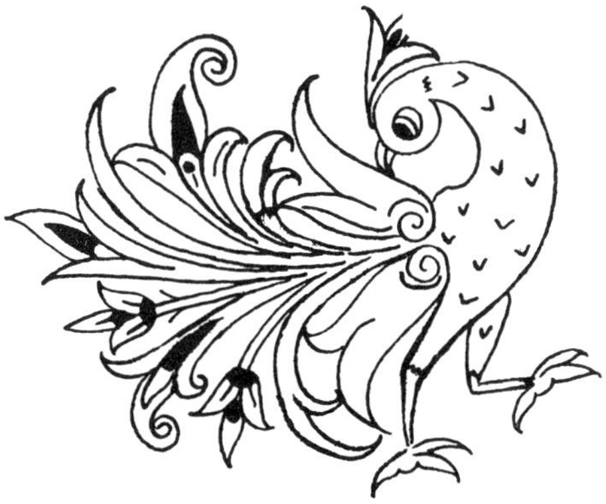

# 1000 DECORATIVE DESIGNS FROM INDIA

DEVI THAPA, KIRAN CHAUDHRI,
AND V. S. NAVALKAR

DOVER PUBLICATIONS, INC.
MINEOLA, NEW YORK

*Bibliographical Note*

This Dover edition, first published in 2007, is a new selection of 124 plates from *Decorative Designs and Craftsmanship of India,* originally published by D. B. Taraporevala Sons & Co., Bombay, in 1968.

DOVER *Pictorial Archive* SERIES



*Library of Congress Cataloging-in-Publication Data*

Bhavnani, Enakshi.
[Decorative designs and craftsmanship of India. Selections]
1000 decorative designs from India / [drawings by] Devi Thapa, Kiran Chaudhri, and V. S. Navalkar.
p. cm. — (Dover pictorial archive series)
Originally published: Decorative designs and craftsmanship of India. Bombay : D. B. Taraporevala Sons & Co., 1968.
ISBN-13: 978-0-486-46040-6
ISBN-10: 0-486-46040-1
1. Decoration and ornament—India. 2. Decorative arts—India. 3. Pattern books. I. Thapa, Devi. II. Chaudhri, Kiran. III. Navalkar, V. S. IV. Title. V. Title: One thousand decorative designs from India.

NK1476.B452 2007
745.40954—dc22

2007016080

Manufactured in the United States of America
Dover Publications, Inc., 31 East 2nd Street, Mineola, N.Y. 11501

# Contents

# Plate 1

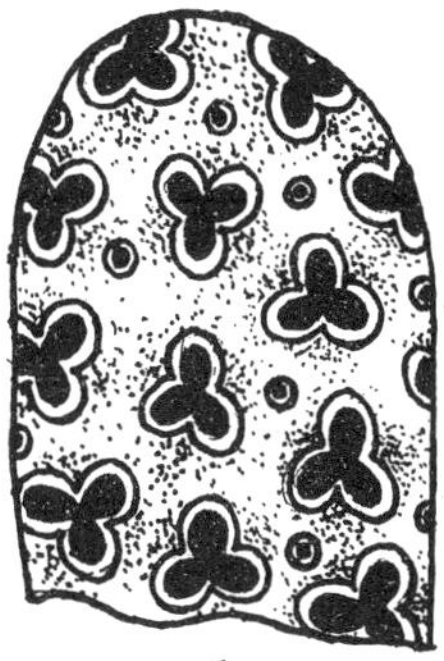

1

2

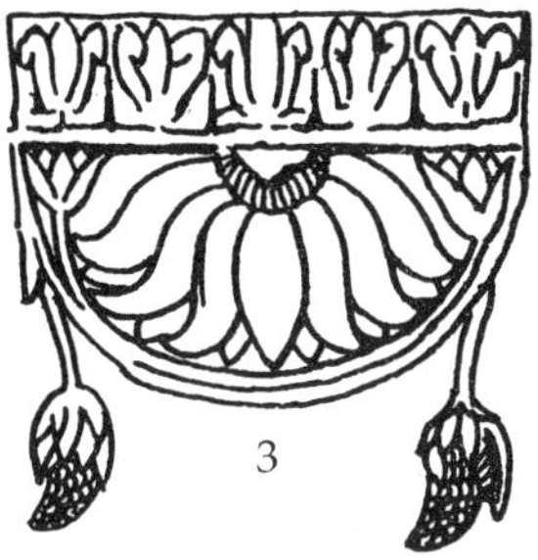

3

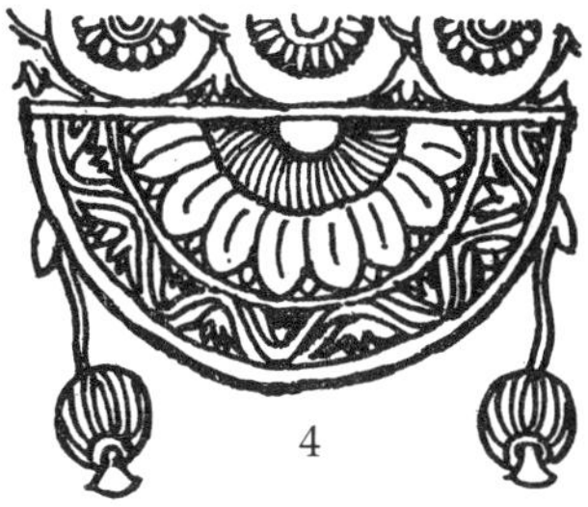

4

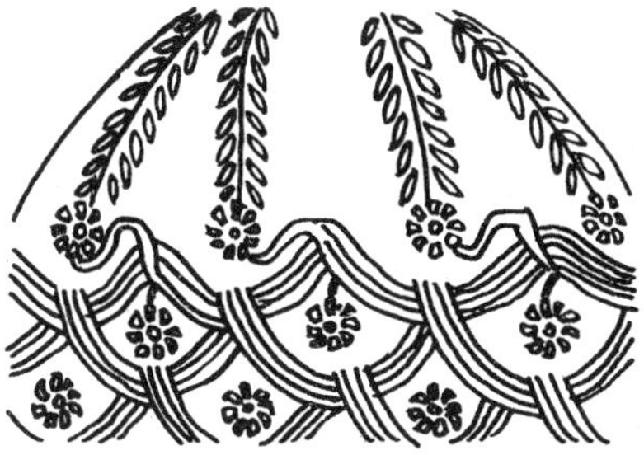

5

6

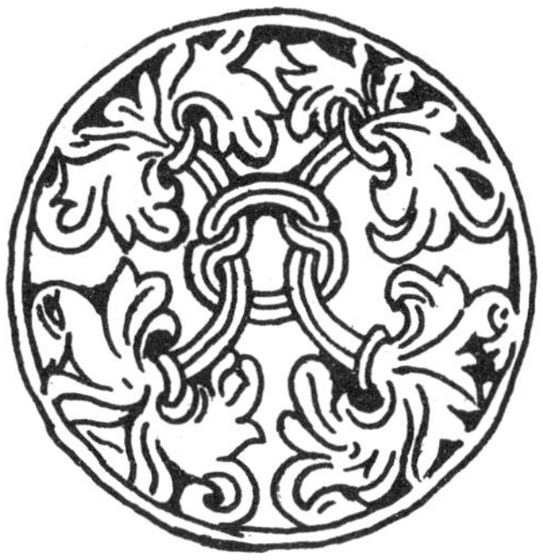

7

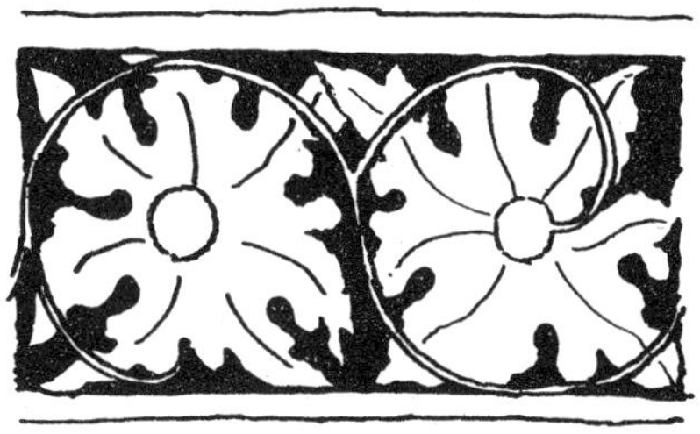

8

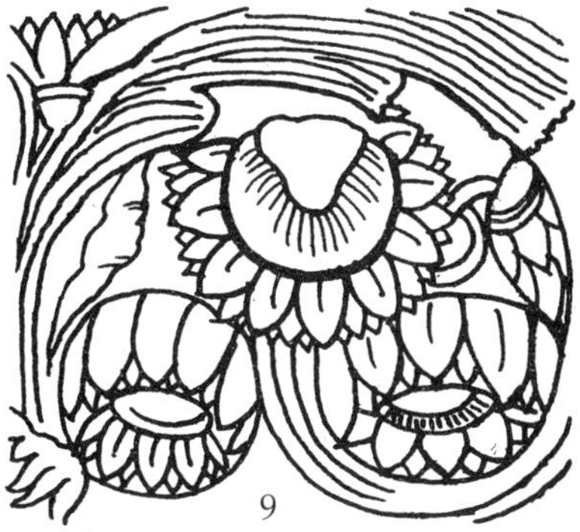

9

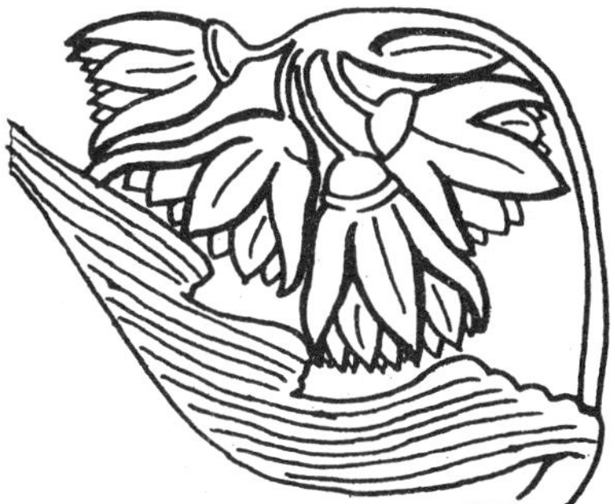

10

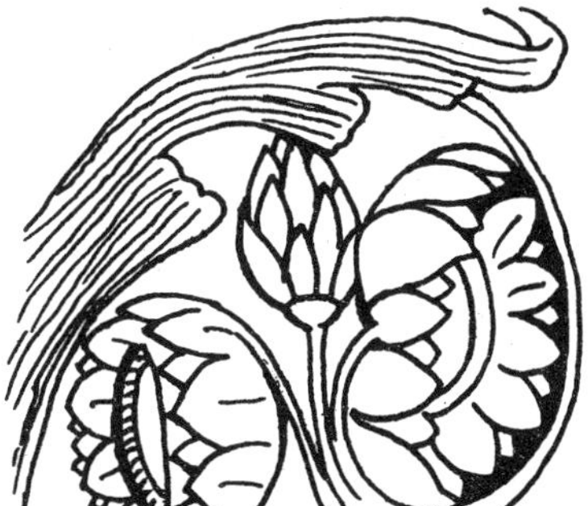

11

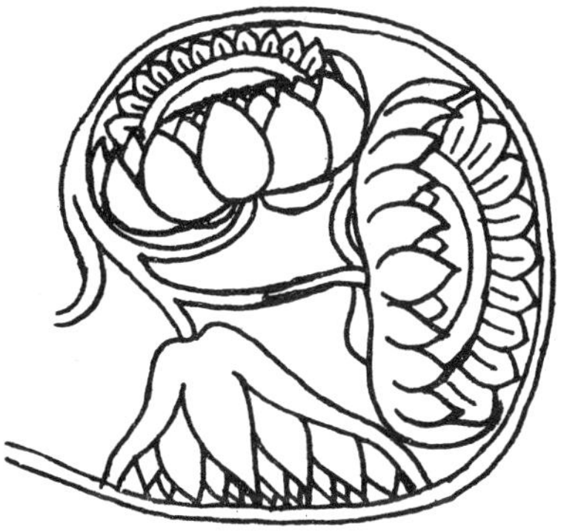

12

STONE SCULPTURE. **1.** Trefoil patterned garment worn by bearded figure from Mohenjo-Daro, 2500–1500 B.C. **2.** Floral frieze on section of Bull capital pillar Rampurva, 3rd century B.C. **3, 4.** Carvings with lotus motifs above Yakshi (Tree goddesses) figures in Bharhut, c. 150 B.C., Sunga period. **5.** Floral decoration on Stupa in Bharhut, c. 150 B.C., Sunga period. **6.** Lotus and honeysuckle on Stupa No. 1. Sanchi, 1st century B.C. **7.** Foliated entwined stems from Jain Stupa, Mathura, late 1st century B.C.—1st century A.D. **8.** Carved panel of Basel leaves, Amaravati, 1st century B.C., Satavahana period. **9–12.** Lotus forms, Amaravati, 1st century B.C., Satavahana period.

# Plate 2

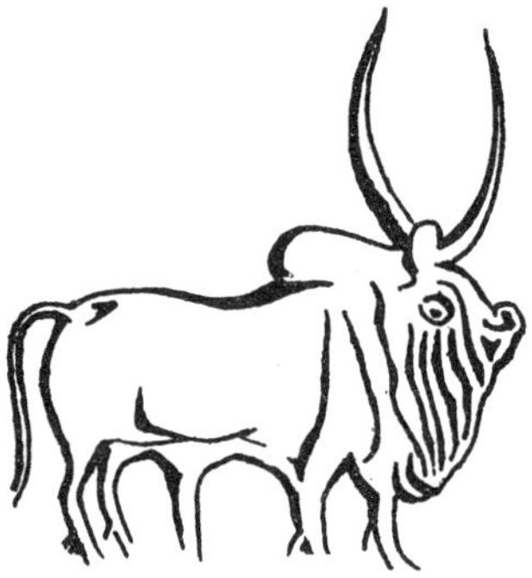
13

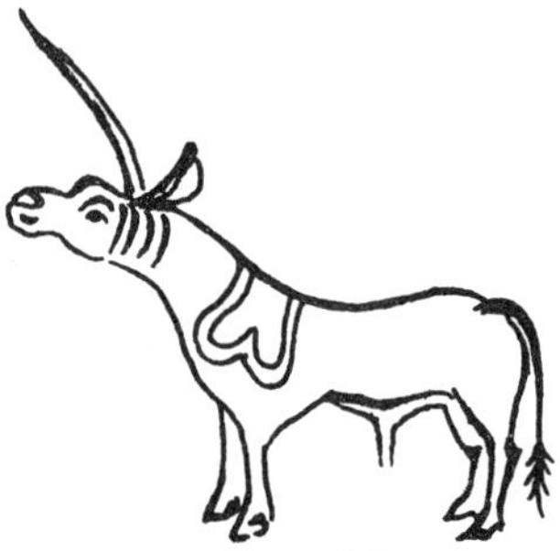
14

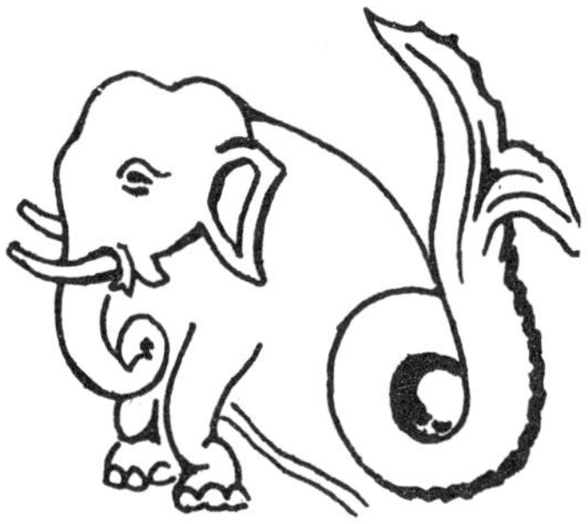
15

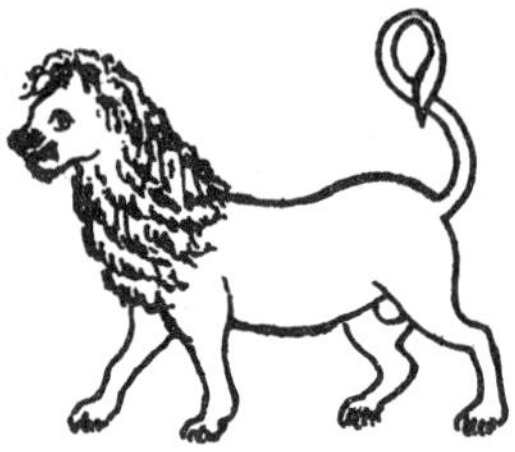
16

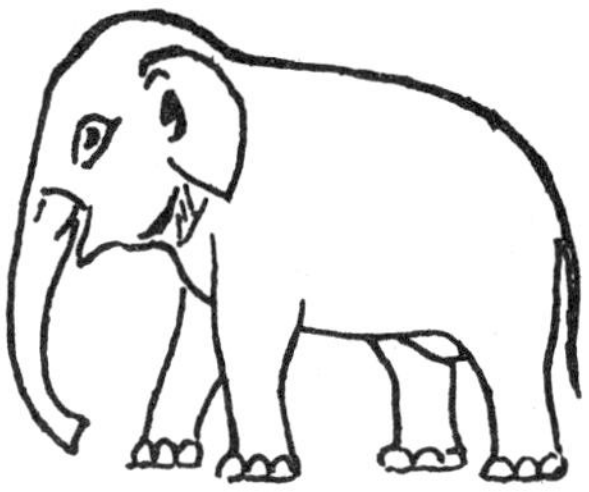
17

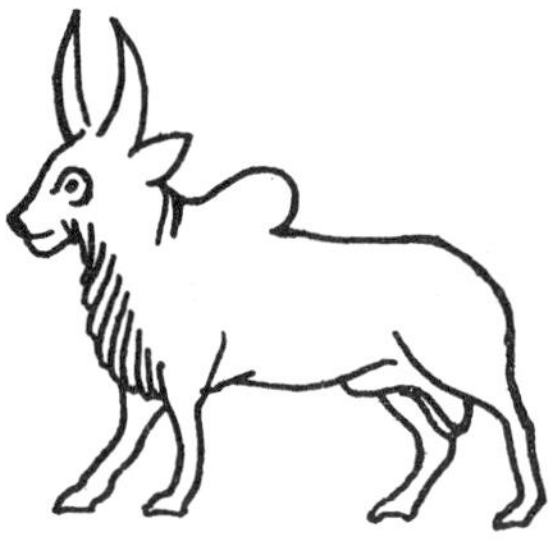
18

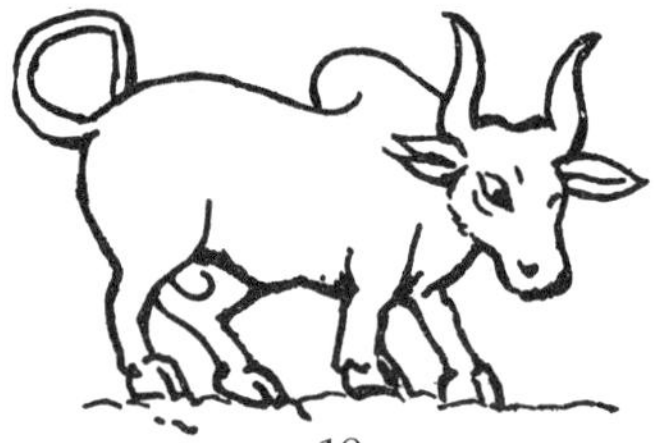
19

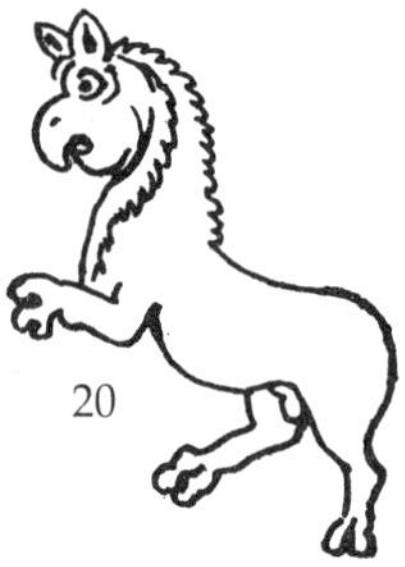
20

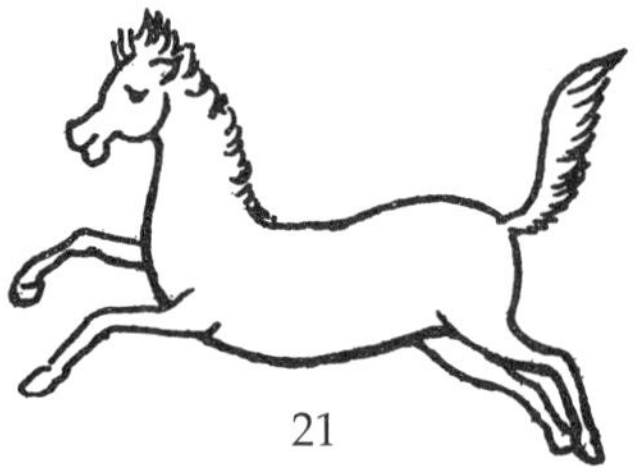
21

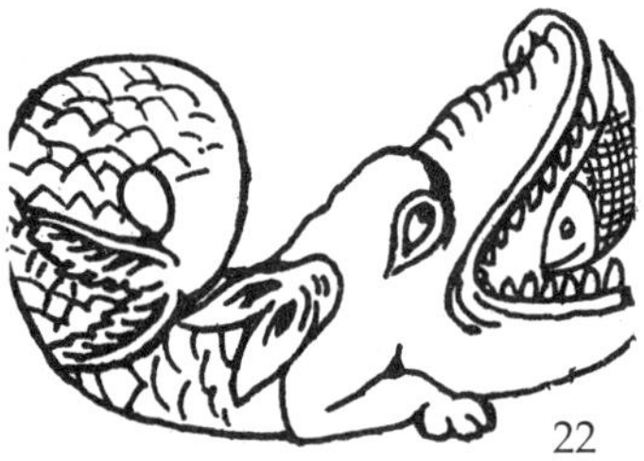
22

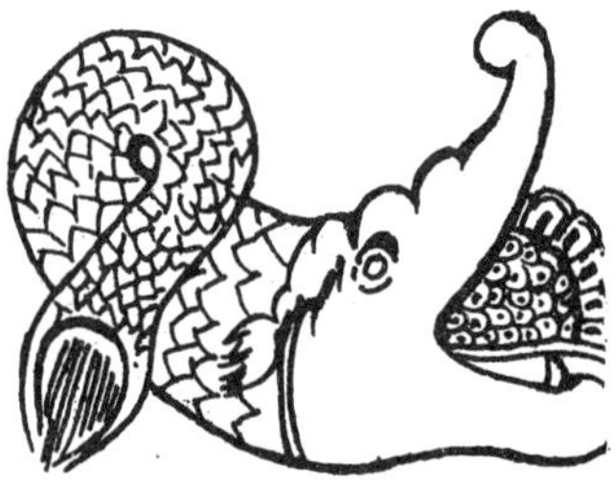
23

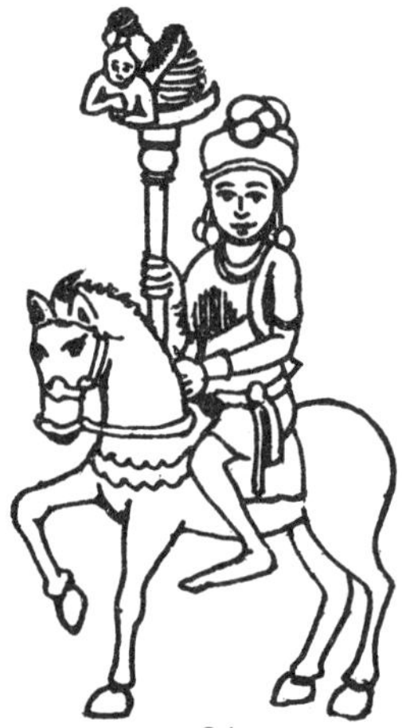
24

STONE SCULPTURE. **13.** Bull on seal, Mohenjo-Daro, 2500–1500 B.C. **14.** Mythological horned animal on seal, Lothal, Saurashtra, 2500–1500 B.C. **15, 19.** Fish-tailed elephant and bull, Jain Stupa, Mathura, 1st century B.C.—1st century A.D. **16, 17, 18, 21.** Lion, elephant, bull and horse motifs from abacus of Sarnath pillar, 3rd century B.C., Mauryan period. **20.** Mythological animal, Stupa No. 1, Sanchi, 1st century B.C. **22.** Crocodile (Makara) and fish, Mathura, 1st century B.C.—1st century A.D. **23.** Crocodile (Makara) and lotus, Amaravati, 1st century B.C. **24.** Figure on horse, inner side of Eastern gateway, Bharhut, c. 150 B.C.

# Plate 3

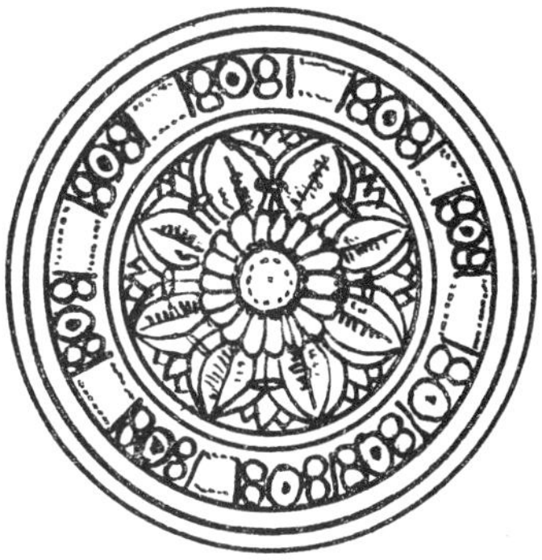

25

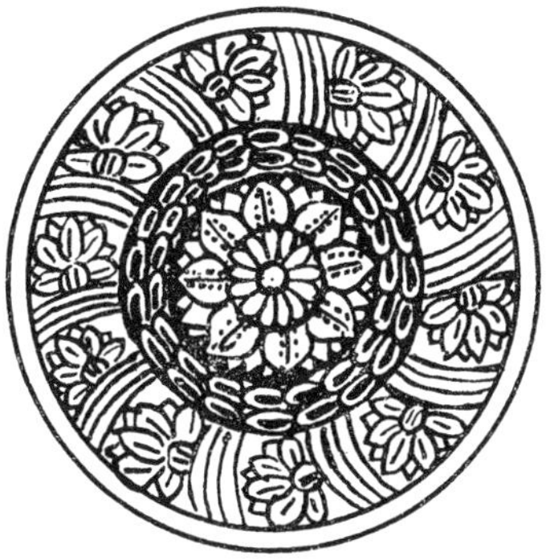

26

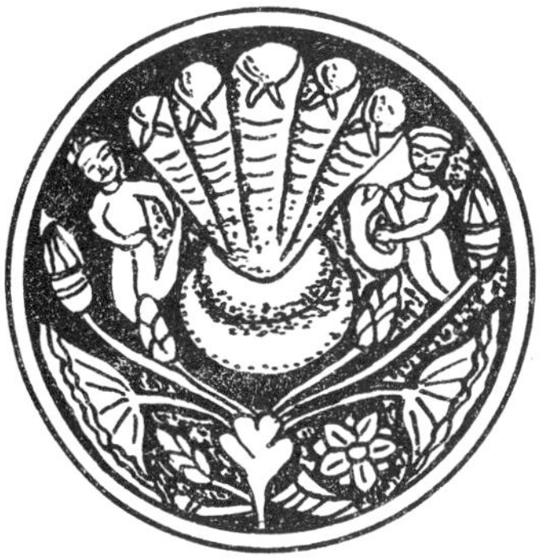

27

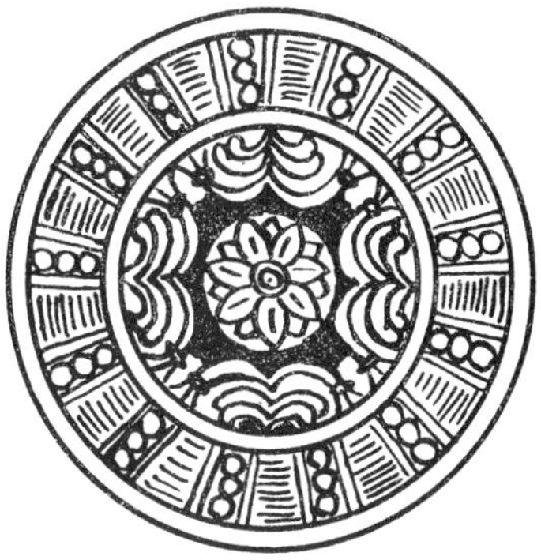

28

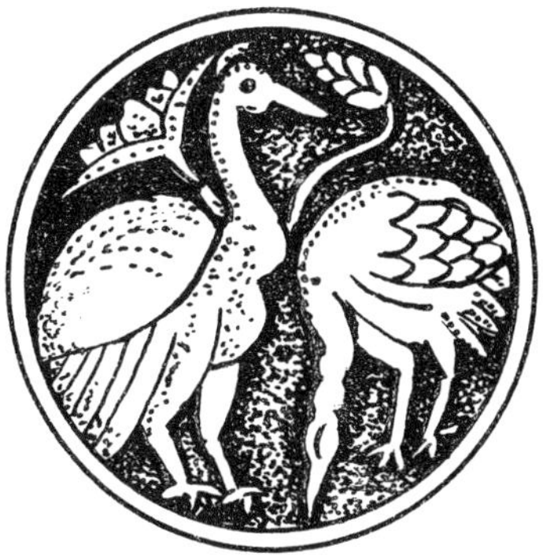

29

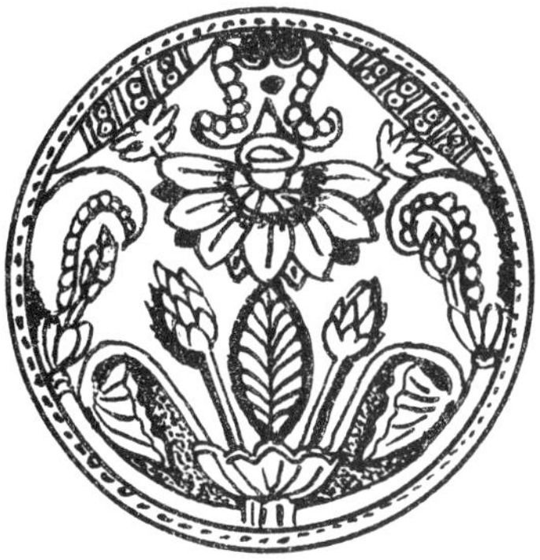

30

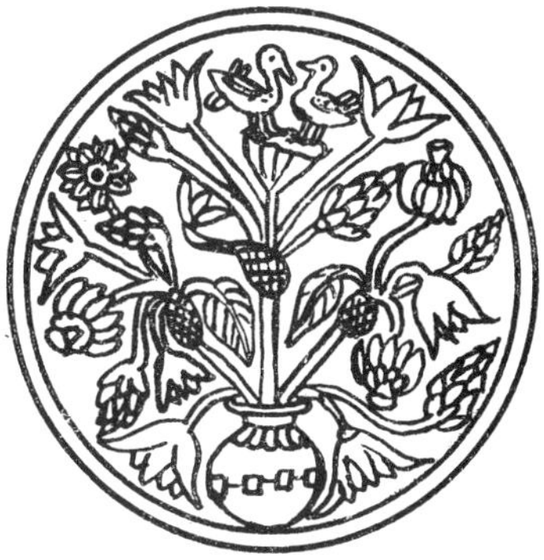

31

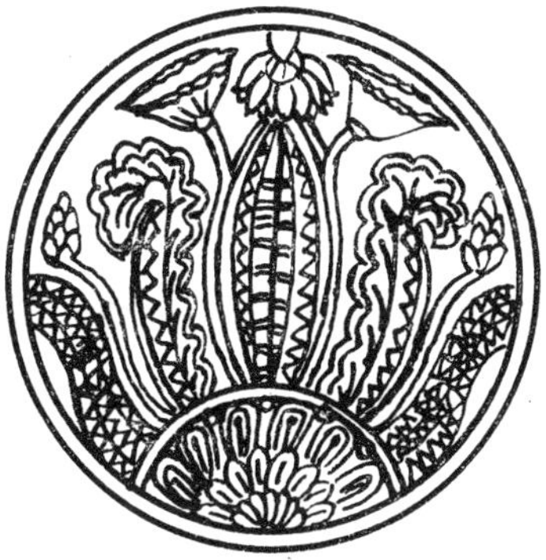

32

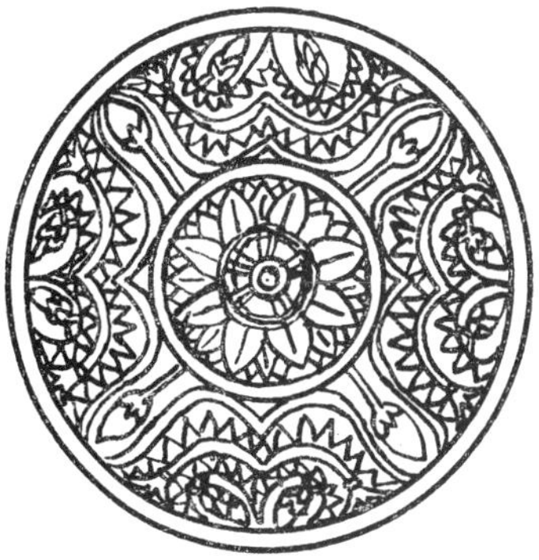

33

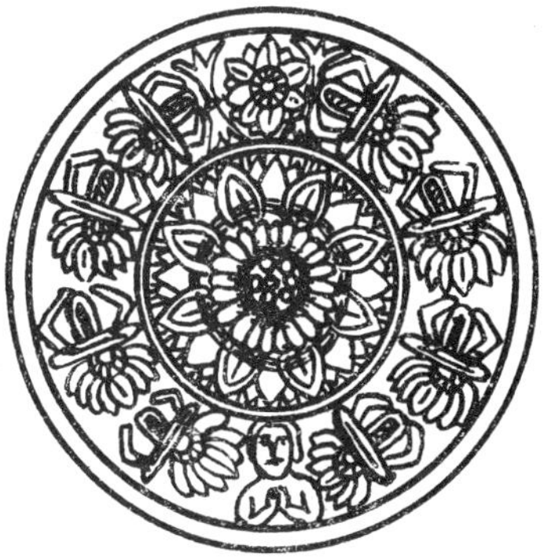

34

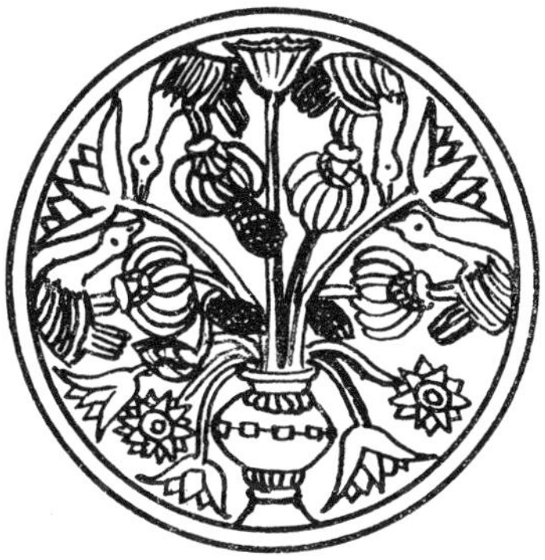

35

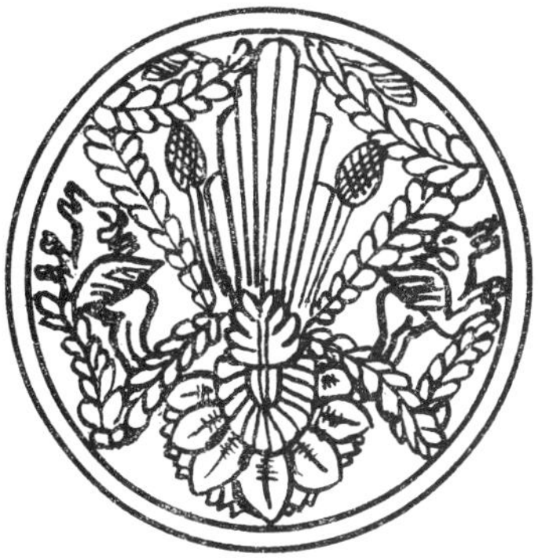

36

STONE SCULPTURE. **25, 28.** Rosettes. **26.** Flower encircled rosette. **27.** Serpent and worshippers in lotus lake. **29.** Geese. **30.** Lotus with sacred symbol, Medallions from Sanchi and Amaravati, 1st century B.C.—1st century A.D. **31, 35.** Lotuses in bowl of Good Fortune with birds. **32.** Lotus and buds. **33.** Rosette with lotus buds. **34.** Rosette and Lotus forms. **36.** Honeysuckle and lotus. Medallions from Bharhut, 2nd century B.C.

# Plate 4

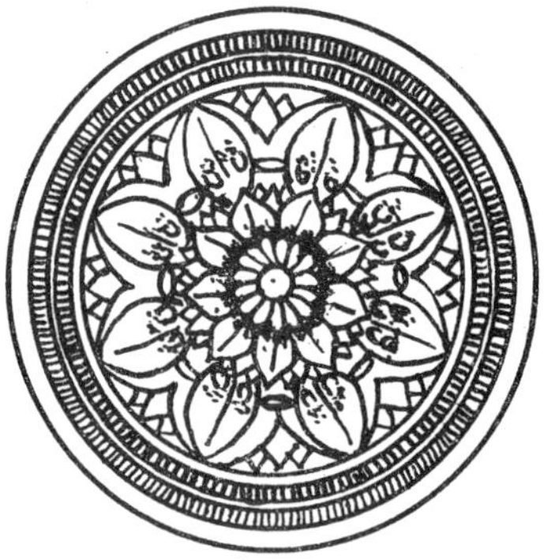
37

38

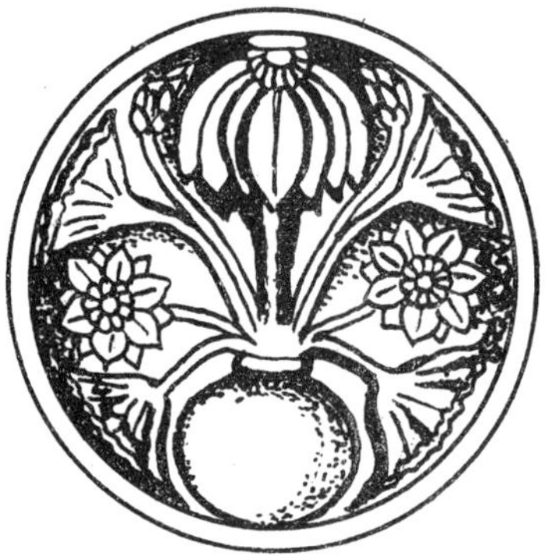
39

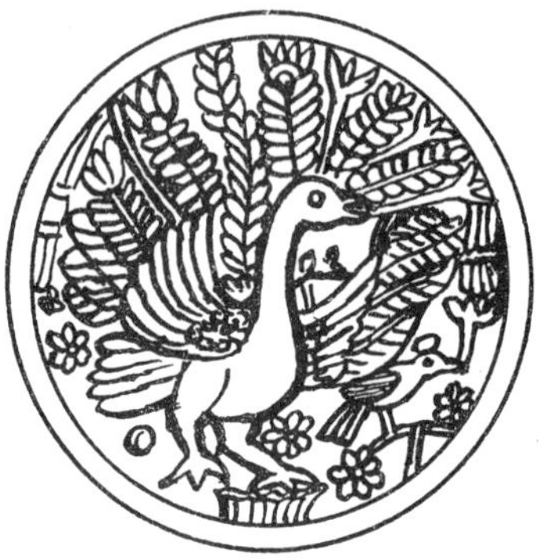
40

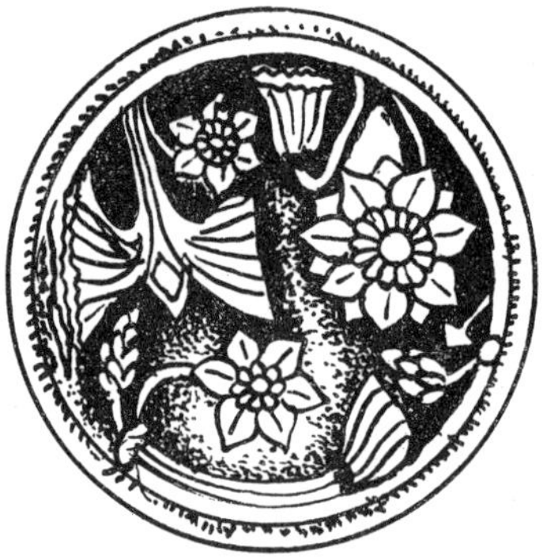
41

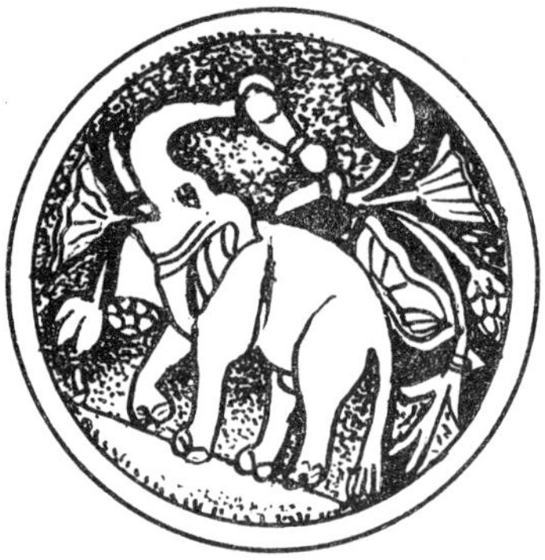
42

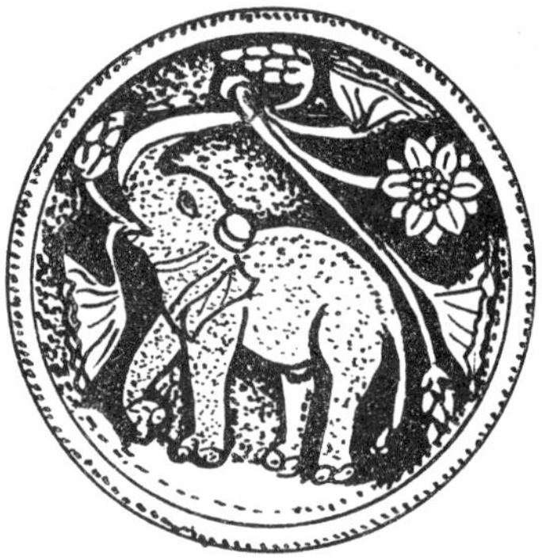
43

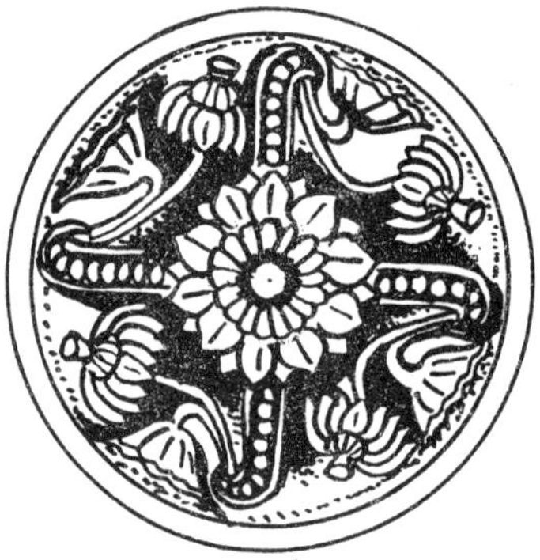
44

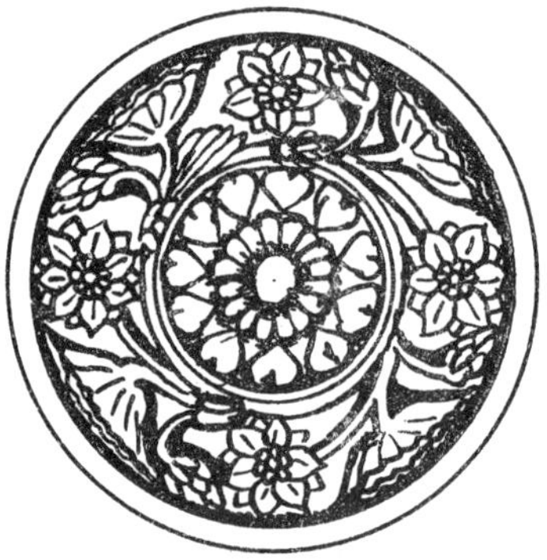
45

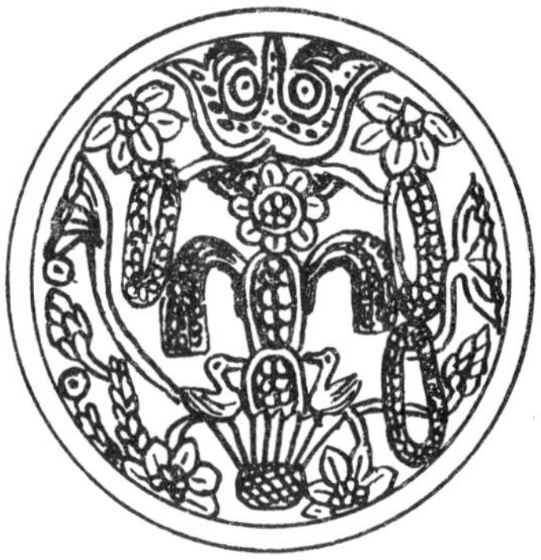
46

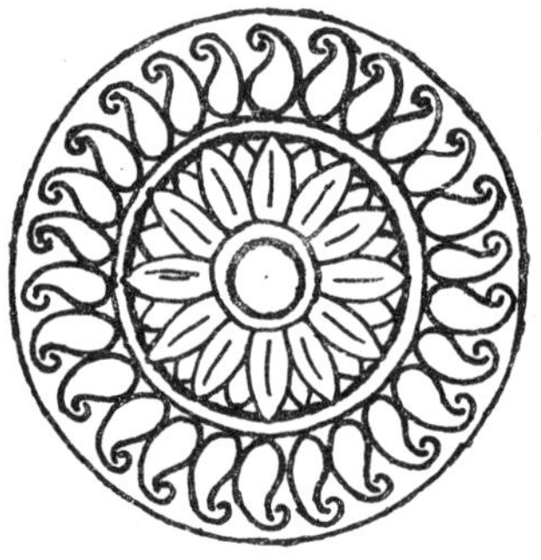
47

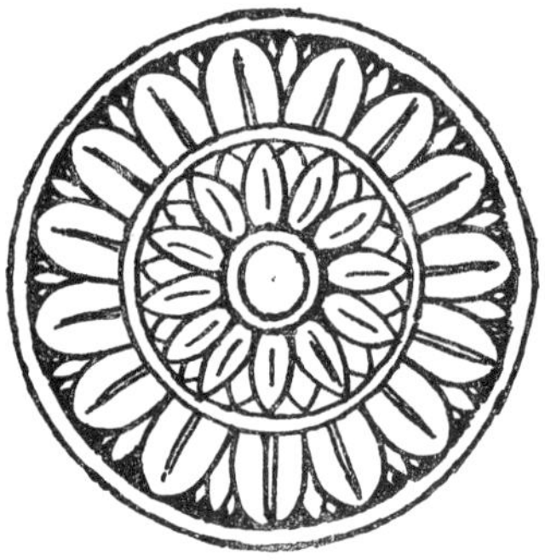
48

STONE SCULPTURE. **37.** Rosette. **38, 39.** Lotuses in bowl of Good Fortune. **40.** Dancing Peacock. **41.** Lotuses. **42, 43.** Elephant with lotuses. **44, 45.** Rosettes with lotuses. **46.** Lotuses with sacred symbol. Medallions from Sanchi Stupa, 1st century B.C. **47, 48.** Lotus forms. Eastern gateway Bharhut, c. 150 B.C.

# Plate 5

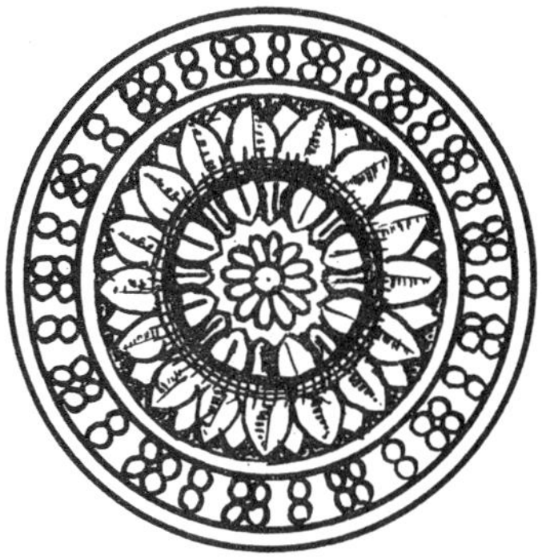

49

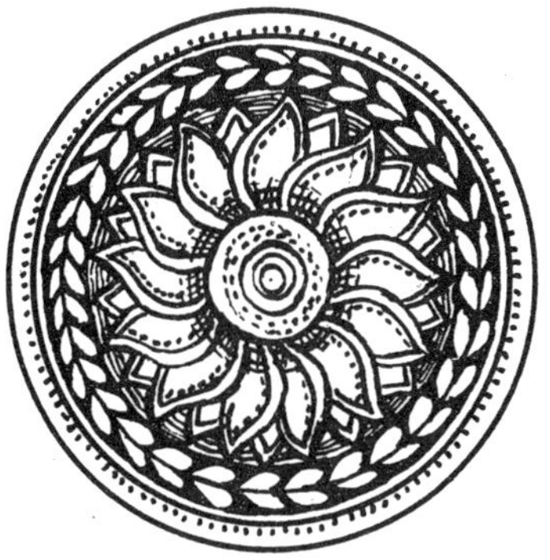

50

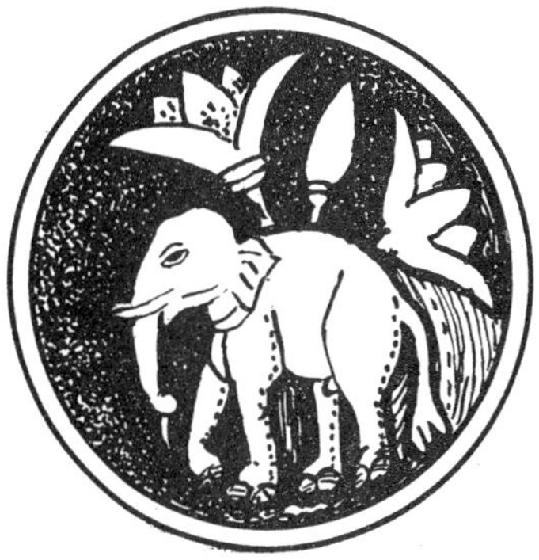

51

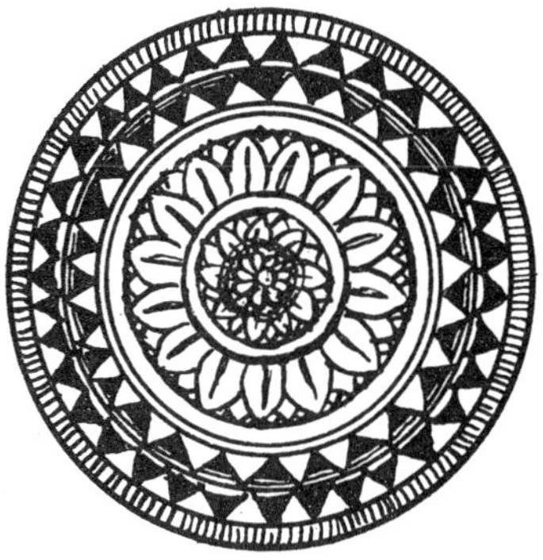

52

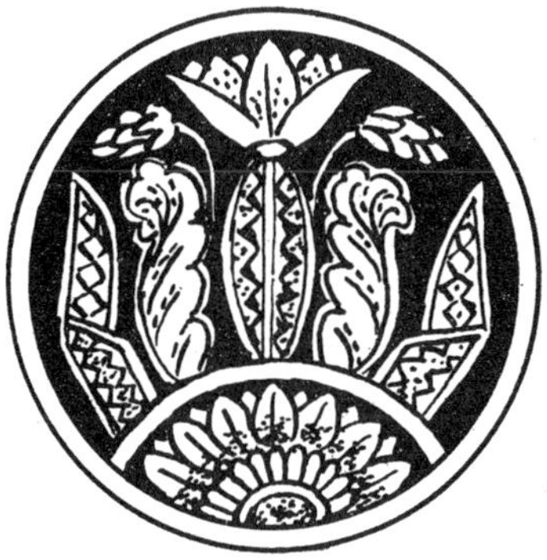

53

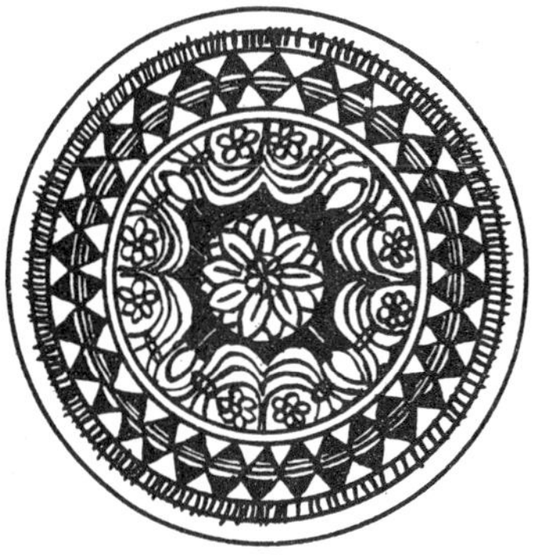

54

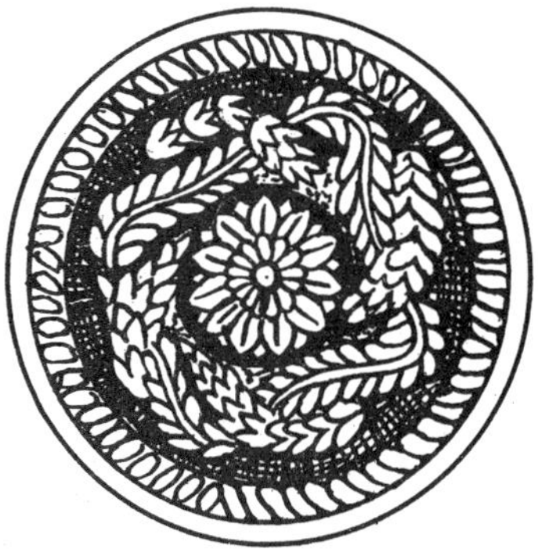

55

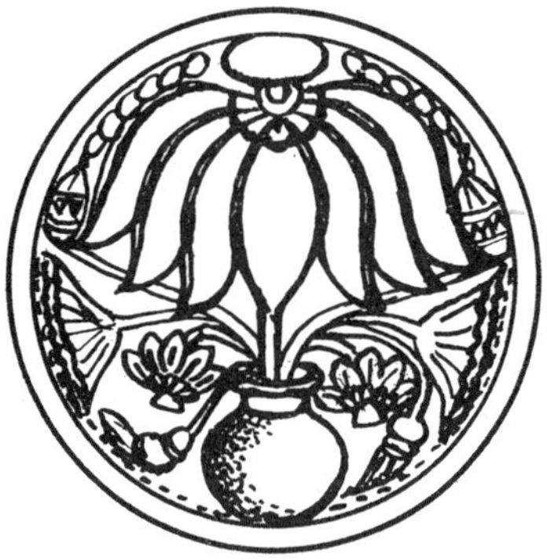

56

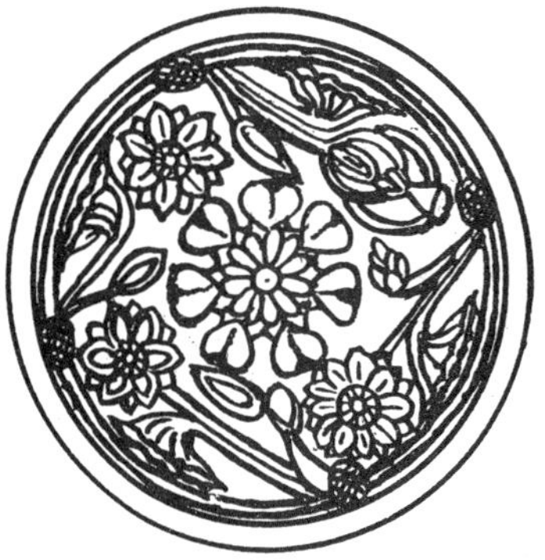

57

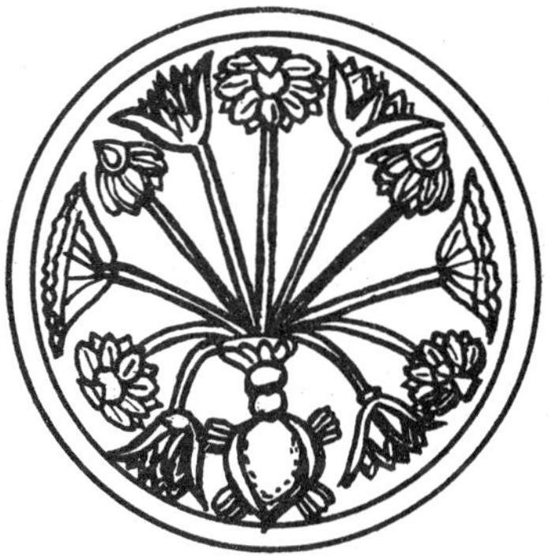

58

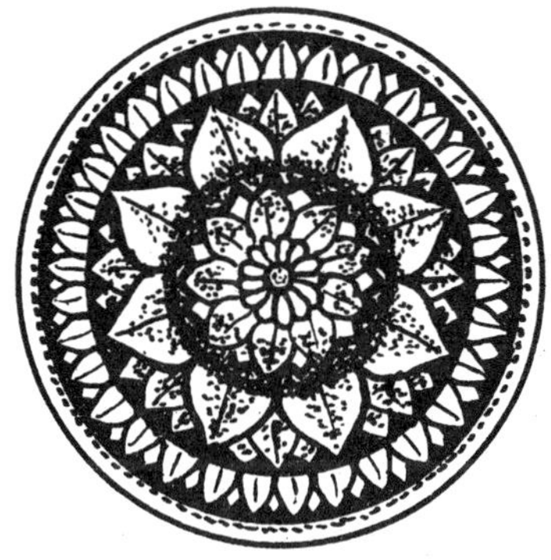

59

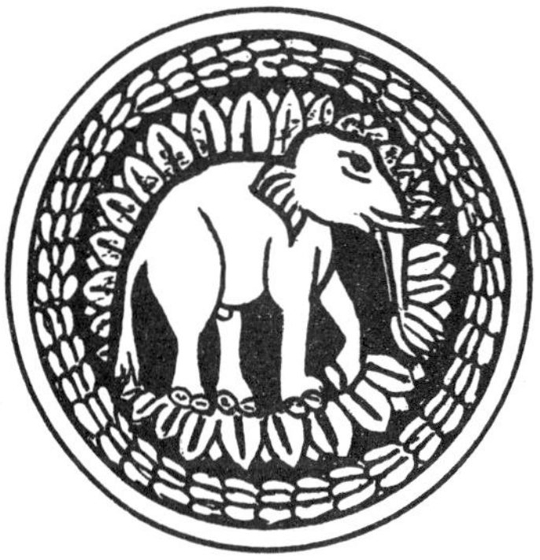

60

STONE SCULPTURE. **49.** Rosette. **50.** Lotus with leaf border. **51.** Elephant in lotus lake. **52, 54.** Rosettes and geometrical pattern. **53.** Rosette and honeysuckle. **55.** Rosette and foliated forms. Medallions from Bharhut, c. 150 B.C. **56, 58.** Lotuses in bowl of Good Fortune. **57.** Lotuses. **59.** Rosette. **60.** Elephant within a lotus. Medallions from Sanchi Stupa, 1st century B.C.

# Plate 6

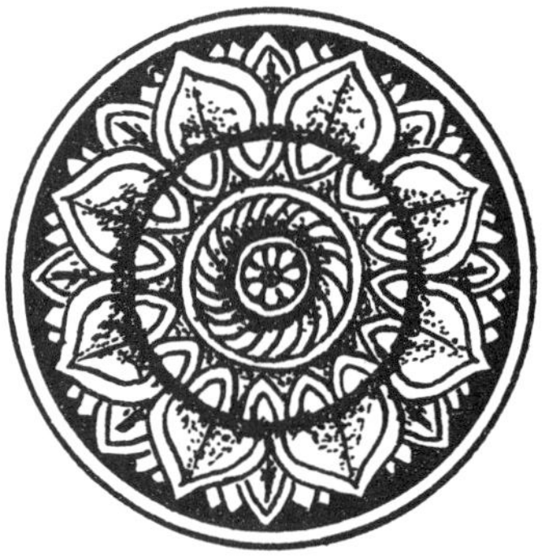

61

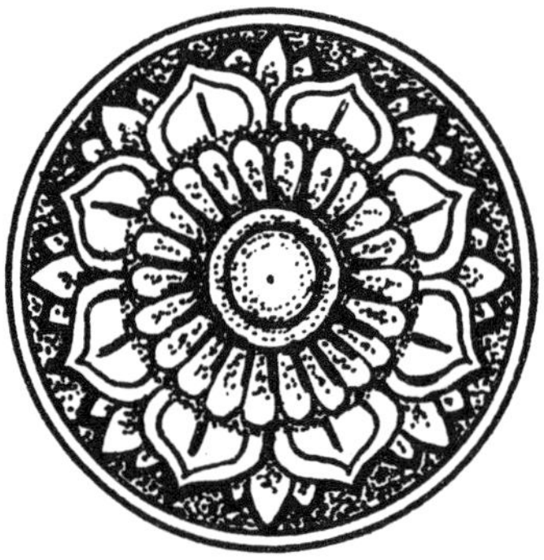

62

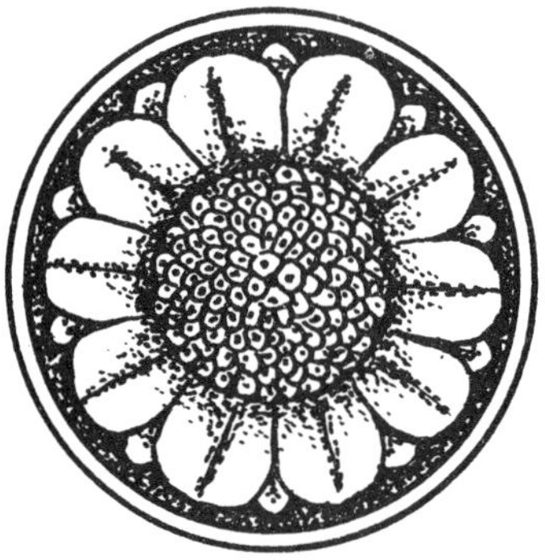

63

64

65

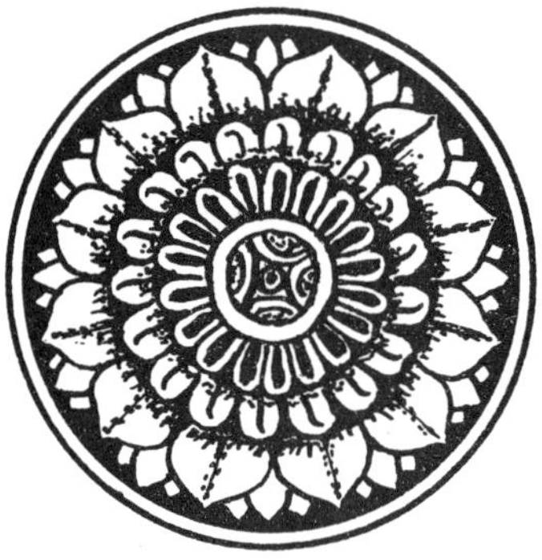

66

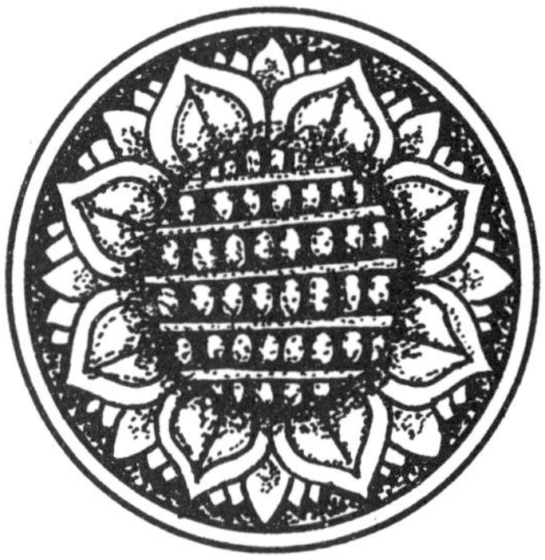

67

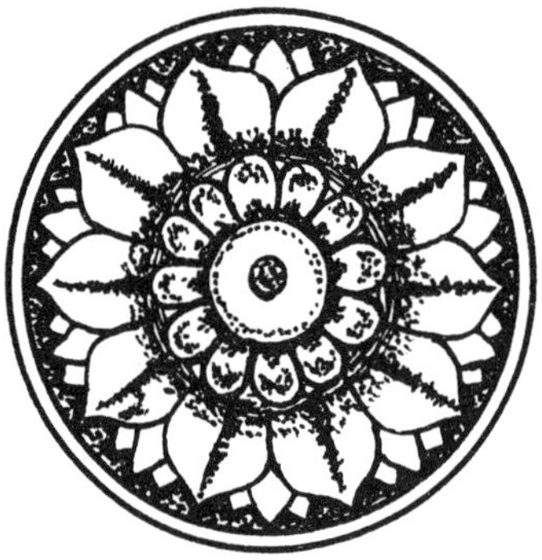

68

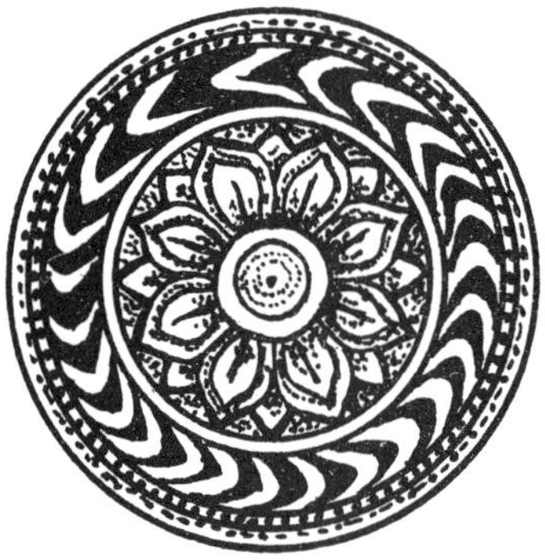

69

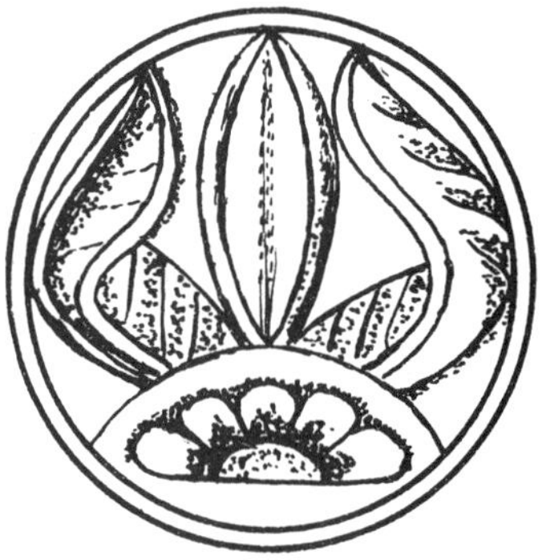

70

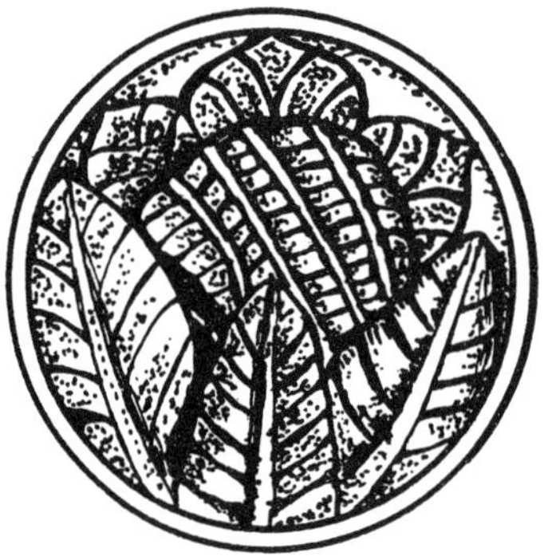

71

72

STONE SCULPTURE. **61–69.** Lotus forms. **70.** Rosette and honeysuckle. **71.** Bud and leaves. **72.** Fleur-de-lis with part of a rosette. Medallions from Mathura, 2nd century A.D.

# Plate 7

73

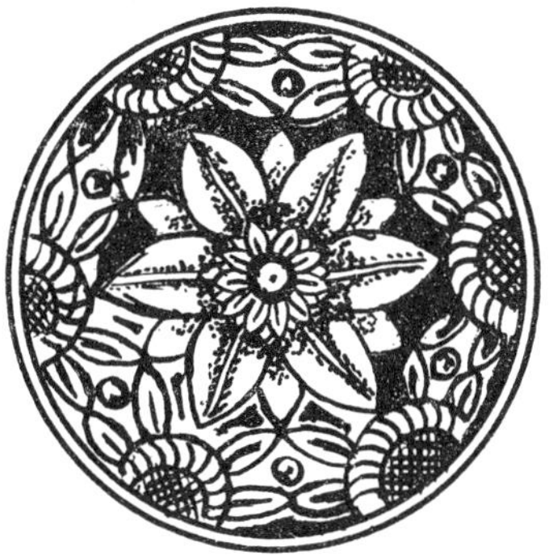

74

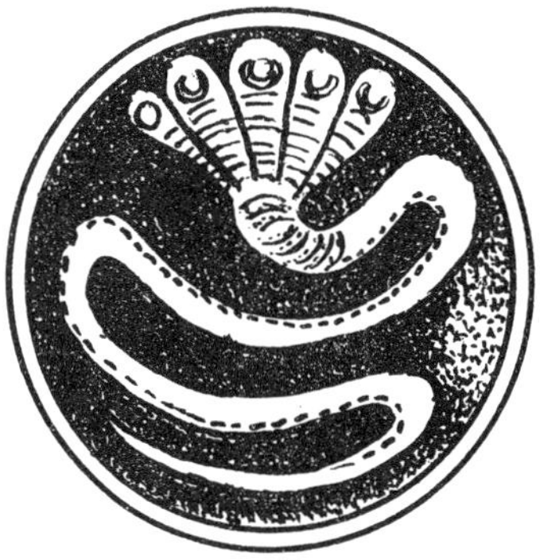

75

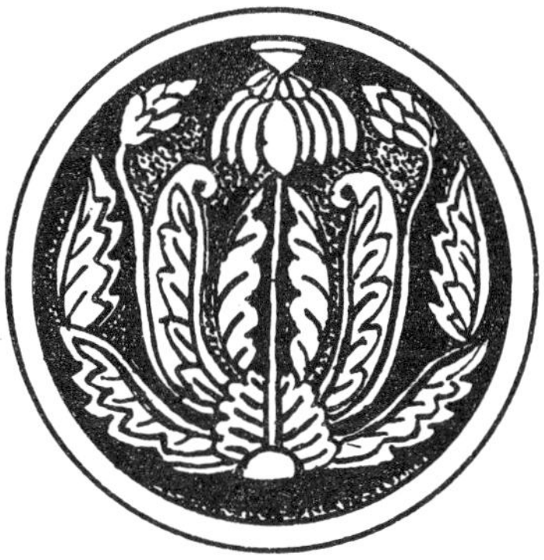

76

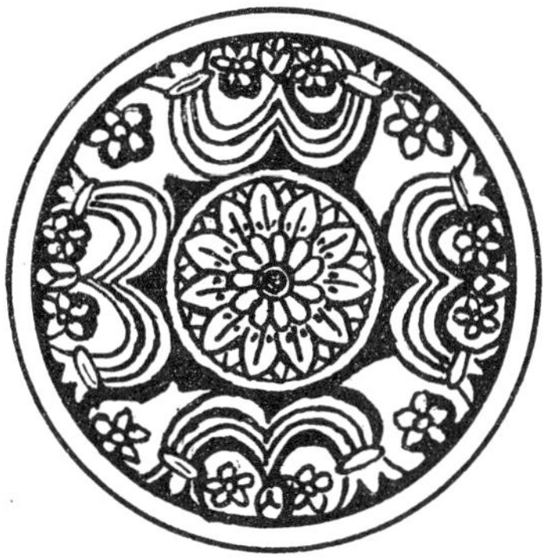

77

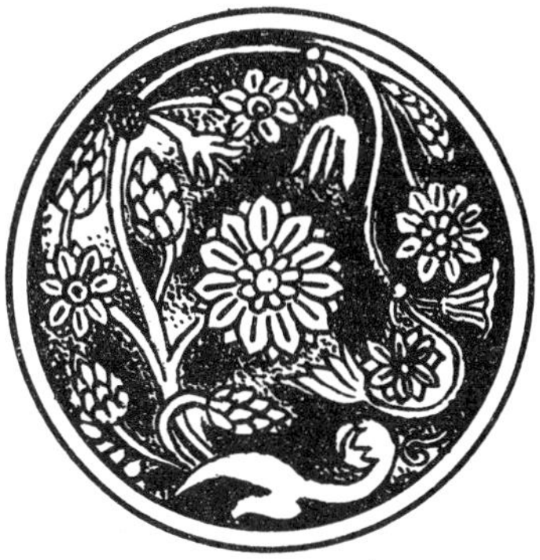

78

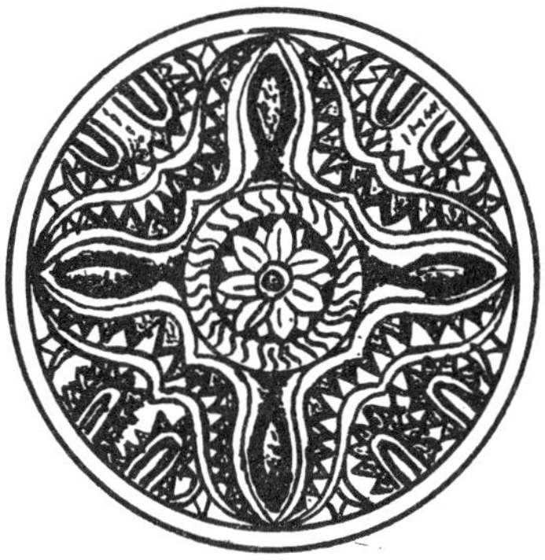

79

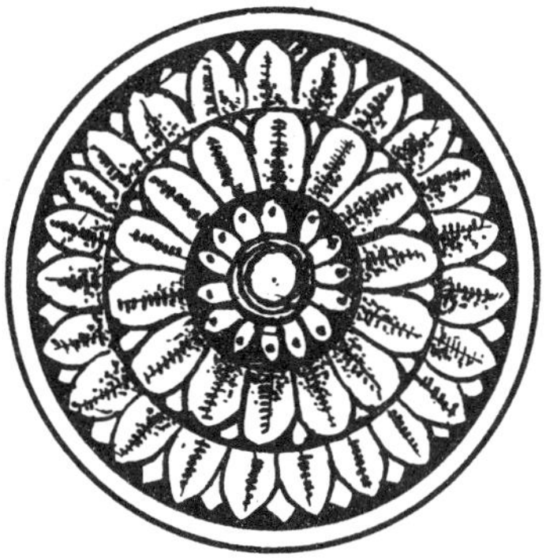

80

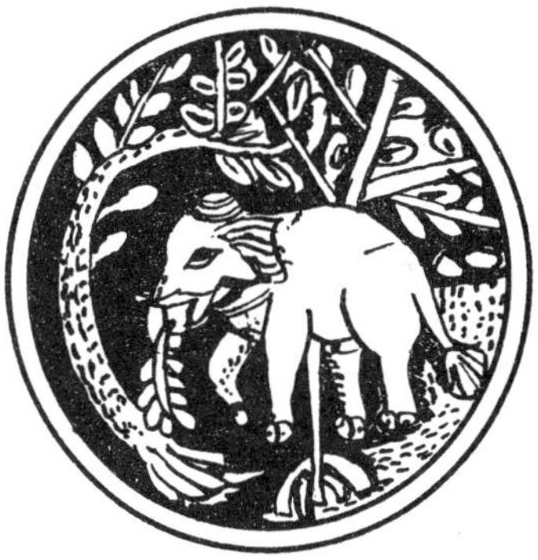

81

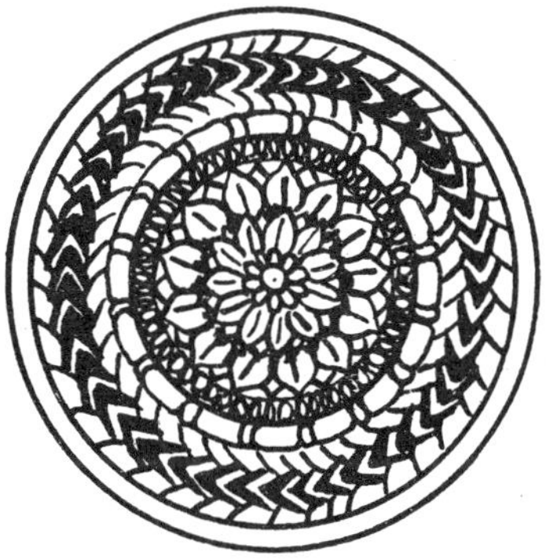

82

83

84

STONE SCULPTURE. **73.** Rosette. **74.** Lotuses in full bloom. **75.** Serpent. **76, 78, 79.** Lotus forms. **77.** Rosette and sacred symbol. Medallions from Sanchi and Mathura, 1st century B.C.—1st century A.D. **80, 83.** Rosettes. **81.** Elephant and tree. **82.** Rosette and geometrical pattern. **84.** Rosette and honeysuckle. Medallions from Bharhut, 2nd century A.D.

# Plate 8

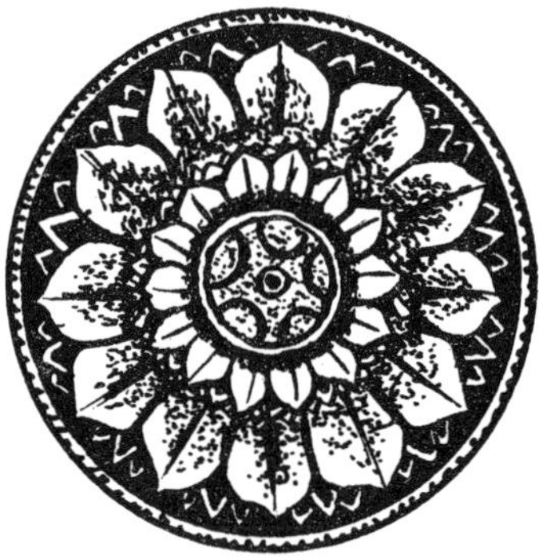
85

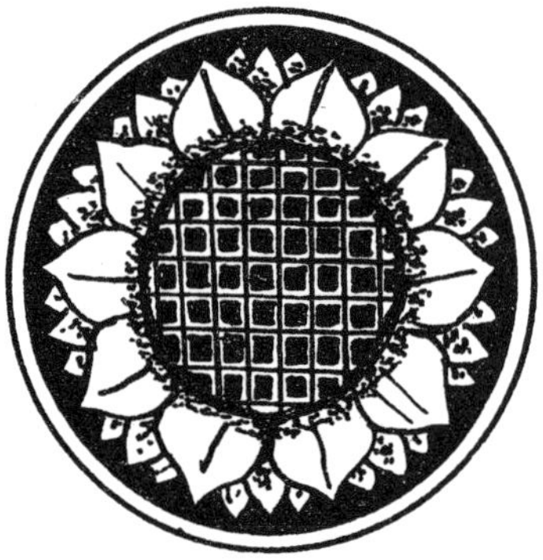
86

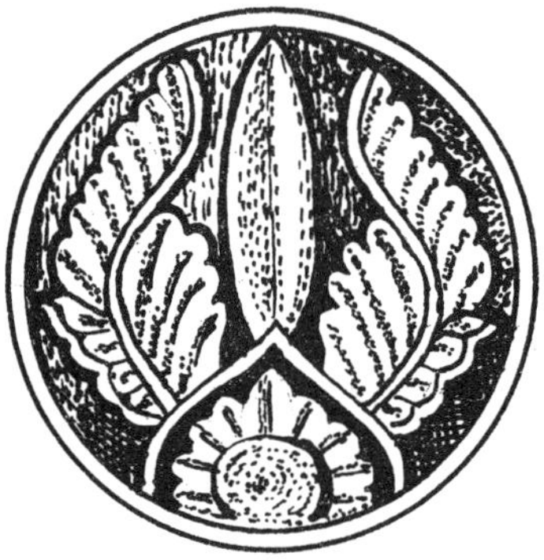
87

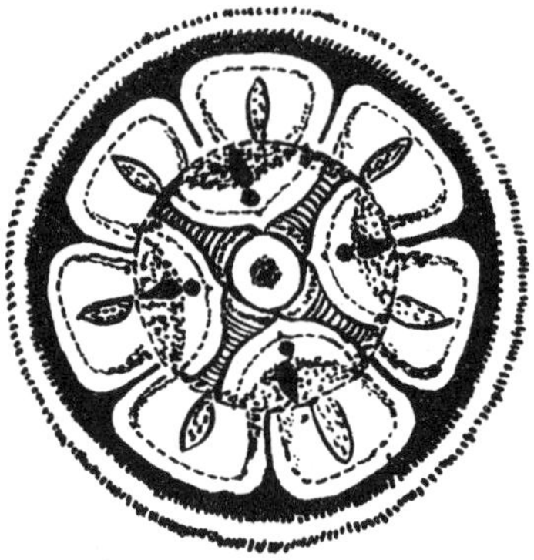
88

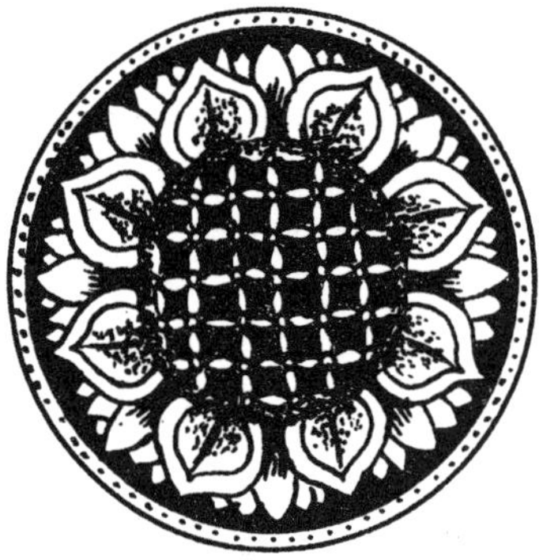
89

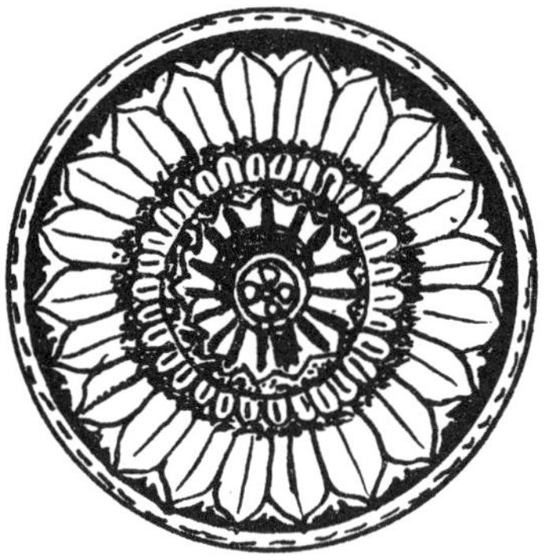
90

91

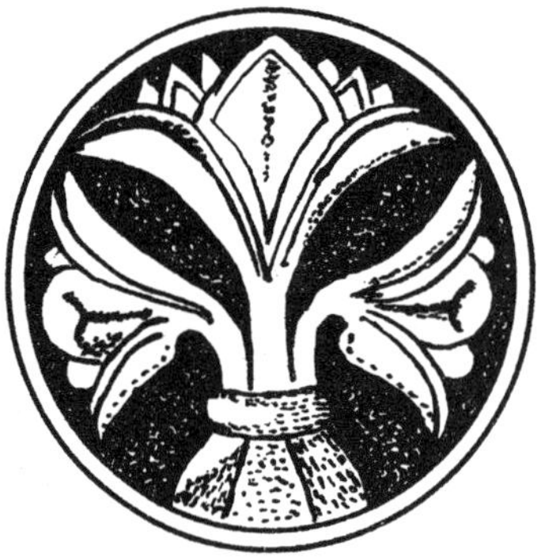
92

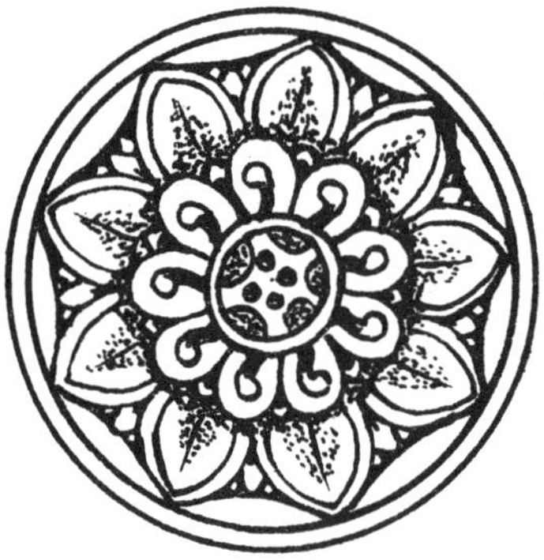
93

94

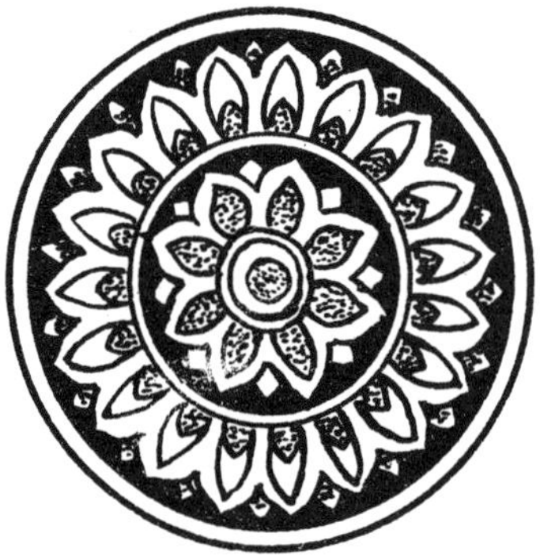
95

96

STONE SCULPTURE. **85, 86.** Lotus forms. **87.** Lotus and honeysuckle. **88, 89, 90.** Rosettes. **91.** Honeysuckle. **92.** Fleur-de-lis. Medallions from Mathura, 1st century A.D. **93, 94, 95.** Rosettes. **96.** Lotus. Medallions from Sanchi and Mathura, 1st century B.C.—2nd century A.D.

# Plate 9

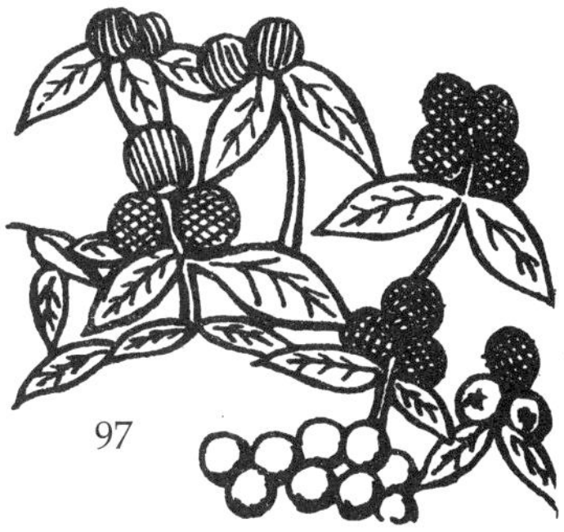

97

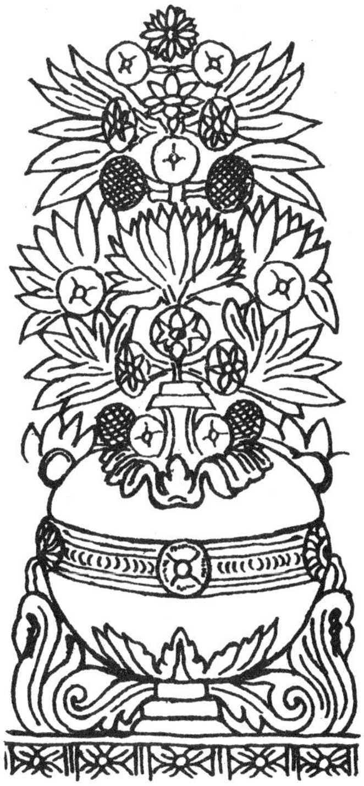

98

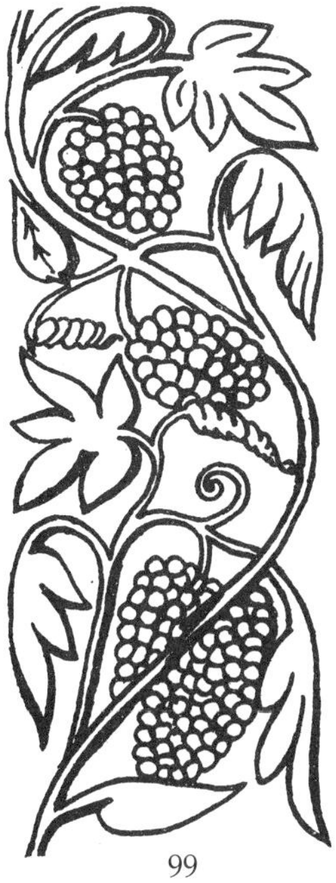

99

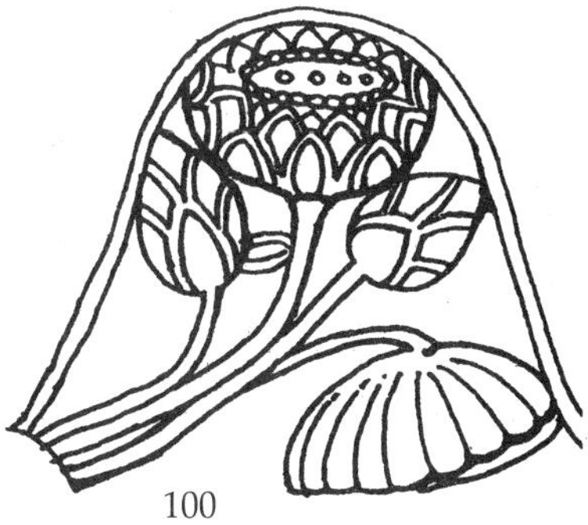

100

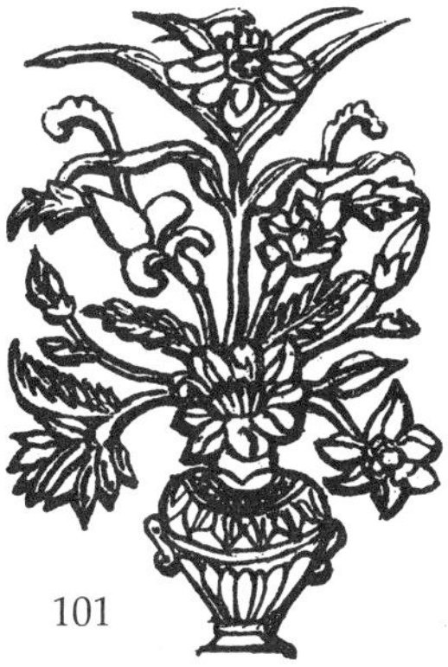

101

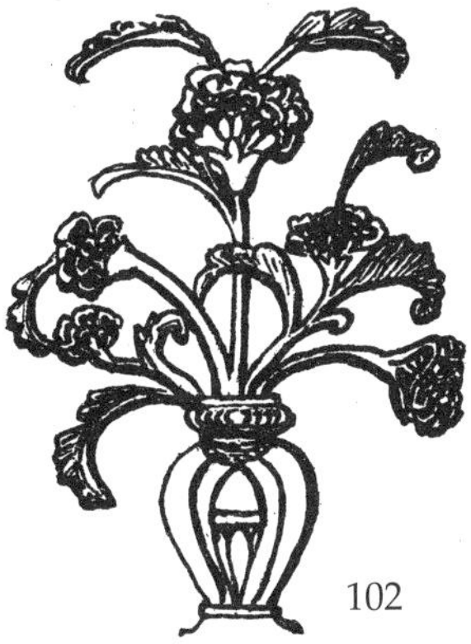

102

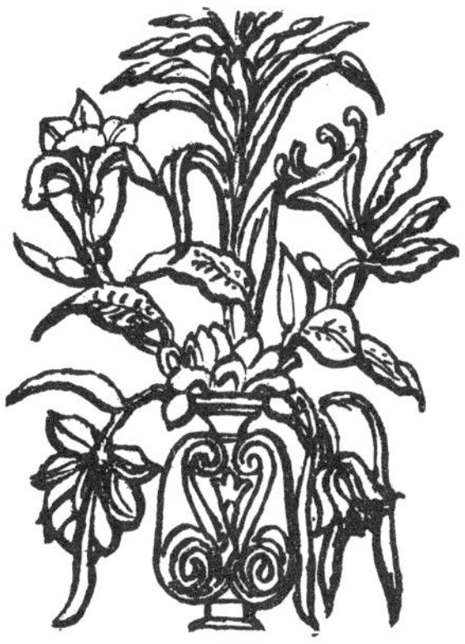

103

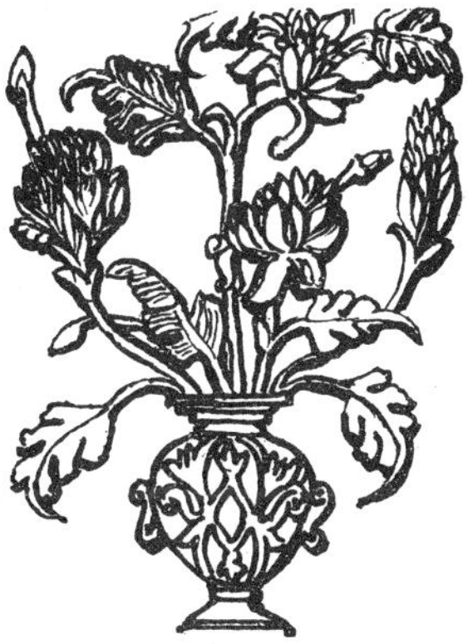

104

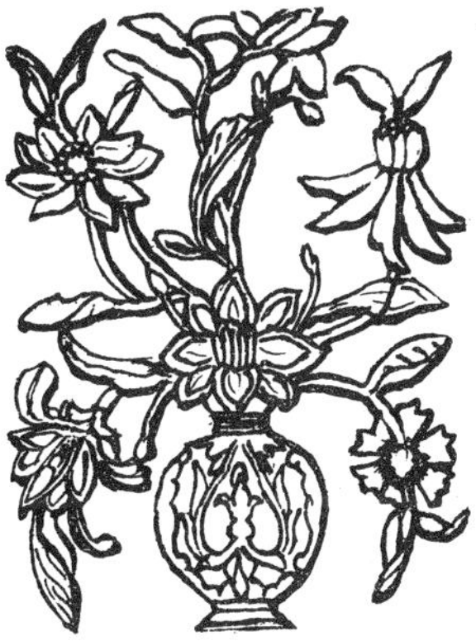

105

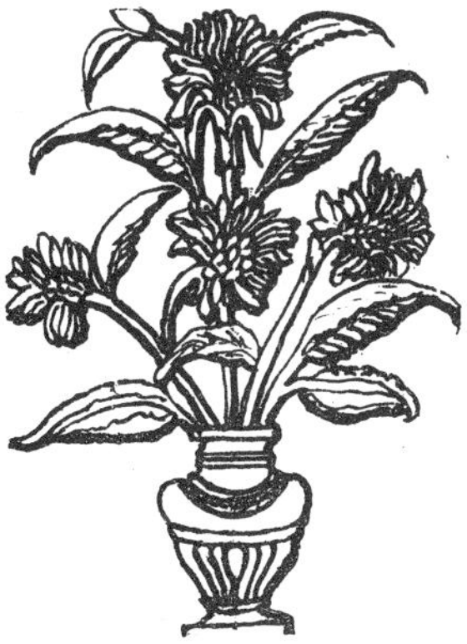

106

STONE SCULPTURE. **97.** Fruit motif on Jain railing pillar, Mathura, late 1st century B.C.—1st century A.D. **98.** Lotuses, leaves and fruit in bowl, Buddhist shrine Ghantasala. **99.** Grave vine on door-jamb, Jain Stupa Mathura, late 1st century B.C.—1st century A.D. **100.** Lotus motif, Mathura, 1st century B.C. **101–106.** Flower arrangements in vases from the palace at Amber, old capital of Jaipur State, Rajasthan, medieval period.

# Plate 10

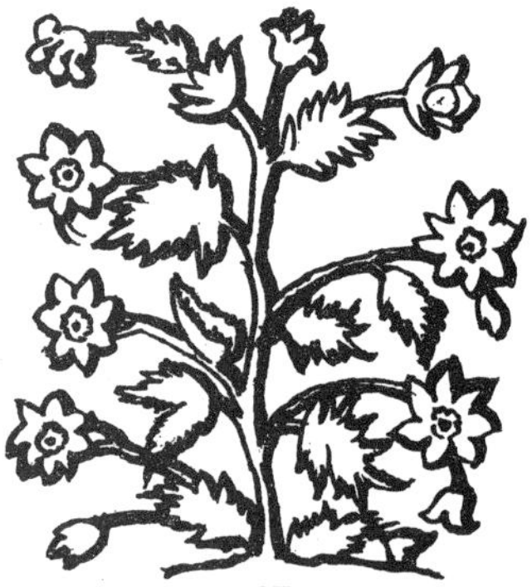
107

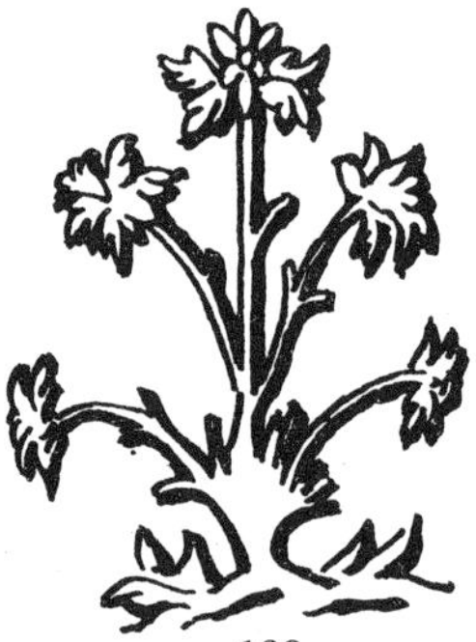
108

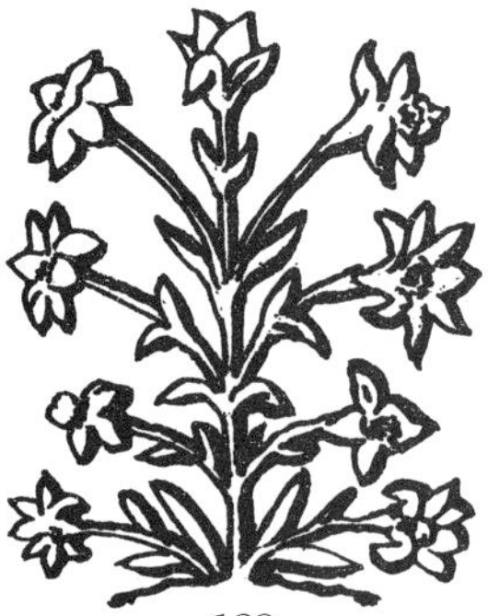
109

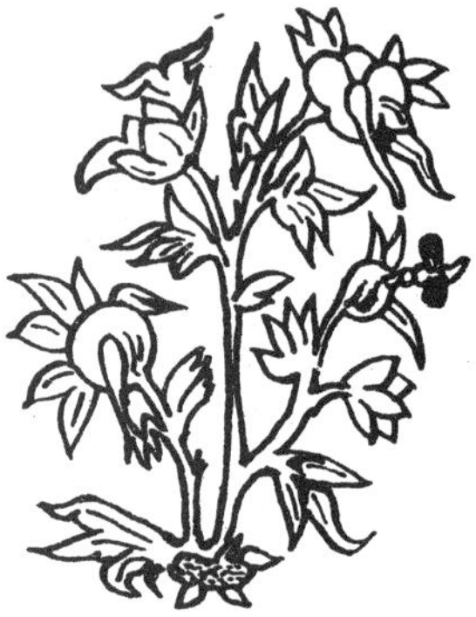
110

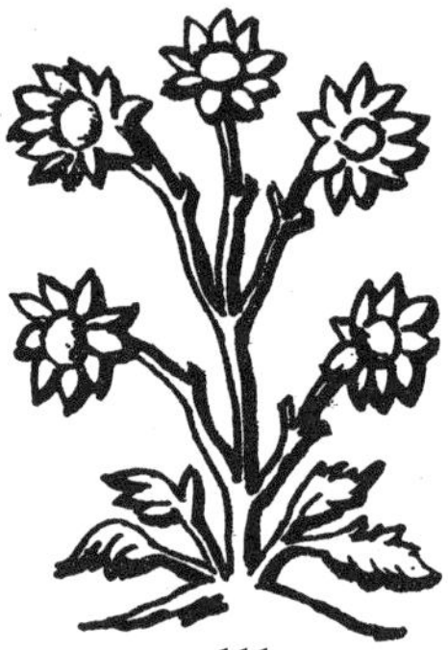
111

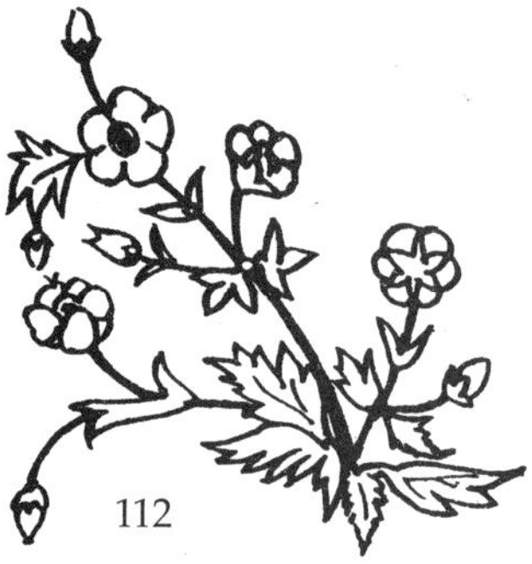
112

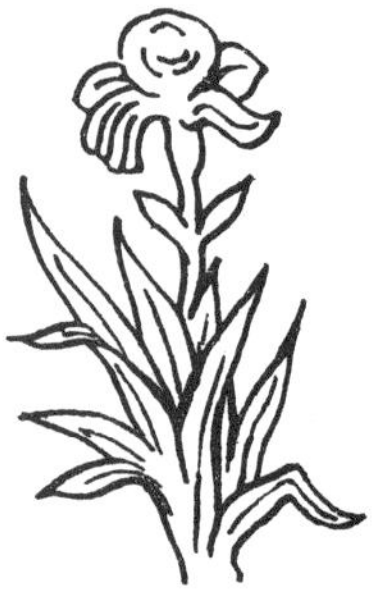
113

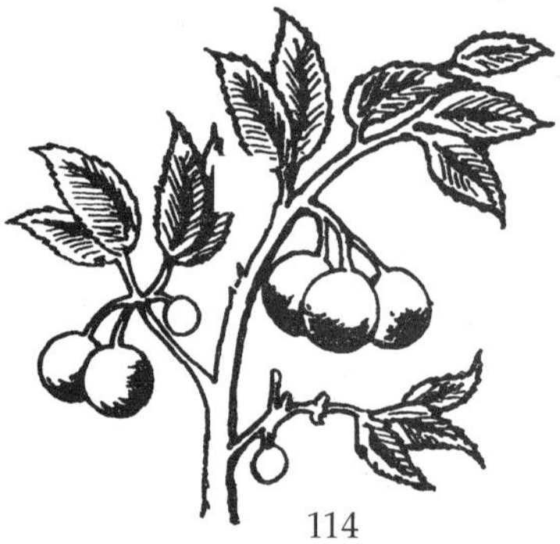
114

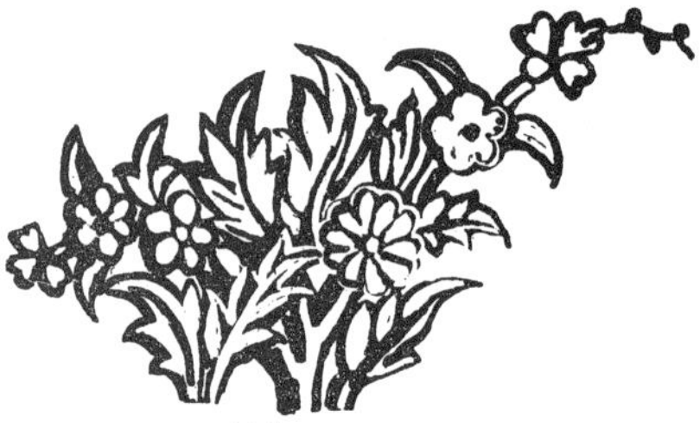
115

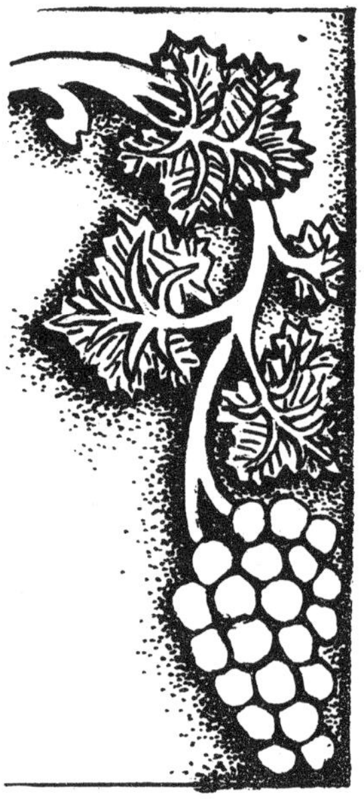
116

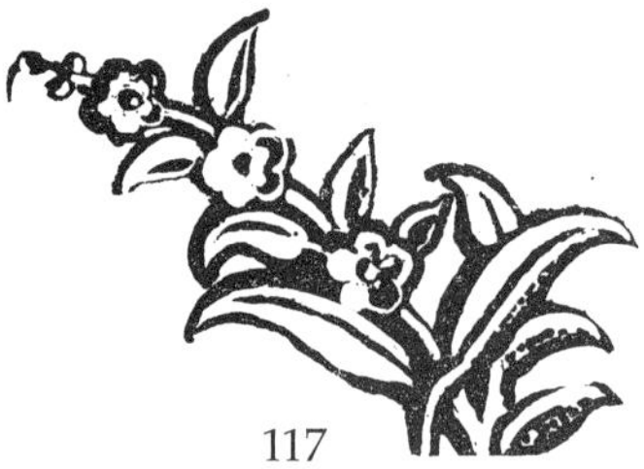
117

STONE SCULPTURE. **107, 109.** Floral motifs of sculptures from the Taj Mahal, Agra. **108, 110–114.** Details of floral ornament from the south end of Emperor Akbar's Cenotaph, Fatehpur Sikri. **115, 116, 117.** Decorative stone work of the grape vine and floral motifs from the Turkish Sultan's palace, Fatehpur Sikri, medieval period.

# Plate 11

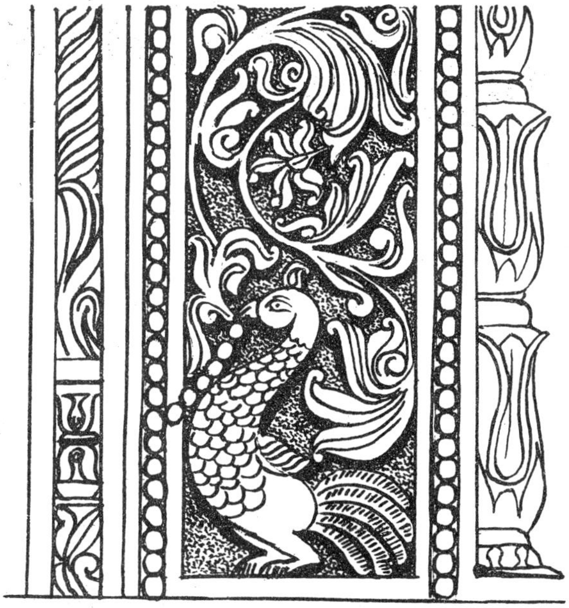

118

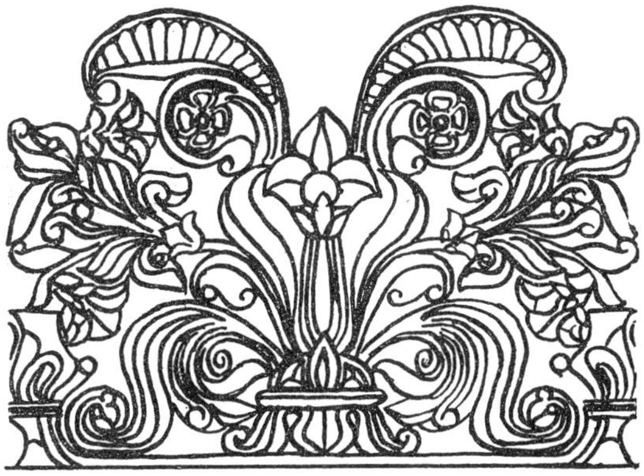

119

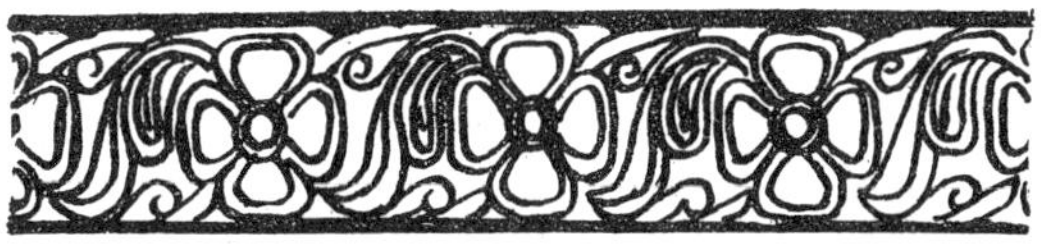

120

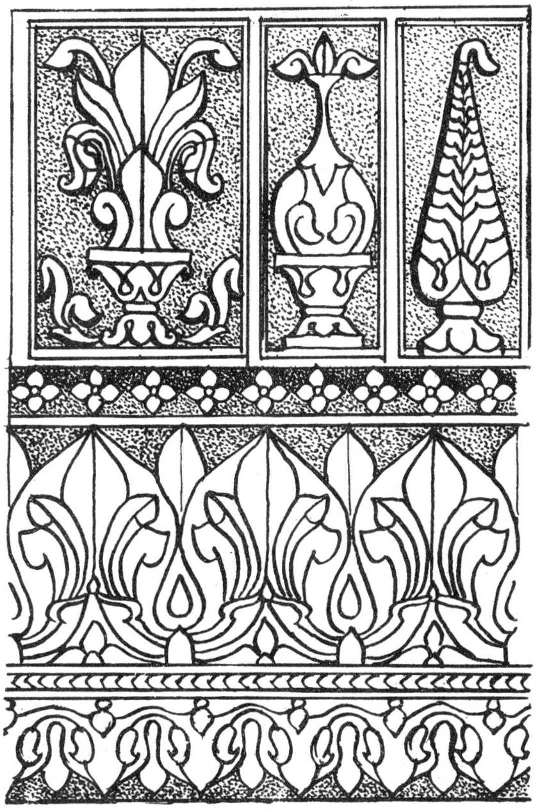

121

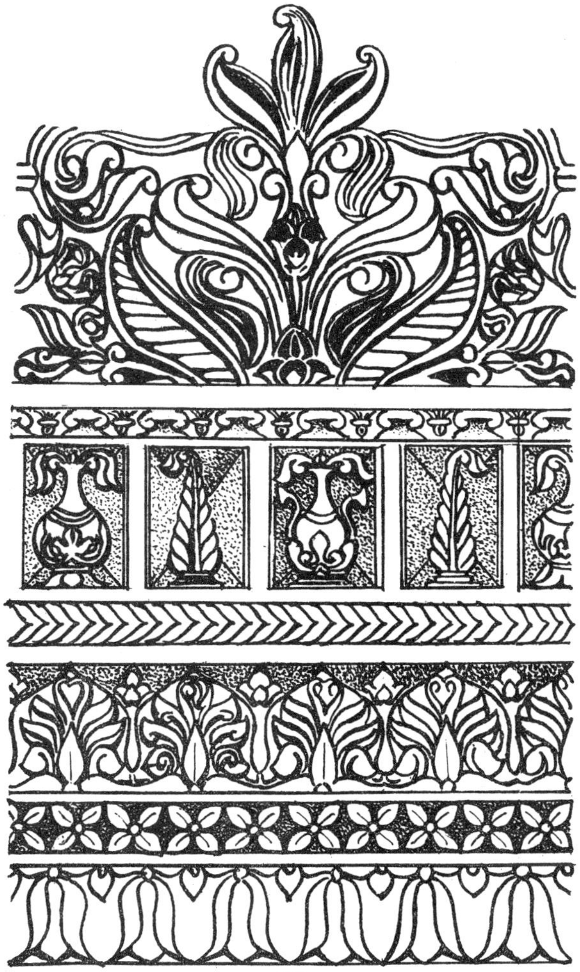

122

123

STONE SCULPTURE. **118–123.** Details of sculpture and carving from Pratapghar, Rajasthan, showing stylized bird, floral, and geometrical forms with decorative vases. Medieval period.

# Plate 12

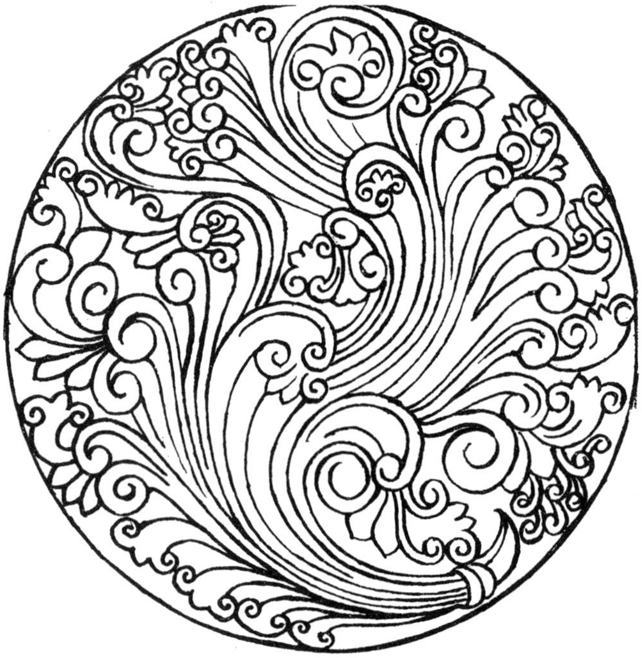

124

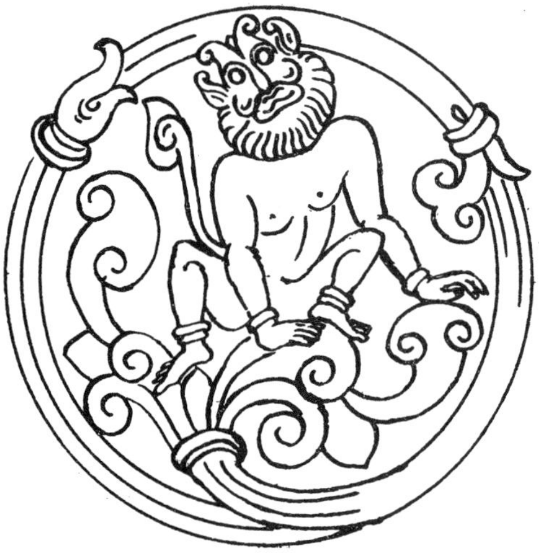

125

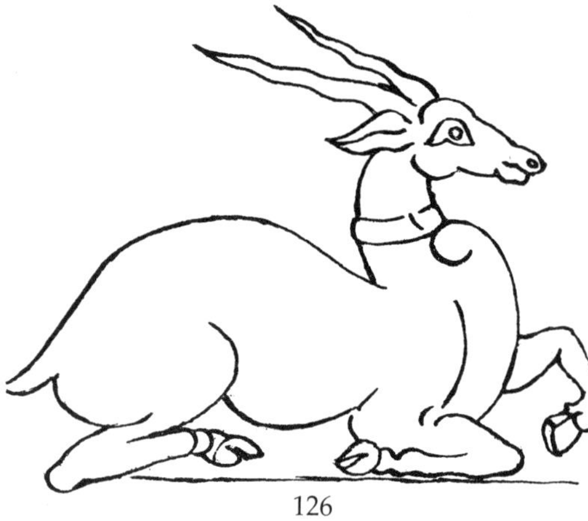

126

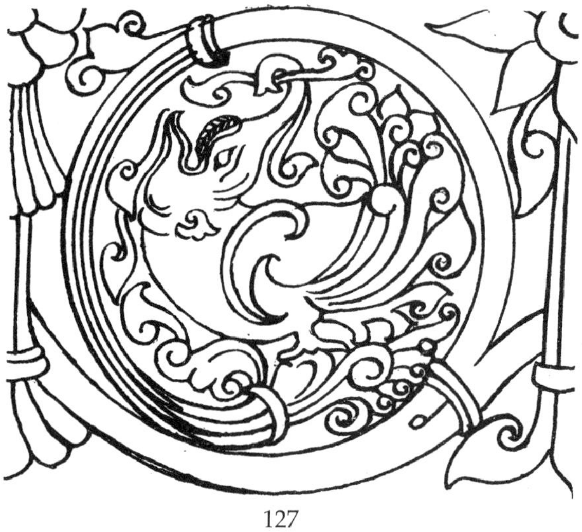

127

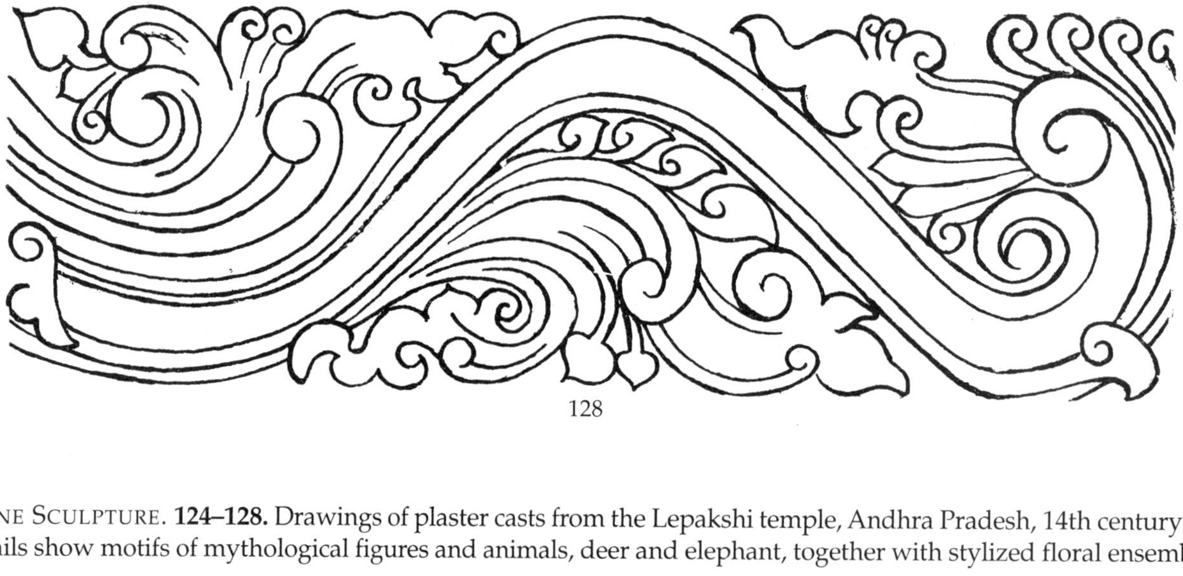

128

STONE SCULPTURE. **124–128.** Drawings of plaster casts from the Lepakshi temple, Andhra Pradesh, 14th century A.D. Details show motifs of mythological figures and animals, deer and elephant, together with stylized floral ensembles.

# Plate 13

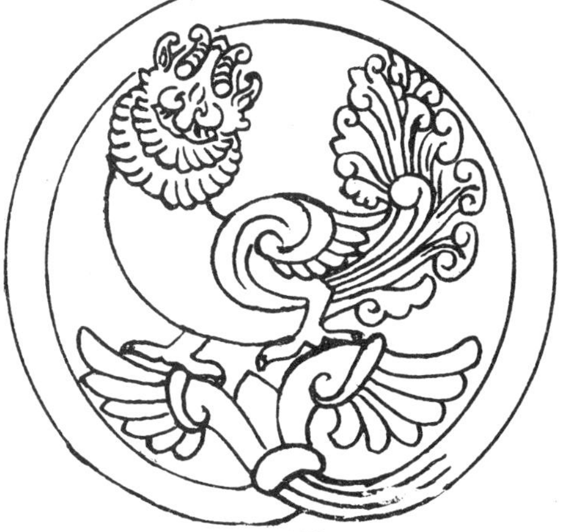

129

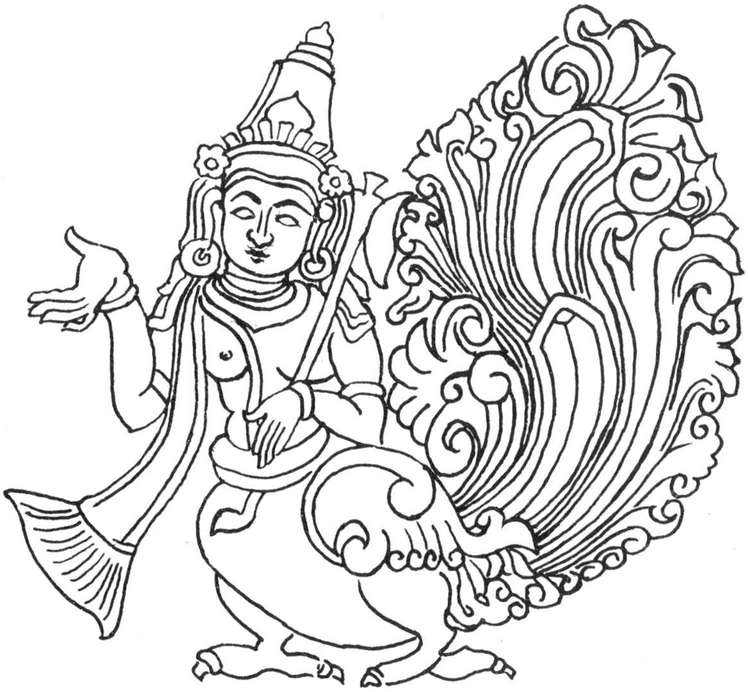

130

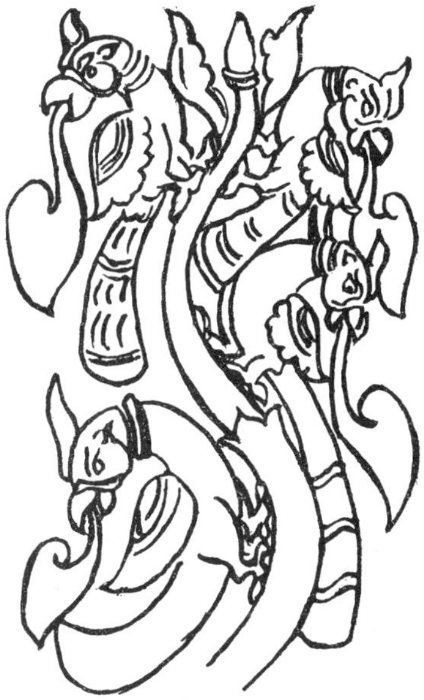

131

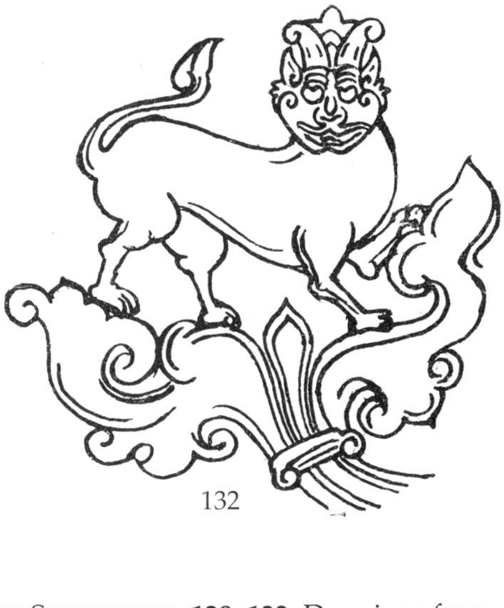

132

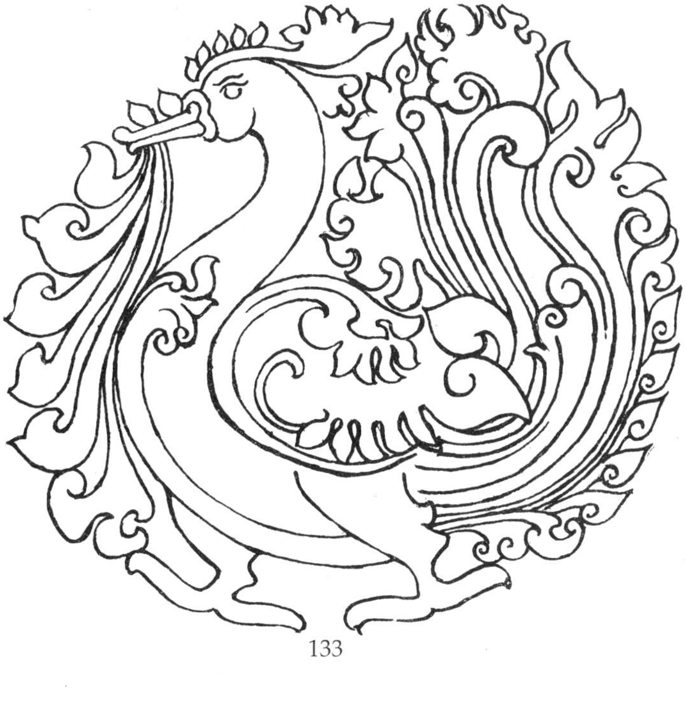

133

STONE SCULPTURE. **129–133.** Drawings from plaster casts from the Lepakshi temple, Andhra Pradesh, 14th century A.D. Details show motifs of mythological figures and animals and the stylized swan.

# Plate 14

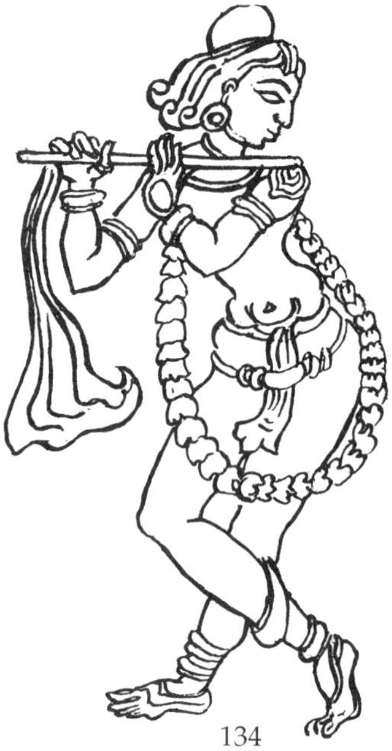

134

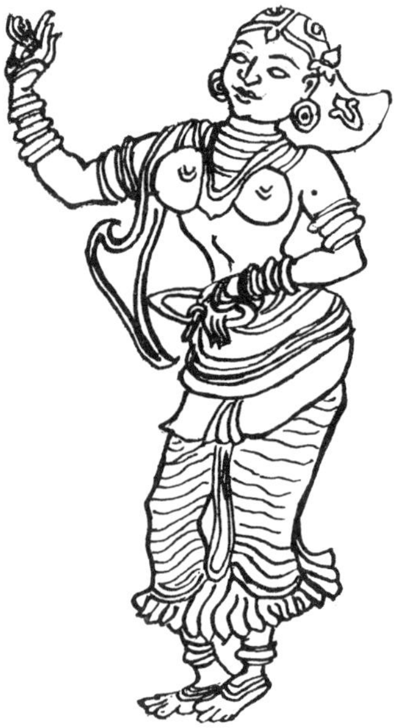

135

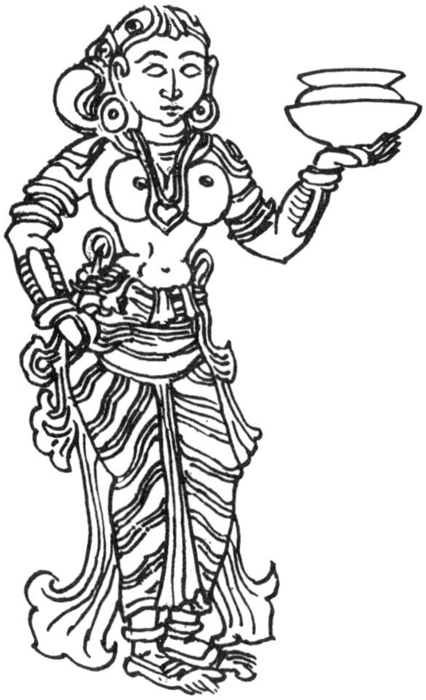

136

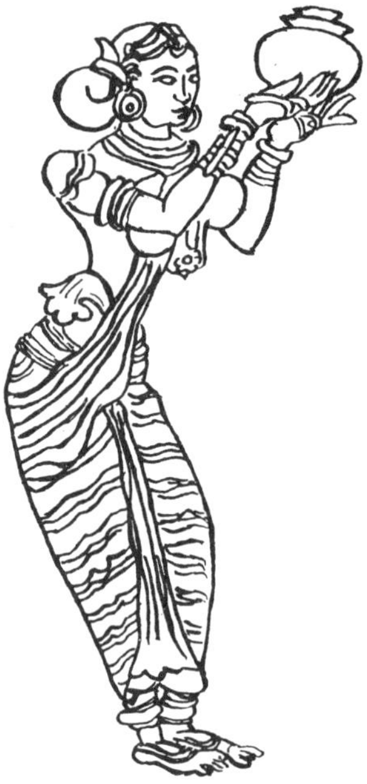

137

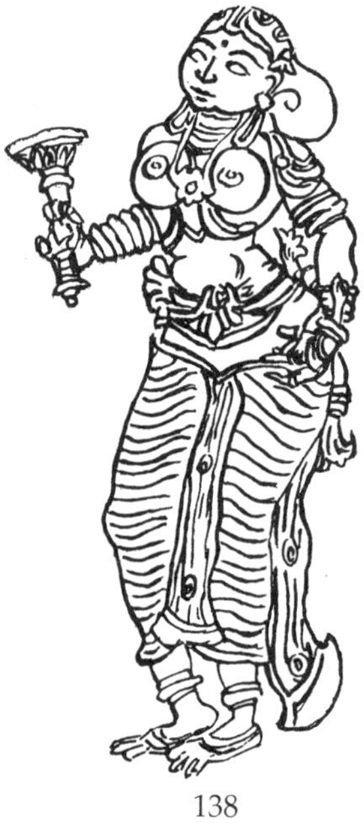

138

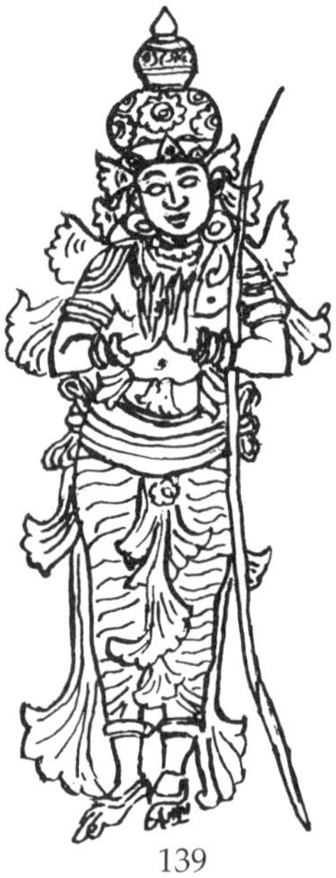

139

STONE SCULPTURE. **134–139.** Drawings from temple sculptures in the Padmanabhaswamy temple, Trivandrum, Kerala, where there are a galaxy of sculptures representing gods and goddesses and characters from sacred story and legend.

# Plate 15

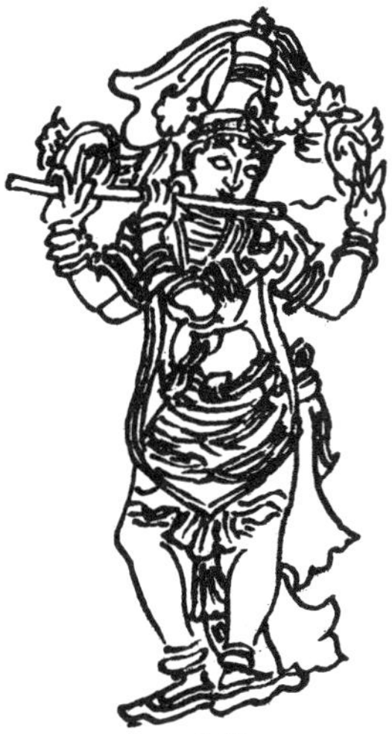

140

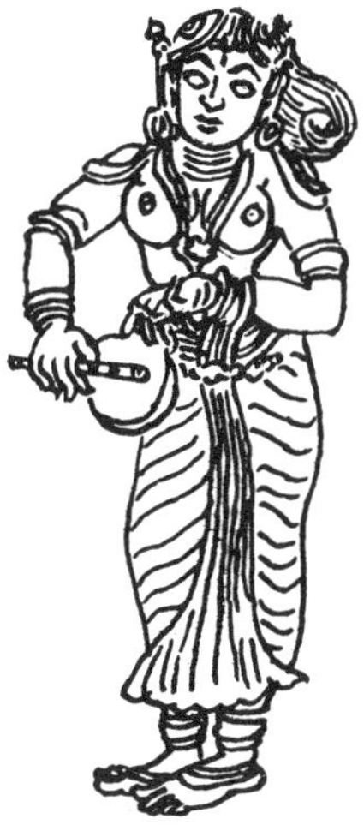

141

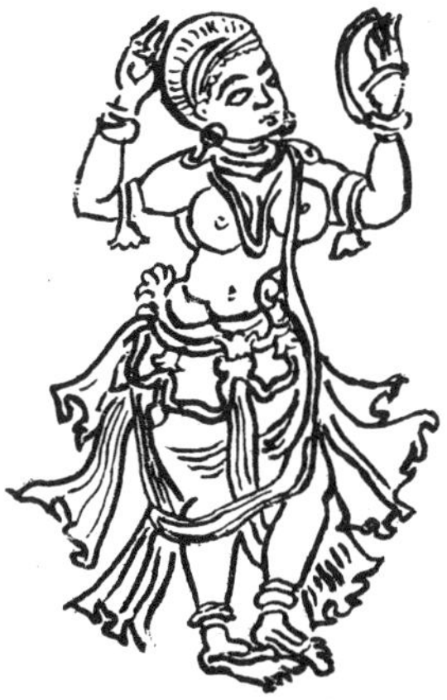

142

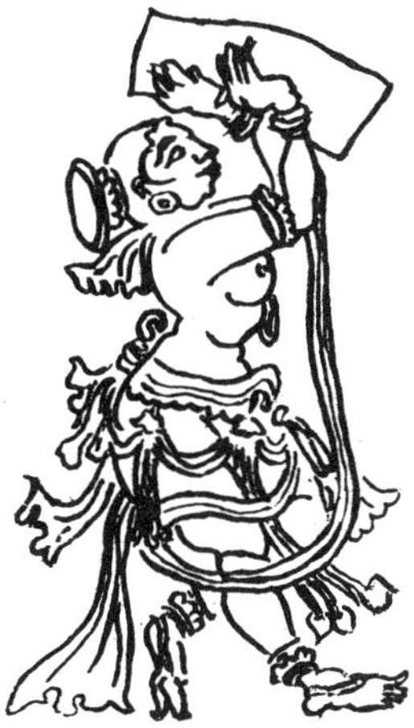

143

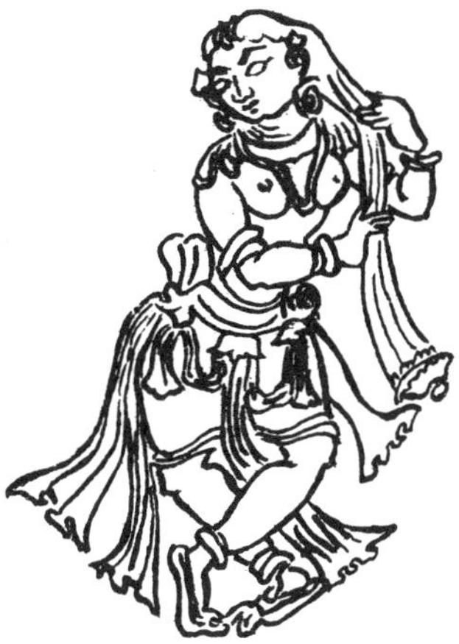

144

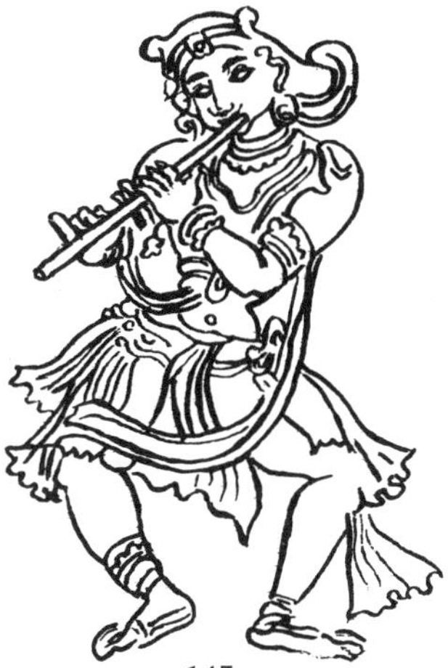

145

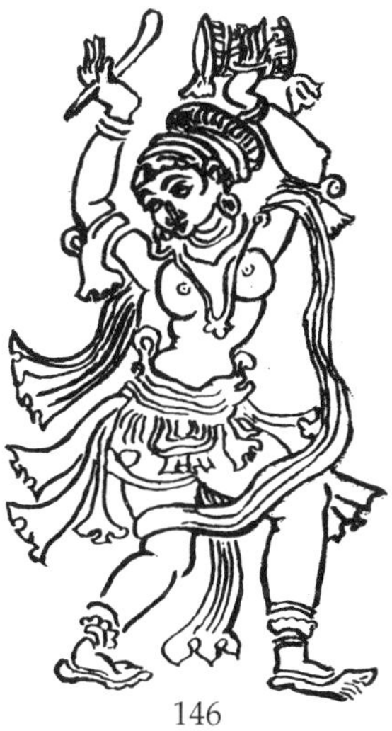

146

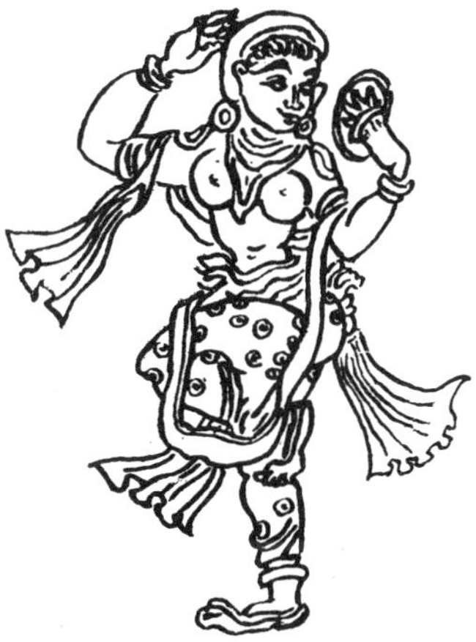

147

STONE SCULPTURE. **140, 141.** Drawings from temple sculptures in the Padmanabhaswamy temple, Trivandrum, Kerala. **142–147.** Drawings from temple sculptures in the Halebid and Belur temples, Mysore State, 12th century A.D. In these temples also sculptures abound portraying gods and goddesses, dancers and characters from sacred story and legend.

# Plate 16

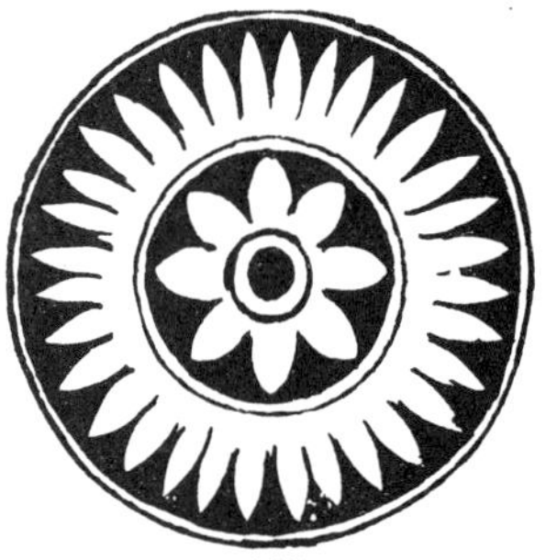
148

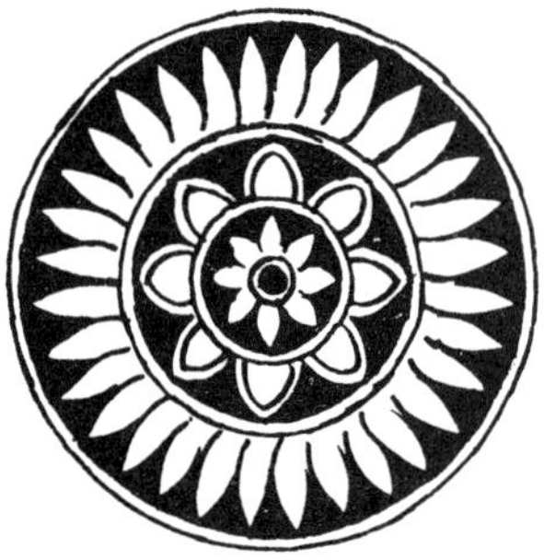
149

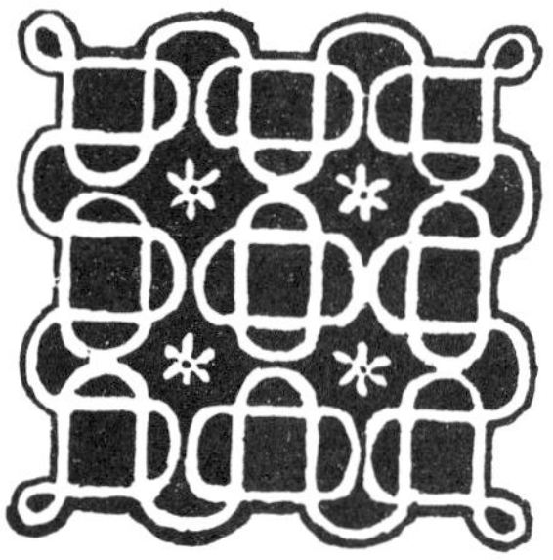
150

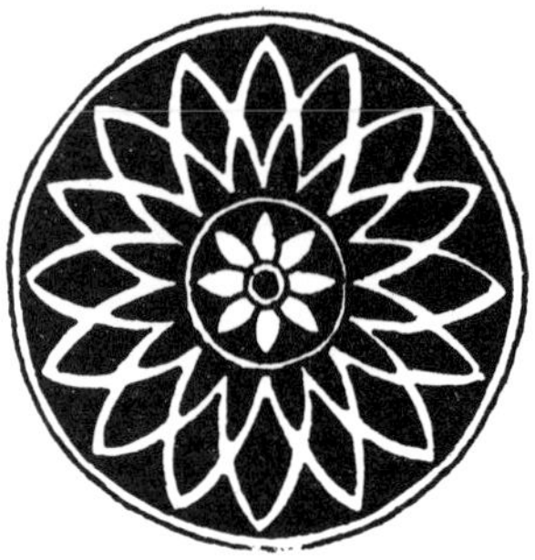
151

152

153

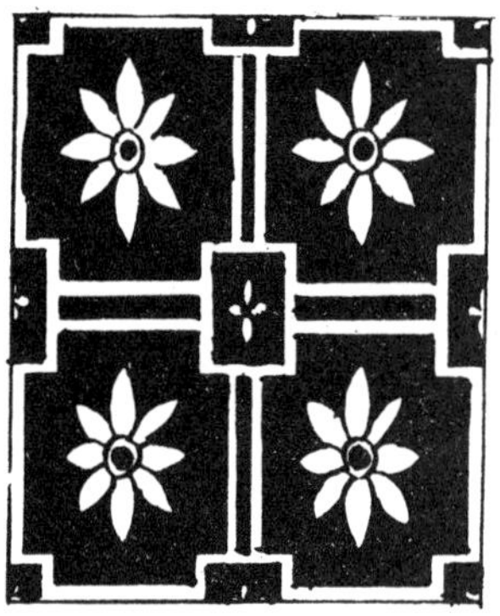
154

155

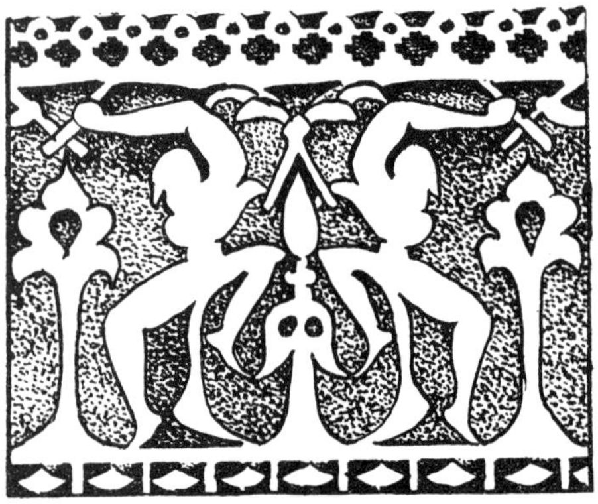
156

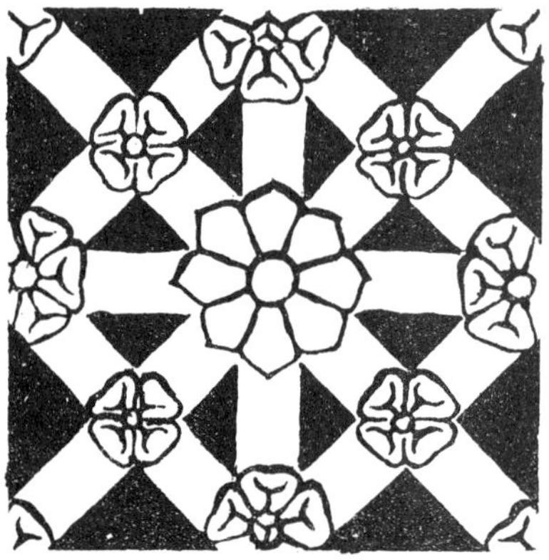
157

STONE SCREENS. **148–154.** Details of designs of stylized floral and geometrical motifs from a window in the Sidi Sayyid's mosque, Ahmadabad, Gujarat, c. 1500 A.D. **155.** Detail of a floral motif from a marble window screen at the tomb of Salim Chisti, Fatehpur Sikri. **156.** Unique stone screen showing dancers from the Man Singh palace, Gwalior, Madhya Pradesh. **157.** Floral and linear patterned screen from Sarnath, 3rd century B.C.

# Plate 17

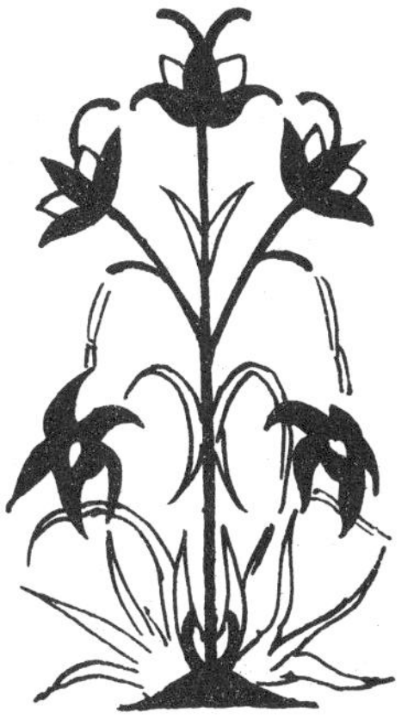
158

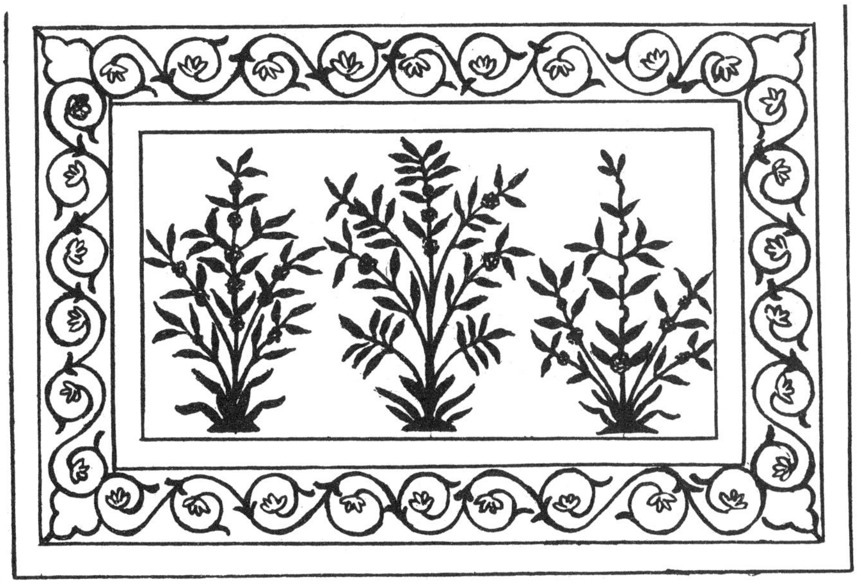
161

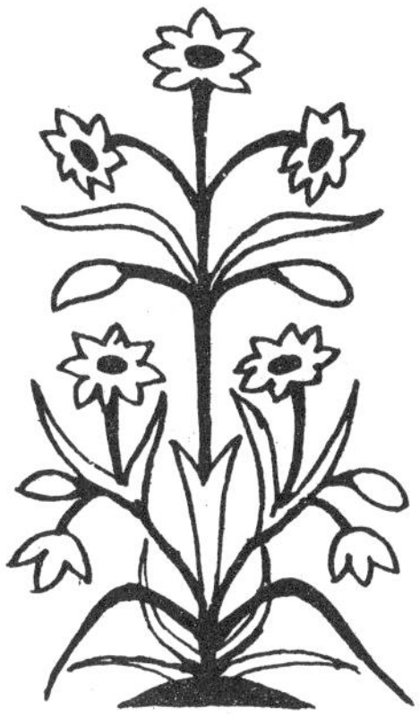
159

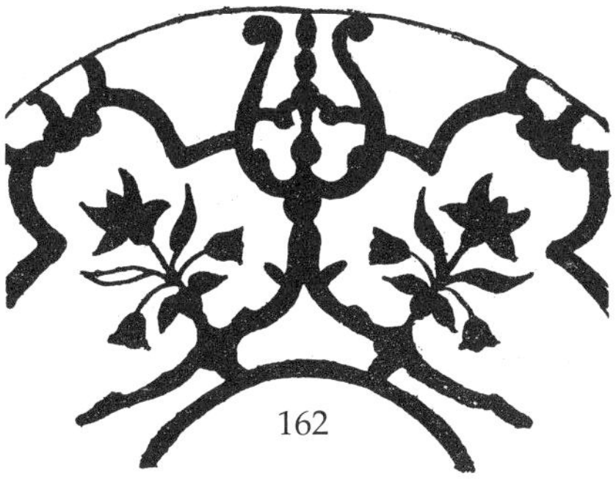
162

164

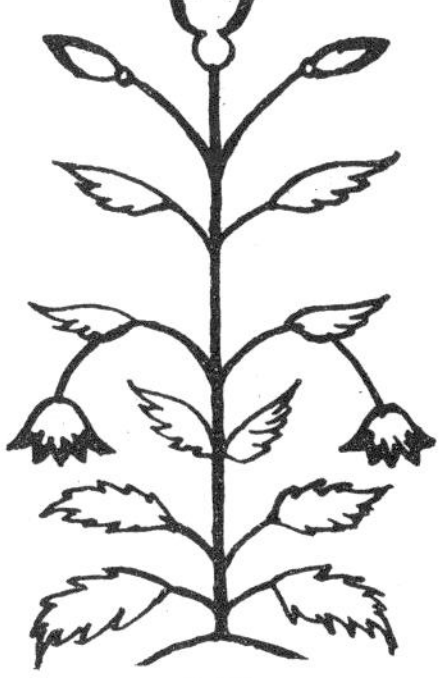
163

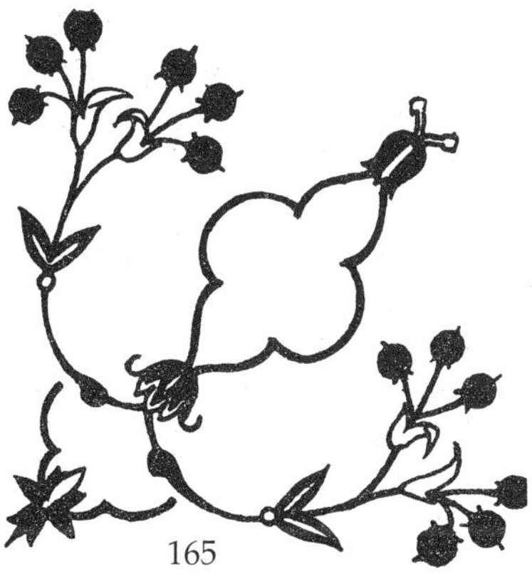
165

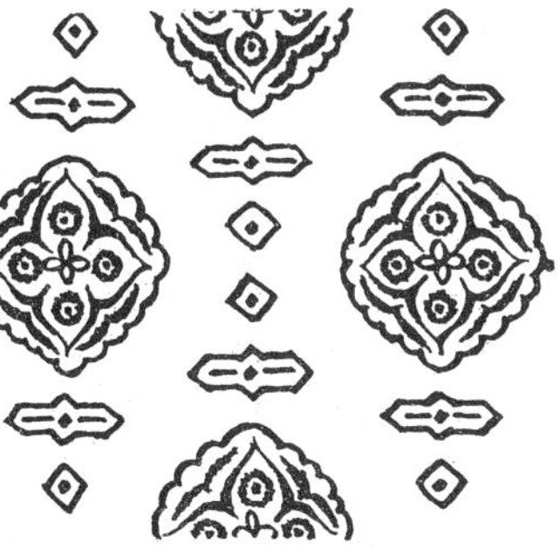
166

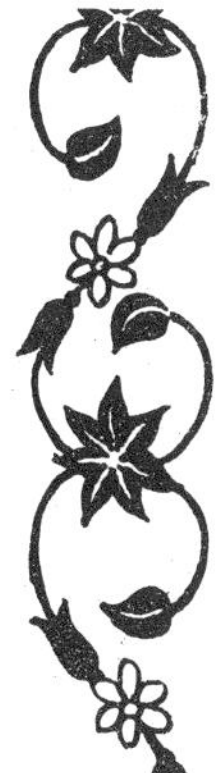

160

STONE INLAY WORK. **158, 159, 163.** Floral mosaics from Chini-ki-Rauza, Agra. **160, 164, 165.** Details of floral leaf and bud mosaics from the Cenotaph, Taj Mahal, Agra. **161, 162.** Floral and plant mosaics from the Hall of Private Audience, Red Fort, Delhi. **166.** Geometrical motifs in the mosaics on the marble turret of the tomb of Itmad-ud-Daula, Agra.

# Plate 18

167

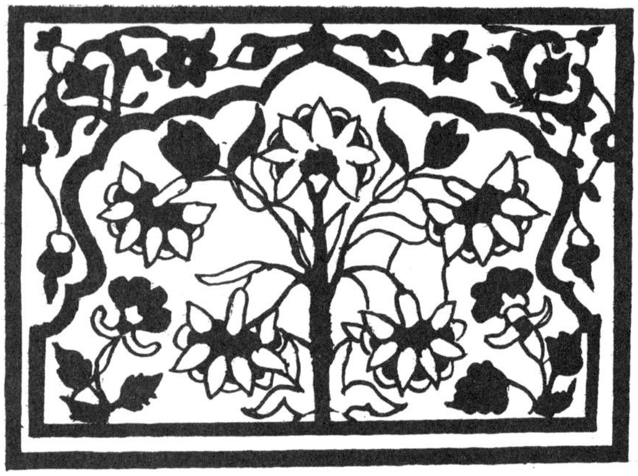

168

169

170

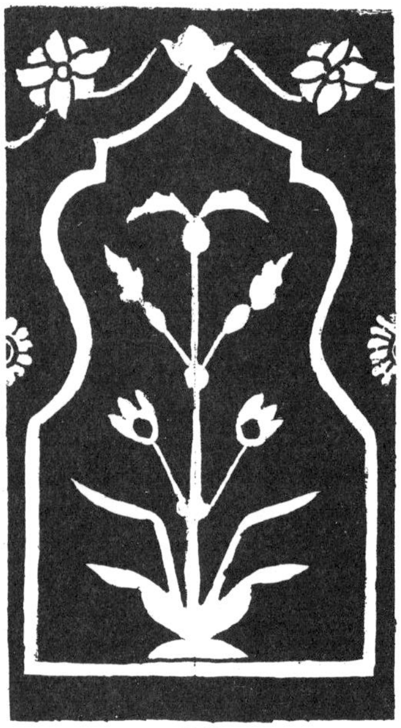

171

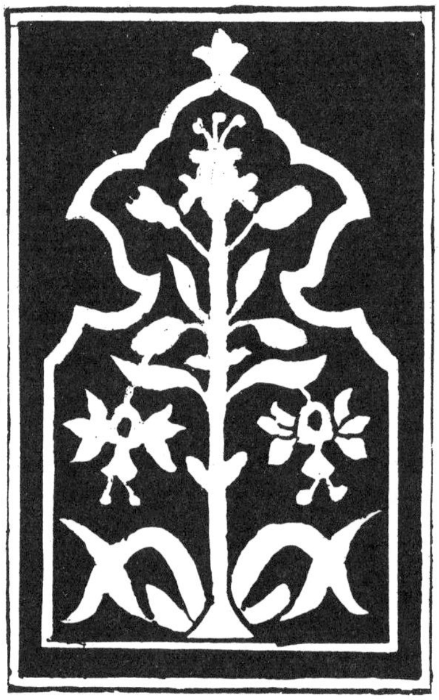

172

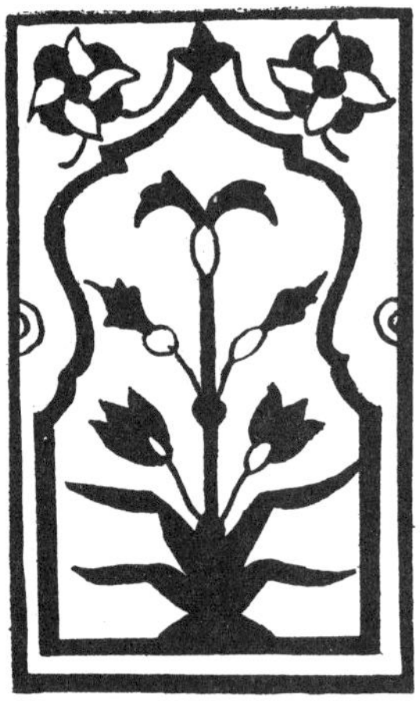

173

174

STONE INLAY WORK. **167–174.** Tile mosaics of different floral ensembles including the iris, lily, narcissus and fuchsia from the west facade north end of Chini-ki-Rauza, Agra.

# Plate 19

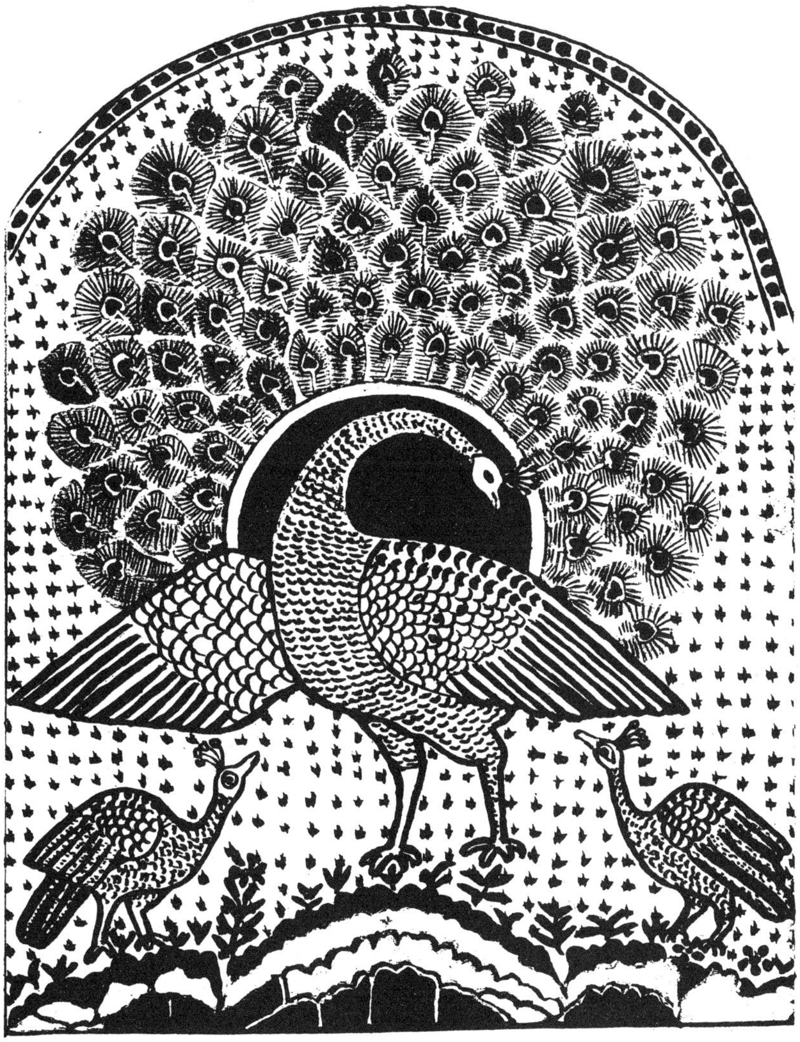

175

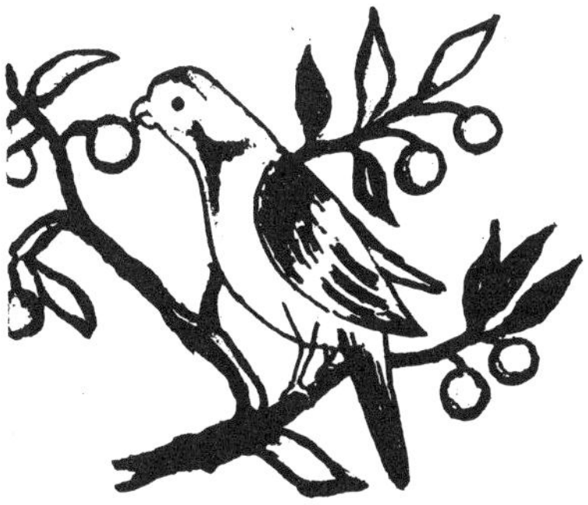

176

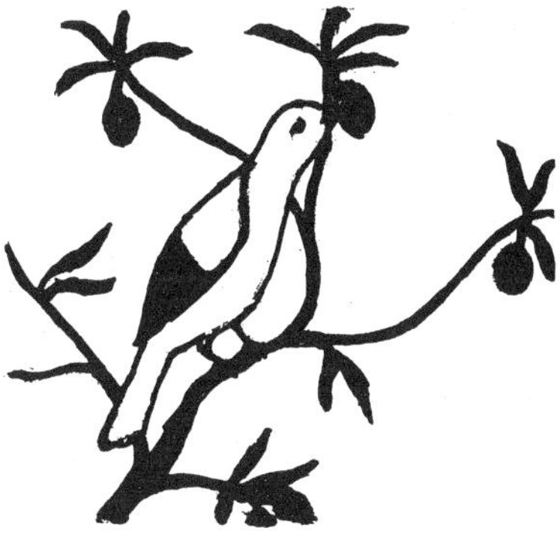

177

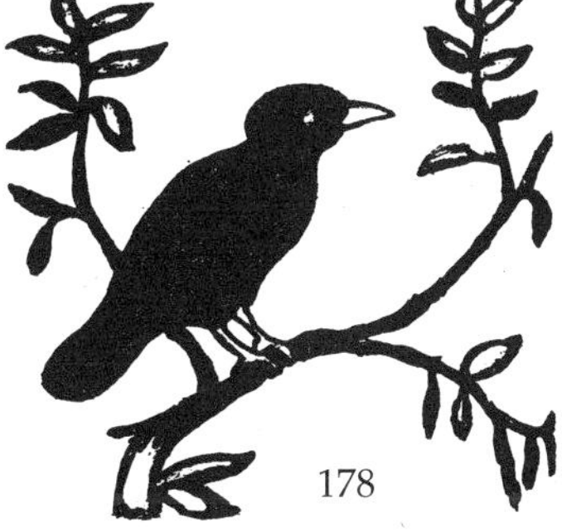

178

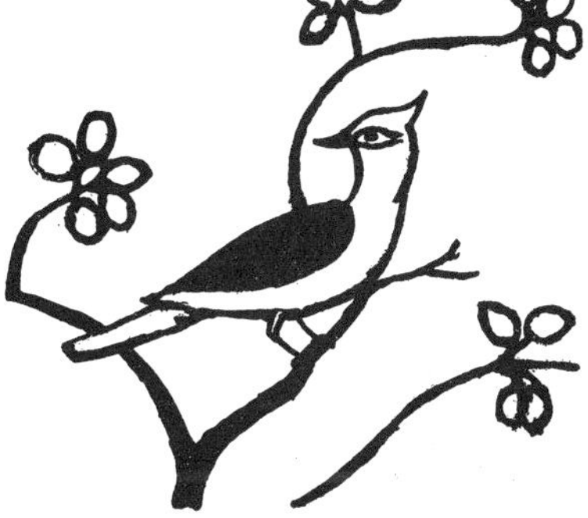

179

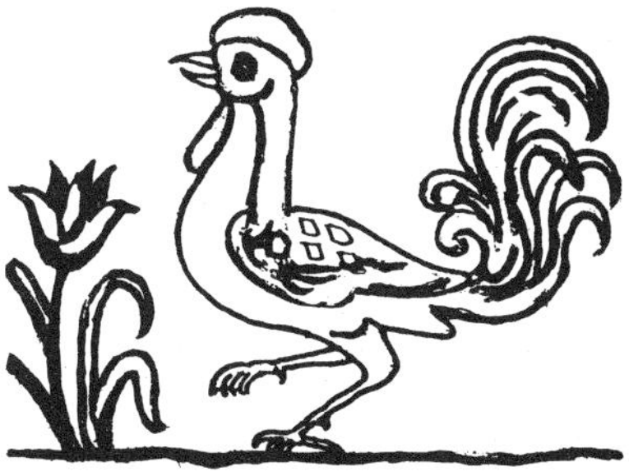

180

STONE INLAY WORK. **175.** Enameled mosaic of peacocks in lapis-lazuli and other semi-precious stones on the wall of a courtyard in the main palace, Udaipur, Rajasthan. **176–180.** Various birds and trees seen in the mosaics from the Throne Room in the Diwan-i-Am, Red Fort, Delhi.

# Plate 20

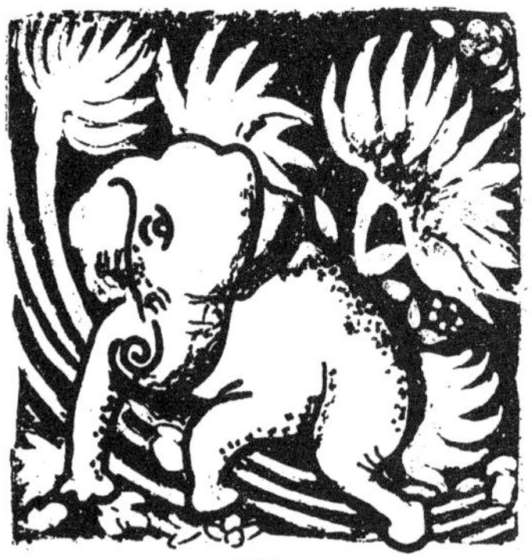
182

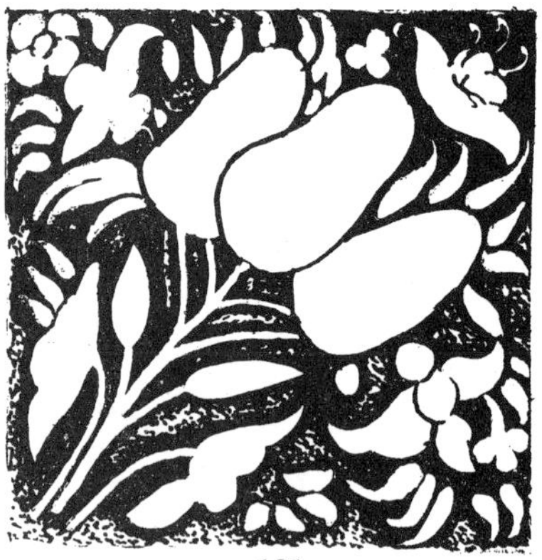
181

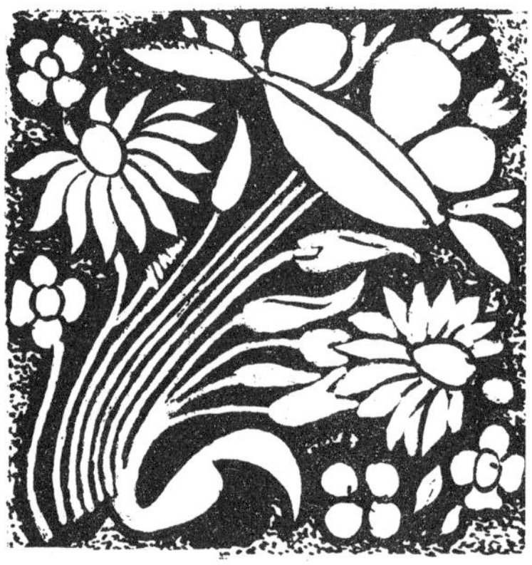
183

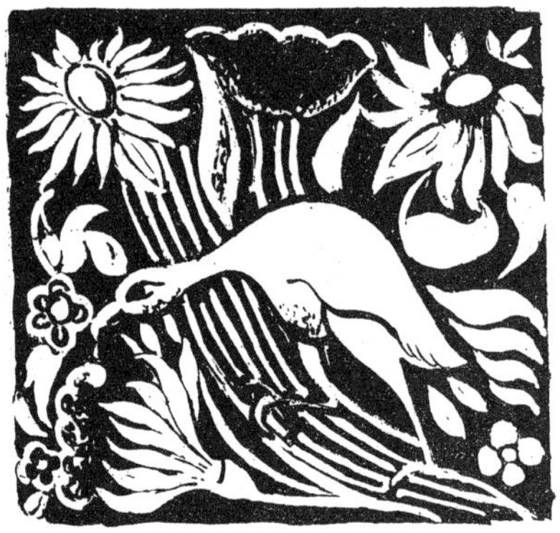
184

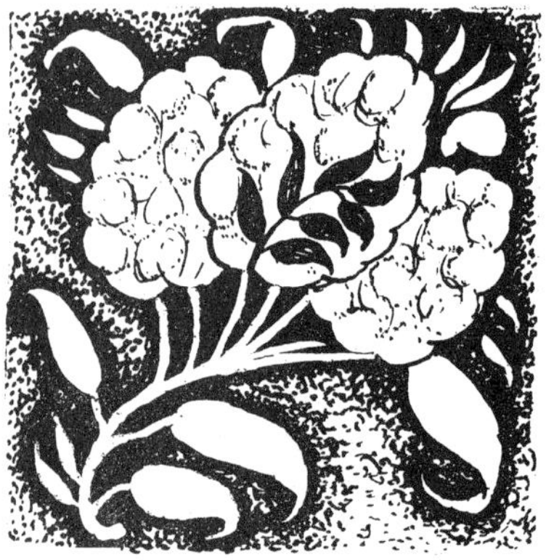
185

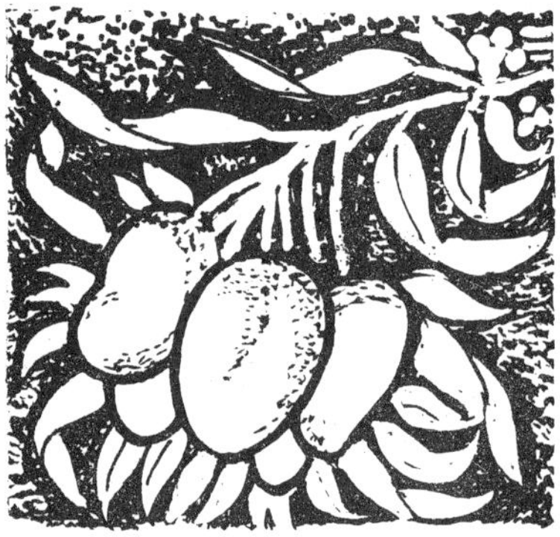
186

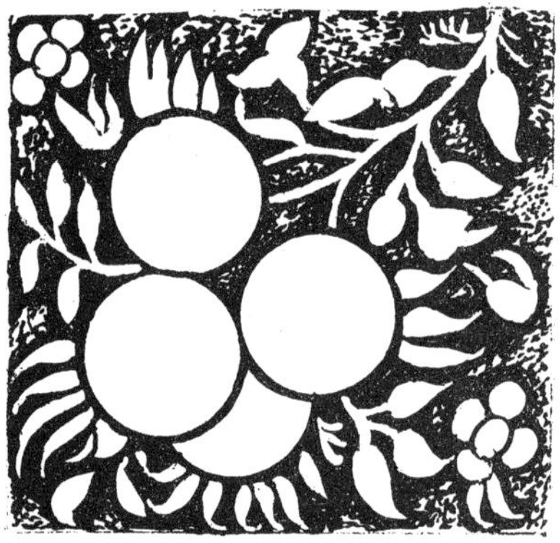
187

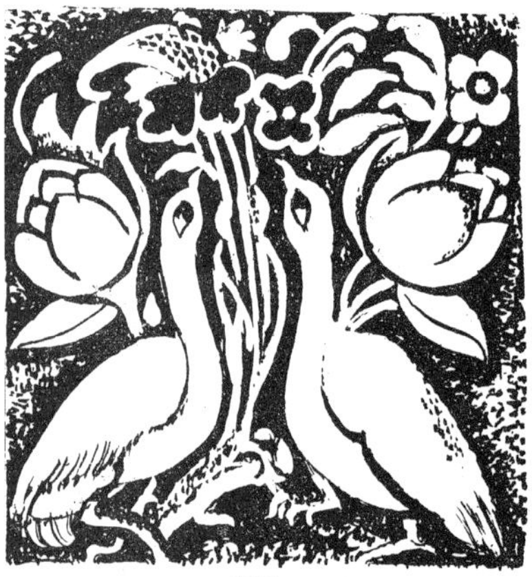
188

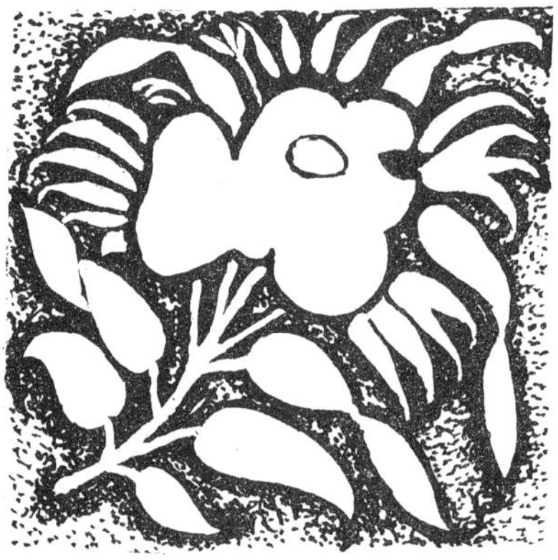
190

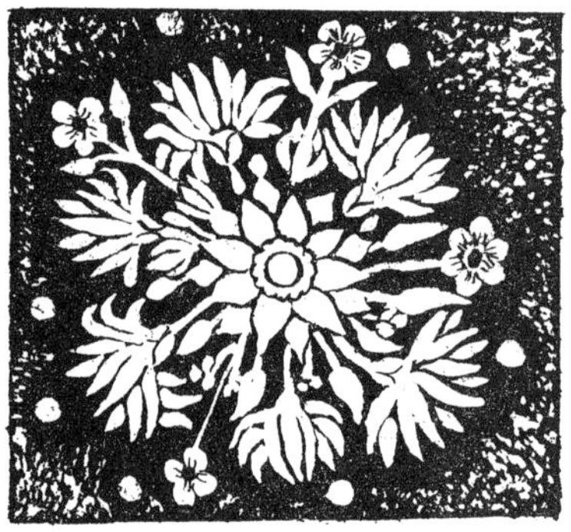
189

FRESCOES. **181–188, 190.** Details of fruit, lotus, bird and elephant motifs from the ceiling of Cave No. 1, Ajanta, c. 6th century A.D. **189.** Lotuses from Cave No. 2, Ajanta, c. 6th century A.D.

# Plate 21

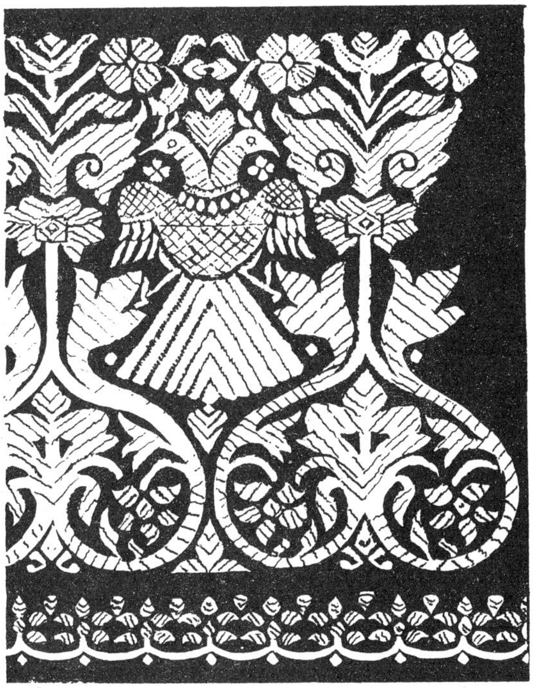

191

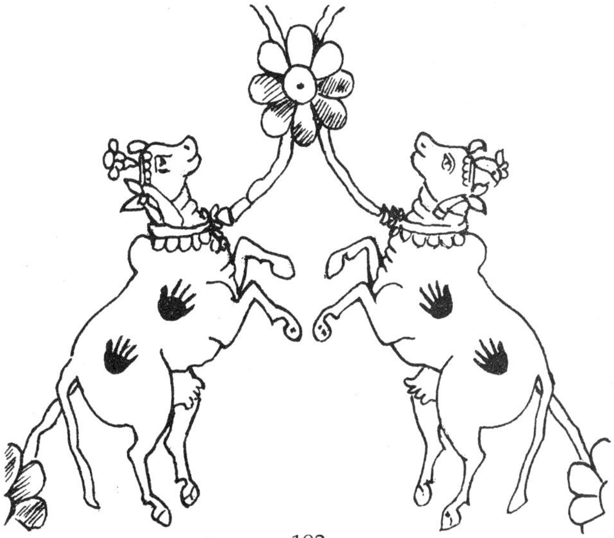

192

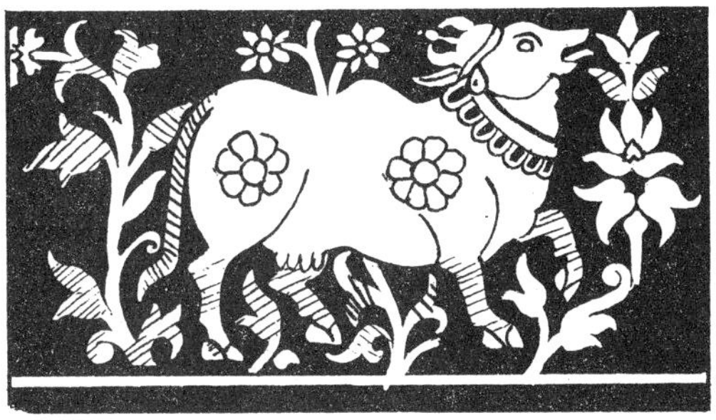

193

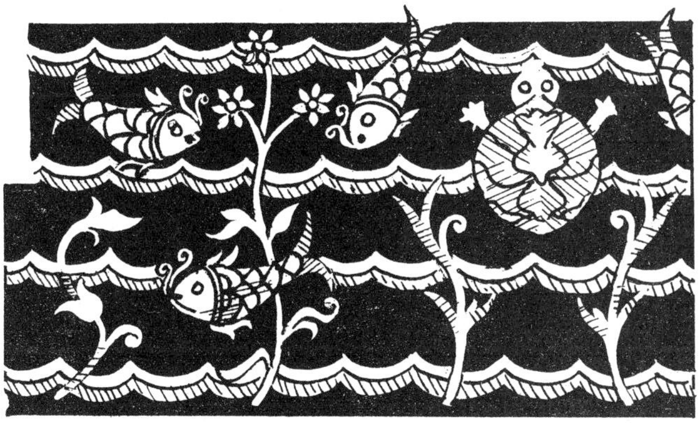

194

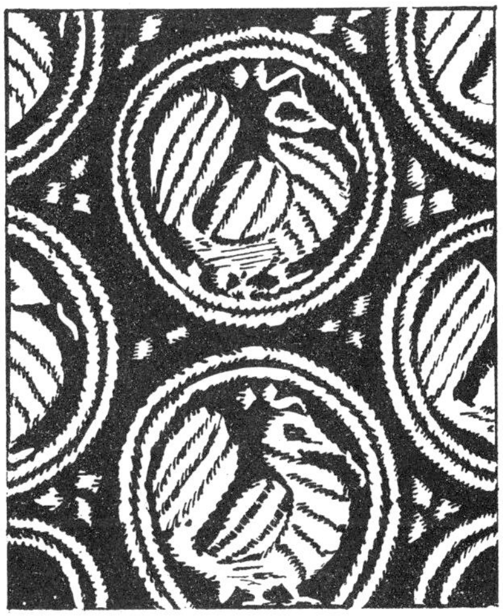

195

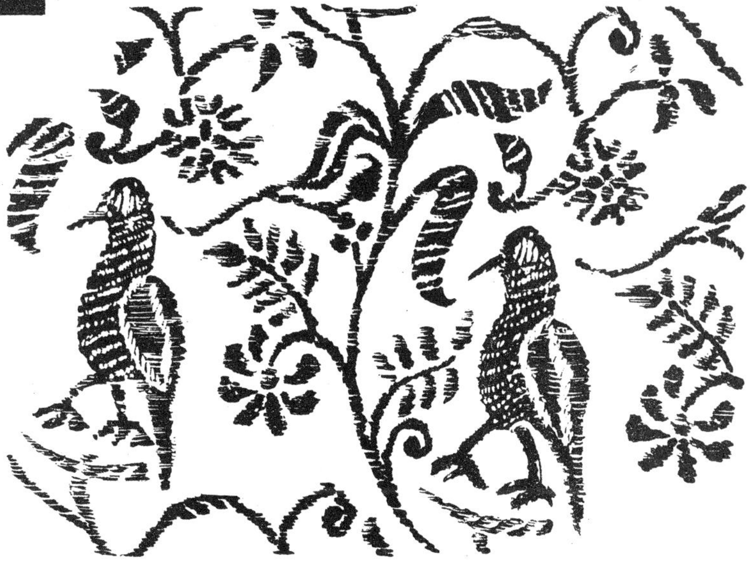

196

WOVEN FABRICS. **191, 195.** Details of stylized flower, eagle and peacock motifs from a traditional gold brocade Sari, Varanasi, Uttar Pradesh. **193, 194.** Details from a gold brocade by Shri Sankalchand Jaichand Bhai Patel of Gujarat, Master-craftsman, winner in the National Awards 1966, All India Handicrafts Board—stylized fauna and flora inspired by Nature. **192.** A Nature subject from a gold brocade from Varanasi, Uttar Pradesh. **196.** Flower and bird motifs are used in this Himru silk brocade from Aurangabad, Maharashtra.

# Plate 22

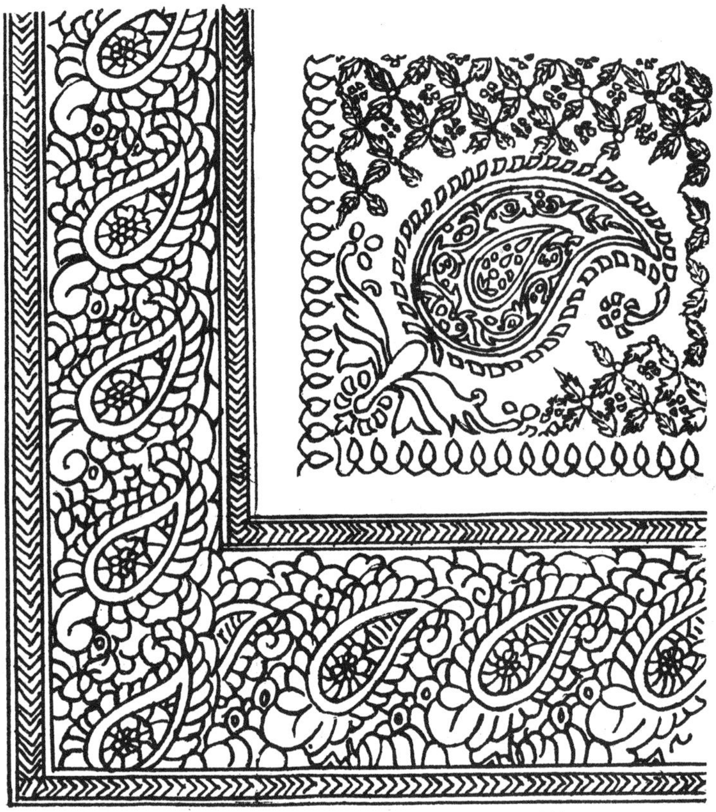

197

198

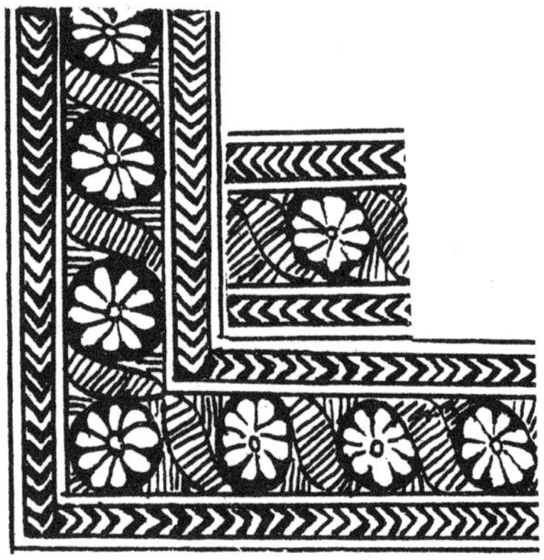

199

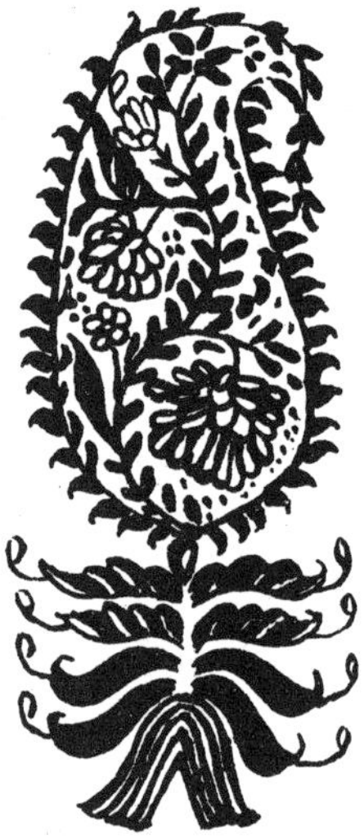

200

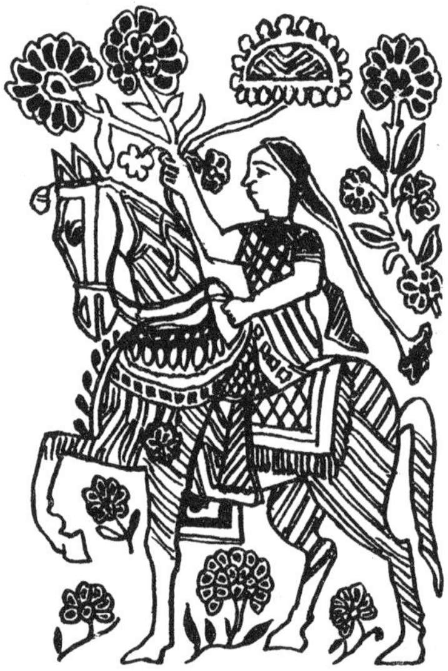

201

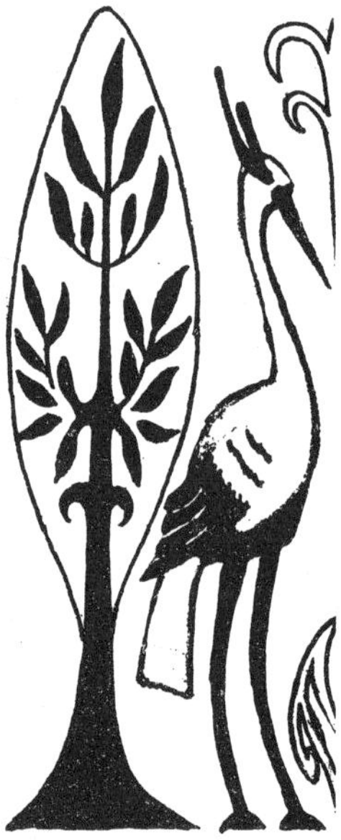

202

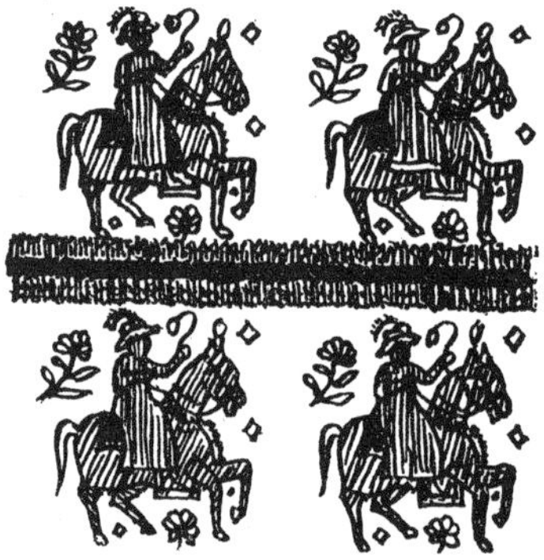

203

WOVEN FABRICS. **197, 198, 199.** Stylized Mango-floral motifs from the border and Pallav of a gold brocade Sari from Gujarat. **200.** Stylized Mango-floral motif from a gold brocade from Varanasi, Uttar Pradesh. **201.** Traditional motif from the Pallav of a Baluchar Sari, West Bengal. **202.** Stylized Crane and tree motif from a traditional Paithani Sari from Paithan, Maharashtra. **203.** Part of the Pallav of a Baluchar Sari from Dacca, 19th century, Bengal.

# Plate 23

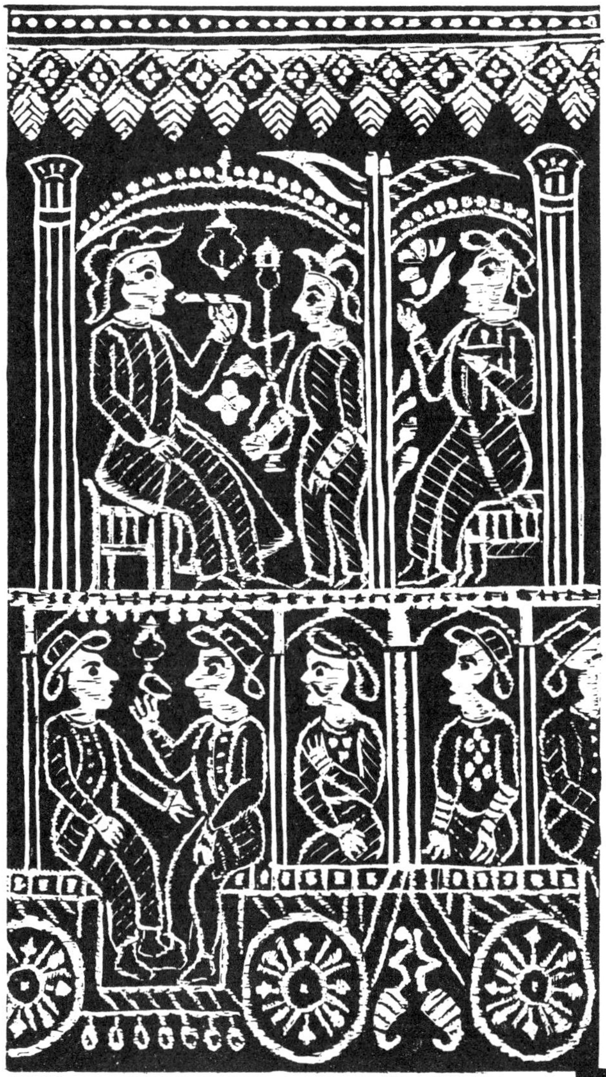

204

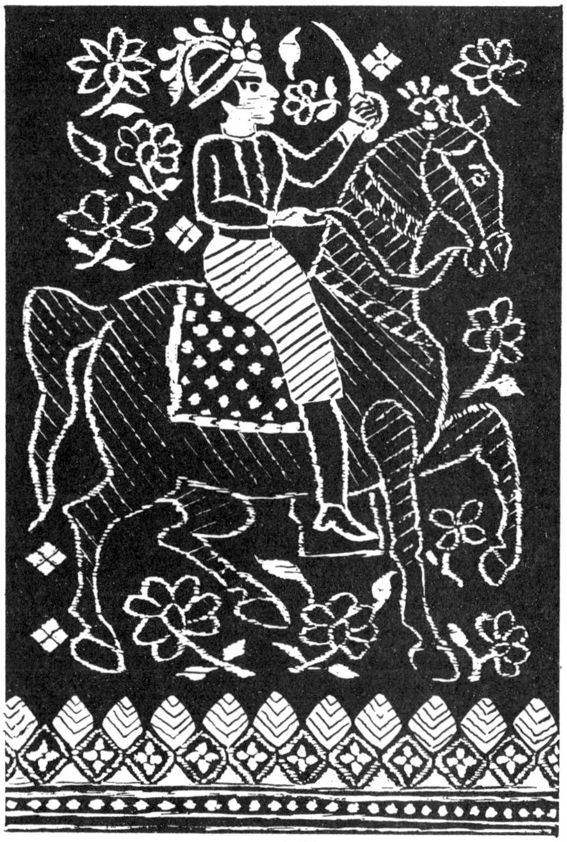

205

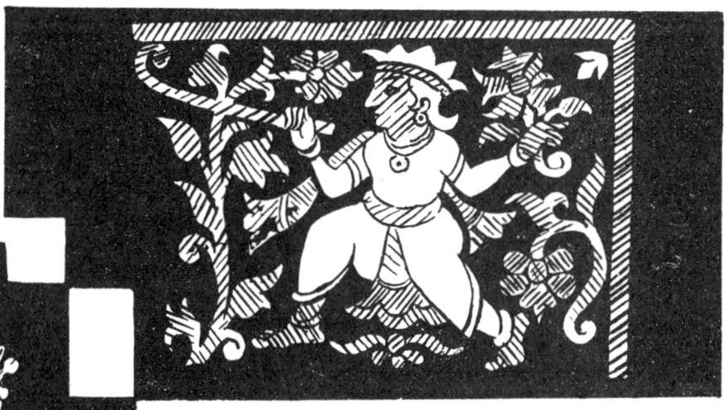

208

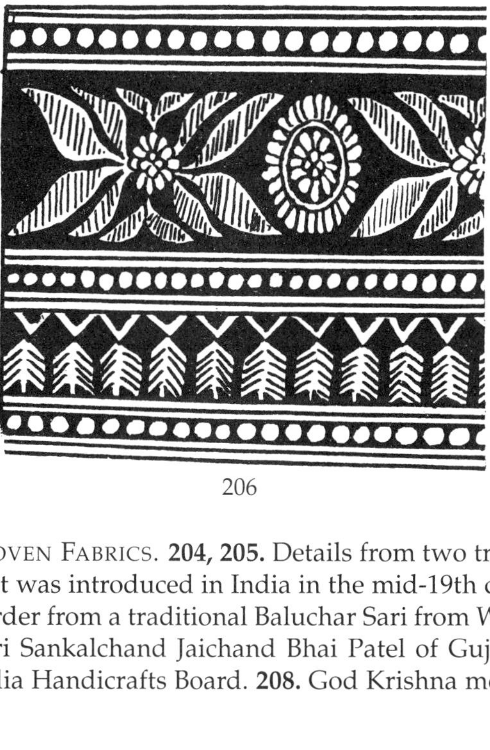

206

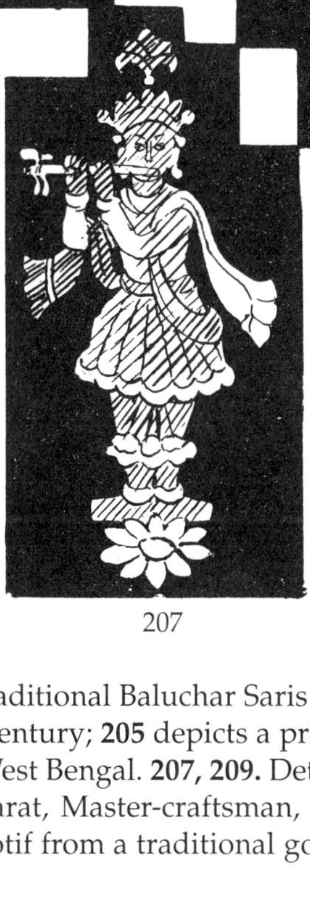

207

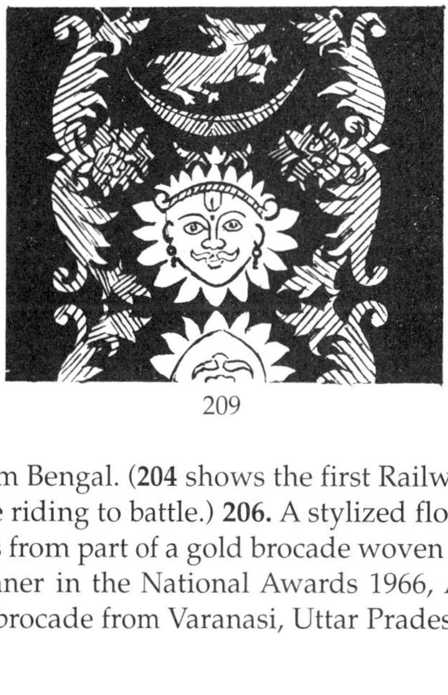

209

WOVEN FABRICS. **204, 205.** Details from two traditional Baluchar Saris from Bengal. (**204** shows the first Railway that was introduced in India in the mid-19th century; **205** depicts a prince riding to battle.) **206.** A stylized floral border from a traditional Baluchar Sari from West Bengal. **207, 209.** Details from part of a gold brocade woven by Shri Sankalchand Jaichand Bhai Patel of Gujarat, Master-craftsman, winner in the National Awards 1966, All India Handicrafts Board. **208.** God Krishna motif from a traditional gold brocade from Varanasi, Uttar Pradesh.

# Plate 24

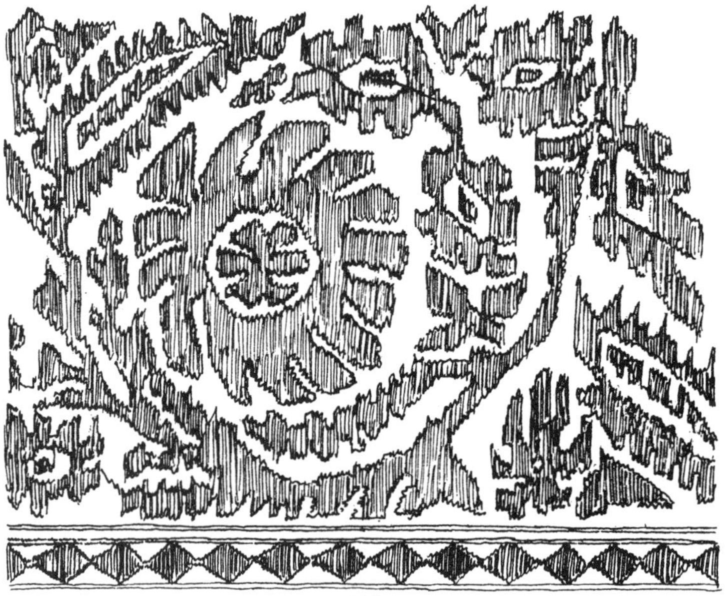

210

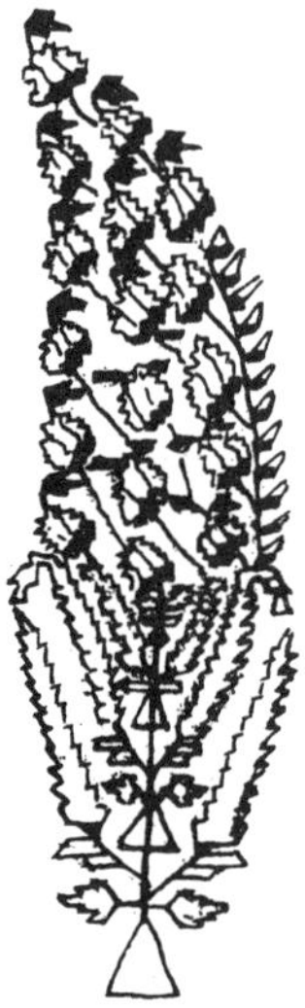

211

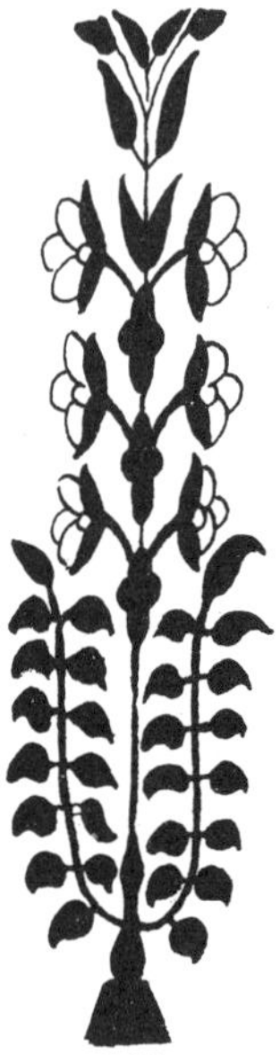

212

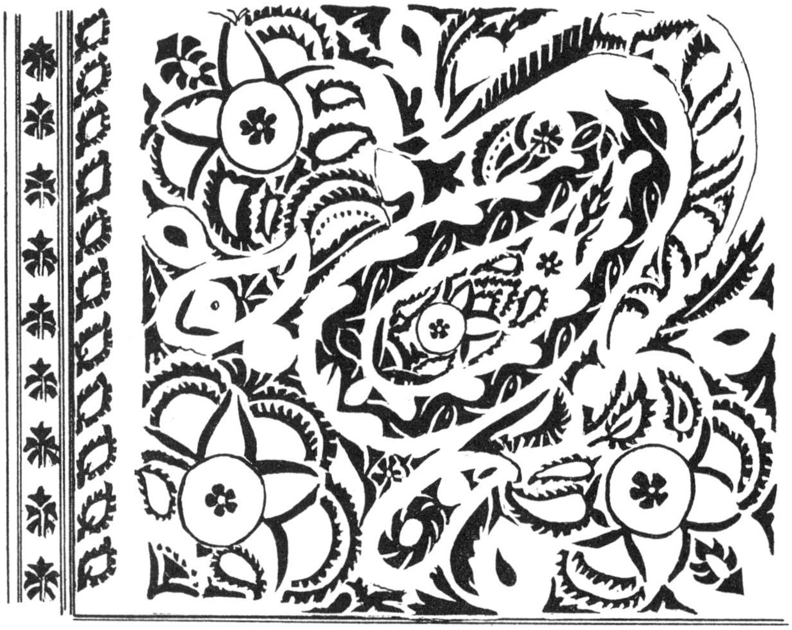

213

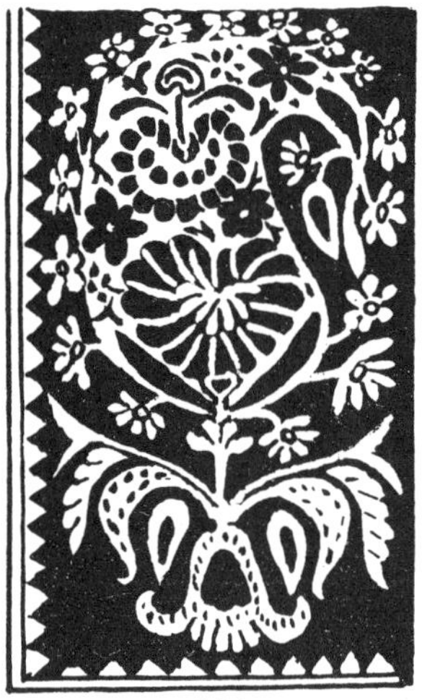

214

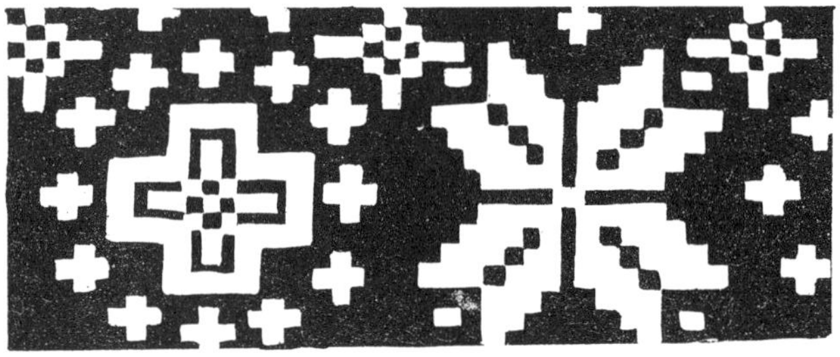

215

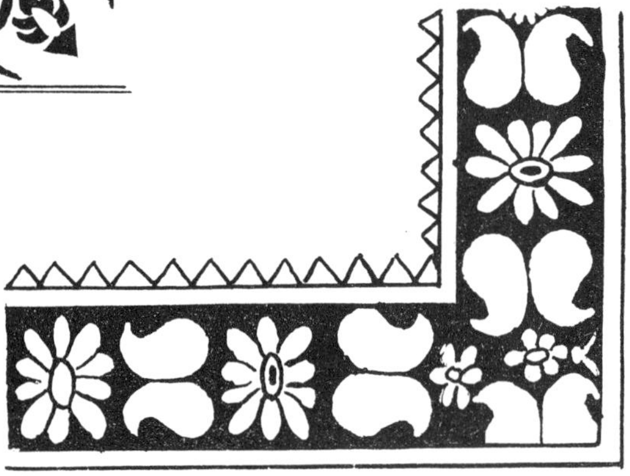

216

WOVEN FABRICS. **210.** Stylized floral ensemble—border of Daccai Jamdani Sari. **211, 212.** Stylized floral motifs from the Pallavs of two Chanderi Saris, Madhya Pradesh. **213.** Stylized mango-floral motif—Daccai Jamdani Sari from West Bengal. **214, 216.** Mango-floral motifs from the Pallav and border of a Daccai Baluchar Sari, Bengal, 19th century. **215.** A woven shadow fabric with geometrical pattern from Varanasi, Uttar Pradesh.

# Plate 25

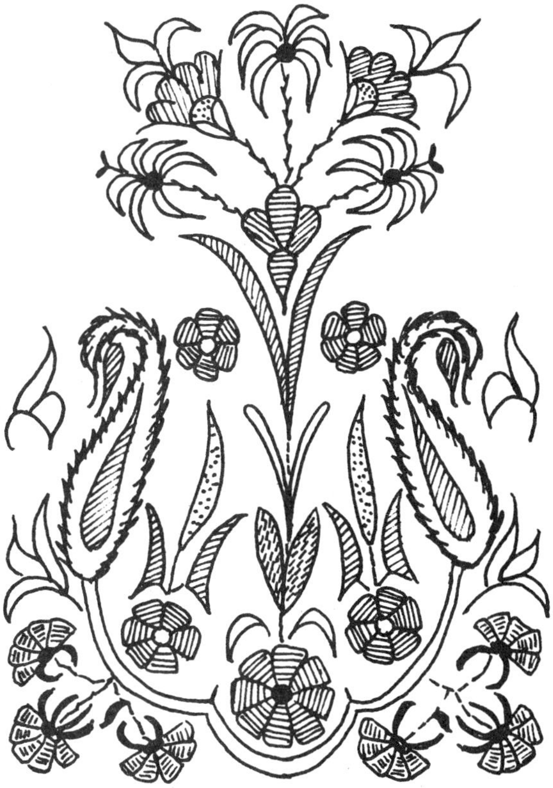

217

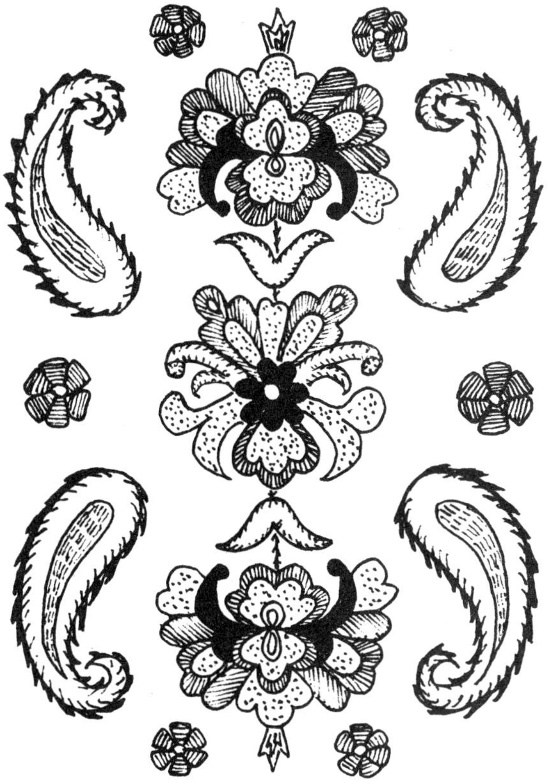

218

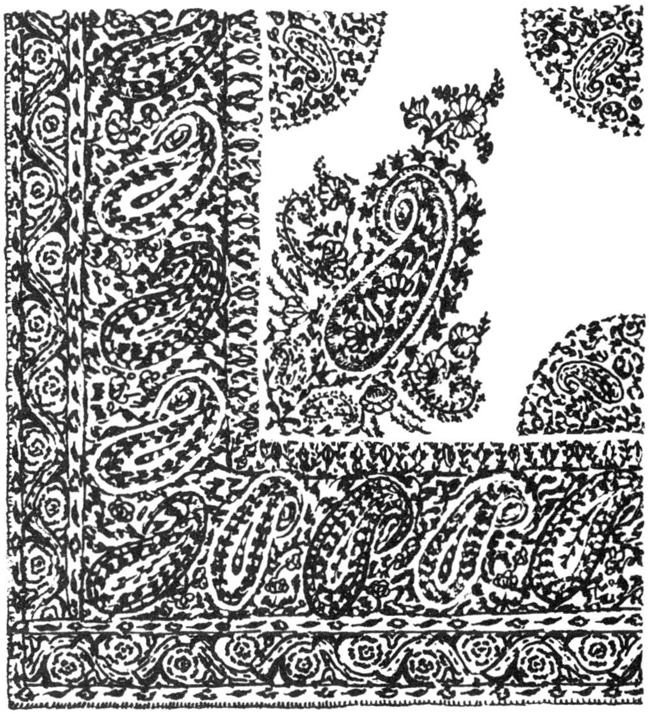

219

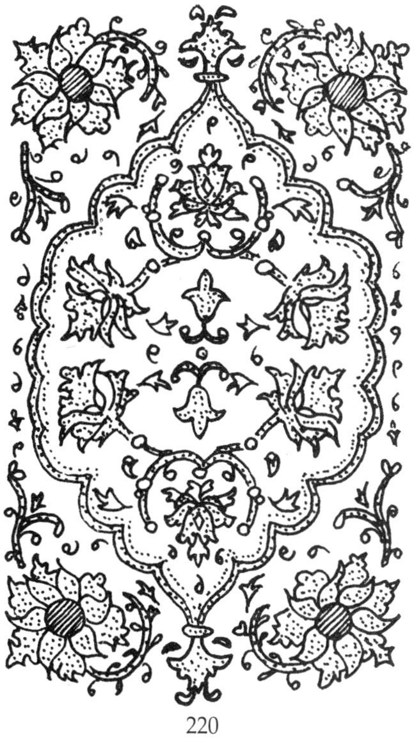

220

EMBROIDERED FABRICS. **217.** Floral, almond and spray motifs from a Kashmir shawl embroidered in mellow tones. **218.** Almond and floral stylized motifs from an embroidered stole, Kashmir. **219.** Details of stylized almond and almond blossom motifs from a traditional embroidered Kashmir shawl based on a woven Jamevar. **220.** Stylized floral motifs from an embroidered Kashmir Choga coat.

# Plate 26

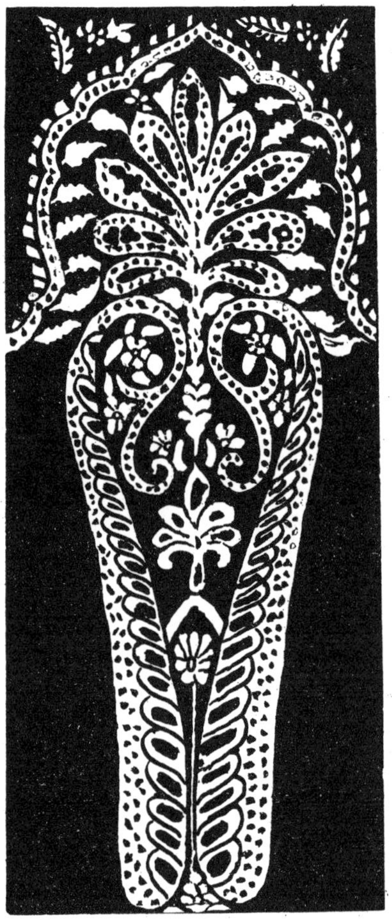

221

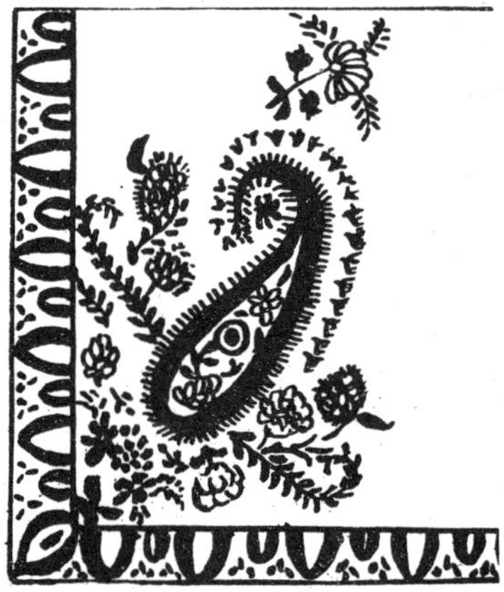

222

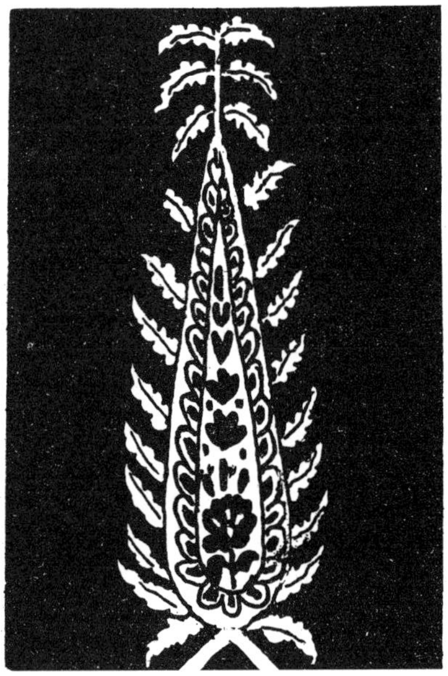

223

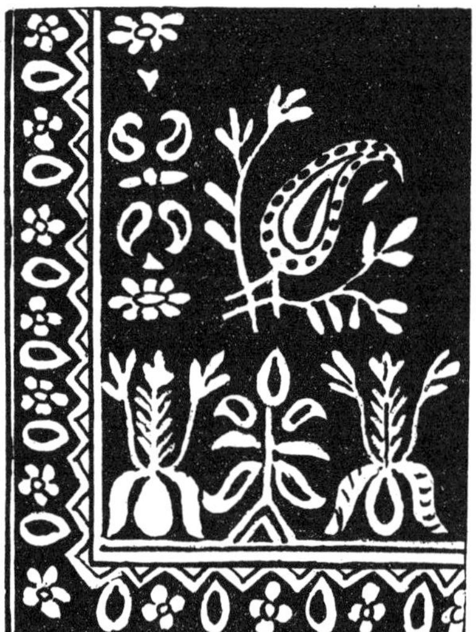

224

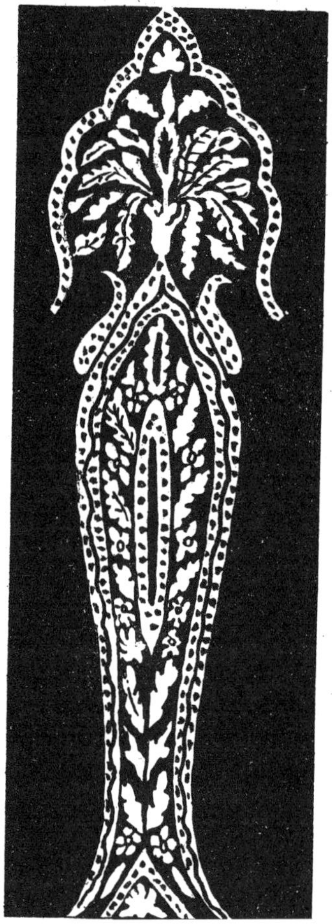

225

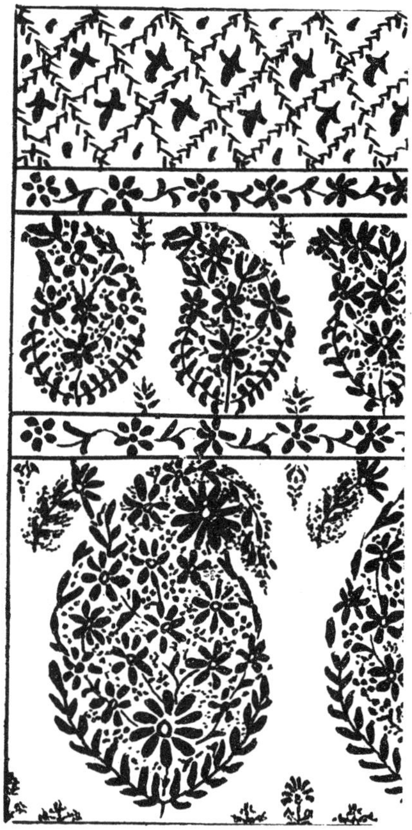

226

EMBROIDERED FABRICS. **221, 223, 224, 225.** Details of Kashmir embroidery in multi-colored silk on a black stole with typical motifs of stylized flowers, the almond and the cyprus tree. **222.** Details of the corner of an old Kashmir embroidered shawl, stylized floral and almond motifs. **226.** Embroidered shawl from Kashmir with traditional Kalka motifs inset with floral ensembles.

# Plate 27

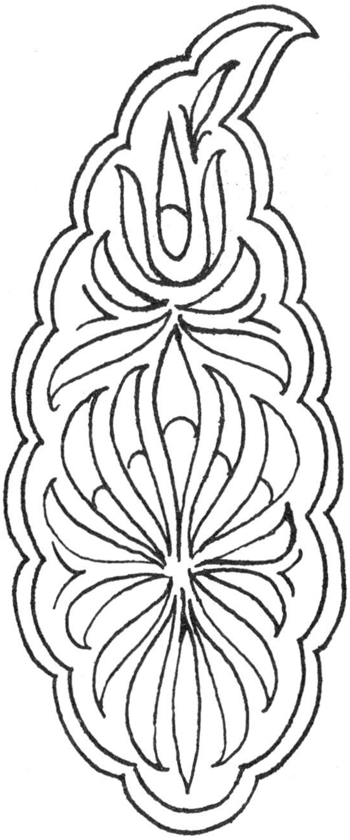

227

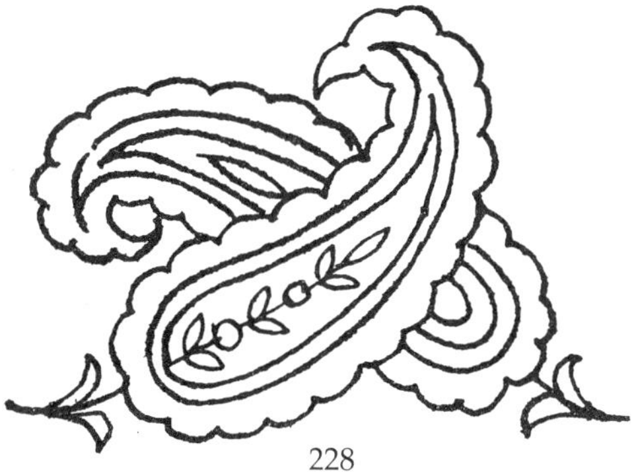

228

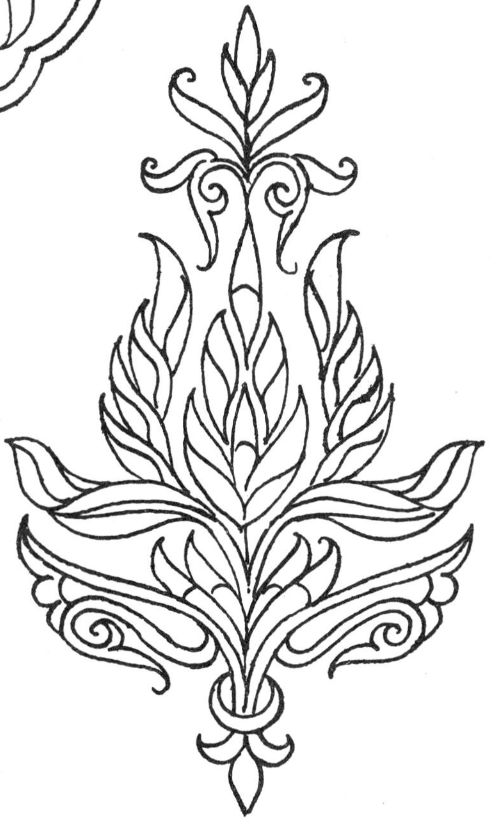

229

230

EMBROIDERED FABRICS. **227.** Pinecone motif taken from a Kashmir Choga coat, worked in Dori embroidery which applies the thread on top, fixed with finer thread. **228.** The double almond (Badam) motif from a traditional Kashmir shawl. **229.** Details of a stylized Iris, an old motif from a Kani traditional Kashmir shawl, in which the weaver and embroiderer (Rafughar) both participate. **230.** The Cyprus tree stylized in this motif taken from a Dourukha traditional woven shawl and adapted to embroidery, with the mode of both sides of the shawl being the same. All motifs **227–230** have been adapted for embroideries by Kashelen Fabrics, Srinagar, Kashmir.

# Plate 28

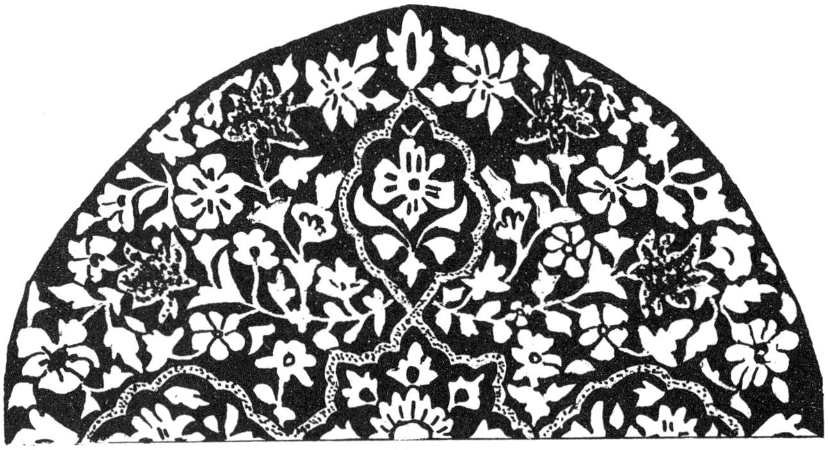

231

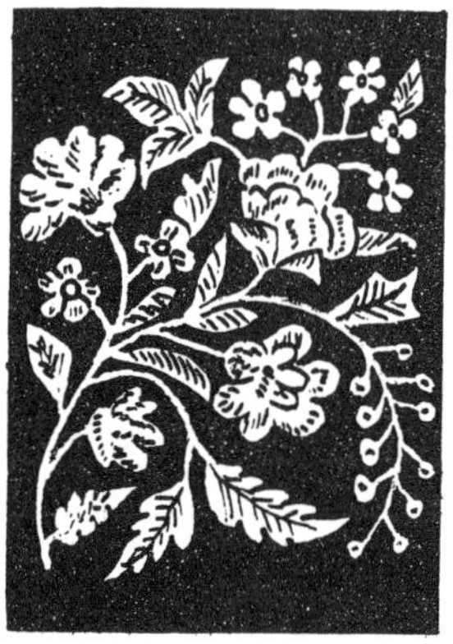

232

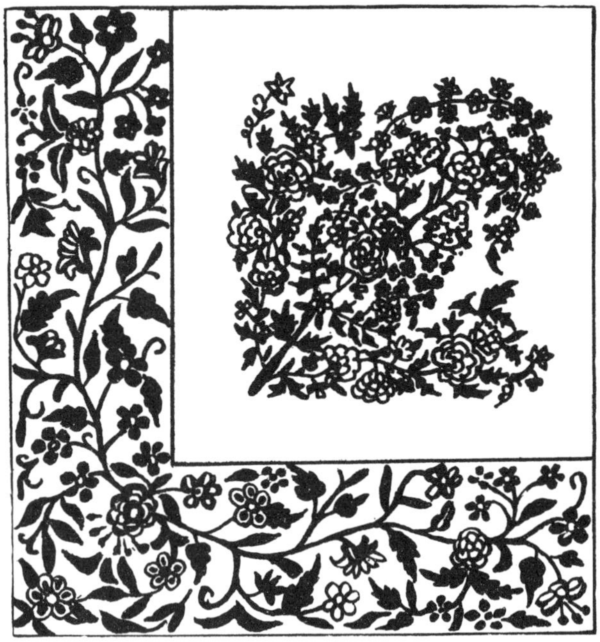

233

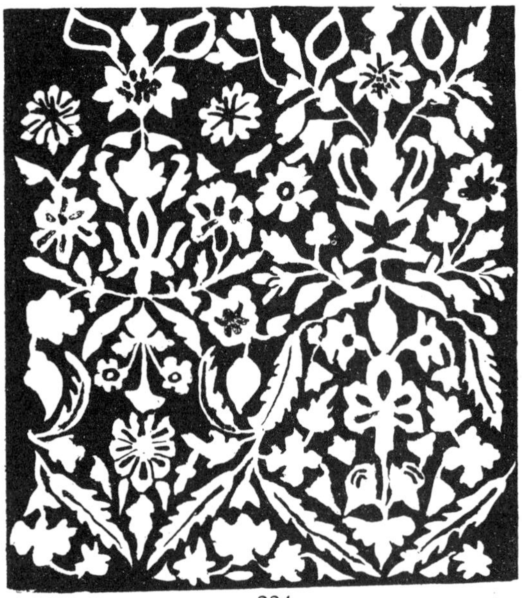

234

235

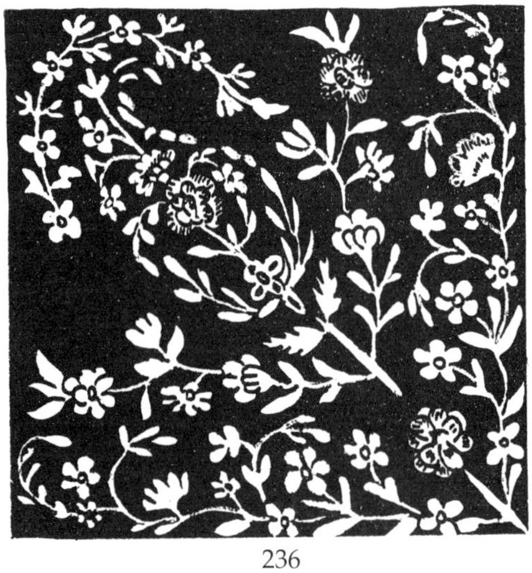

236

EMBROIDERED FABRICS. **231, 234.** Details of embroidered floral ensembles with multi-colored silks on black material, 19th century. **232, 235, 236.** Details of borders and corner of combinations of floral sprays done in white silk on black net, Dacca, 19th century. **233.** Details of rose, forget-me-not and honeysuckle motifs on curving stems embroidered in contrasting tones, 19th century.

# Plate 29

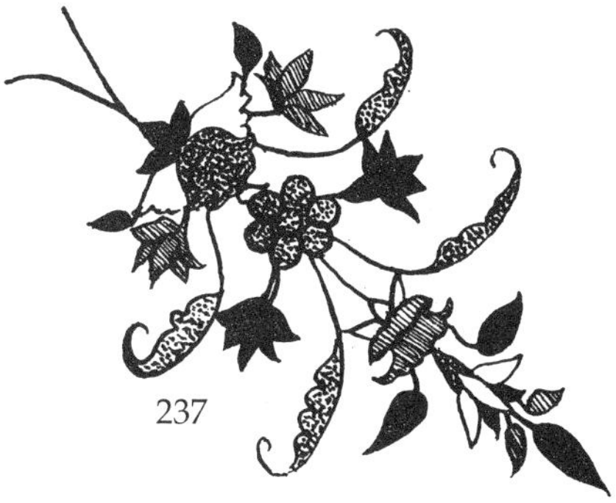
237

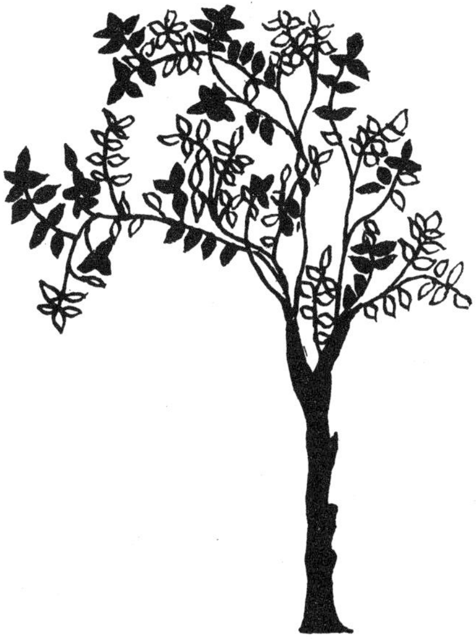
238

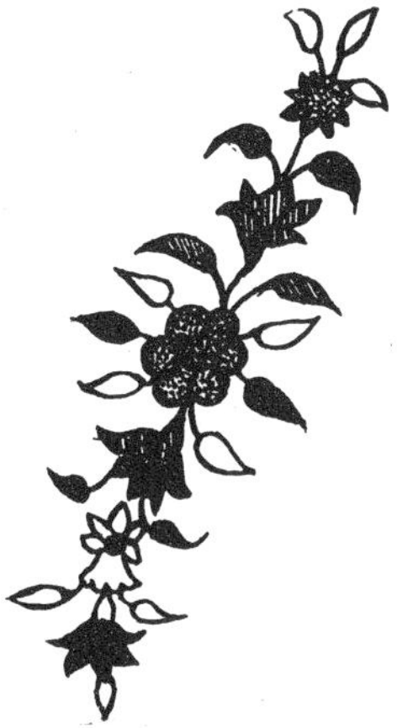
239

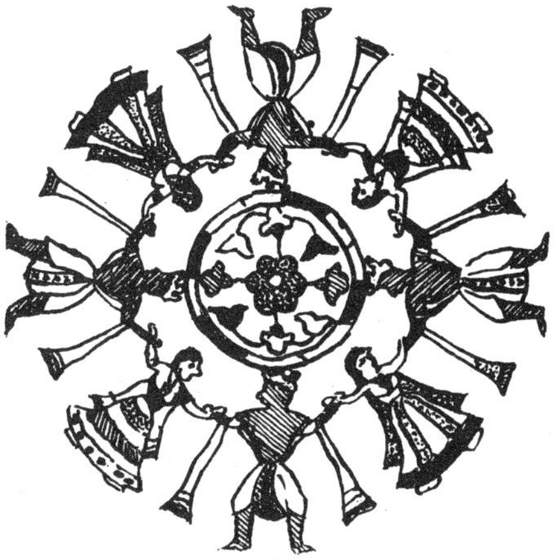
240

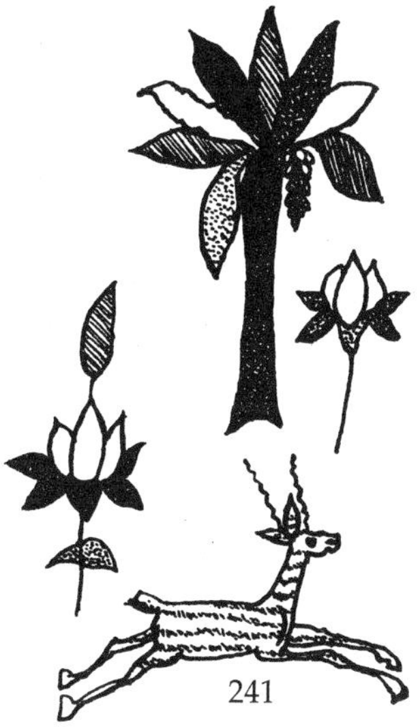
241

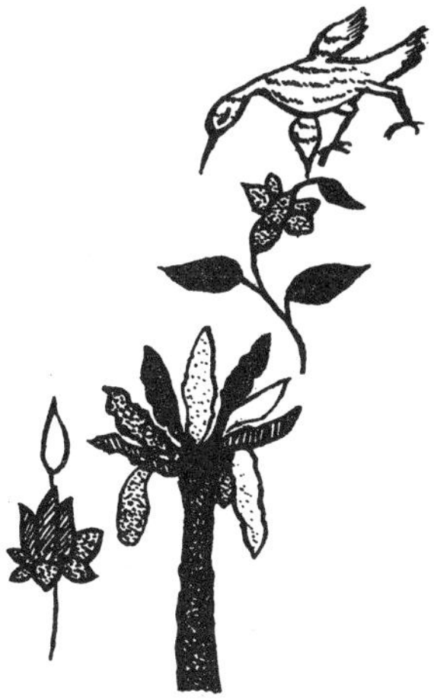
242

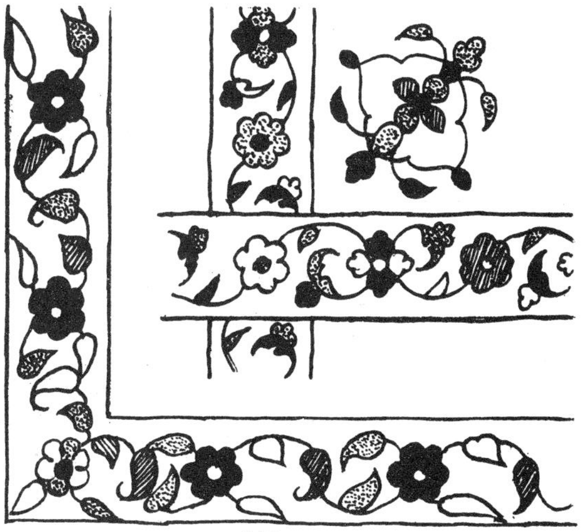
243

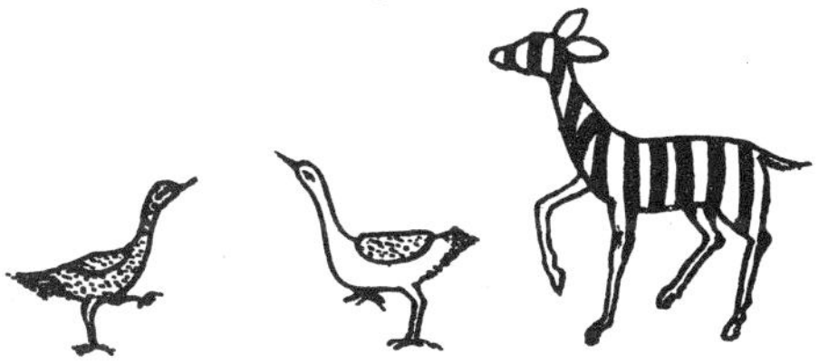
244

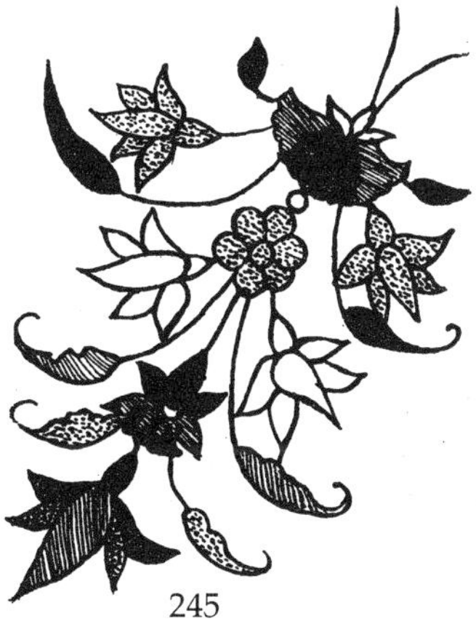
245

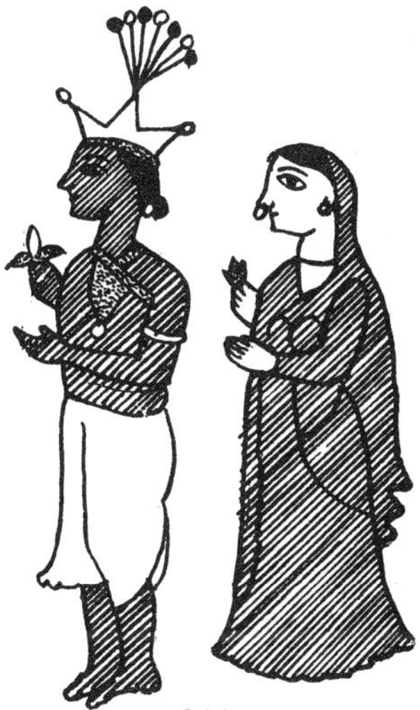
246

EMBROIDERED FABRICS. **237, 238, 239, 241, 242, 244, 245, 246.** Details of motifs of sprays, trees, the lotus ducks, deer and Krishna and Radha from a traditional embroidered Chamba Rumal. **240, 243.** Details of motifs of the Group Dance of Krishna, Radha and the Gopis (Ras Mandla) and floral borders from a traditional Chamba Rumal Himachal Pradesh.

# Plate 30

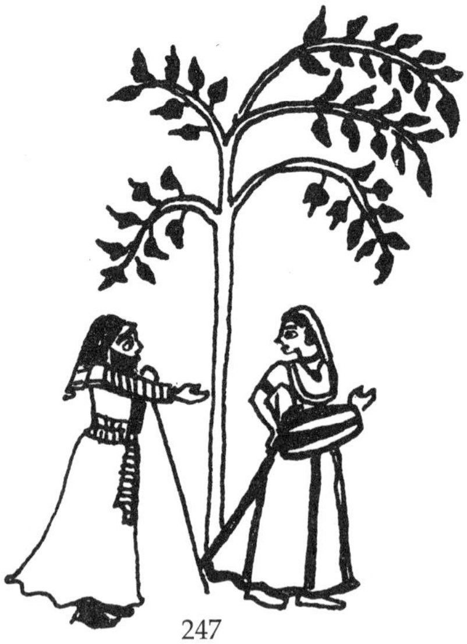
247

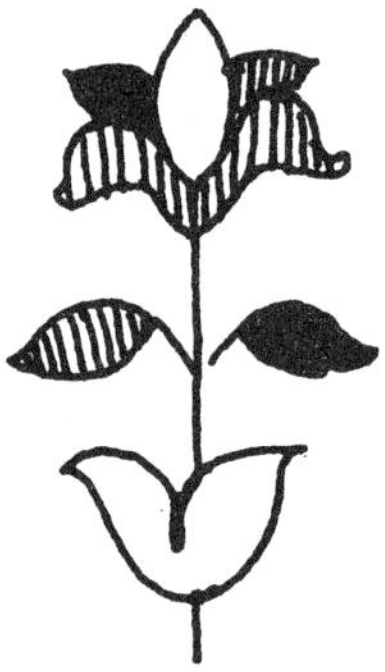
248

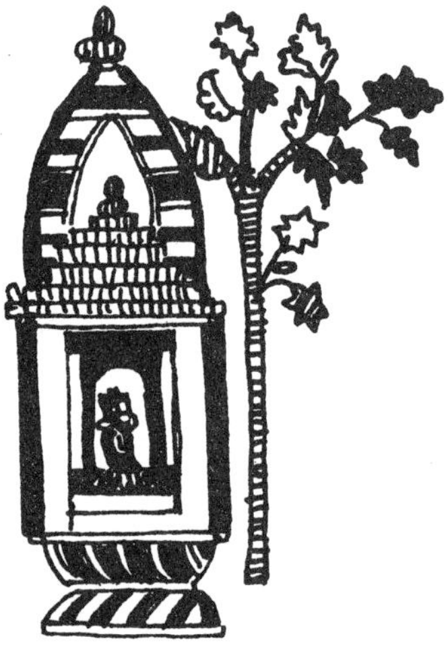
249

250

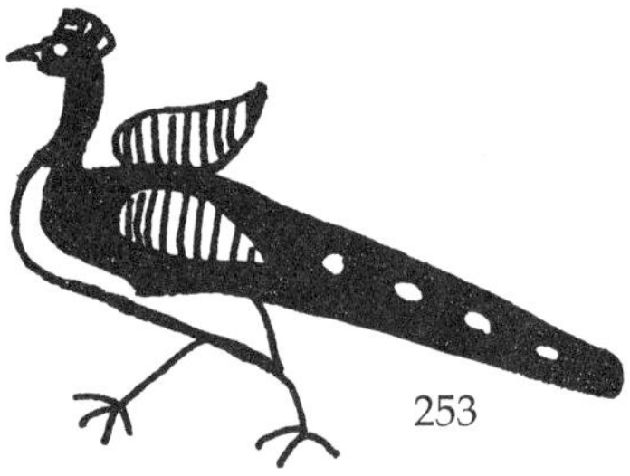
253

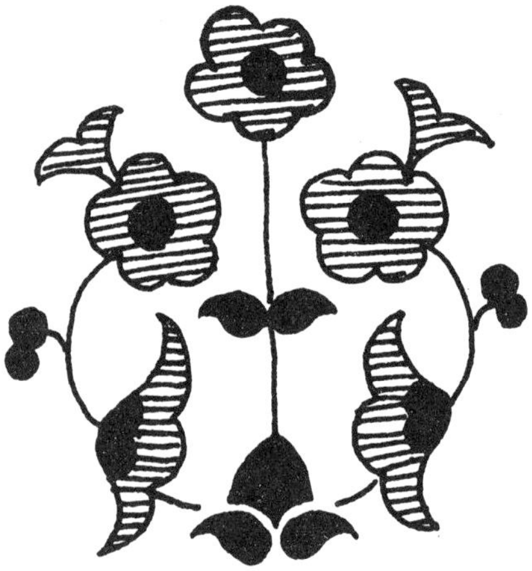
251

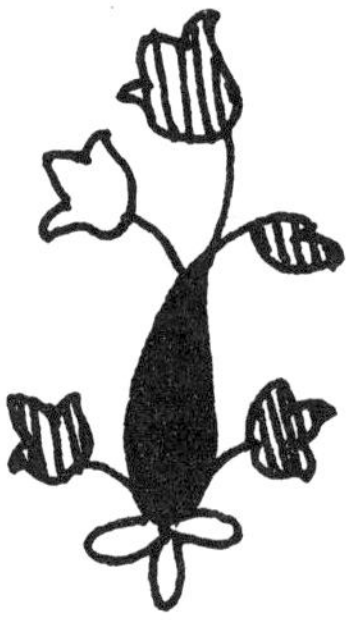
252

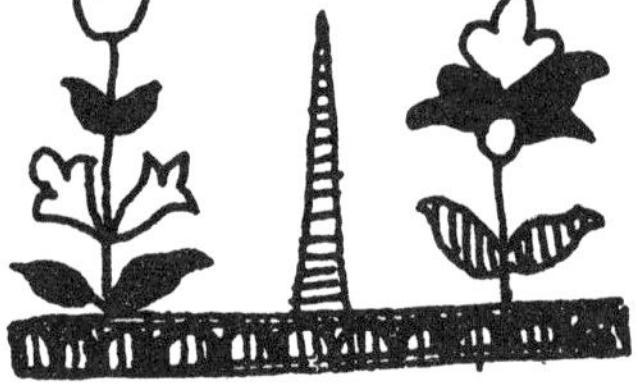
255

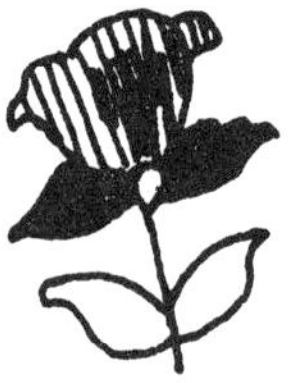
256

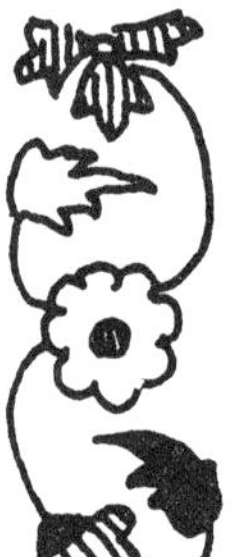

254

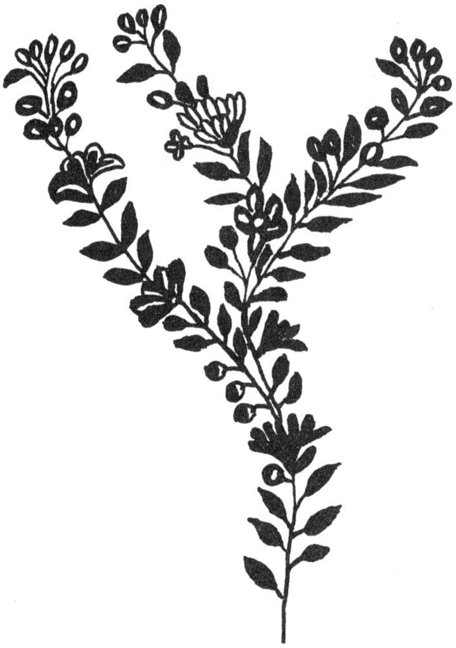
257

EMBROIDERED FABRICS. **247–252, 254, 255, 256.** Details of motifs of floral borders and sprays, trees, temple and human figures from a traditional embroidered Chamba Rumal depicting the marriage of Rukmani (Rukmani Haran). **253.** Bird motif. **257.** Stylized jasmine spray sometimes adapted from a Miniature painting to a traditional embroidered Chamba Rumal, Himachal Pradesh.

# Plate 31

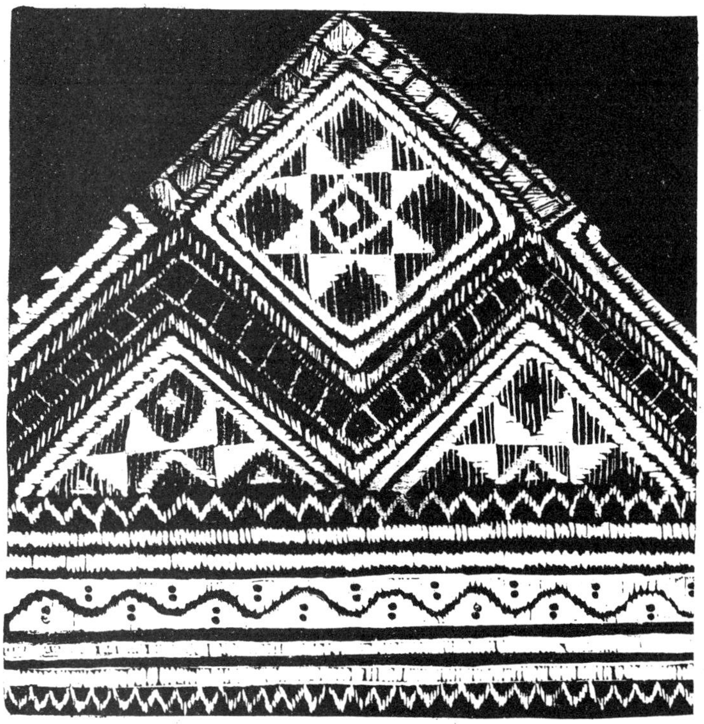

258

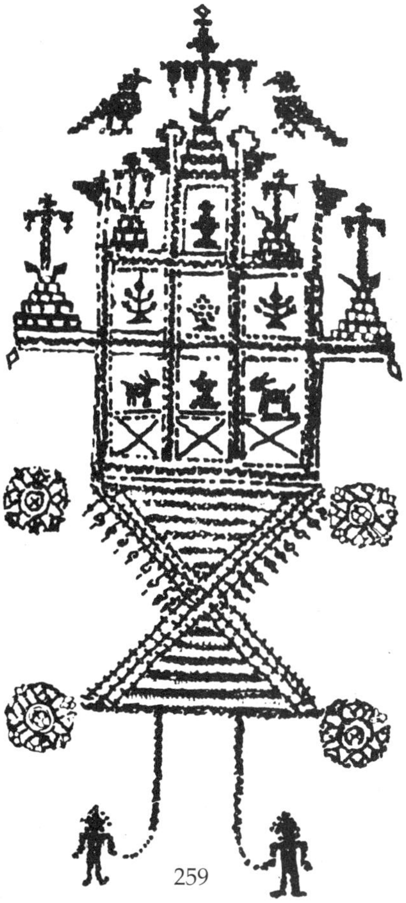

259

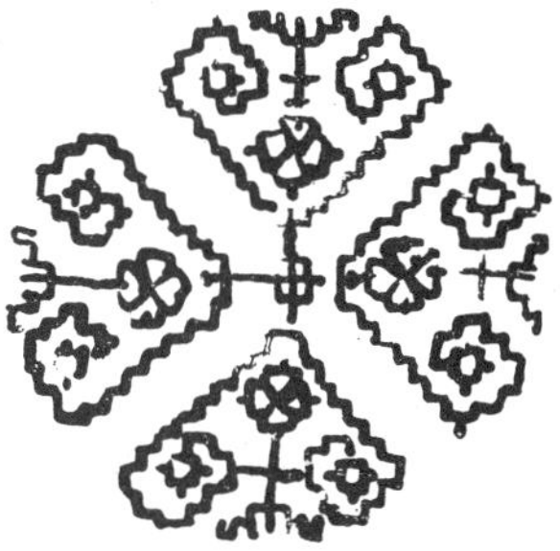

260

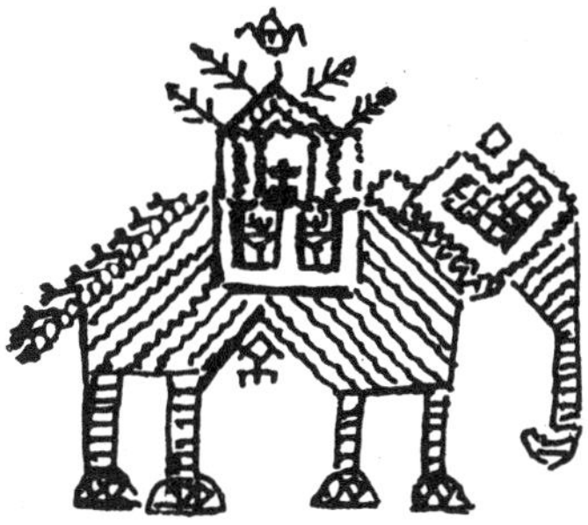

261

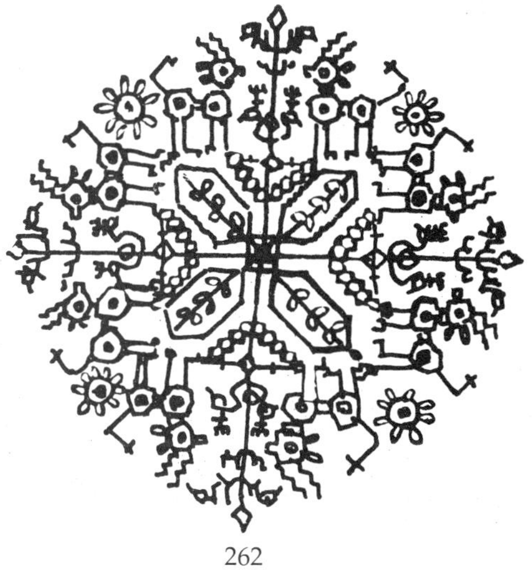

262

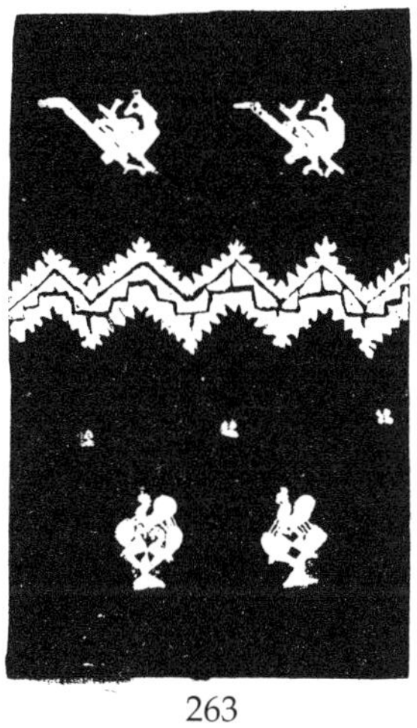

263

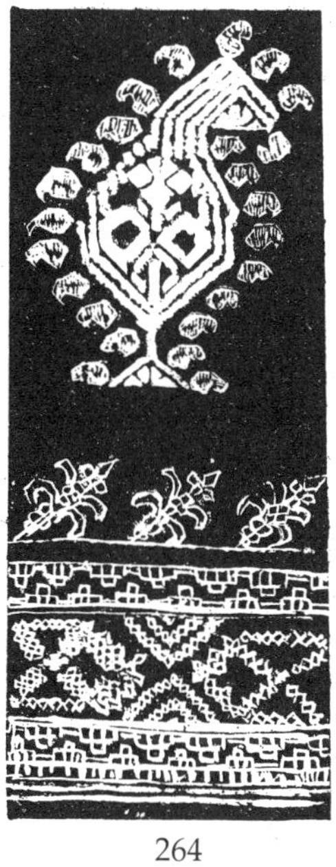

264

EMBROIDERED FABRICS. **258.** Details of geometrical pattern in Kashida embroidery on a Sari, Bihar. **259–264.** Varied traditional motifs of a chariot, lotus, elephant and howdah, lotus and deer, peacocks and cashew-nut (Godambi) in Kashuti embroidery, Karnatak Districts, Mysore State.

# Plate 32

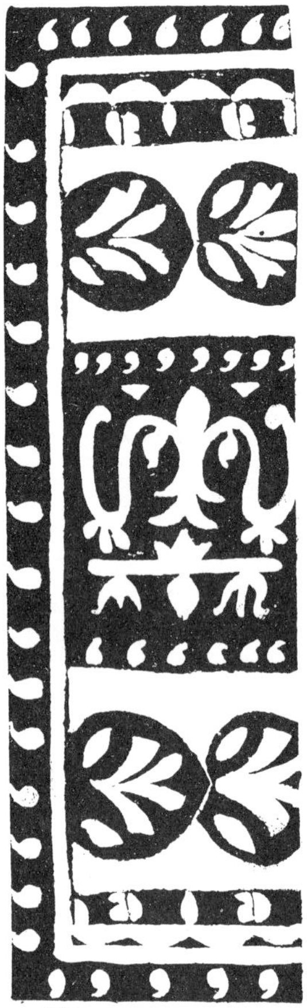
265

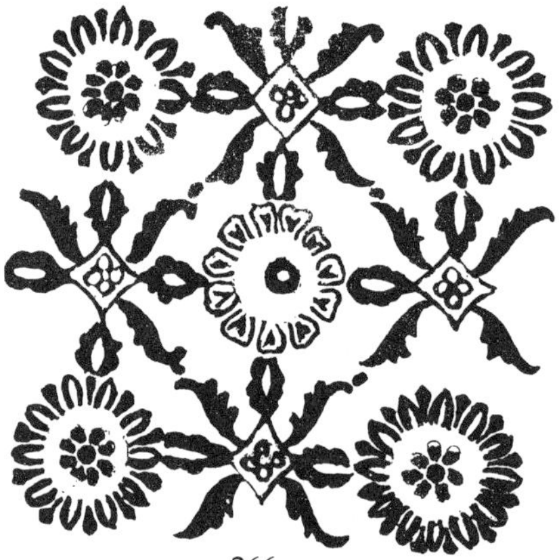
266

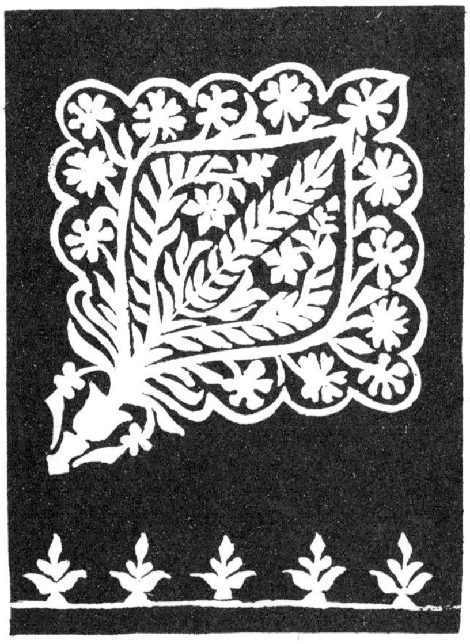
267

268

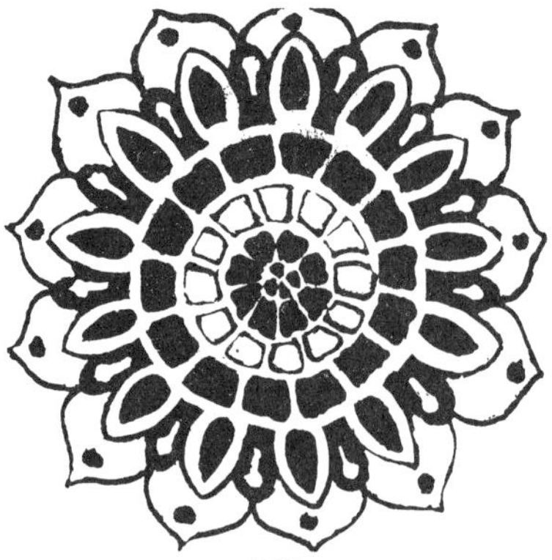
269

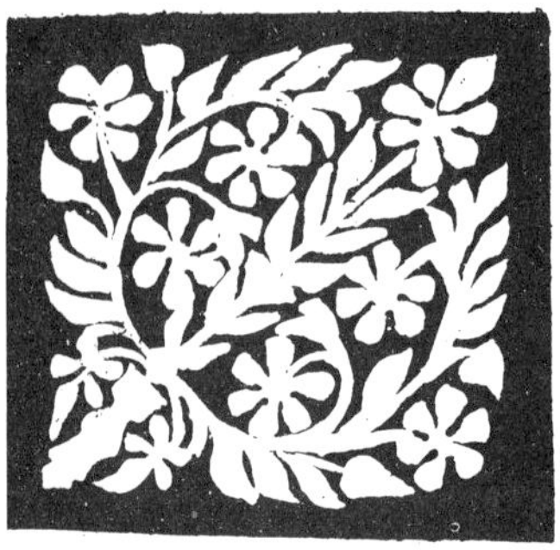
270

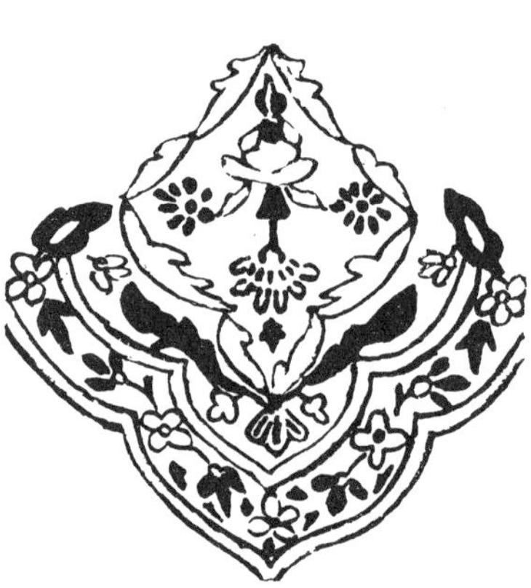
272

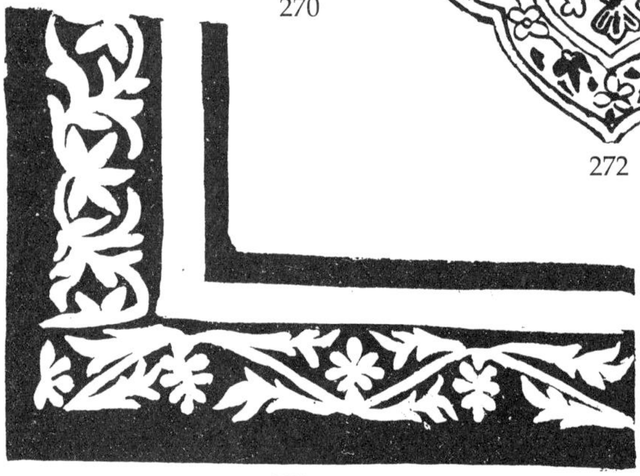
271

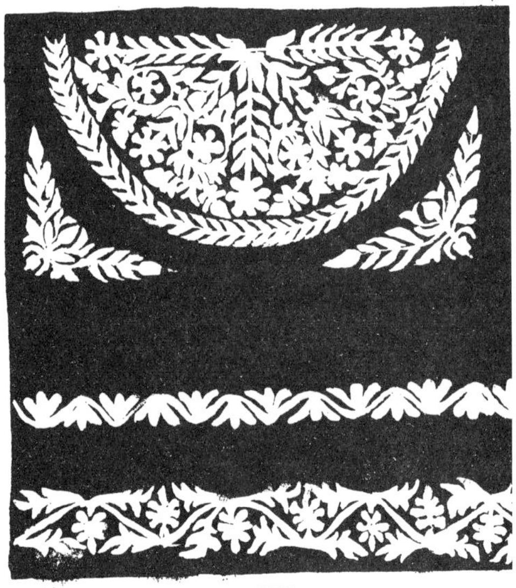
273

EMBROIDERED FABRICS. **265.** Stylized traditional floral appliqué work from Haveli Kharagpur, Bihar. **266, 268, 269, 272.** Details of central motif and section of background appliquéd in multi-colors on crimson silk, 19th century. **267.** Detail of stylized floral spray and border appliquéd on a bed cover, Bihar. **270, 271.** Details of appliqué of stylized floral spray on the background and border of a Shamiana decoration, Bihar. **273.** Details of appliquéd floral ensembles on a table cloth, Bihar.

# Plate 33

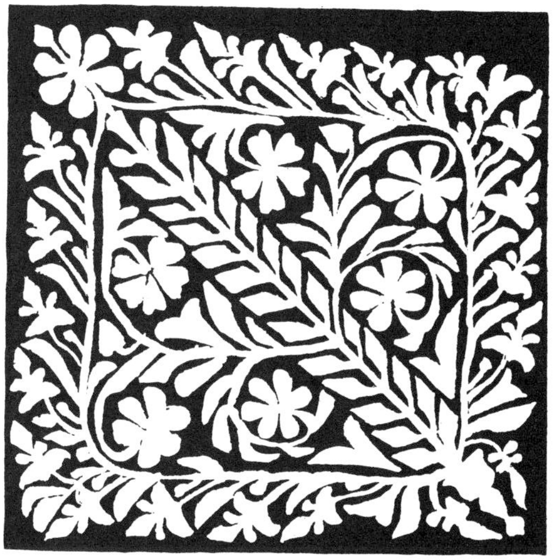

274

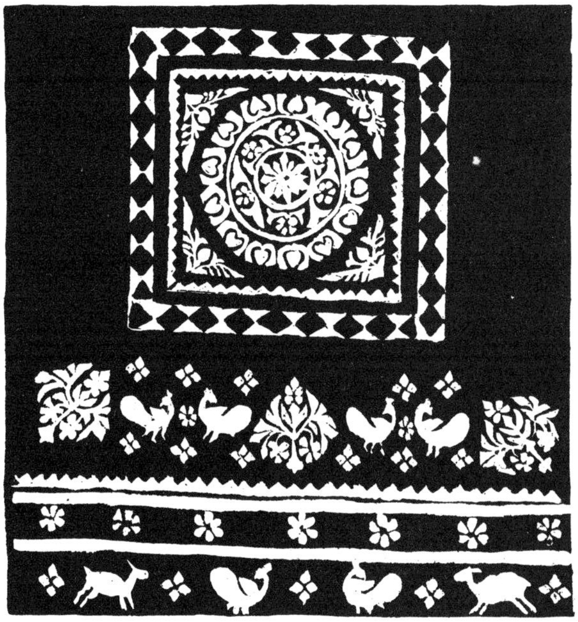

275

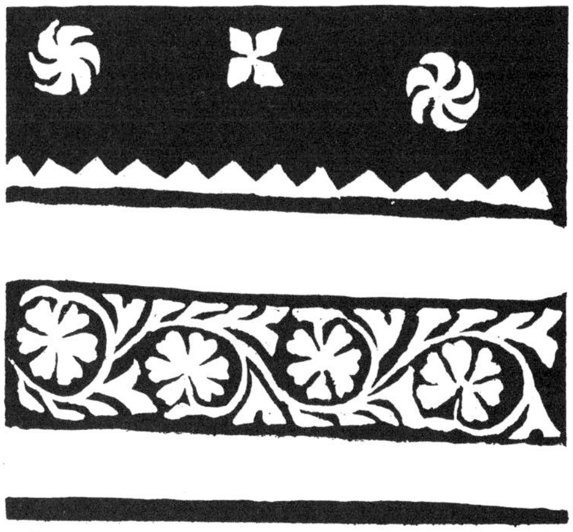

276

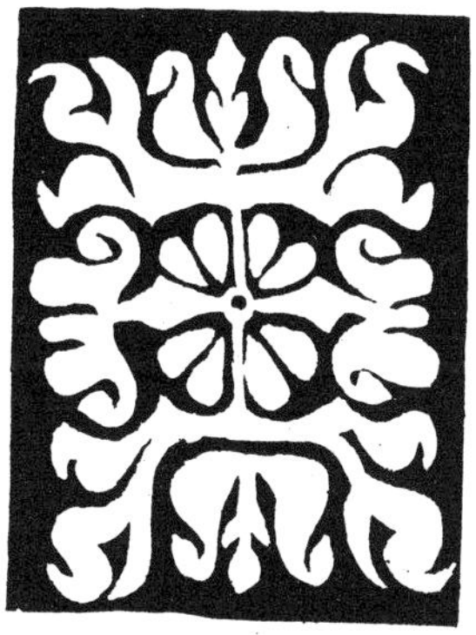

277

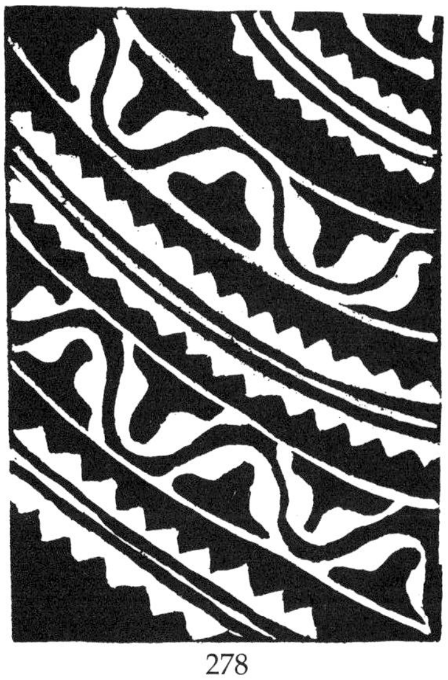

278

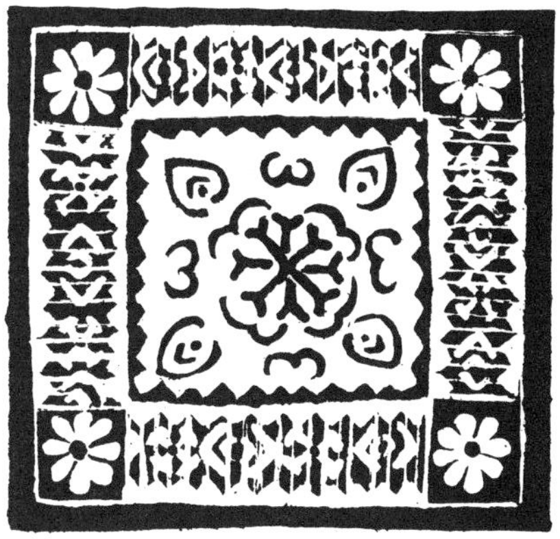

279

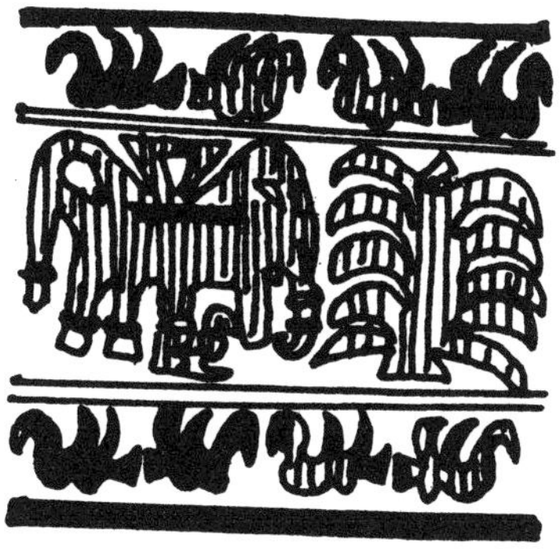

280

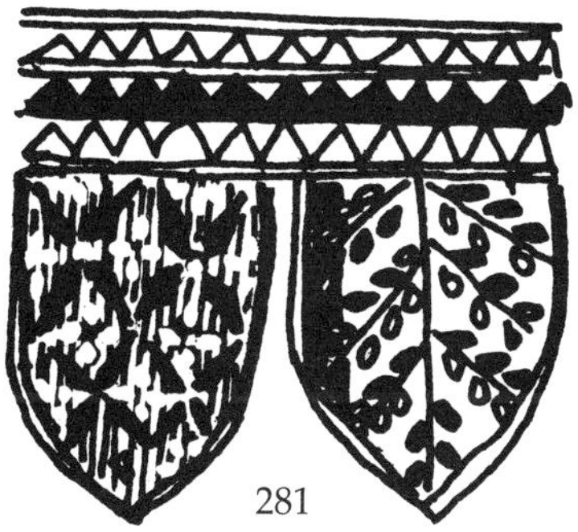

281

EMBROIDERED FABRICS. **274, 276.** Details of appliquéd stylized star and floral spray motifs on the background and border of a Shamiana decoration, Bihar. **275.** Details of appliquéd floral ensembles, trees and peacocks on a table cloth, Bihar. **277, 278.** Stylized floral mode and abstract forms appliquéd on two pillow covers, Bihar. **279.** Stylized floral motifs appliquéd on a quilt, Ahmadabad, Gujarat. **280, 281.** Appliquéd stylized elephants and trees and peacocks on a Thoran (door hanging), Saurashtra, Gujarat.

# Plate 34

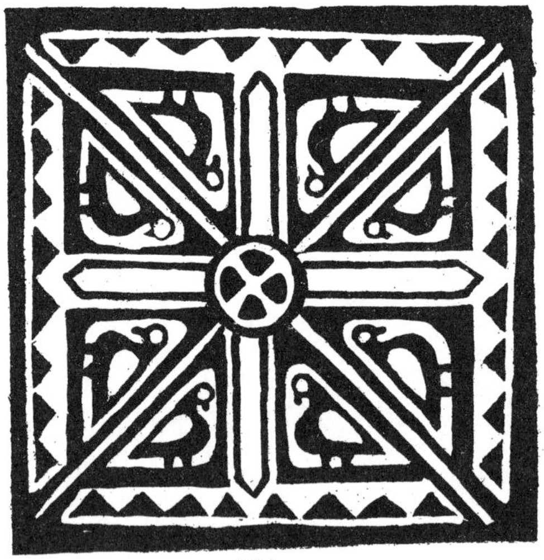
282

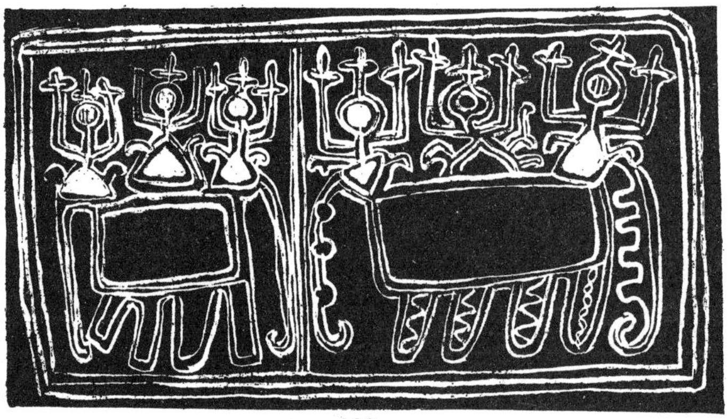
283

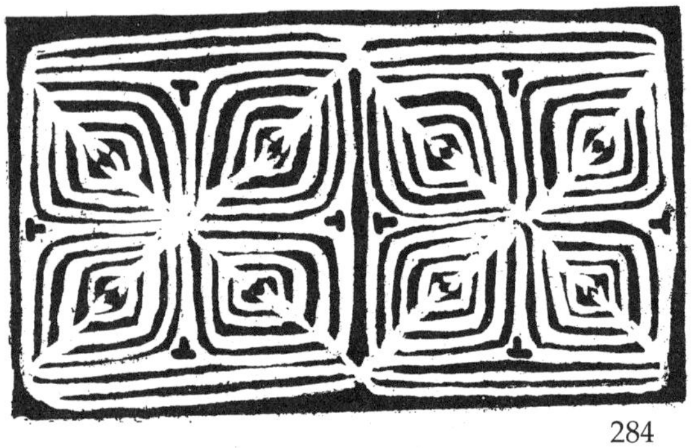
284

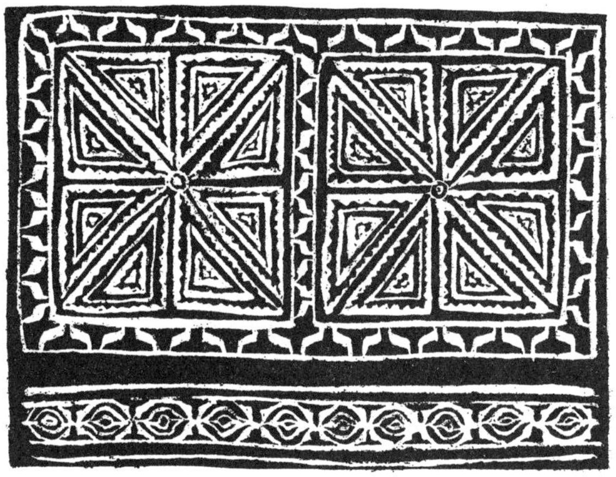
285

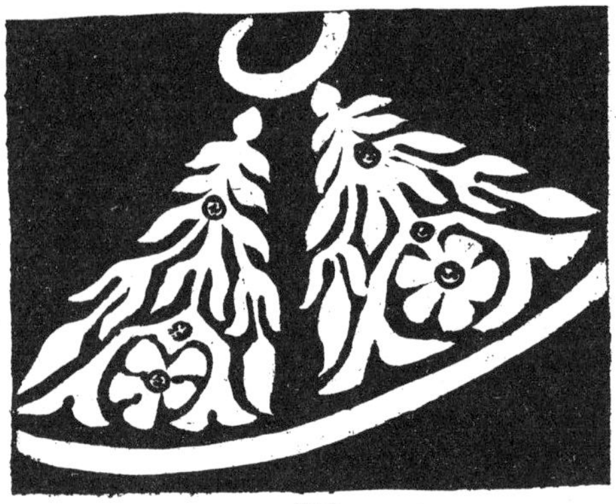
286

287

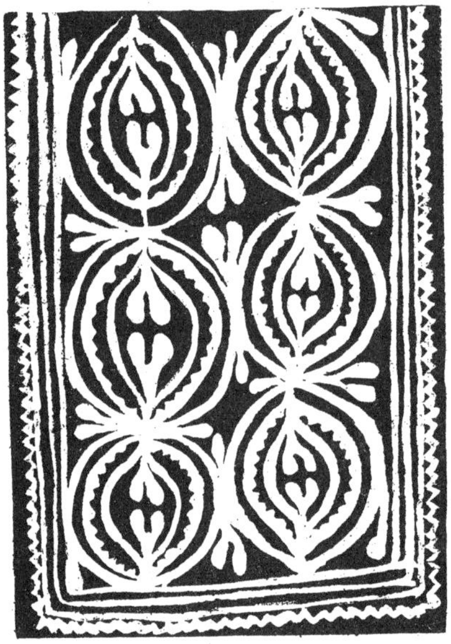
289

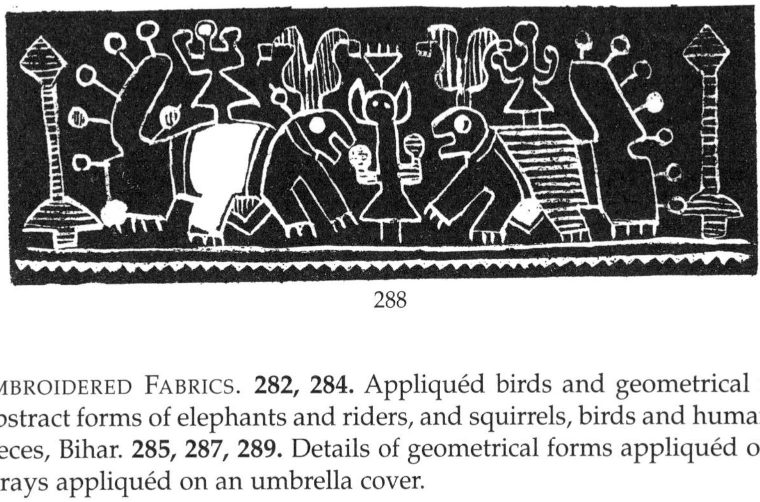
288

EMBROIDERED FABRICS. **282, 284.** Appliquéd birds and geometrical motifs on cushion covers, Bihar. **283, 288.** Abstract forms of elephants and riders, and squirrels, birds and human figures appliquéd on two decorative wall pieces, Bihar. **285, 287, 289.** Details of geometrical forms appliquéd on pillow covers, Bihar. **286.** Detail of floral sprays appliquéd on an umbrella cover.

# Plate 35

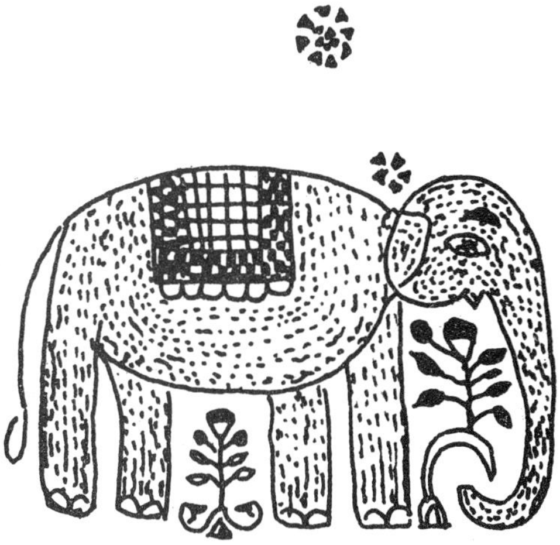

290

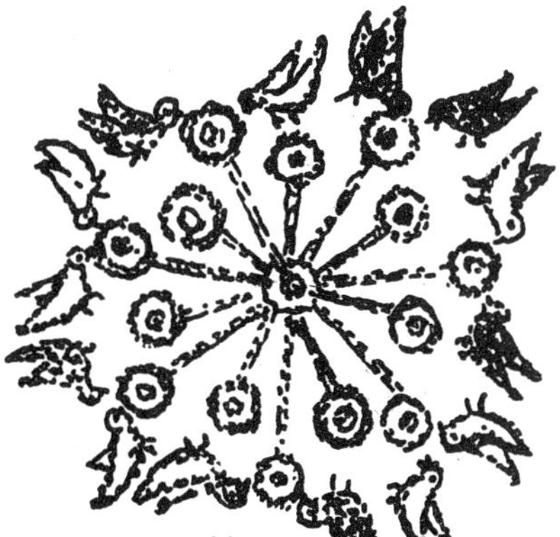

291

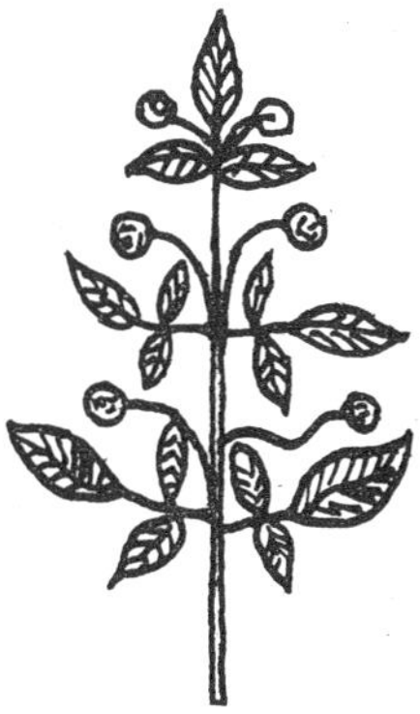

292

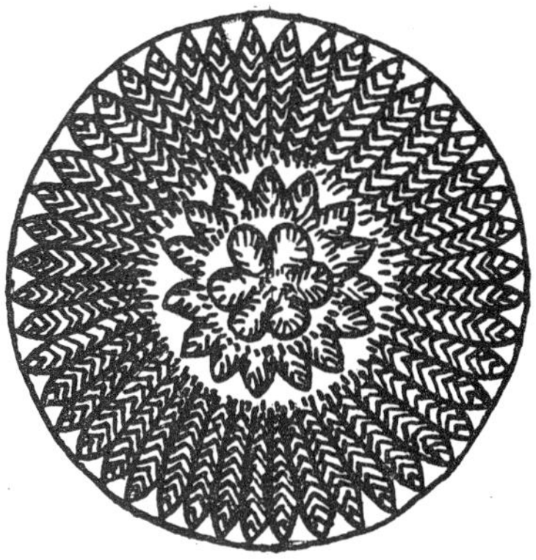

293

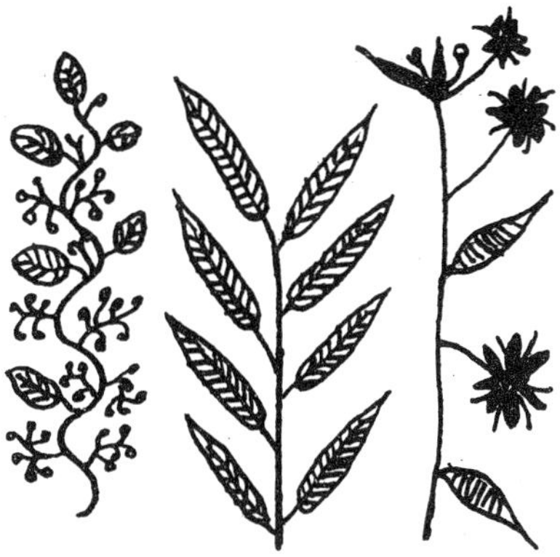

294

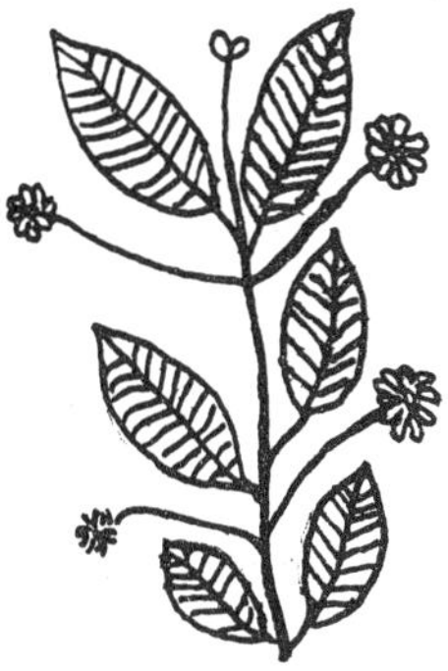

295

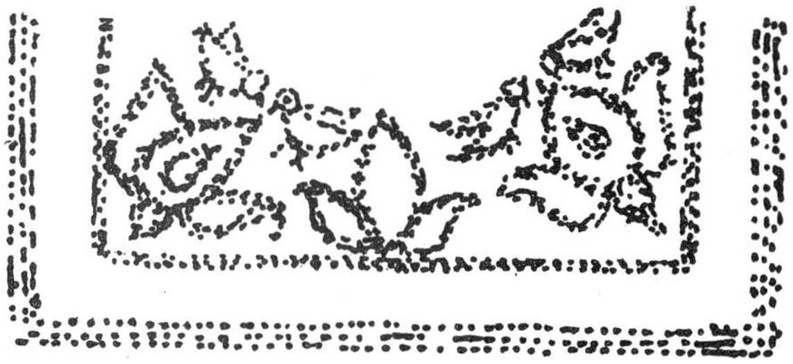

296

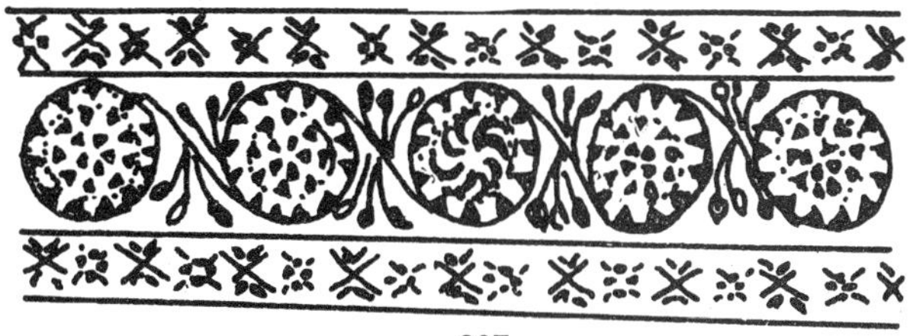

297

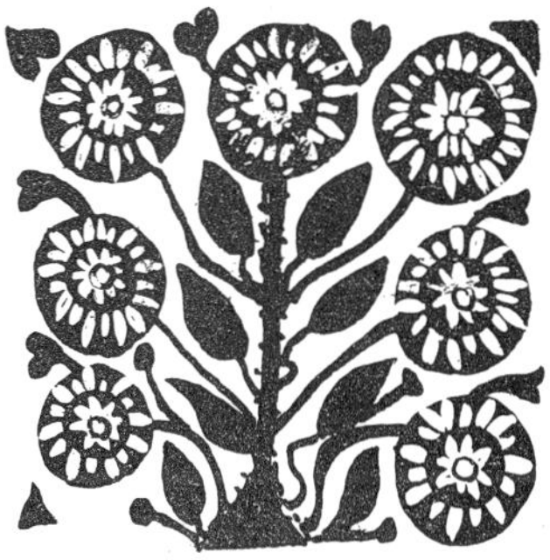

298

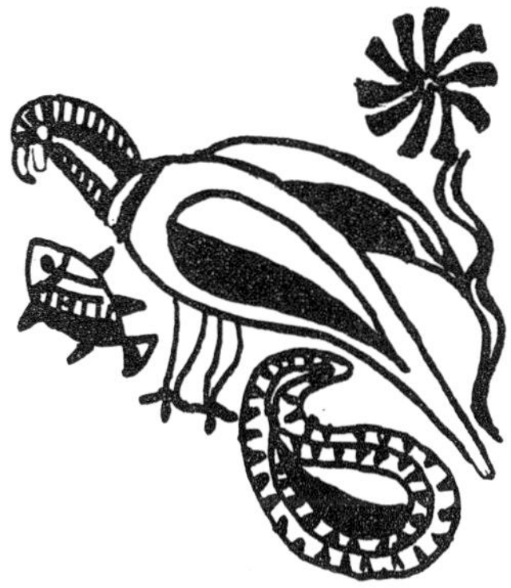

299

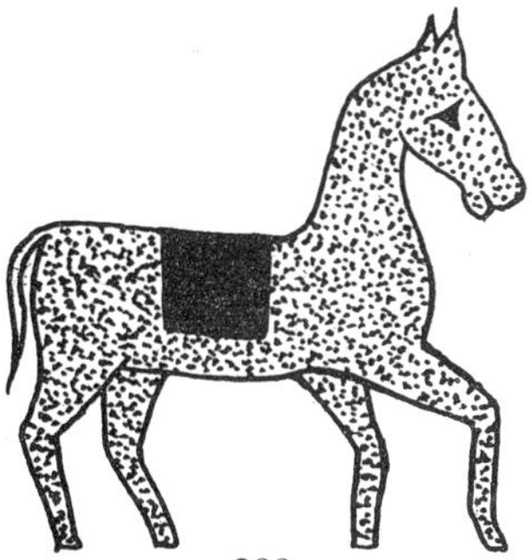

300

EMBROIDERED FABRICS. **290, 297.** An elephant motif and floral border from a traditional Bengal Kantha. **291, 296.** Stylized birds, floral and rose bud motifs from a Bihar Kantha. **292–295, 300.** Stylized lotus, leaf and flower sprays, and a horse from a traditional Bengal Kantha. **298, 299.** Stylized flowering tree, bird, fish and mango from a traditional Bengal Kantha.

# Plate 36

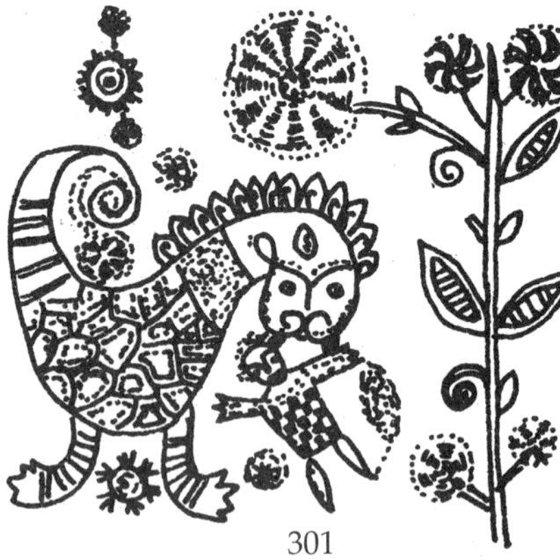

301

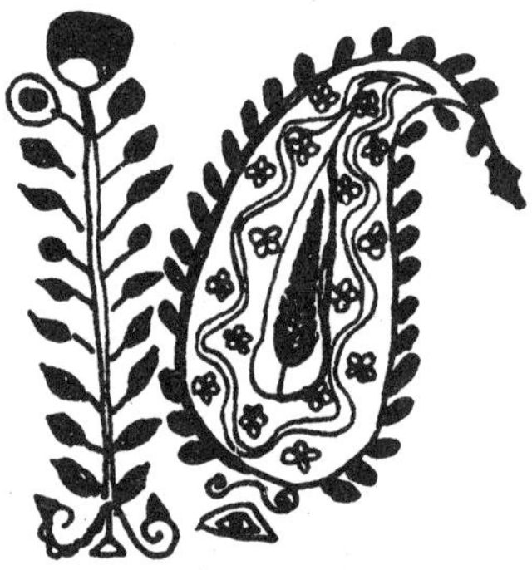

302

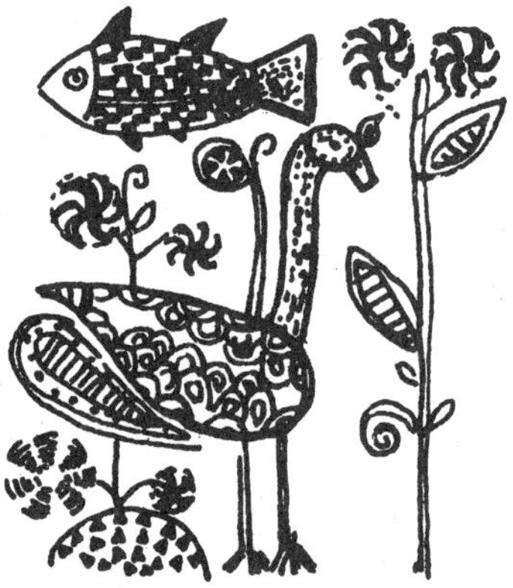

303

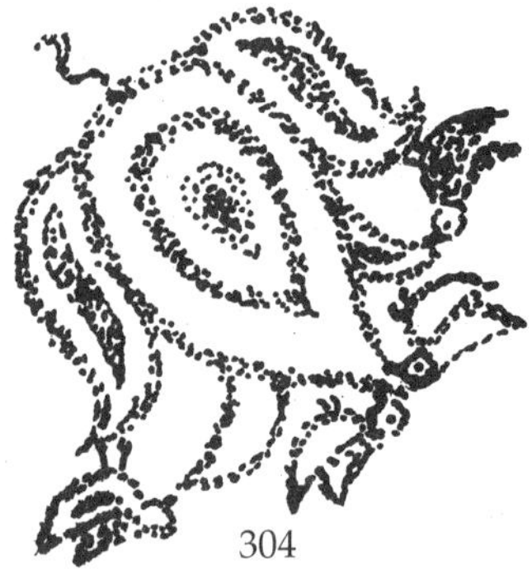

304

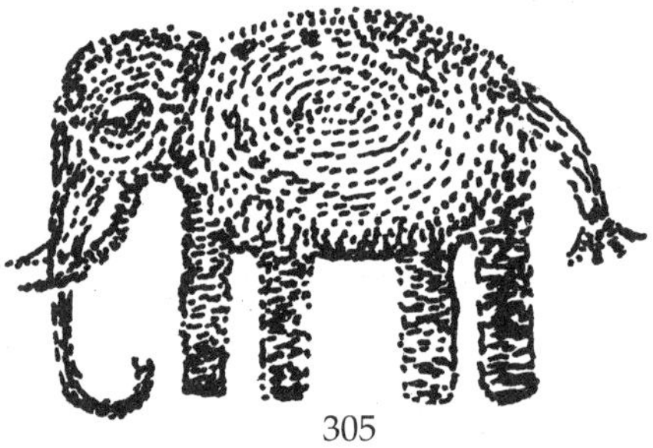

305

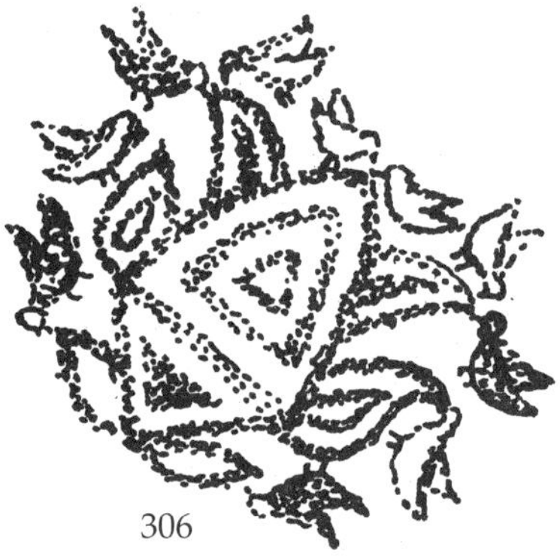

306

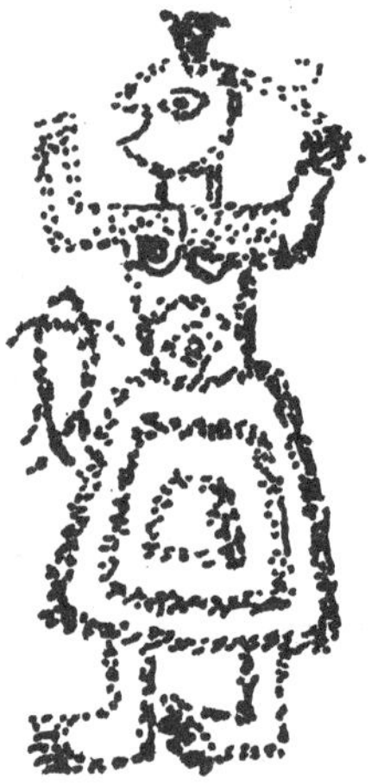

307

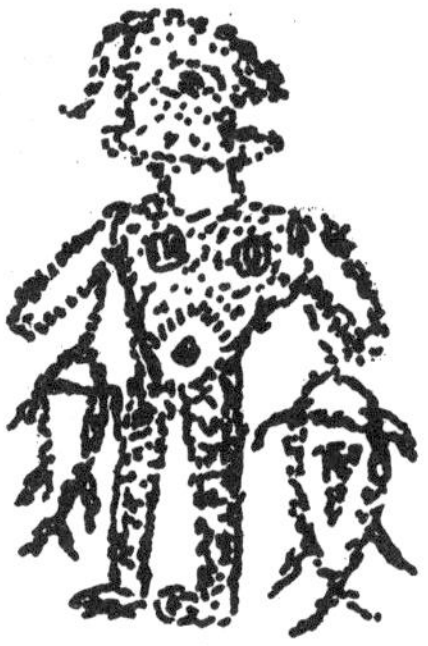

308

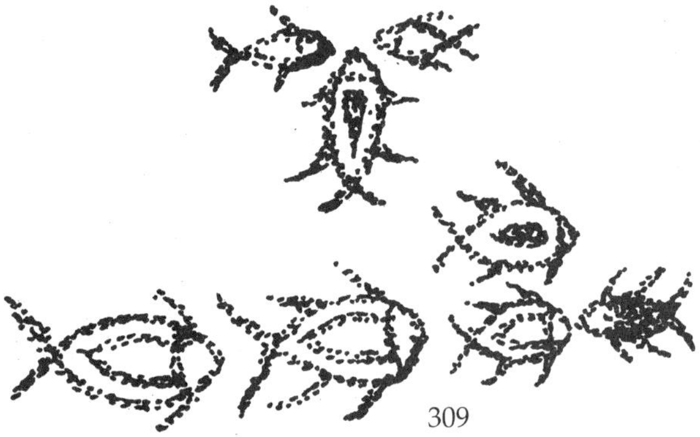

309

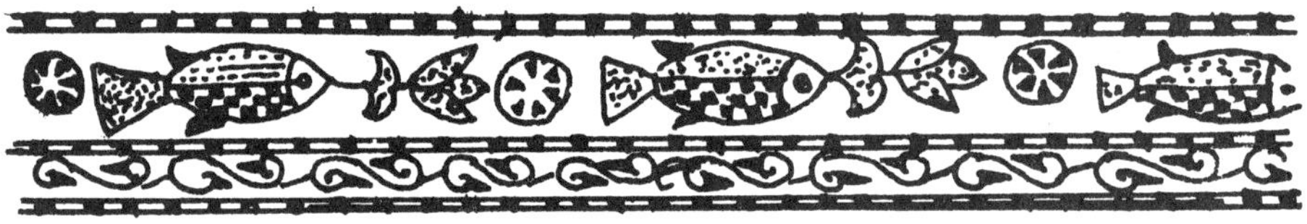

310

EMBROIDERED FABRICS. **301, 302, 303, 310.** Stylized motifs of birds, fish, almond, trees and human figure from a traditional Bengal Kantha. **304–309.** Stylized rose buds, fish, elephant and human figures from a traditional Bihar Kantha.

# Plate 37

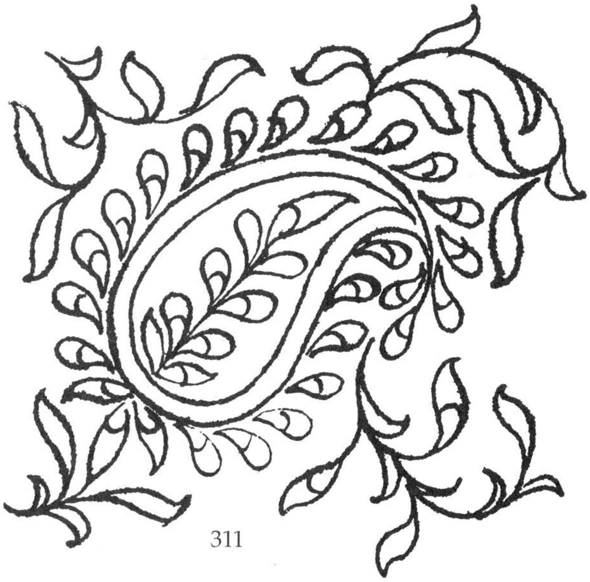

311

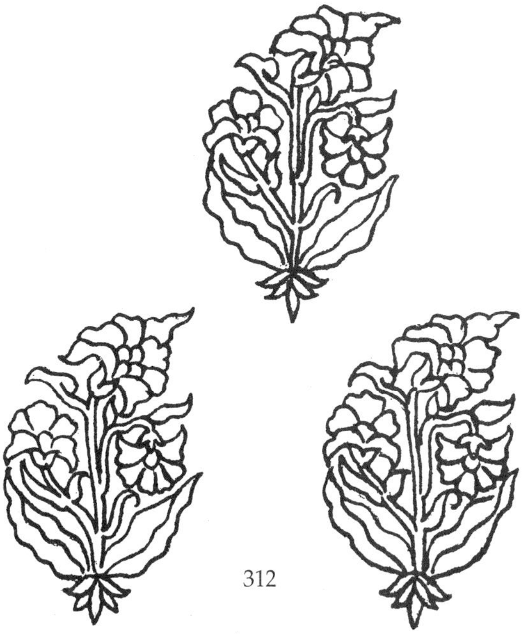

312

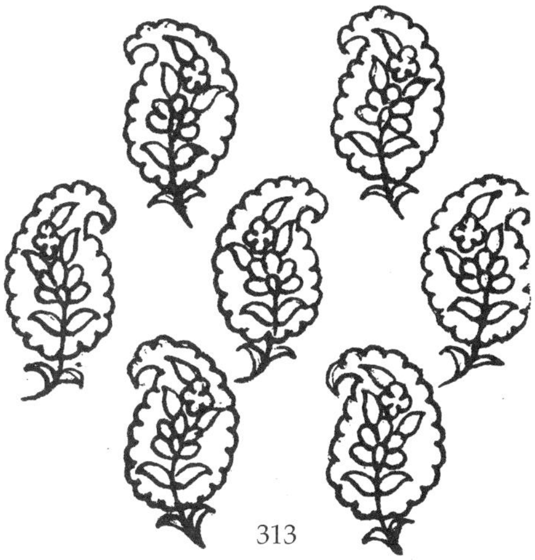

313

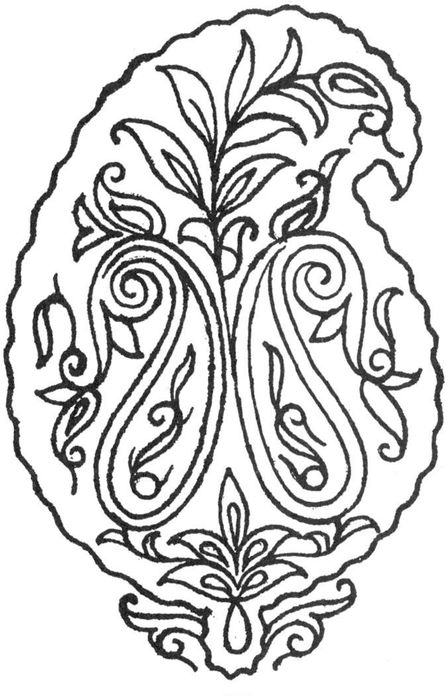

315

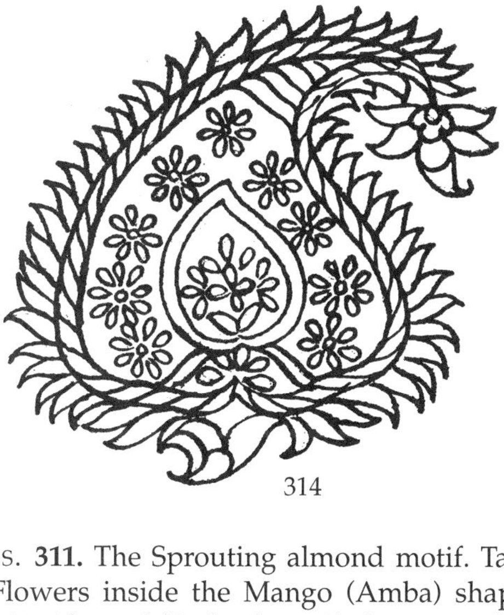

314

EMBROIDERED FABRICS. **311.** The Sprouting almond motif. Taken from an old cotton print from Farrukhabad, Uttar Pradesh. **312.** Flowers inside the Mango (Amba) shape. Taken from a traditional cotton print, Jaipur Museum, Rajasthan. **313.** Almond (Badam) motifs from a traditional printed muslin, Jaipur Museum, Rajasthan. **314.** The Mango (Amba) motif taken from an old Benares brocade. **315.** The Mango (Amba) motif. Taken from an old Bidri Metal piece from Hyderabad, Andhra Pradesh. All motifs **311–315** have been adapted for embroideries by Kashelen Fabrics, Srinagar, Kashmir.

# Plate 38

316

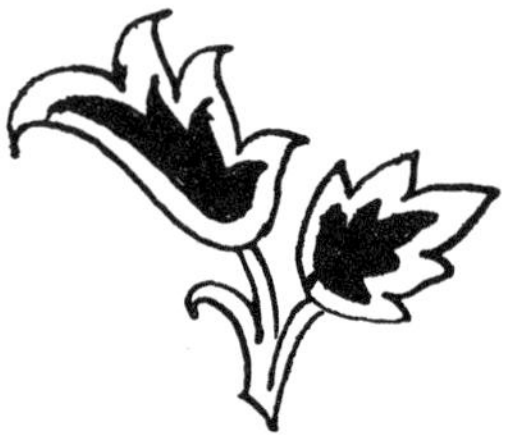

317

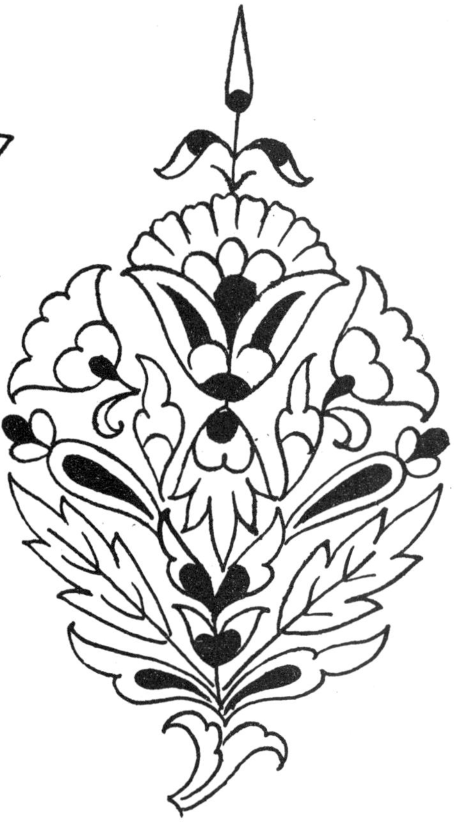

318

319

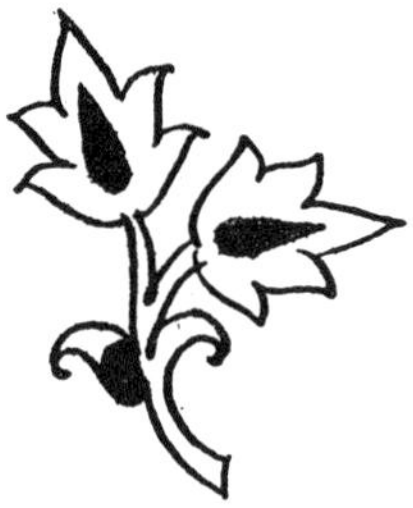

320

321

EMBROIDERED FABRICS. **316–321.** Designs are taken from a Rajasthani woman's wide skirt (Ghagra), made from a printed fabric. An old piece. The motifs are stylized peacock feathers. All motifs have been adapted for embroidery by Kashelen Fabrics, Srinagar, Kashmir.

# Plate 39

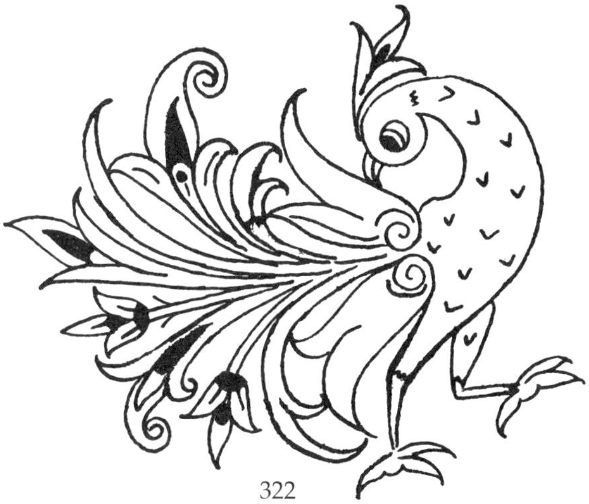

322

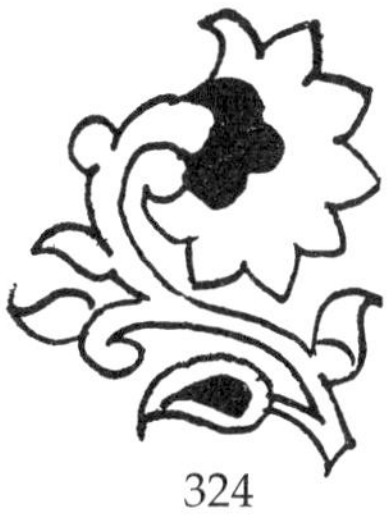

324

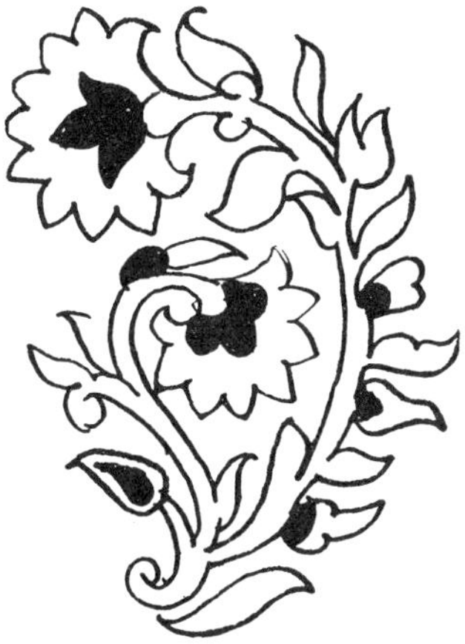

325

323

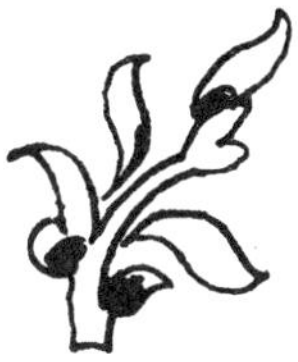

326

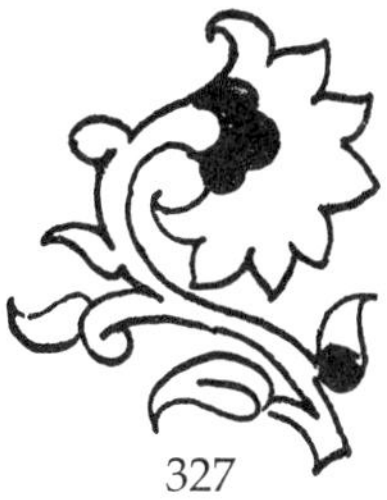

327

329

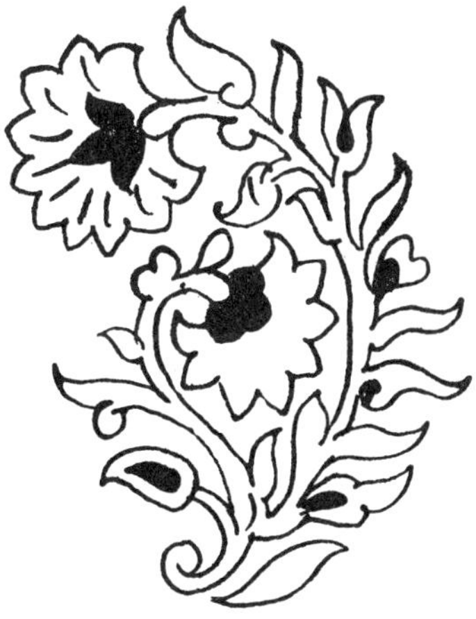

328

330

EMBROIDERED FABRICS. **322, 323.** Motifs of stylized peacock and floral border taken from a Jaipur Inlay work box. An old traditional piece in a private collection. **324–328.** Motifs taken from a silk Himru brocade Achkan coat, worked with stylized floral sprays. An heirloom piece. **329, 330.** Design taken from the embroidery of a Gilgit Choga coat. This stylized floral form is also used in Central Asia, Asia Minor and the Balkans. All motifs **322–330** have been adapted for embroideries by Kashelen Fabrics, Srinagar, Kashmir.

# Plate 40

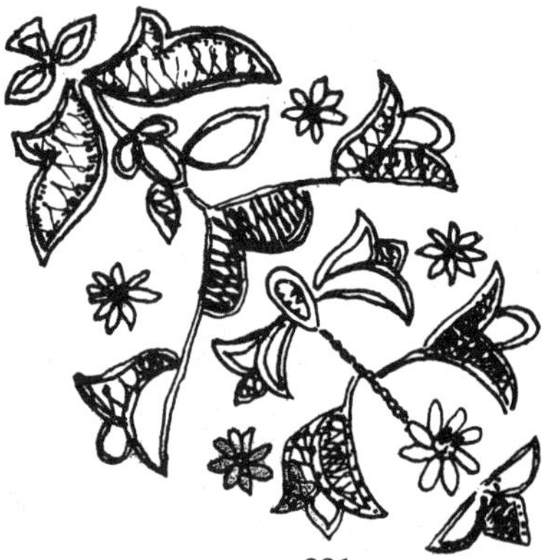

331

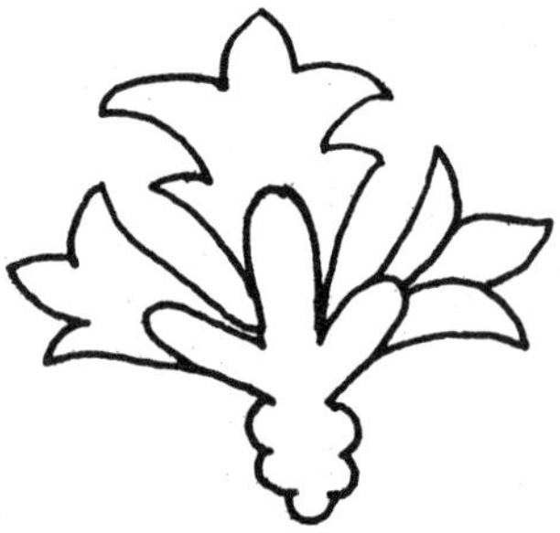

332

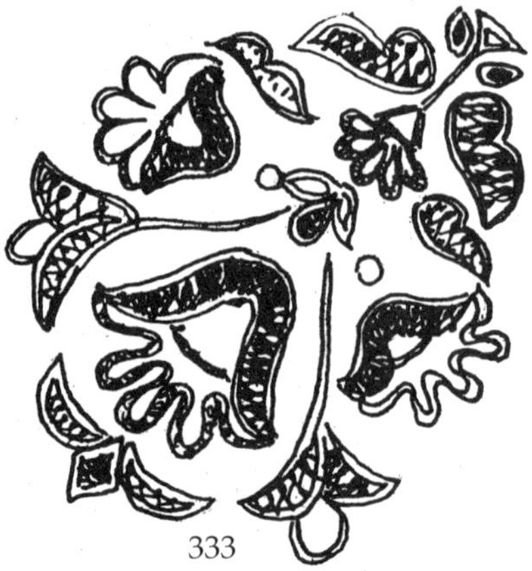

333

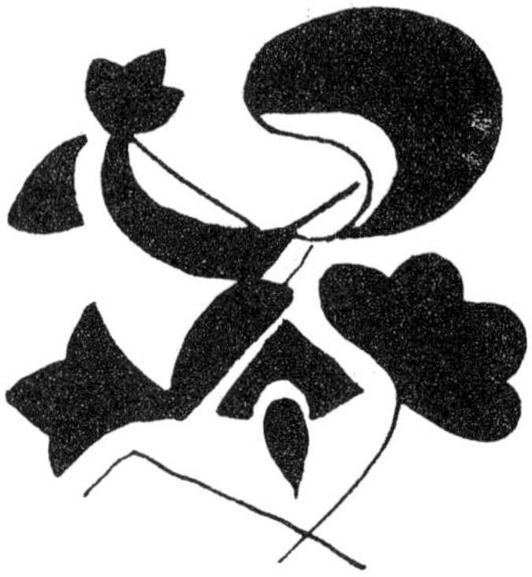

334

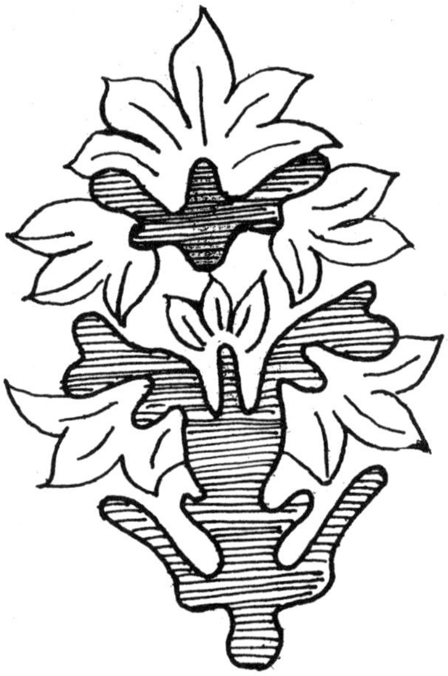

335

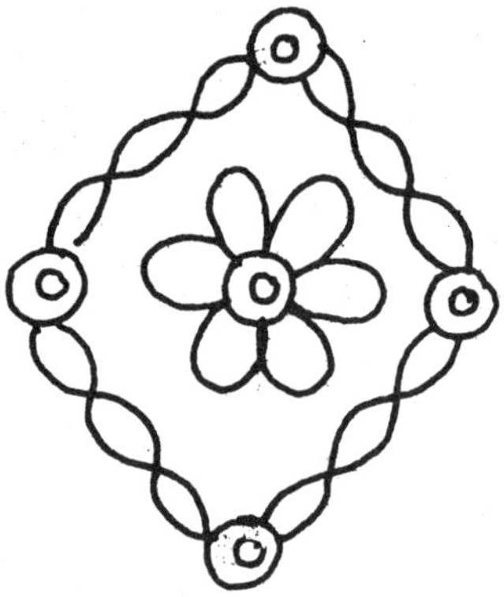

336

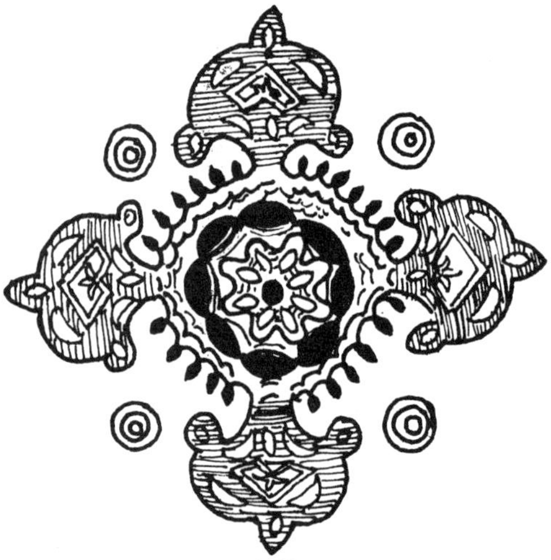

337

338

339

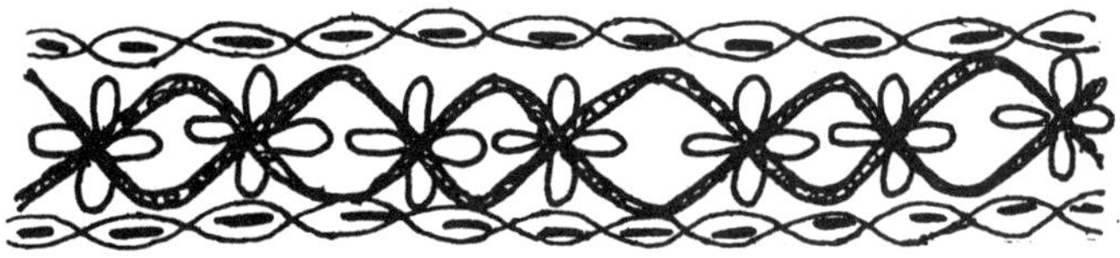

340

EMBROIDERED FABRICS. **331, 333, 338–340.** Folk embroideries from decorative wall pieces (Chandtawa) with motifs of floral sprays, Saurashtra, Gujarat. **332, 336.** Simple motifs for Cholie blouses, Saurashtra, Gujarat. **334.** An abstract motif representing a peacock seated on a flower, Sabarkantha district, Gujarat; worked on a simple tie-and-dye background, for skirts (Ghagras). **335, 337.** Stylized flower motifs from Kathiawar, Gujarat, used on women's top draperies (Odhnis).

# Plate 41

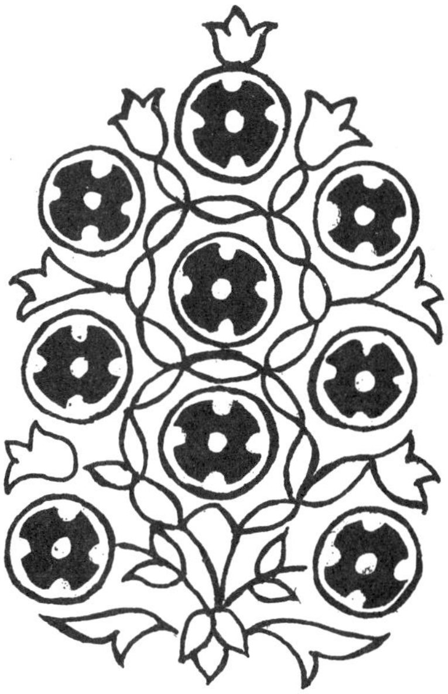

341

342

344

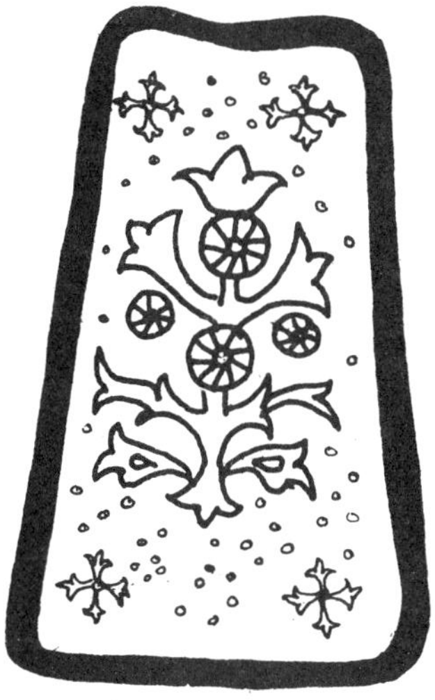

345

343

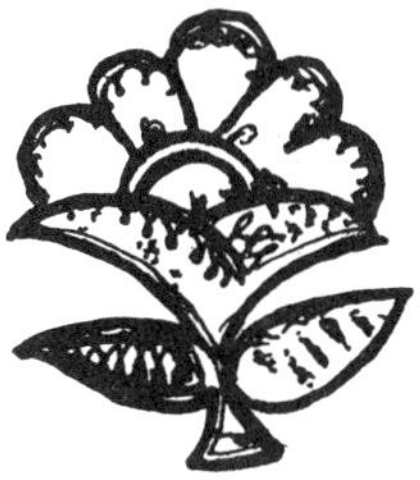

346

347

348

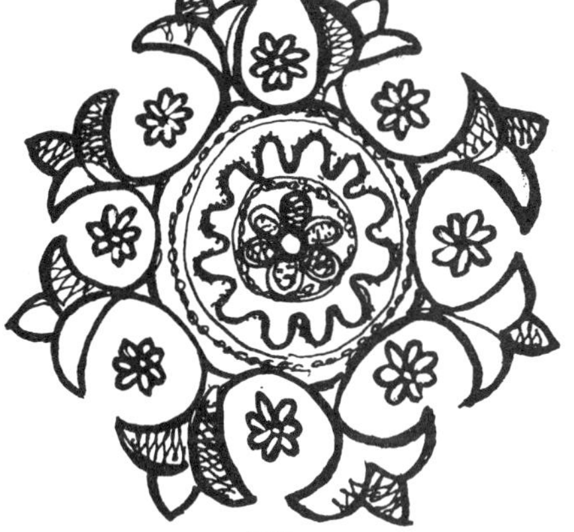

349

EMBROIDERED FABRICS. **341.** Stylized flowering tree, Cutch, Gujarat, with mirror inset work (Abla) for center of each flower. **342.** Dainty shadow work (Chikkan-kari) with flowers and buds on curving lines, Lucknow, Uttar Pradesh. **343–347, 349.** Embroidered stylized floral ensembles from decorative wall pieces (Chandtawa), Saurashtra, Gujarat. **348.** An abstract motif representing a double peacock, Kathiawar, Gujarat.

# Plate 42

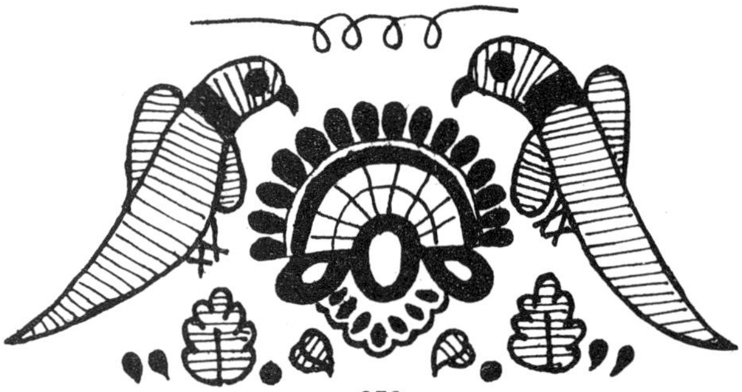

350

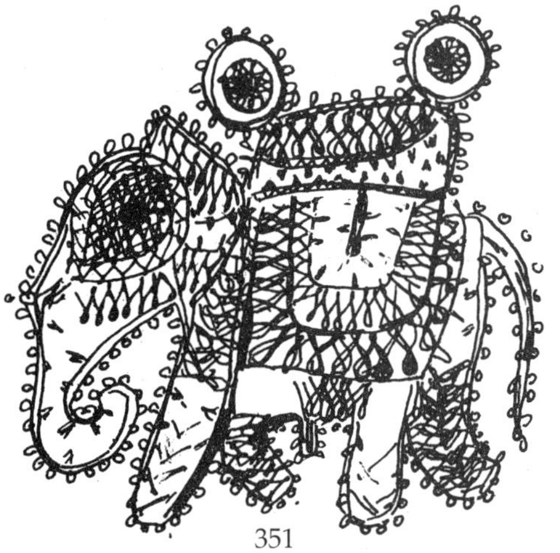

351

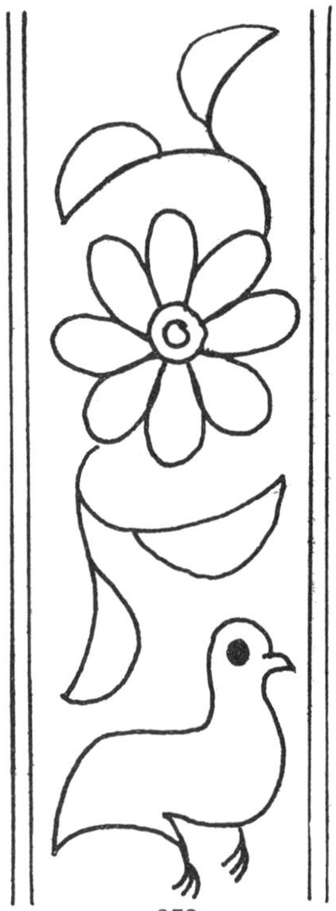

352

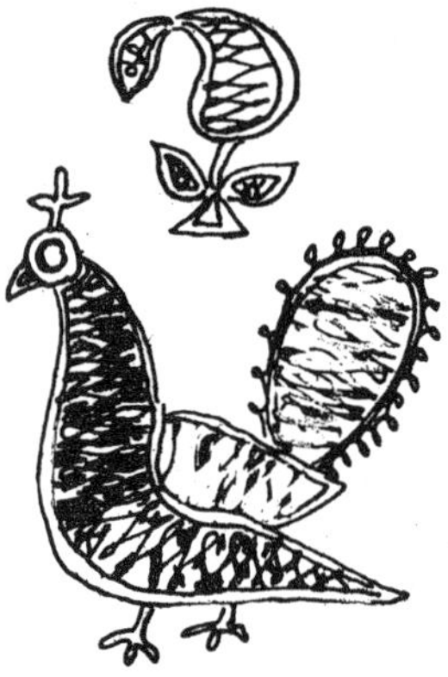

353

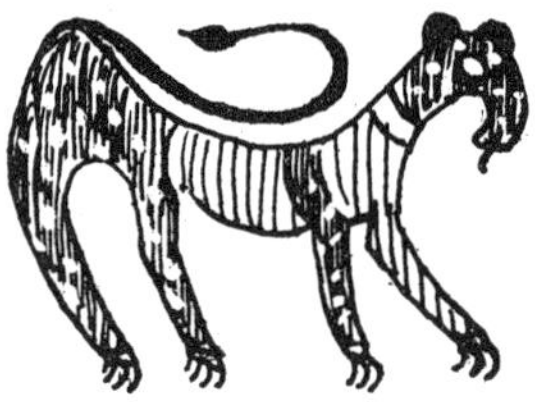

354

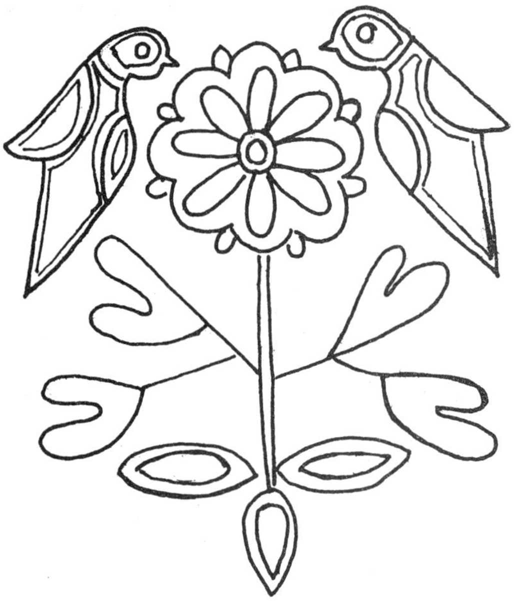

355

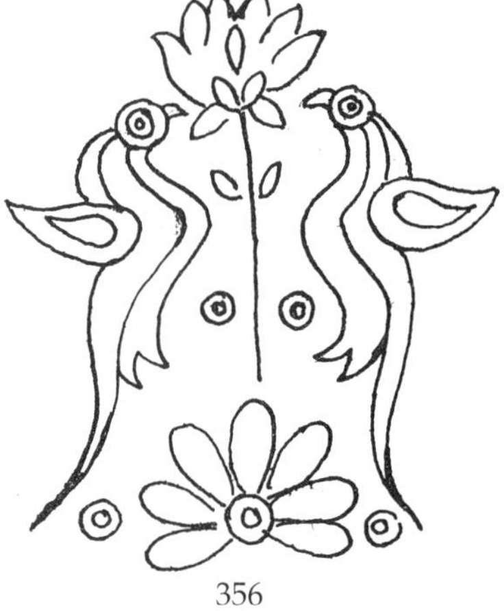

356

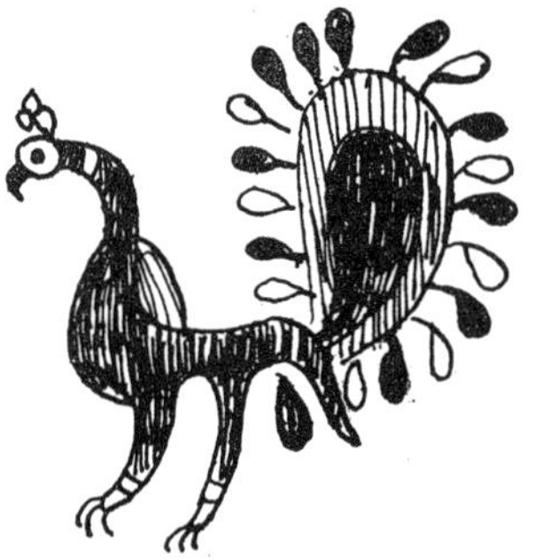

357

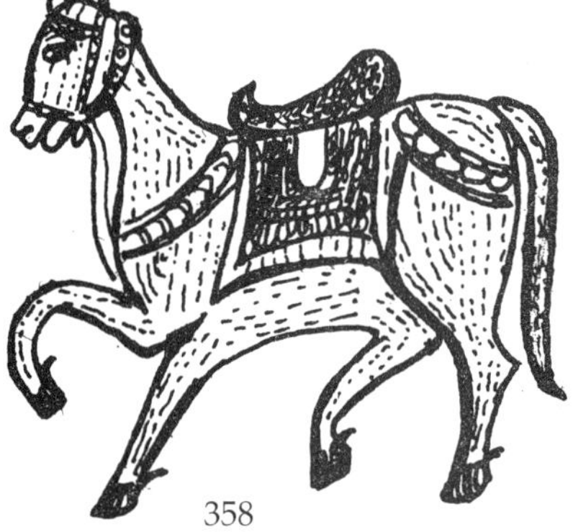

358

EMBROIDERED FABRICS. **350.** Stylized parrots and flower motif from a decorative piece (Chakla), Gujarat. **351, 353, 354, 357, 358.** Motifs of an elephant, peacocks, lion and horse from wall pieces (Chandtawa), used in interior decoration, Saurashtra, Gujarat. **352, 355, 356.** Details of stylized flowers, trees, duck and parrots used on decorative pieces in the home, Saurashtra, Gujarat.

# Plate 43

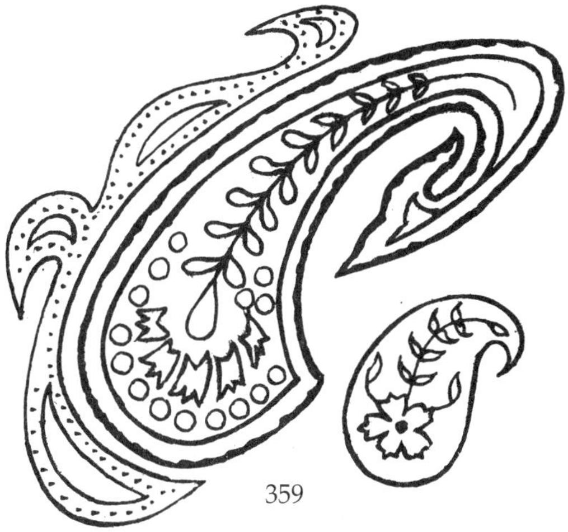
359

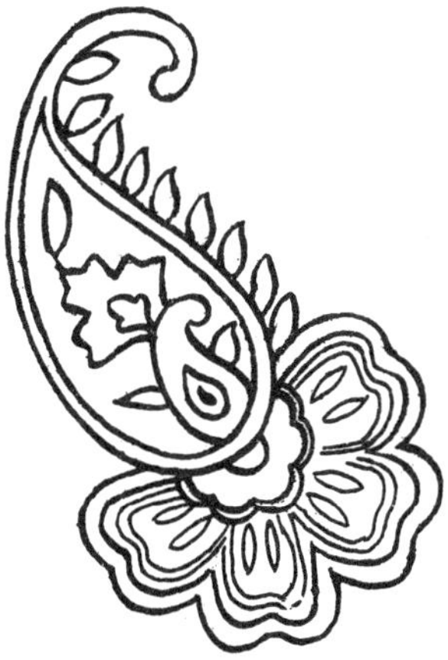
360

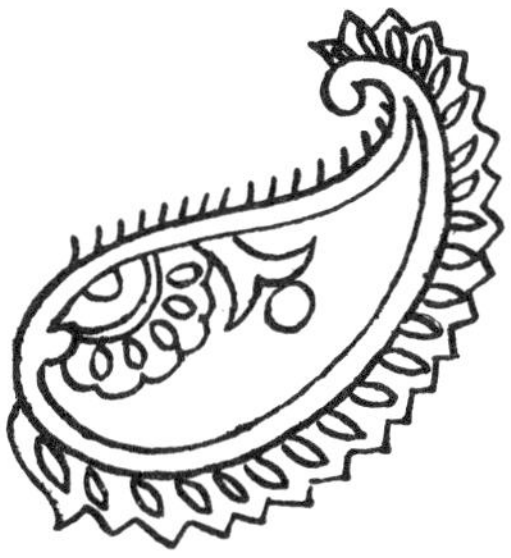
361

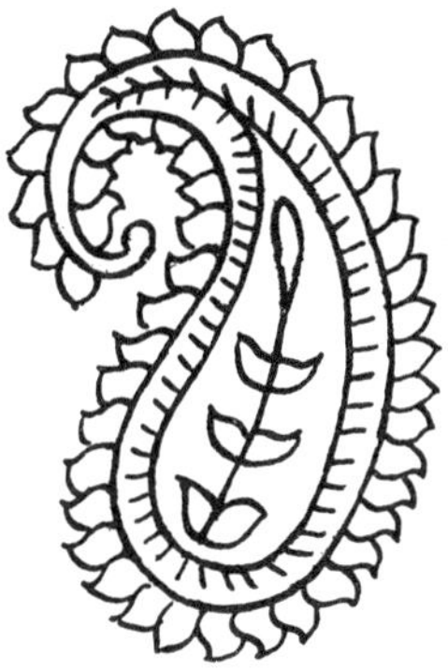
364

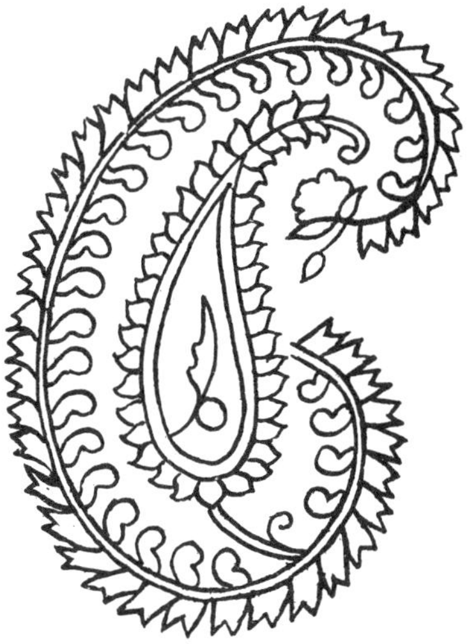
362

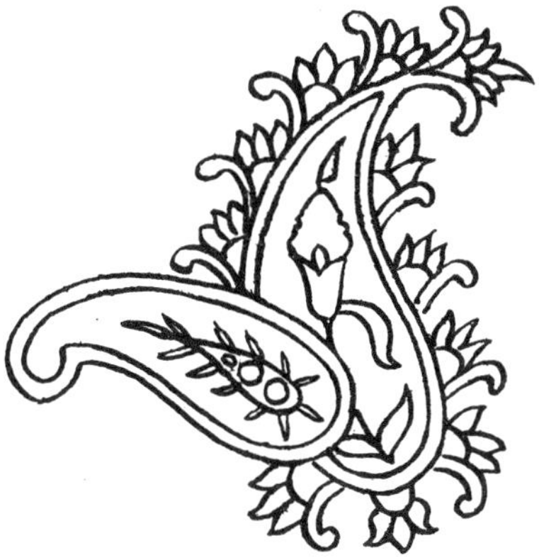
363

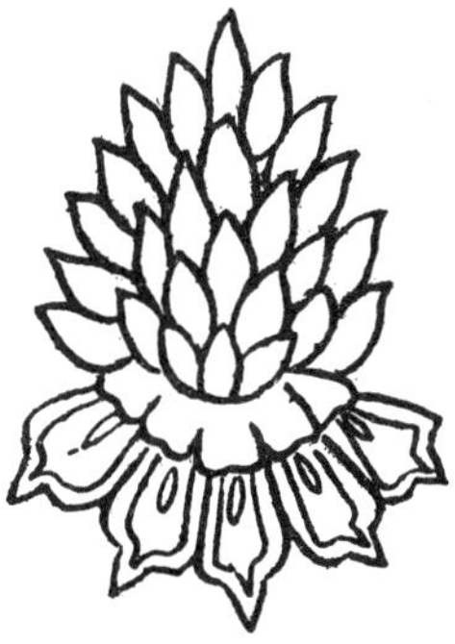
367

365

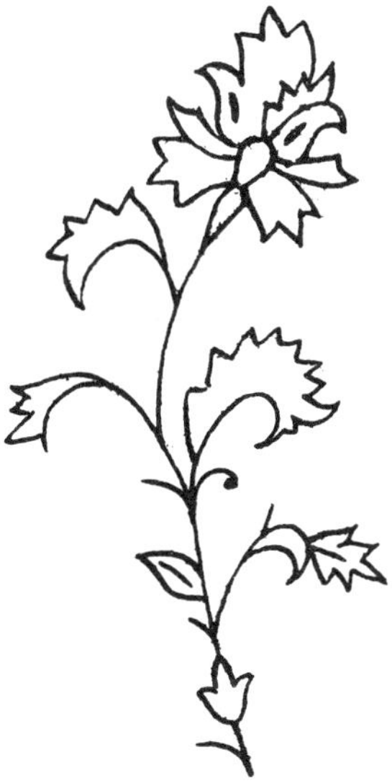
366

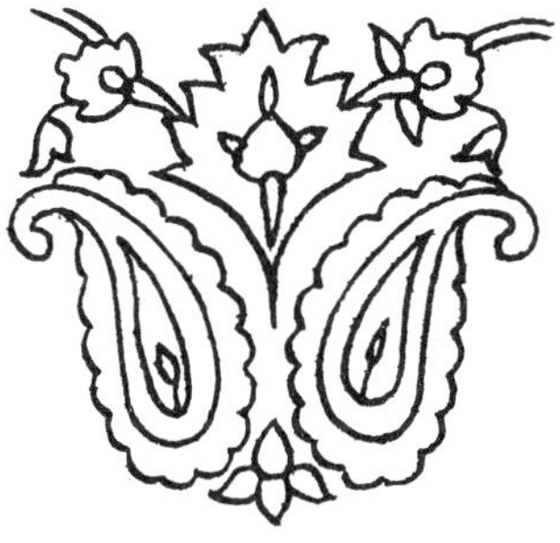
368

WOOD BLOCK PRINTS. **359–368.** Stylized Mango (Amba) and floral motifs from traditional hand-printed cotton textiles from Farrukhabad, Uttar Pradesh.

# Plate 44

369

370

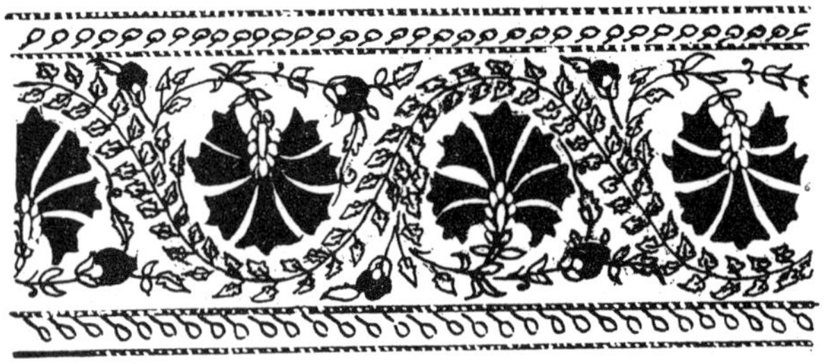

371

372

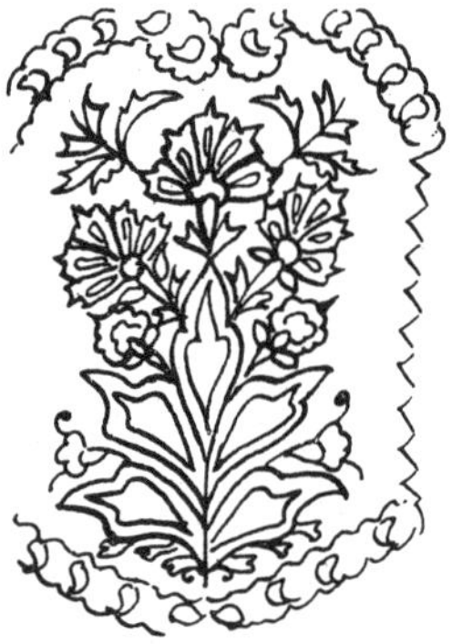

373

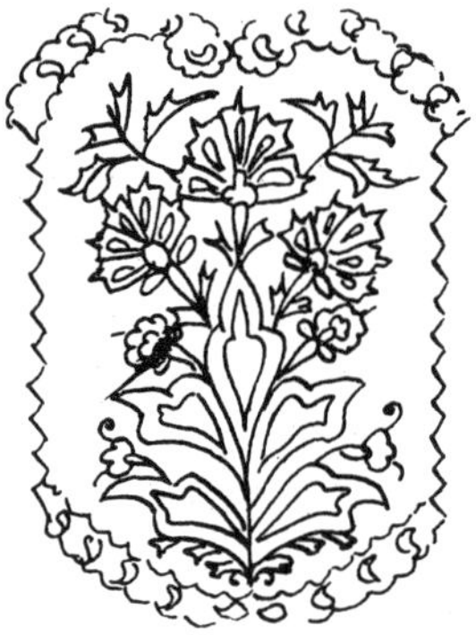

374

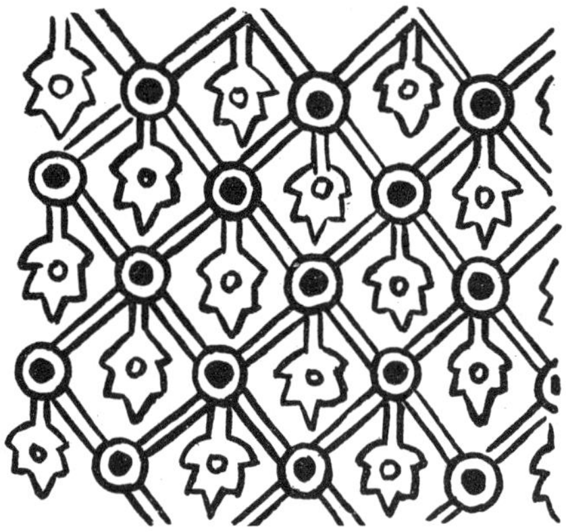

375

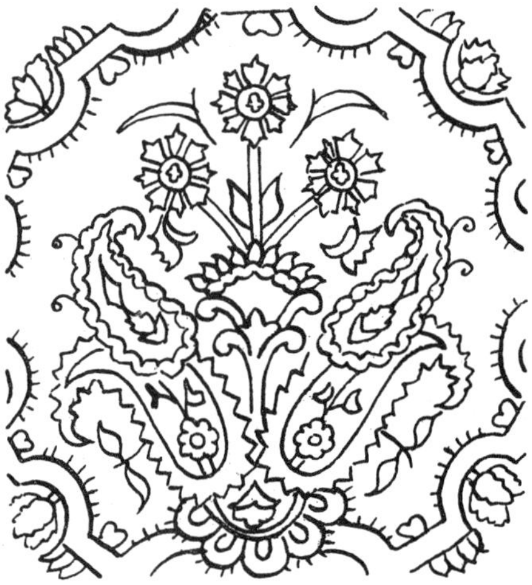

376

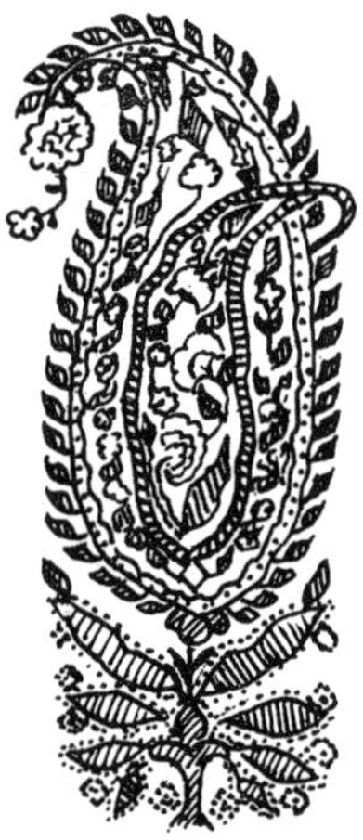

377

378

WOOD BLOCK PRINTS. **369–374, 376.** Stylized floral border and background motifs from traditional hand-printed cotton textiles, Farrukhabad, Uttar Pradesh. **375, 378.** Floral and geometrical motifs from a hand-printed cotton textile, Rajasthan. **377.** Detail of a stylized Mango motif from a hand-printed silk Sari, adapted from the traditional woven Baluchar silk Sari, West Bengal.

# Plate 45

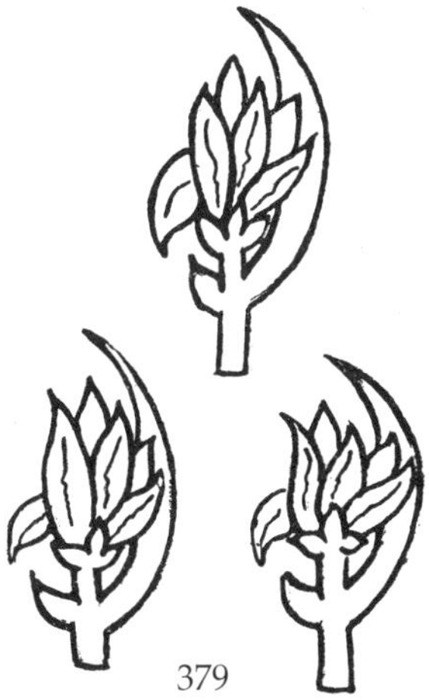

379

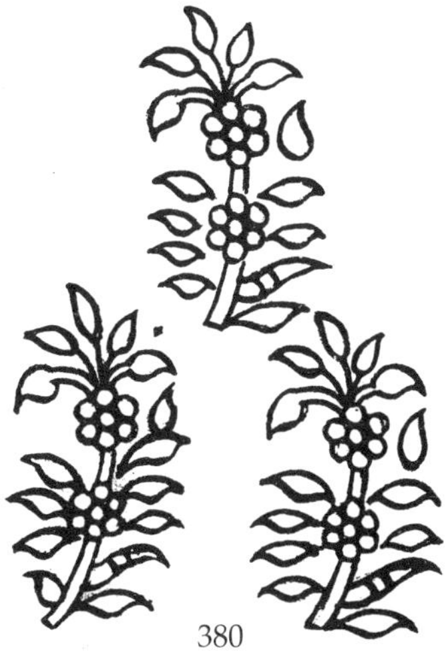

380

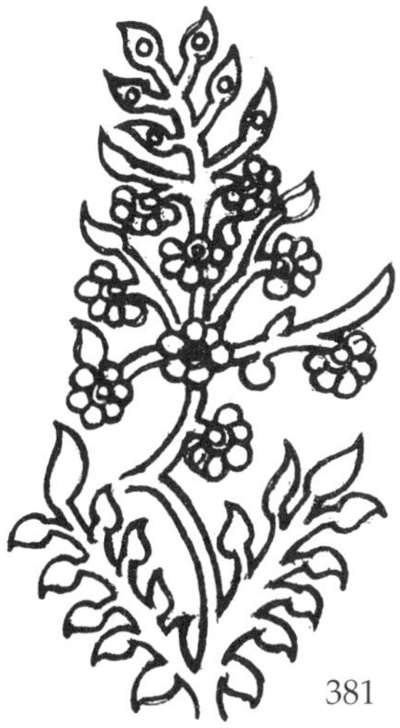

381

382

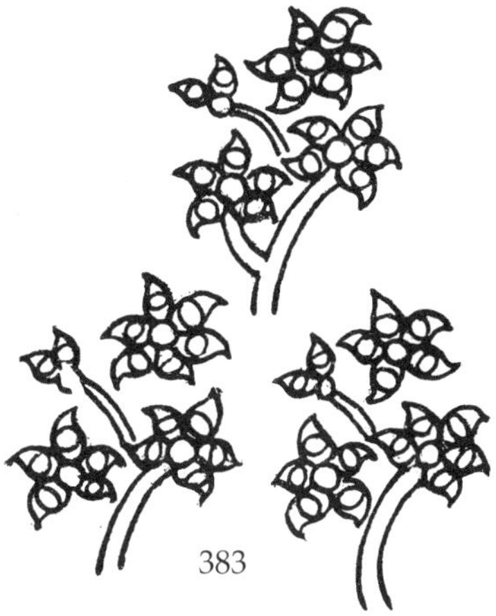

383

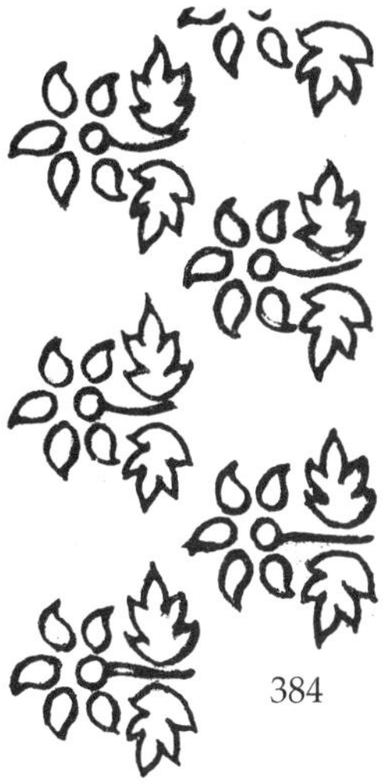

384

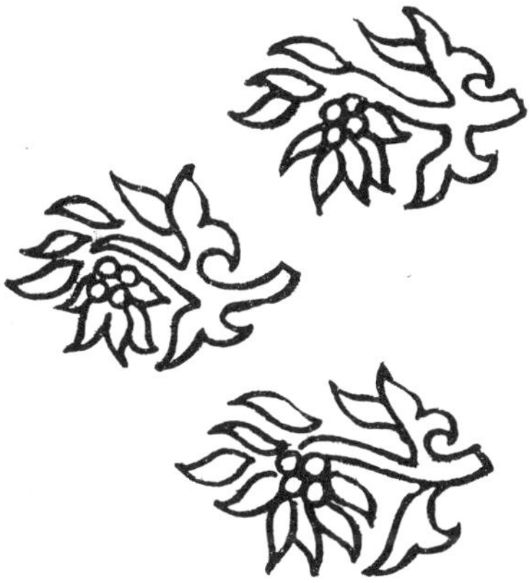

385

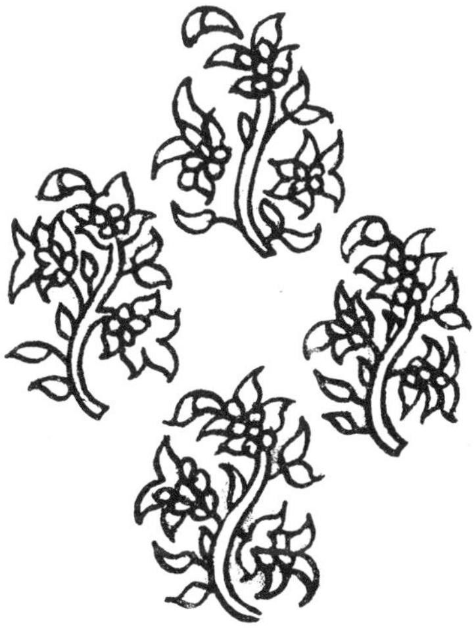

386

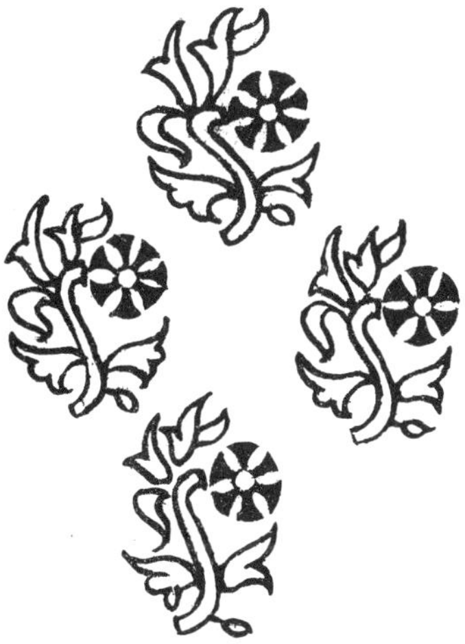

387

WOOD BLOCK PRINTS. **379–387.** Stylized floral and leaf motifs from hand-printed cotton textiles, Rajasthan.

# Plate 46

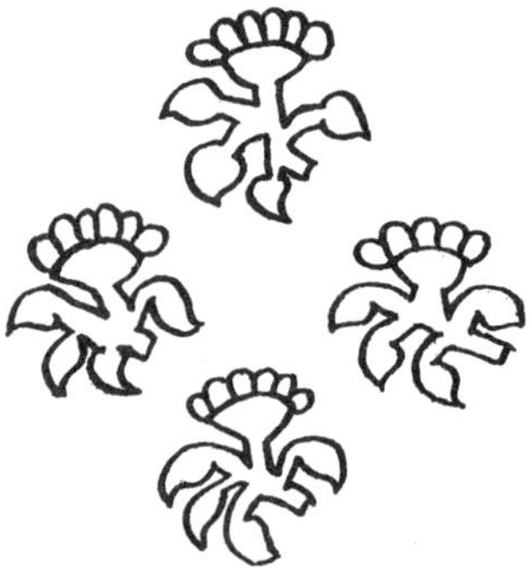
388

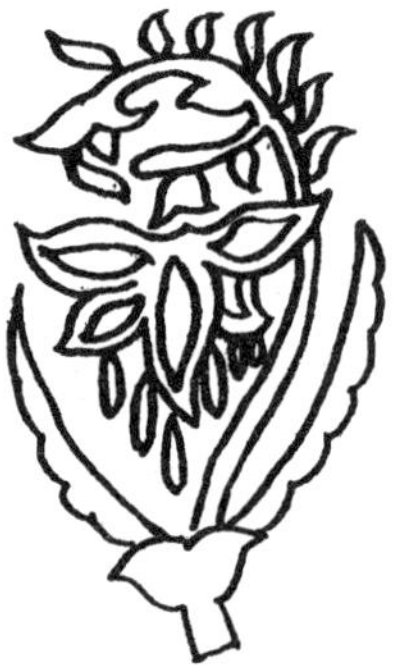
389

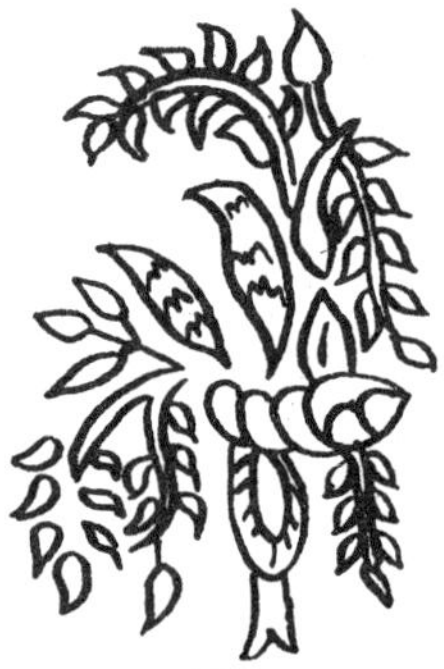
390

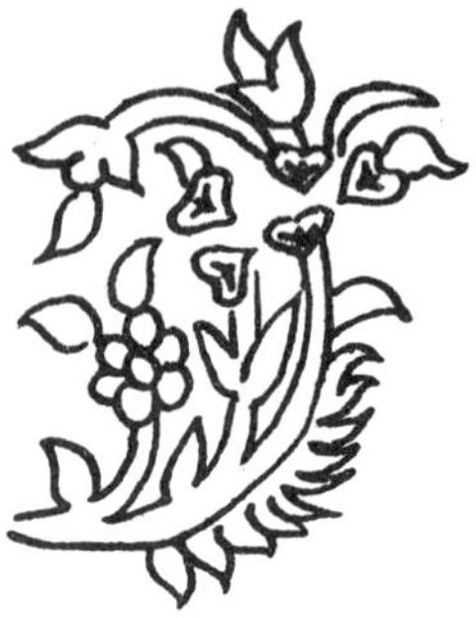
391

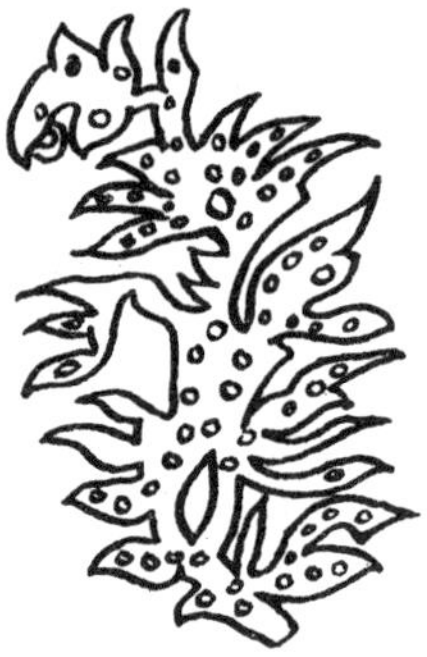
392

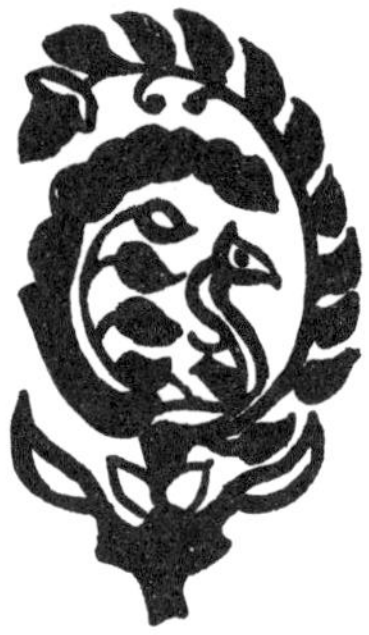
393

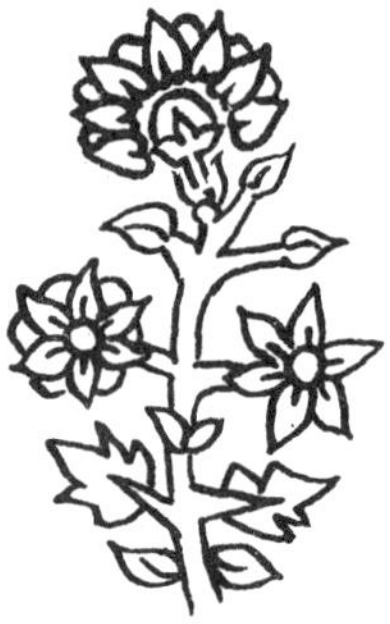
394

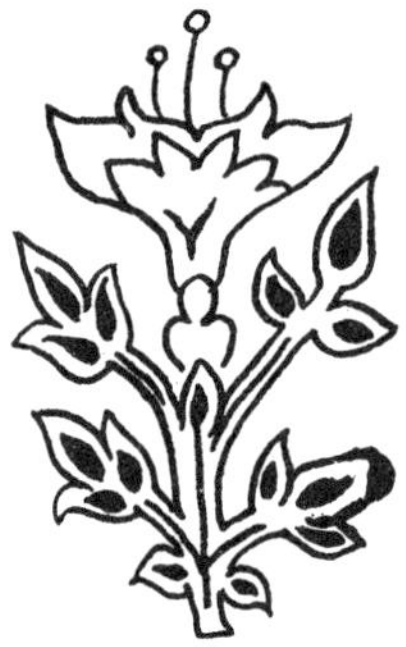
395

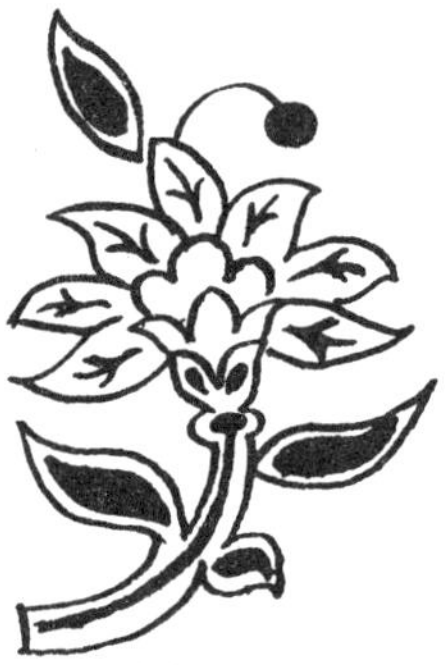
396

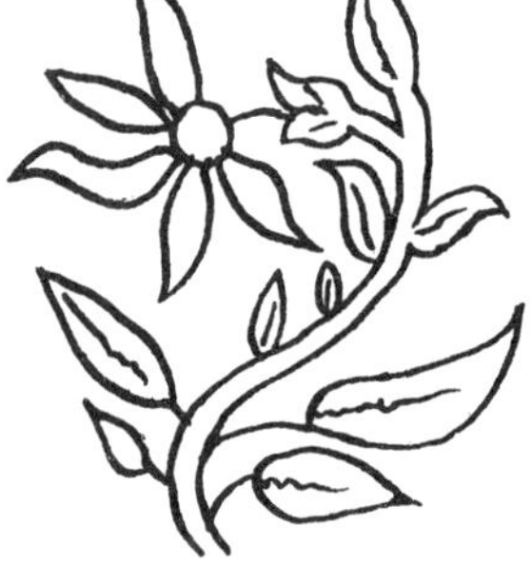
397

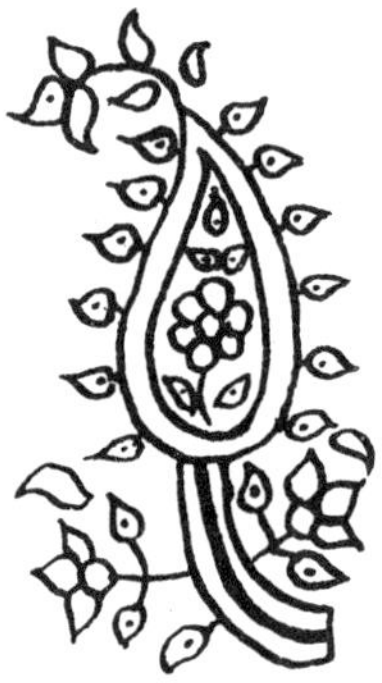
398

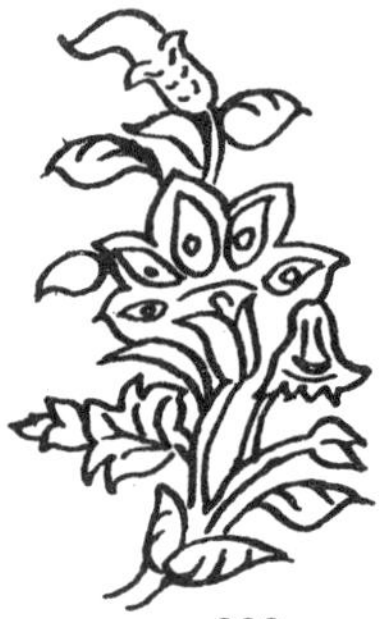
399

Wood Block Prints. **388–399.** Stylized floral and leaf and almond (Badam) motifs from hand-printed cotton textiles, Rajasthan.

# Plate 47

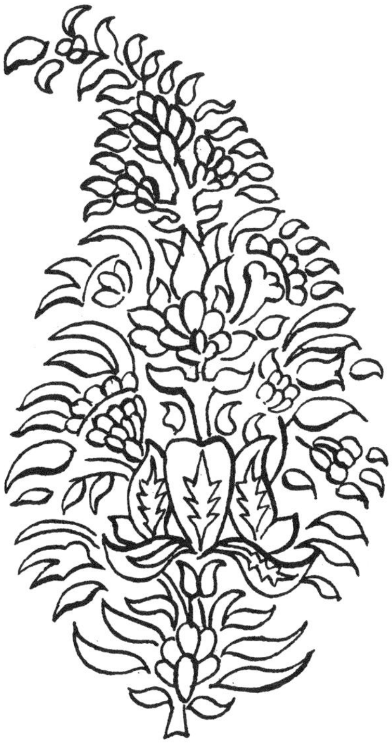
400

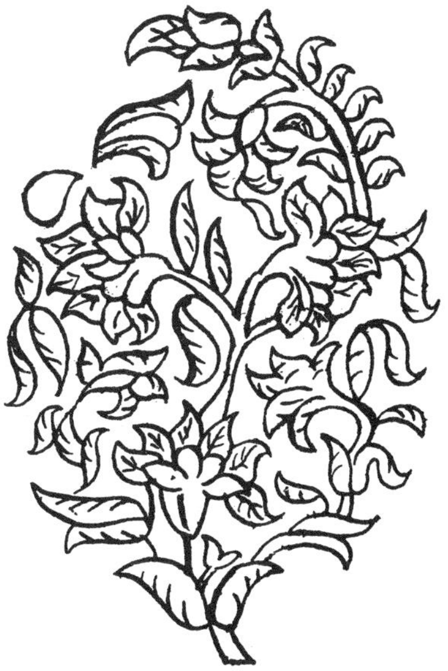
401

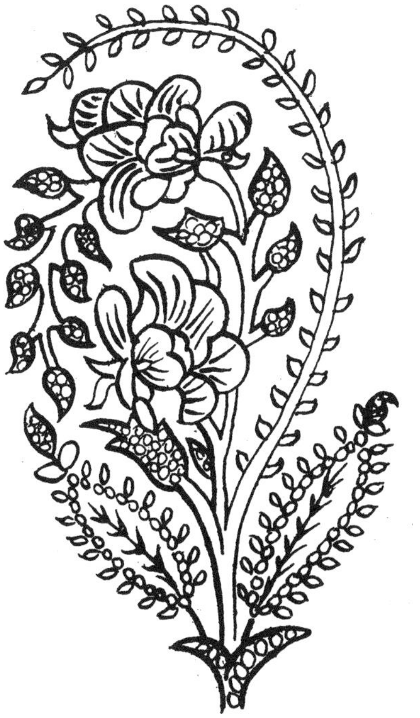
402

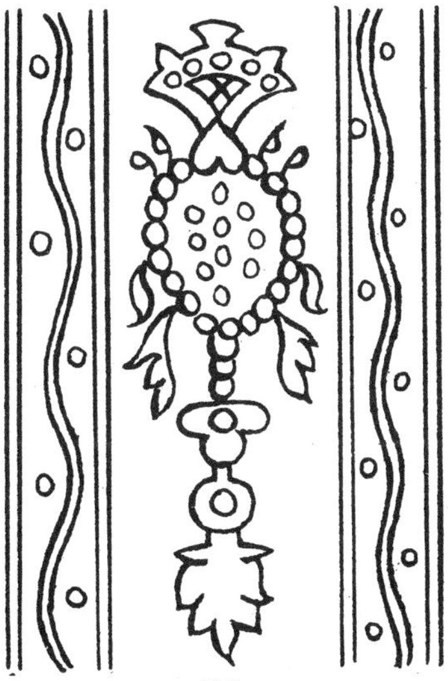
403

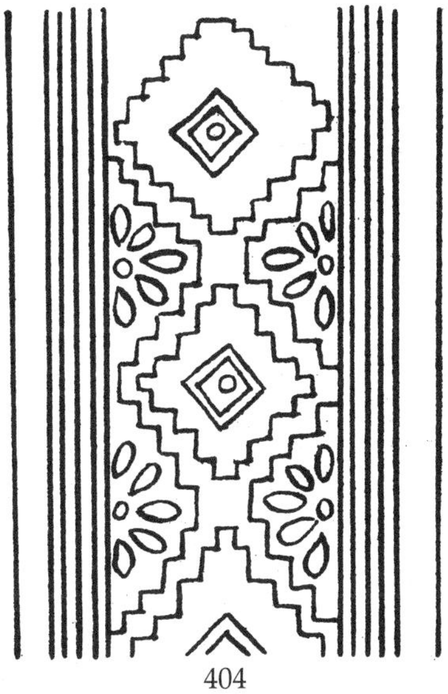
404

405

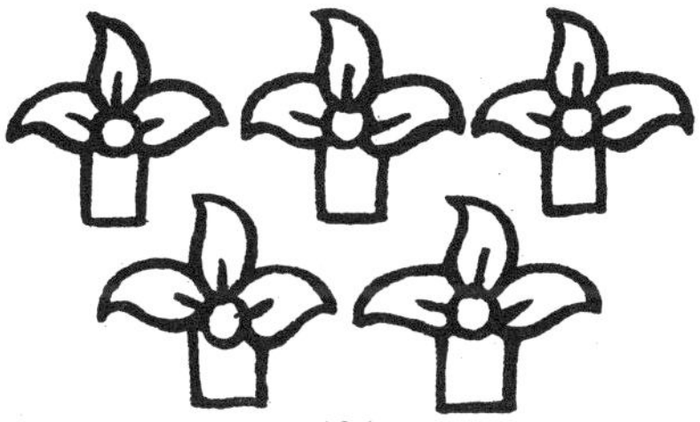
406

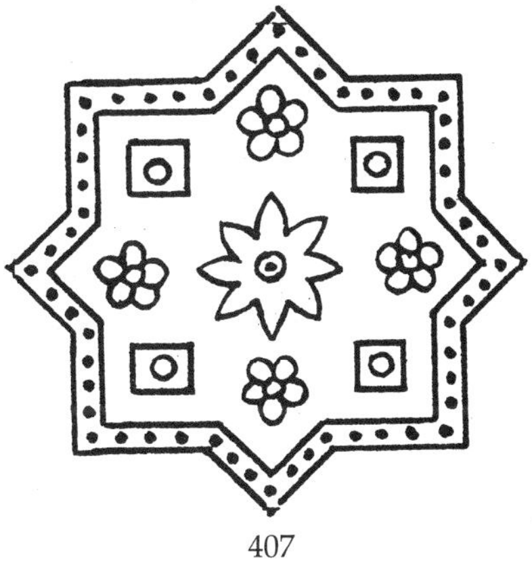
407

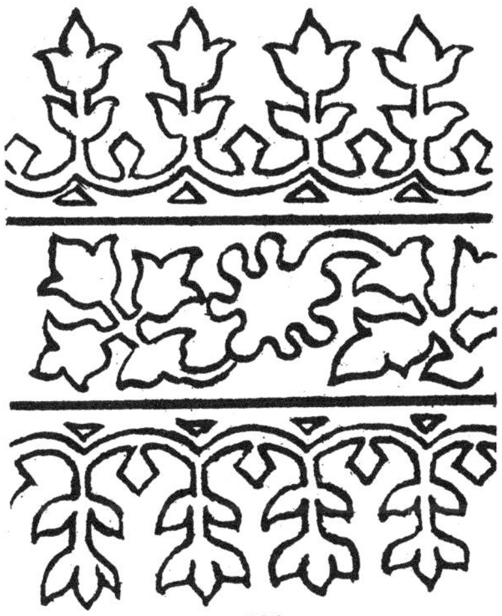
408

WOOD BLOCK PRINTS. **400–408.** Stylized floral, spray and geometrical motifs from the backgrounds and borders of hand-printed cotton textiles, Rajasthan.

# Plate 48

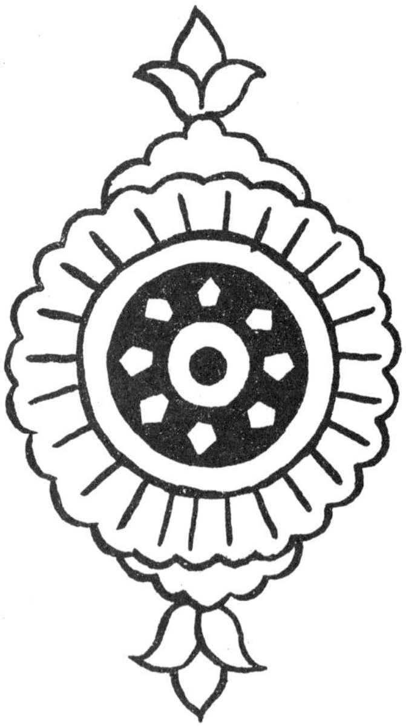

409

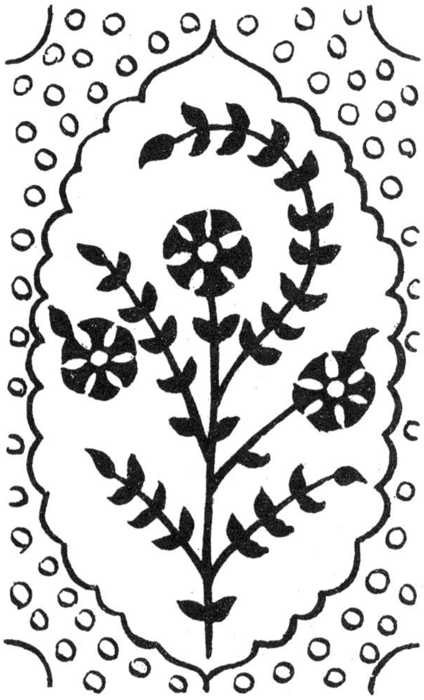

410

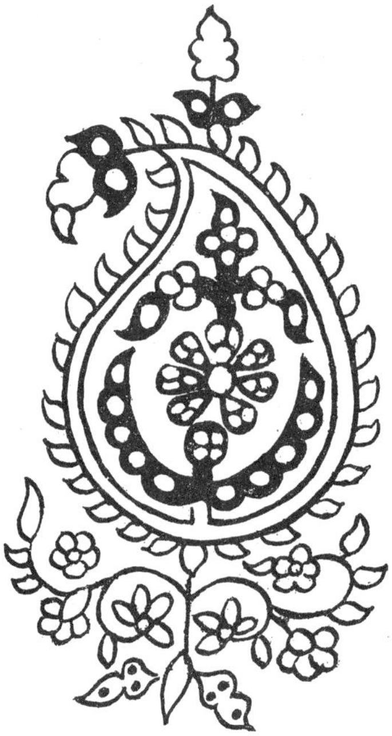

411

412

413

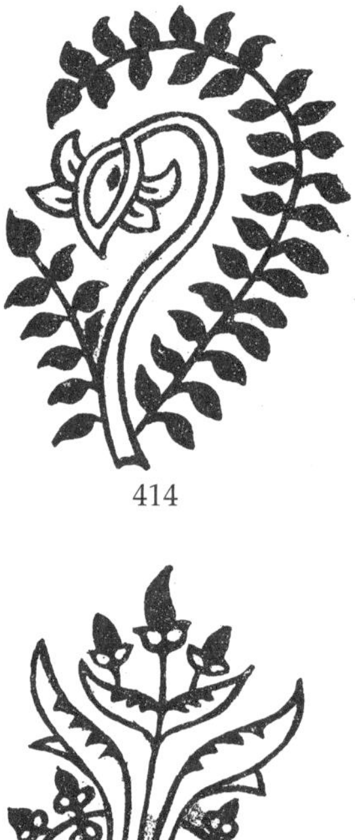

414

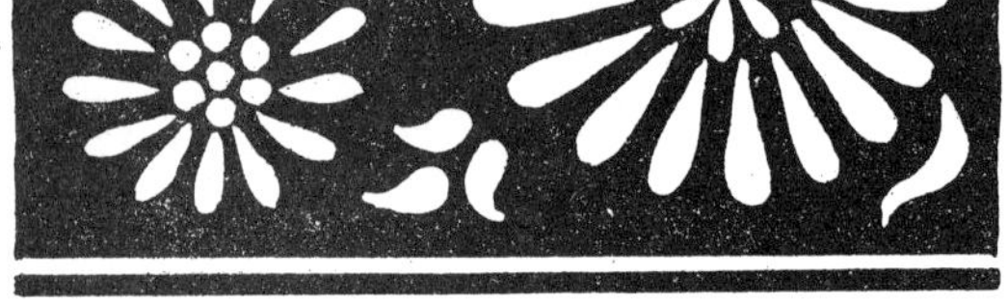

415

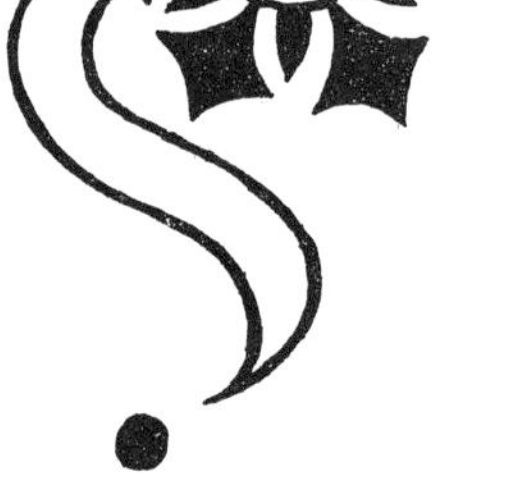

416

417

Wood Block Prints. **409–417.** Stylized floral, mango and spray motifs from the backgrounds and borders of hand-printed cotton textiles, Rajasthan.

# Plate 49

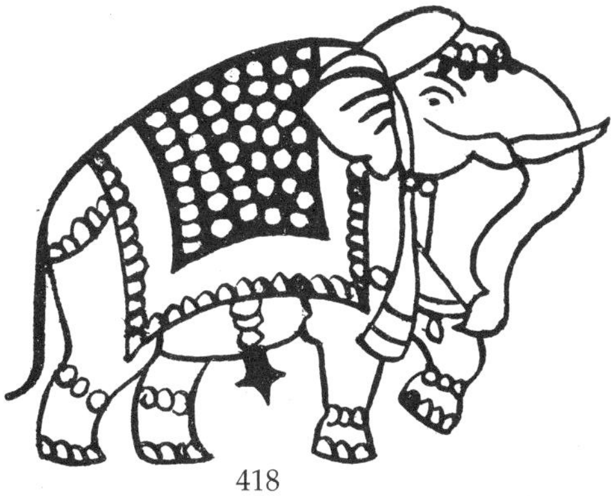

418

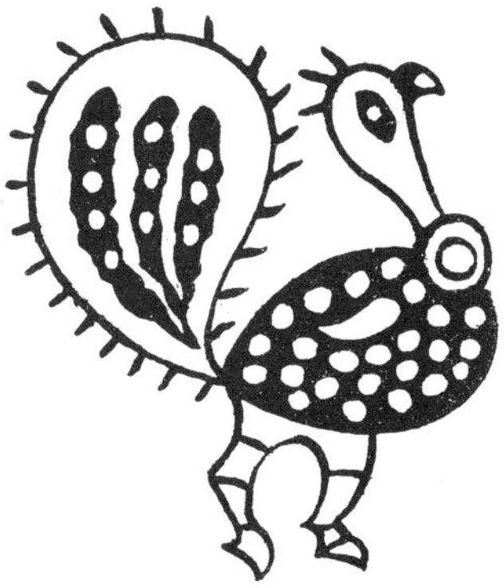

419

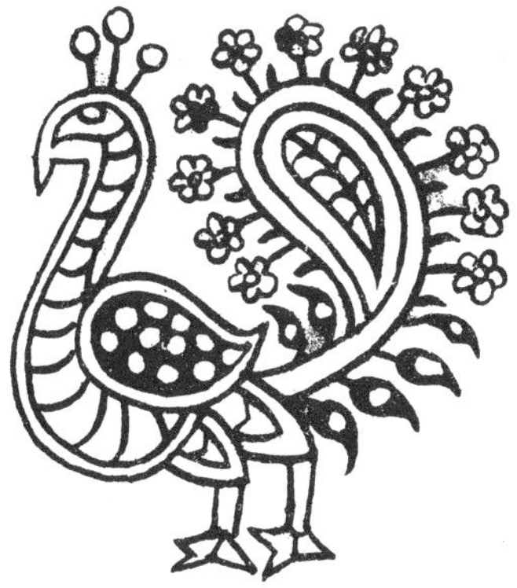

420

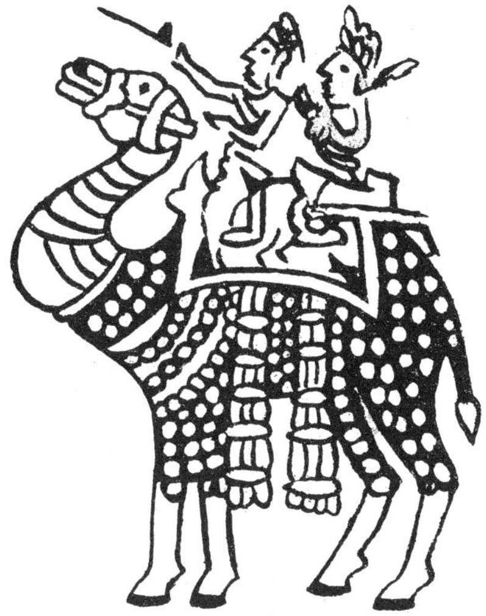

421

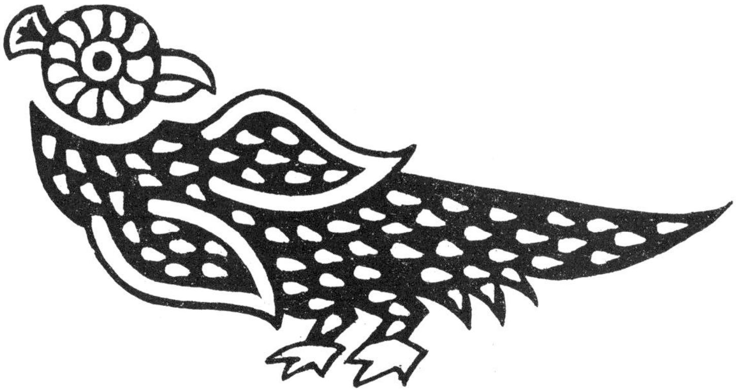

422

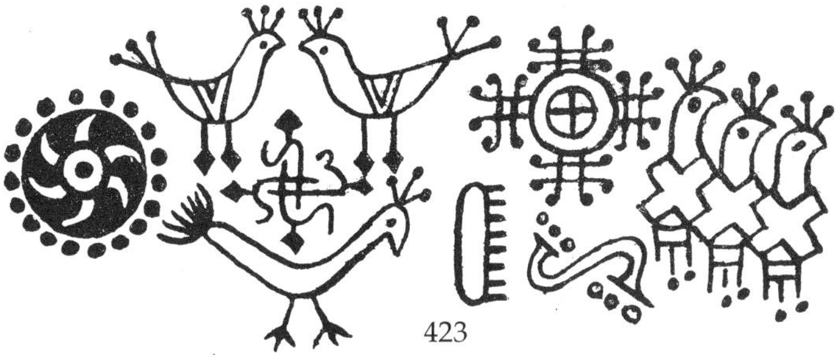

423

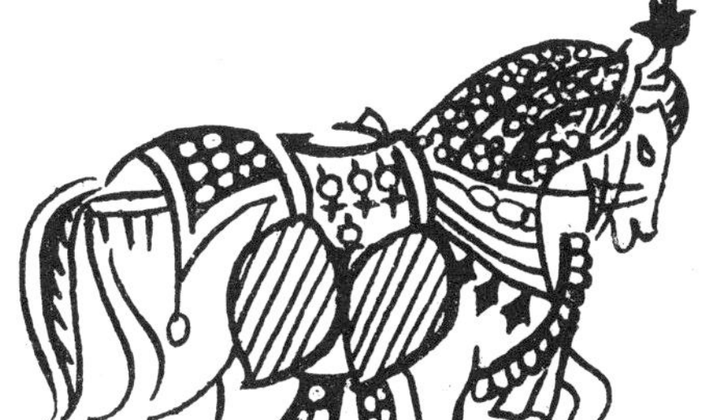

424

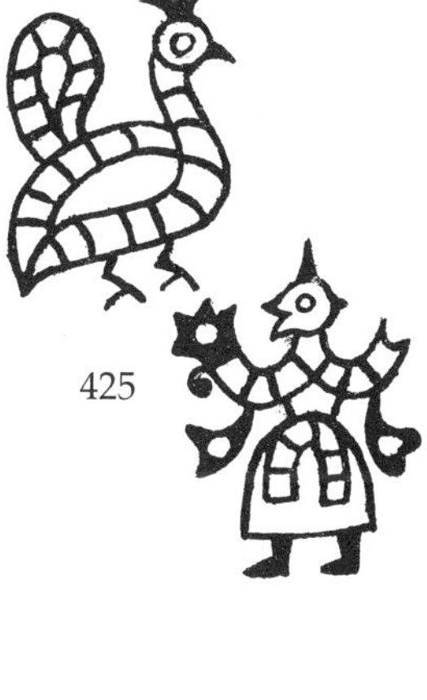

425

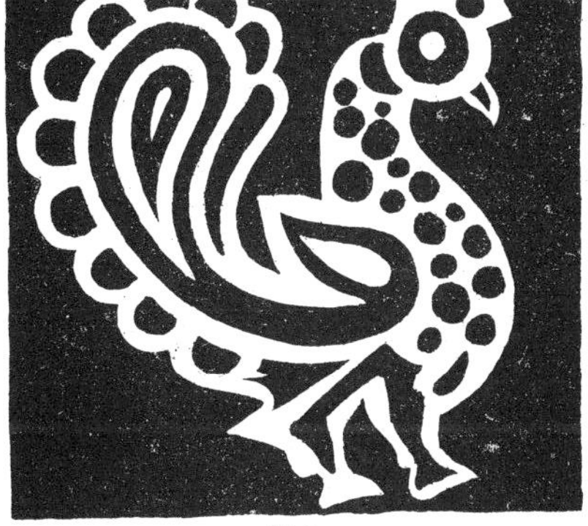

426

WOOD BLOCK PRINTS. **418–424.** Stylized elephant, peacocks, camel with riders, birds and horse from hand-printed cotton textiles, Rajasthan. **425, 426.** Stylized peacocks and human figures, hand printed in folk style on cotton textiles, Maharashtra.

# Plate 50

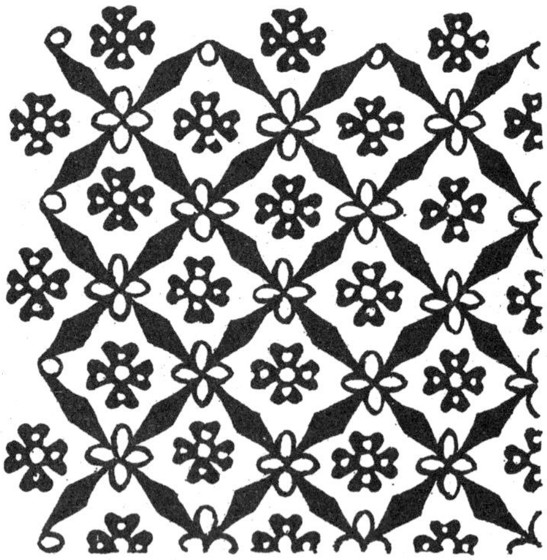

427

428

429

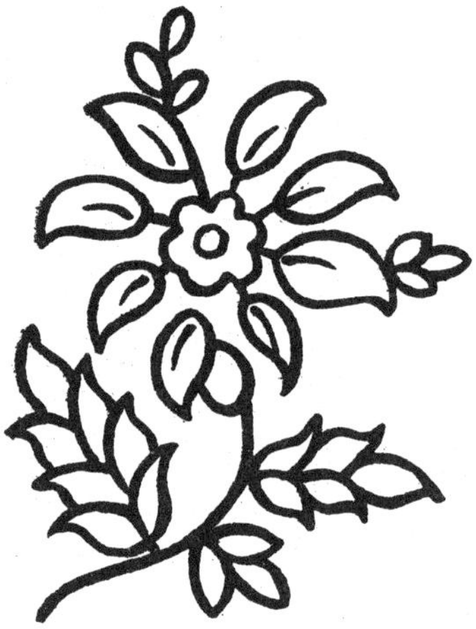

430

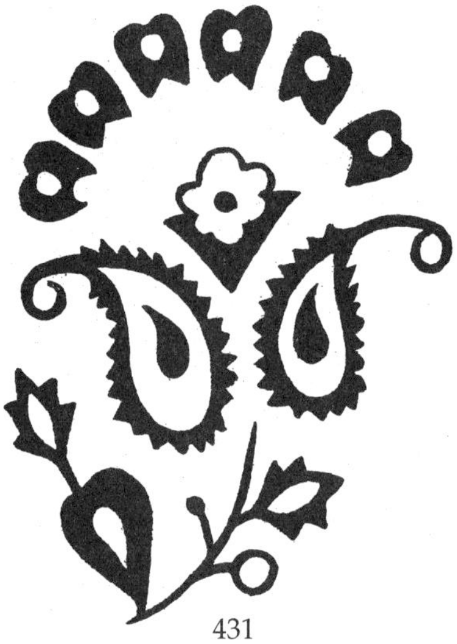

431

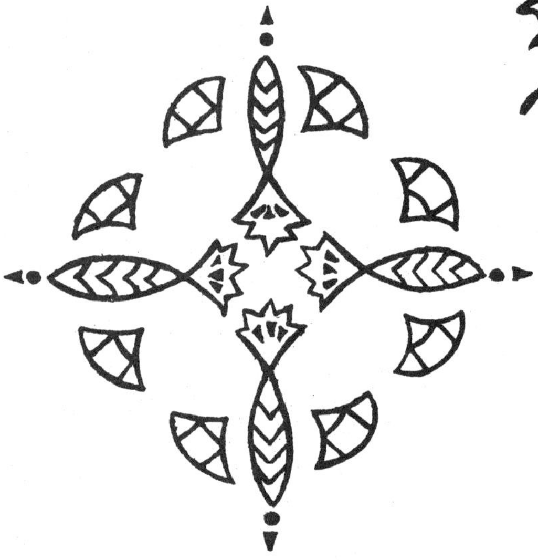

432

433

WOOD BLOCK PRINTS. **427–433.** Stylized floral, spray, leaf and geometrical motifs from hand-printed cotton textiles, Madhya Pradesh.

# Plate 51

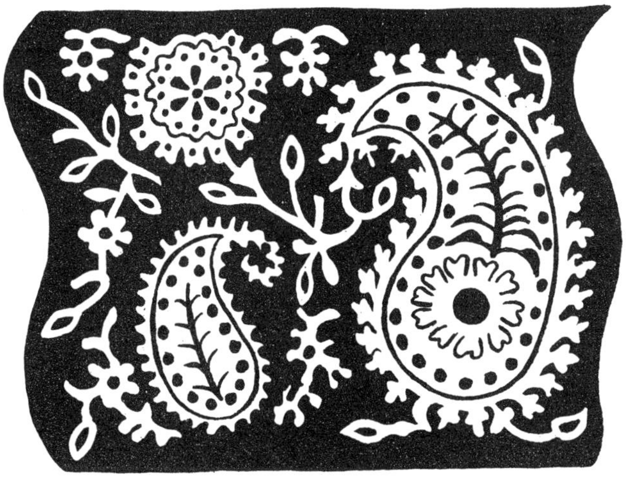

434

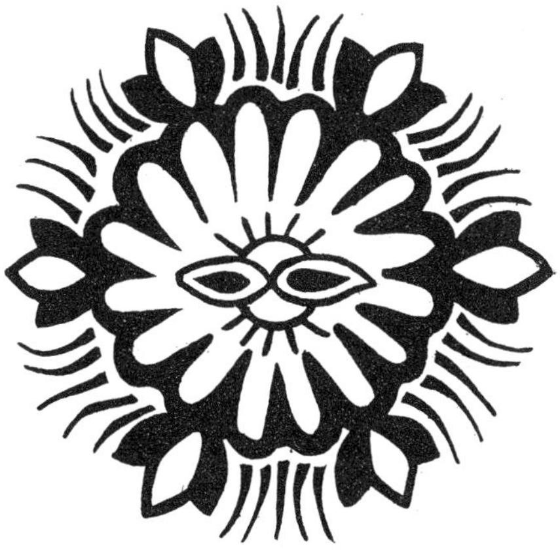

435

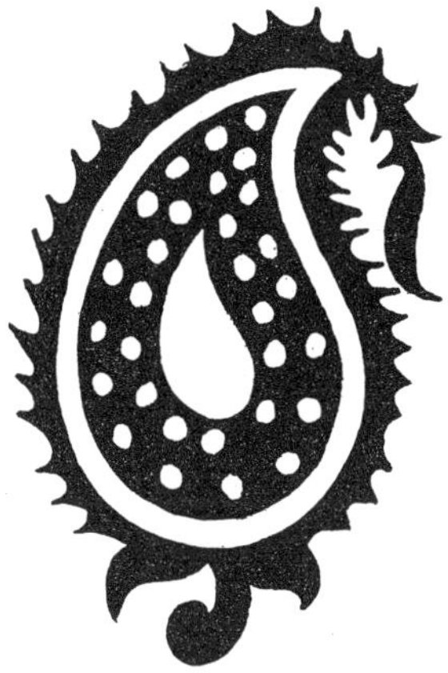

436

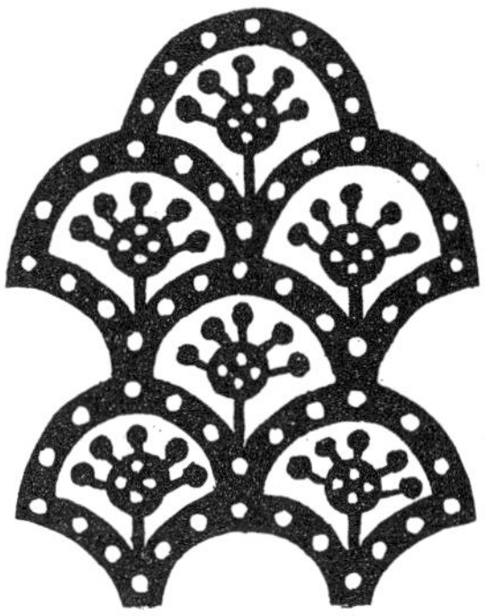

437

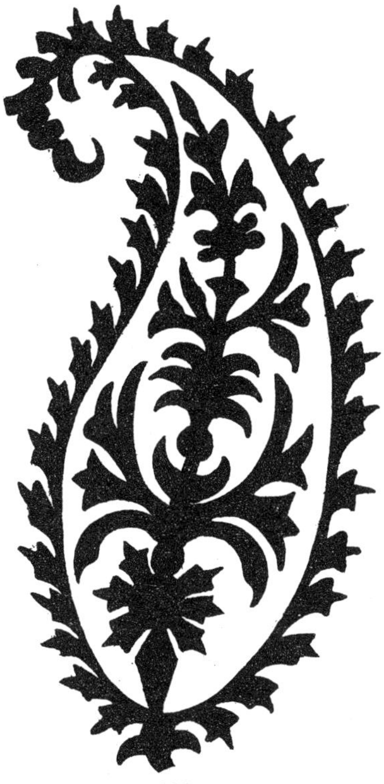

438

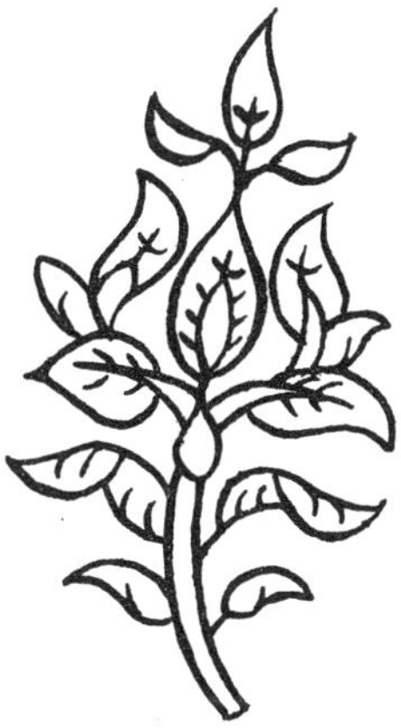

439

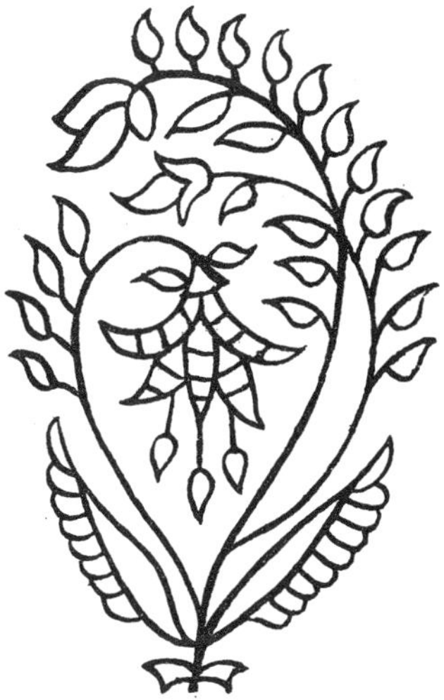

440

441

WOOD BLOCK PRINTS. **434–441.** Stylized Mango, floral and spray motifs from hand-printed cotton textiles, Madhya Pradesh.

## Plate 52

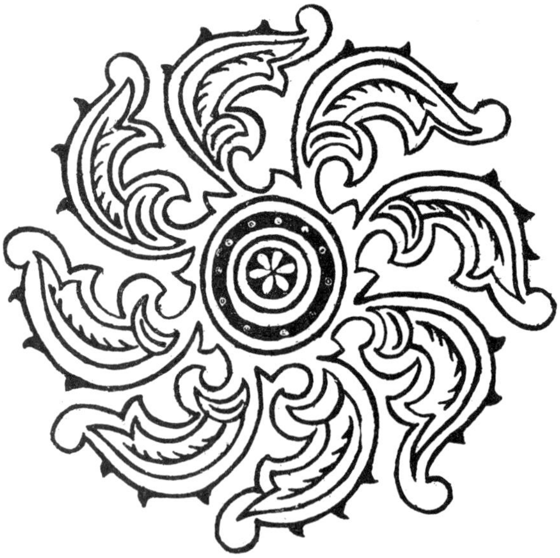
442

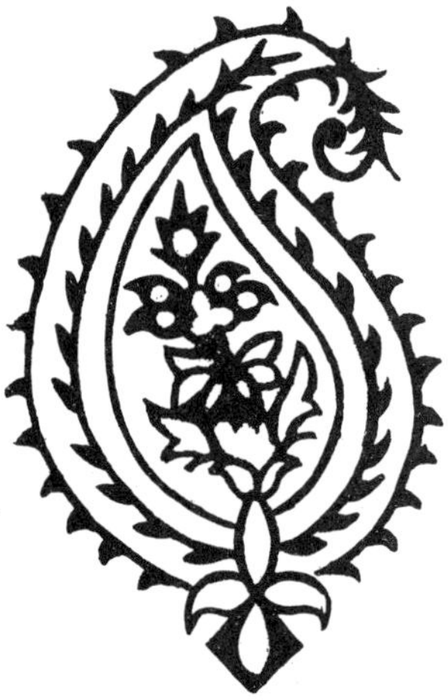
443

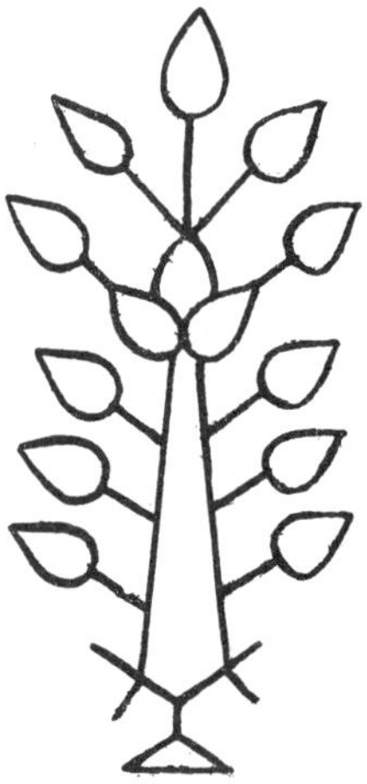
444

445

446

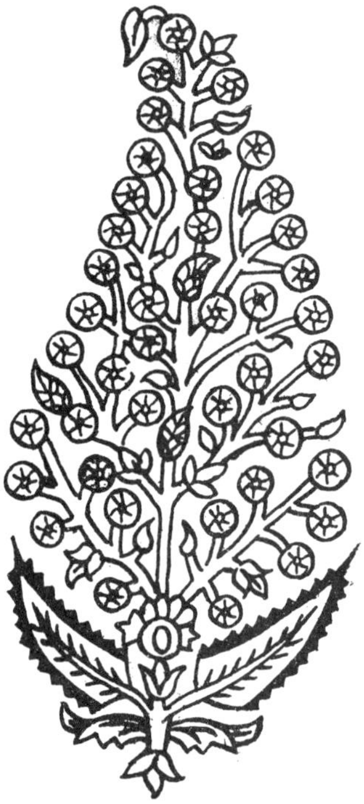
447

448

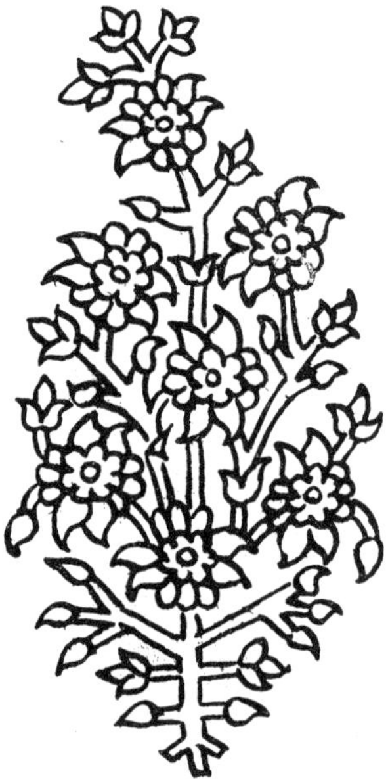
449

450

WOOD BLOCK PRINTS. **442, 443, 445–450.** Stylized geometrical, floral and flowering tree motifs from hand-printed cotton textiles, Madhya Pradesh. **444.** Abstract tree from a hand-printed cotton textile, Gujarat.

# Plate 53

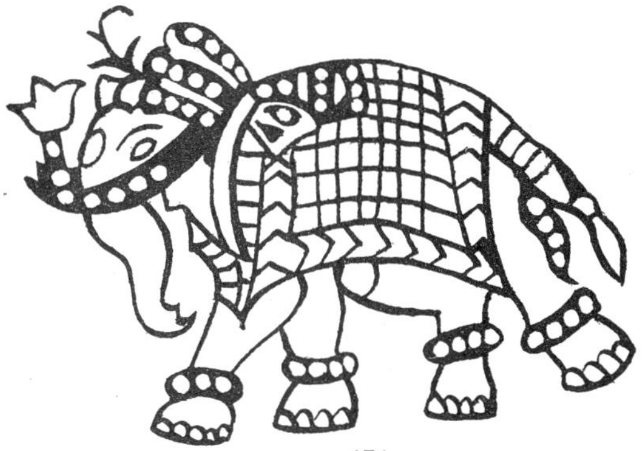

451

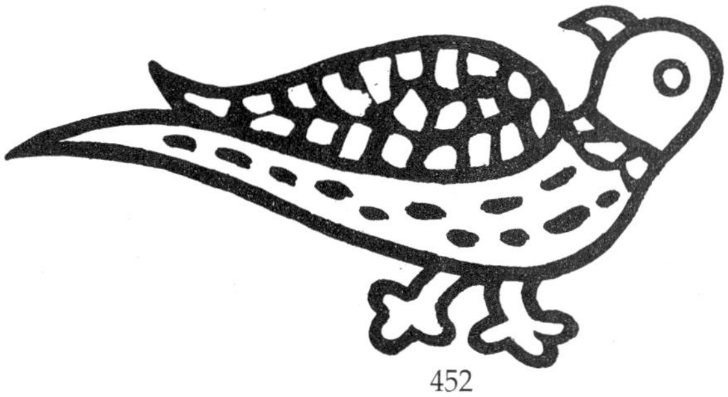

452

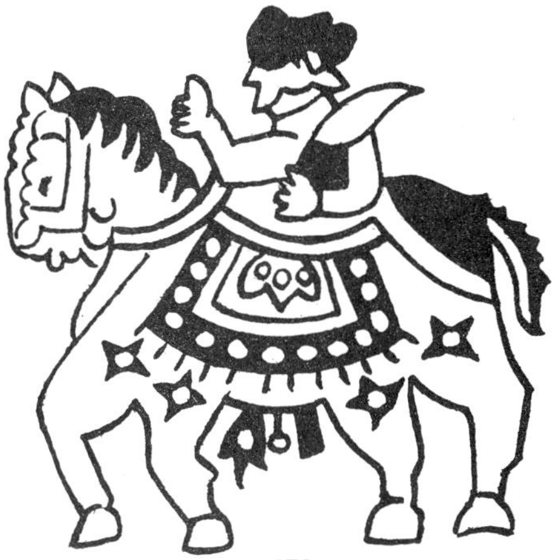

453

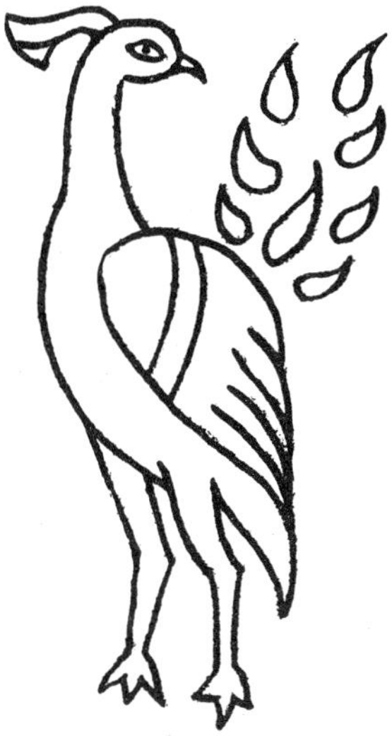

454

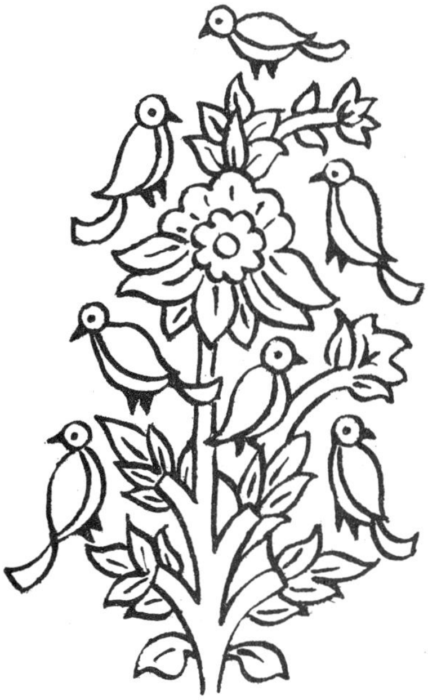

455

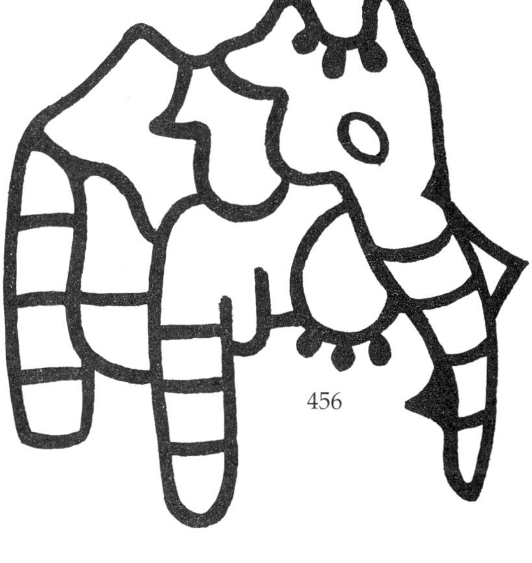

456

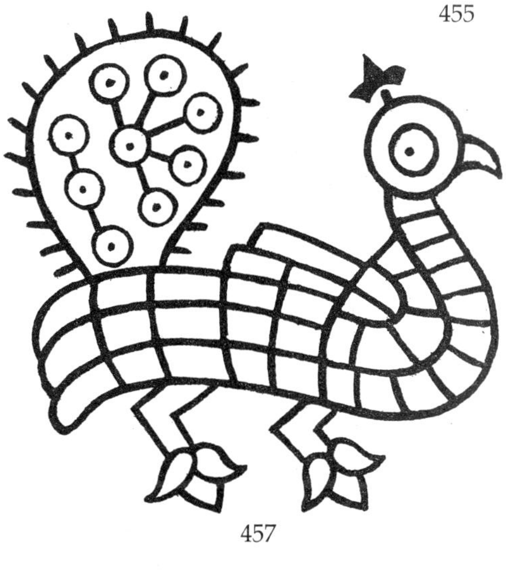

457

WOOD BLOCK PRINTS. **451, 452, 457.** Decorative elephant, bird and peacock folk style motifs from hand-printed cotton textiles, Maharashtra. **453–456.** Decorative horse and rider, crane, flowering tree with birds and elephant folk style hand-printed cotton textile motifs, Madhya Pradesh.

# Plate 54

458

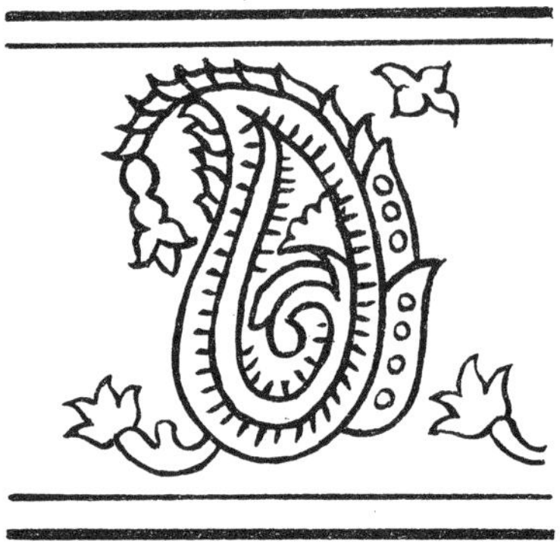

459

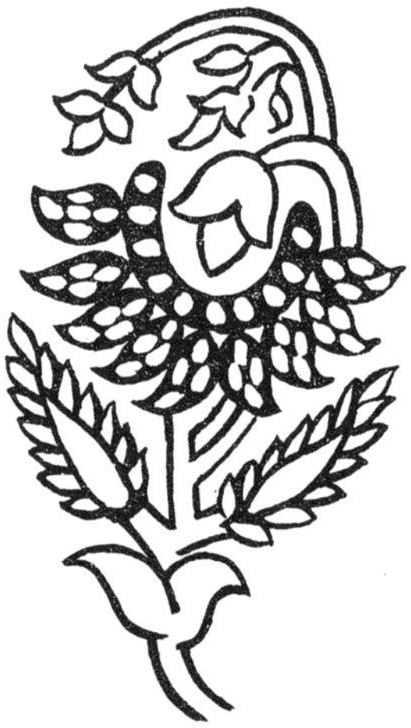

460

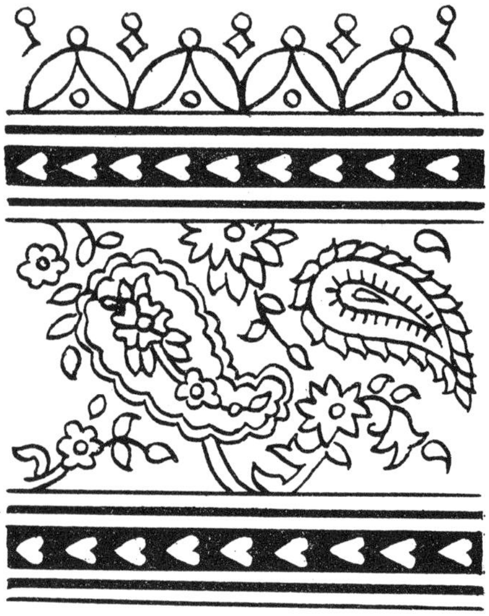

461

462

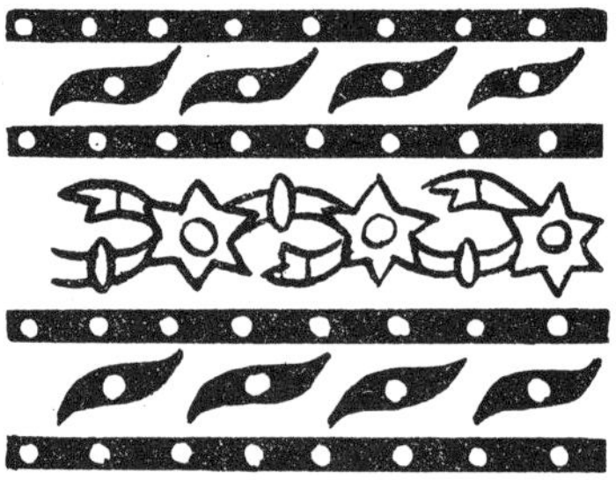

463

464

465

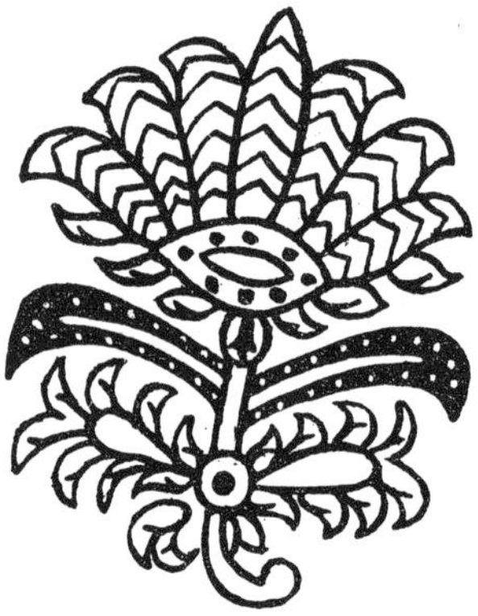

466

467

WOOD BLOCK PRINTS. **458–461.** Stylized mango and floral hand-printed motifs from the backgrounds and borders of cotton textiles, Maharashtra. **462–467.** Stylized floral and geometrical motifs on hand-printed cotton textiles, Madhya Pradesh.

# Plate 55

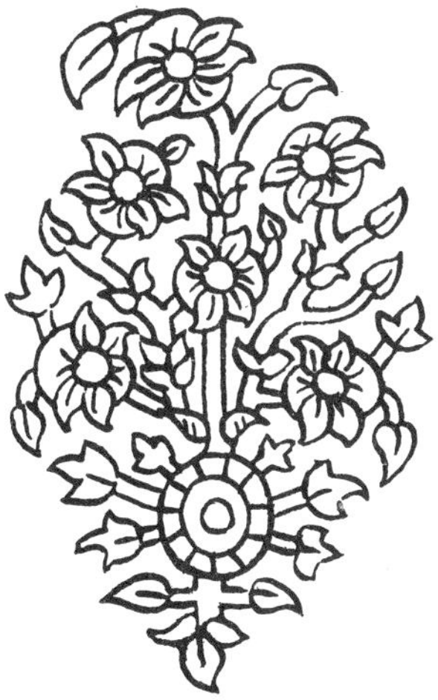

468

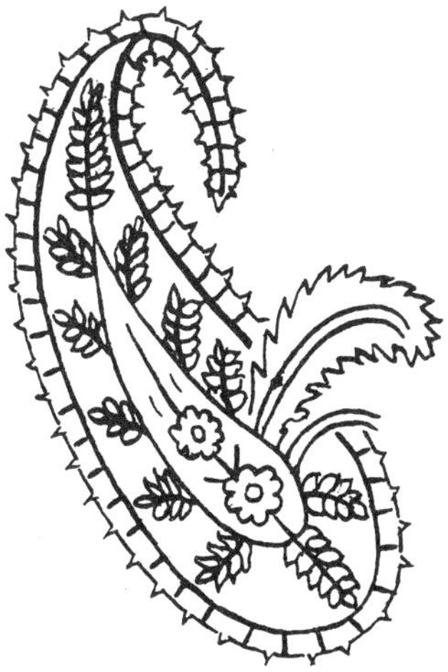

469

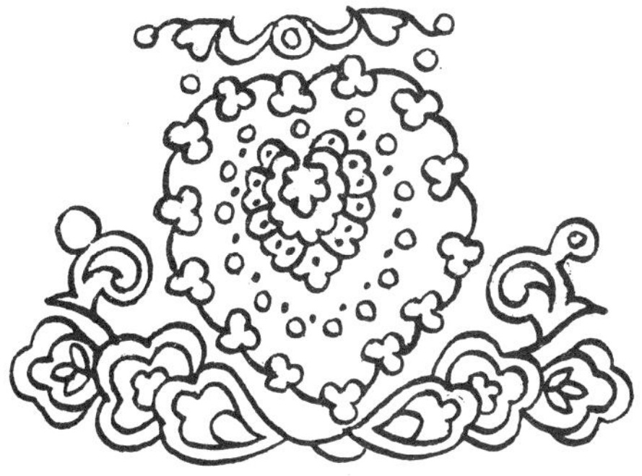

470

471

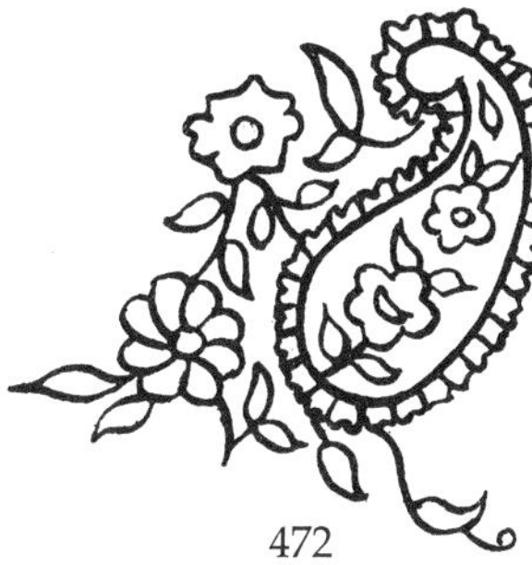

472

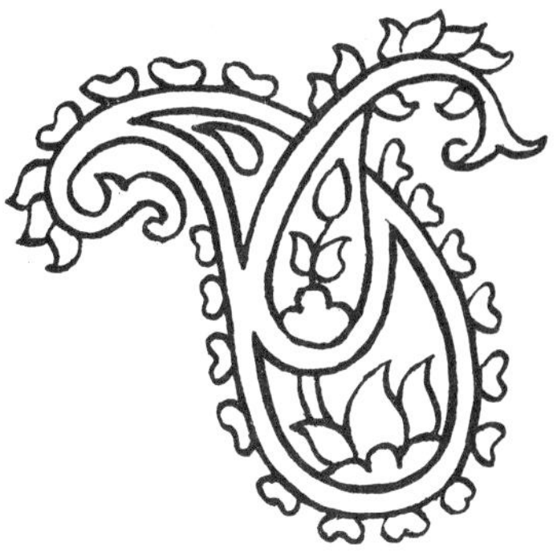

473

474

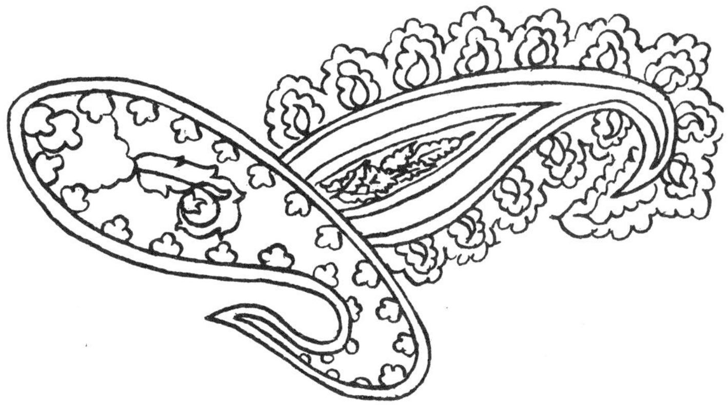

475

476

477

Wood Block Prints. **468–471, 474, 477.** Stylized floral spray, mango and flower motifs from hand-printed cotton textiles, Gujarat. **472, 473, 475, 476.** Stylized mango, floral and geometrical hand-printed motifs from cotton textiles, Maharashtra.

# Plate 56

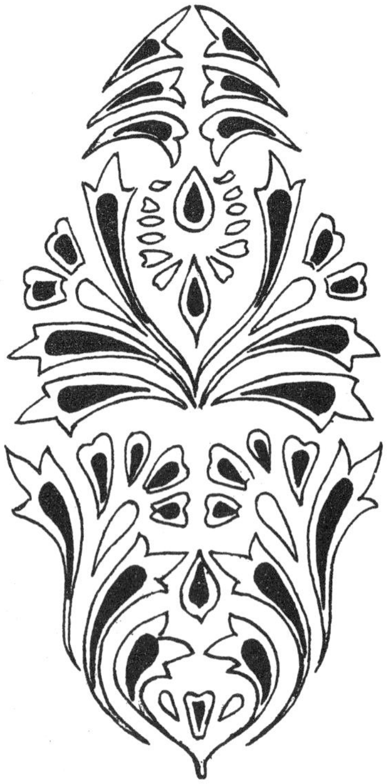

478

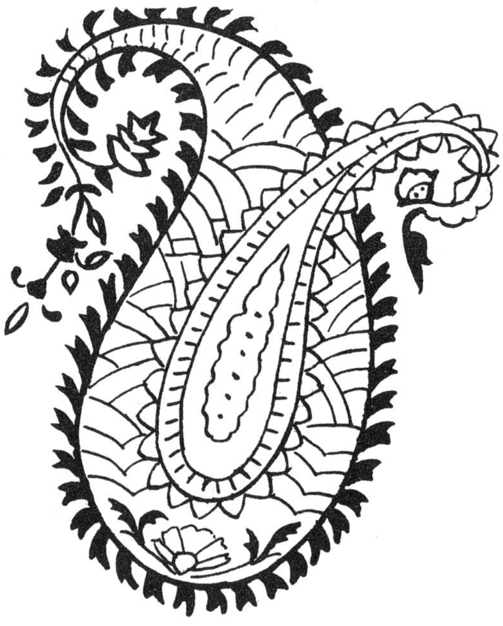

479

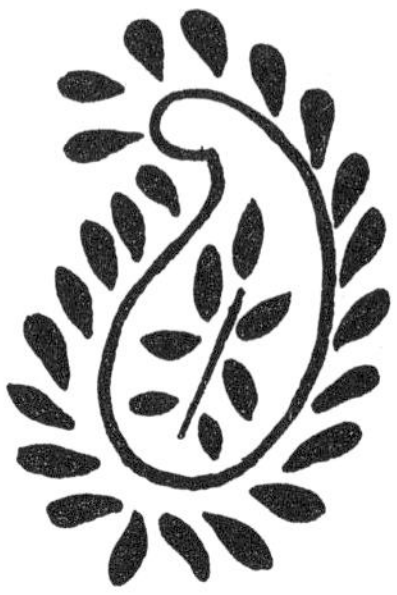

480

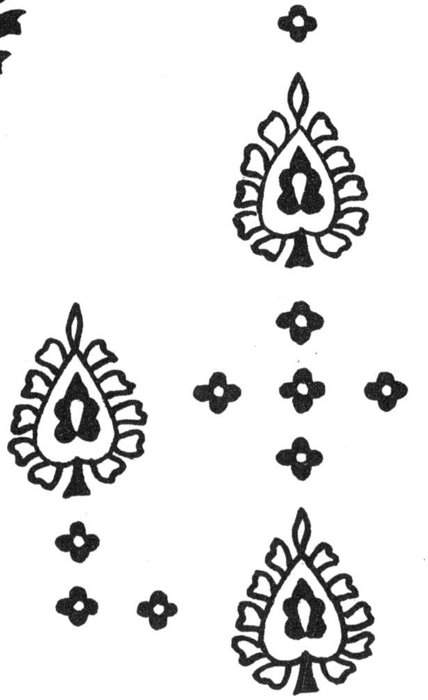

483

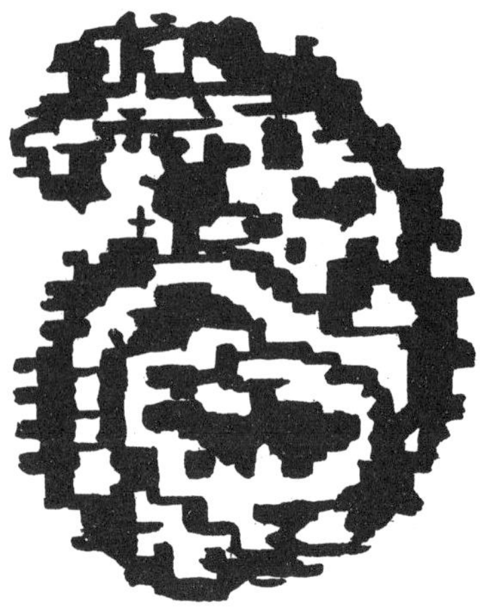

481

482

484

485

WOOD BLOCK PRINTS. **478–483, 485.** Stylized mango and floral hand-printed motifs from traditional wood cut blocks. **484.** Miniature floral hand-printed motifs from a cotton textile, West Bengal.

# Plate 57

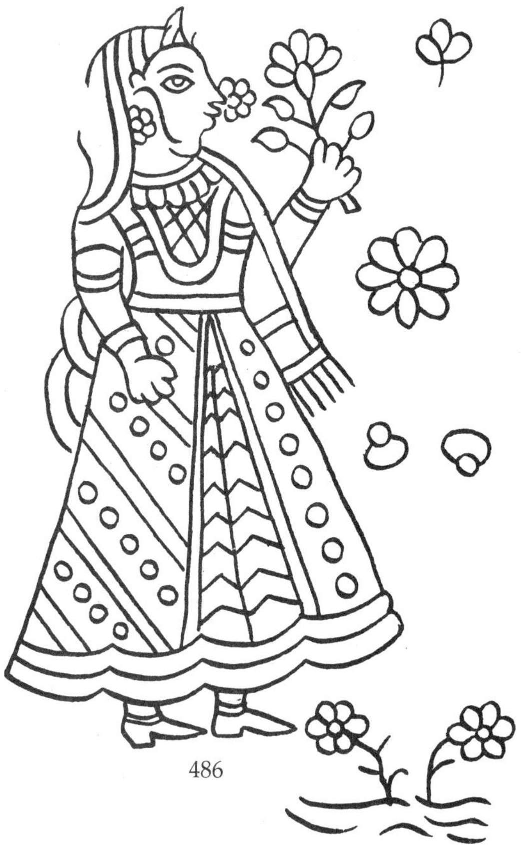

486

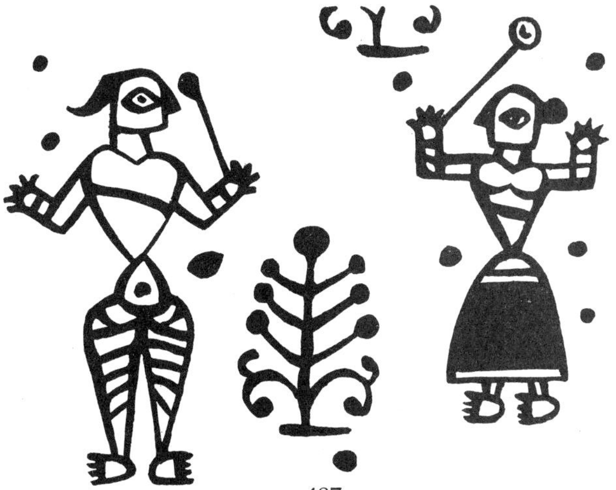

487

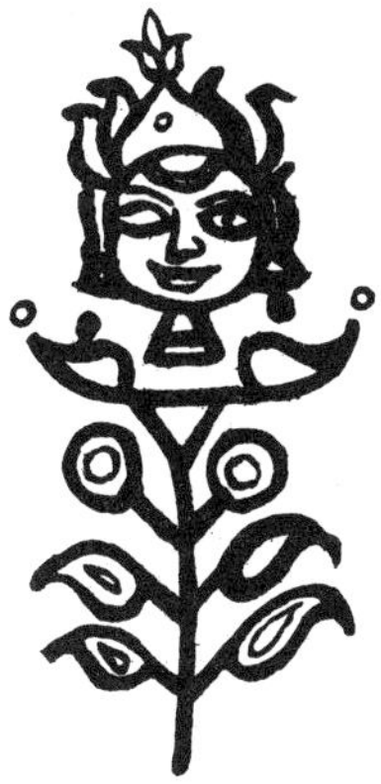

488

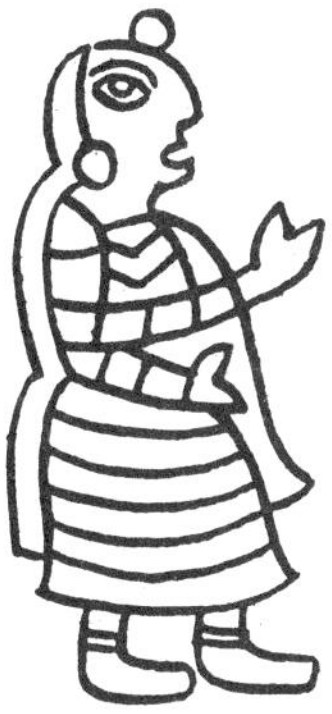

489

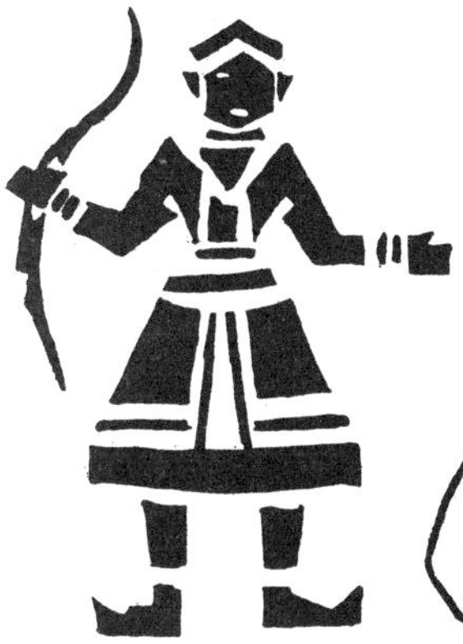

490

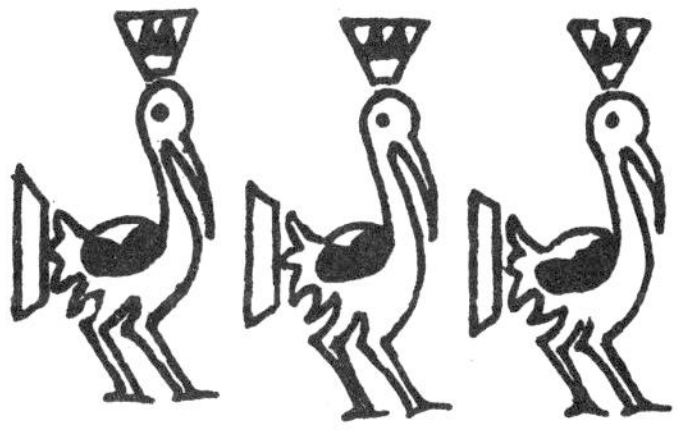

491

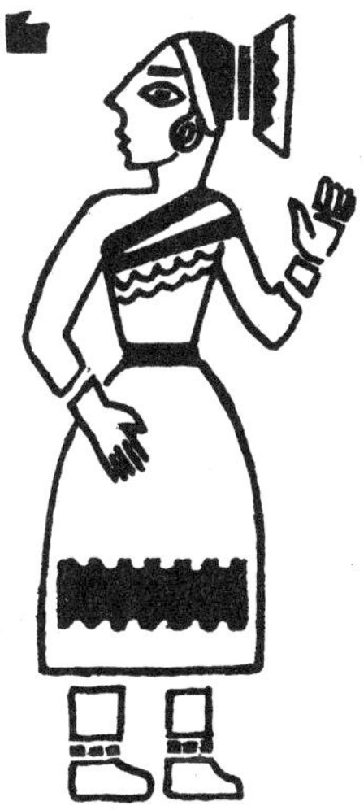

492

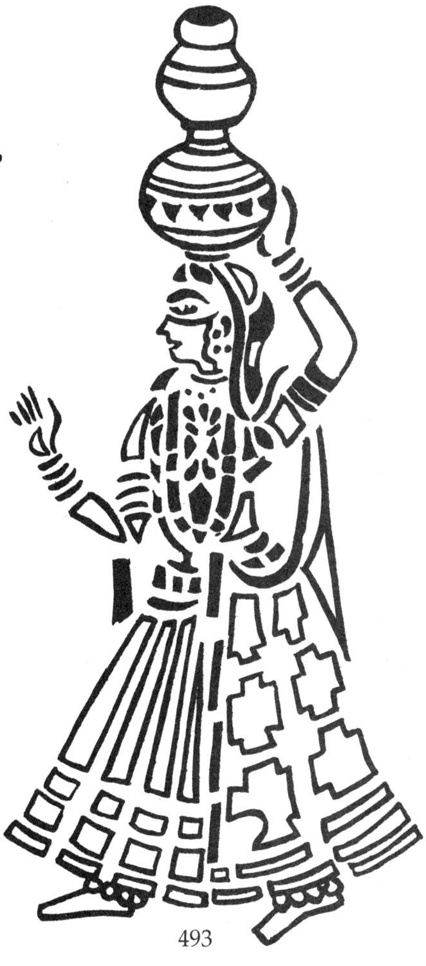

493

WOOD BLOCK PRINTS. **486.** Human figure and floral motifs from a hand-printed cotton textile, Maharashtra. **487, 488, 490.** Stylized human figures and trees in motifs from hand-printed cotton textiles, Bihar. **489.** A woman in this impressionistic folk motif from a hand-printed textile, Gujarat. **491.** Stylized birds from a hand-printed cotton textile, West Bengal. **492.** A woman in this folk inspired hand-printed cotton textile, Assam. **493.** A milkmaid carrying her clay pots, from a hand-printed cotton textile, Rajasthan.

# Plate 58

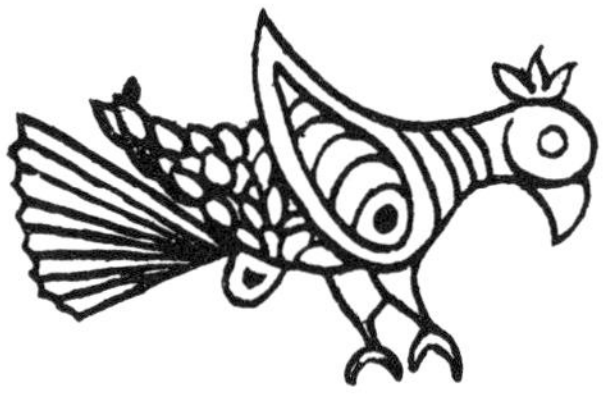

494

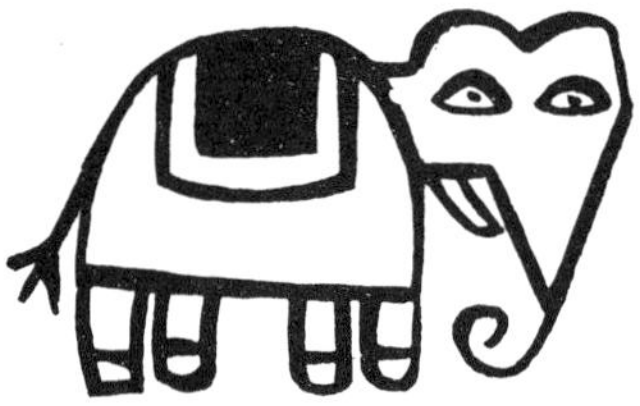

495

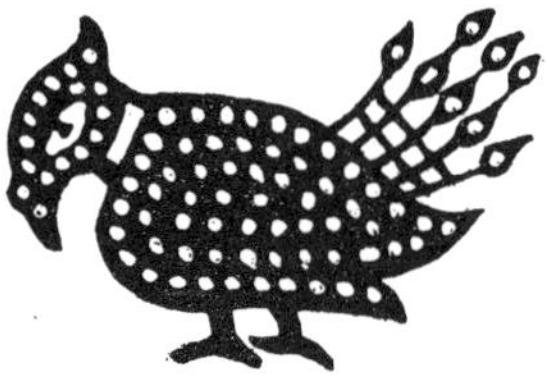

496

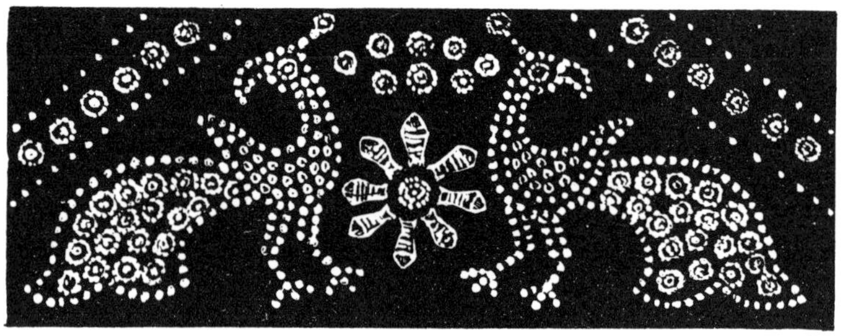

497

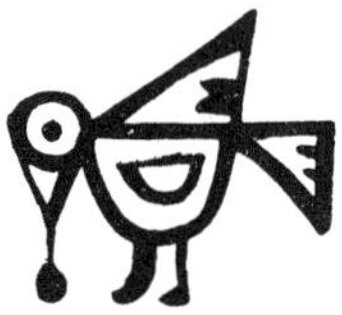

498

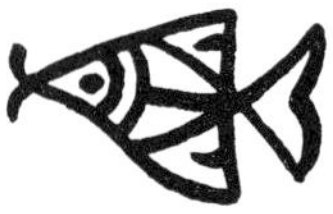

499

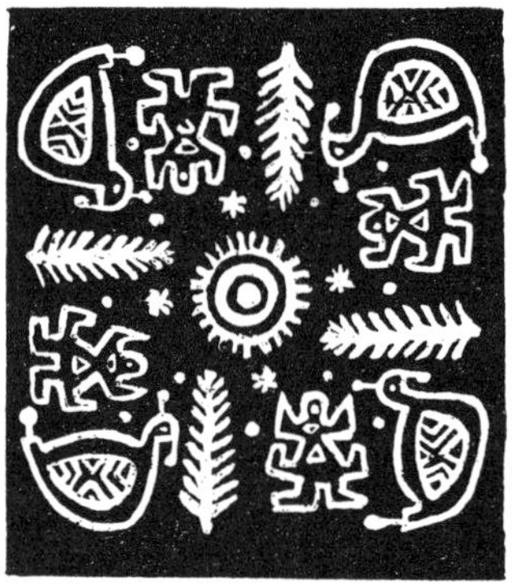

502

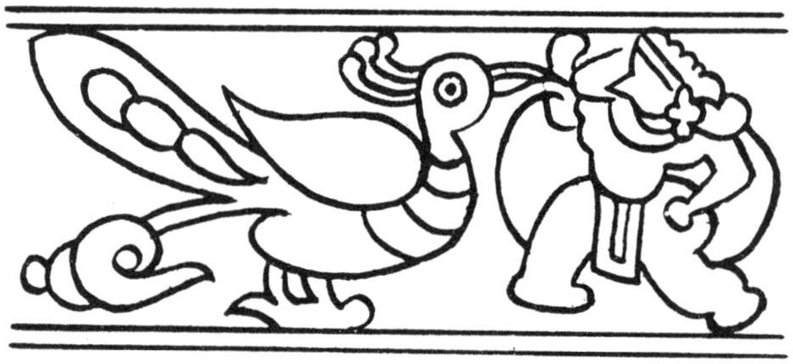

500

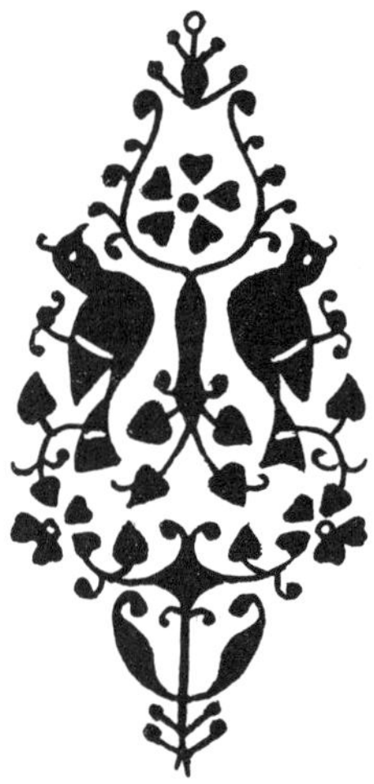

501

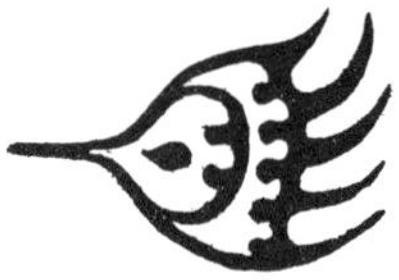

503

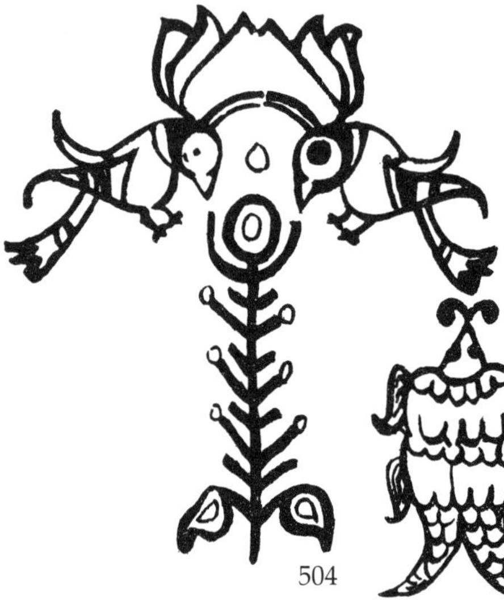

504

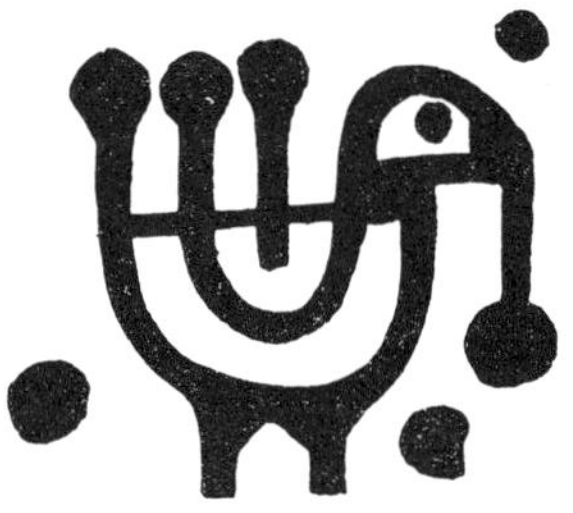

505

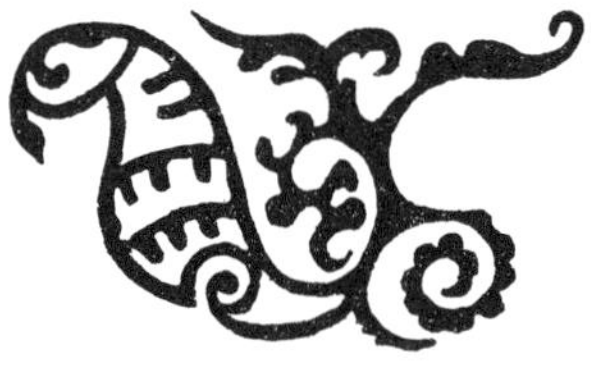

506

Wood Block Prints. **494–496, 498, 499, 502, 504, 505.** Various stylized folk form motifs of birds, elephant, fish, trees and human figures from hand-printed cotton textiles, Bihar. **497.** Stylized motifs of peacocks and stars adapted from the tie and dye mode from a cotton textile, Bihar. **500.** Stylized bird and human figure hand-printed motif from a cotton textile, Maharashtra. **501.** Stylized motifs of birds on a tree from a hand-printed cotton Sari, West Bengal. **503, 506.** Stylized fish and bird motifs from a hand-printed silk fabric, West Bengal.

# Plate 59

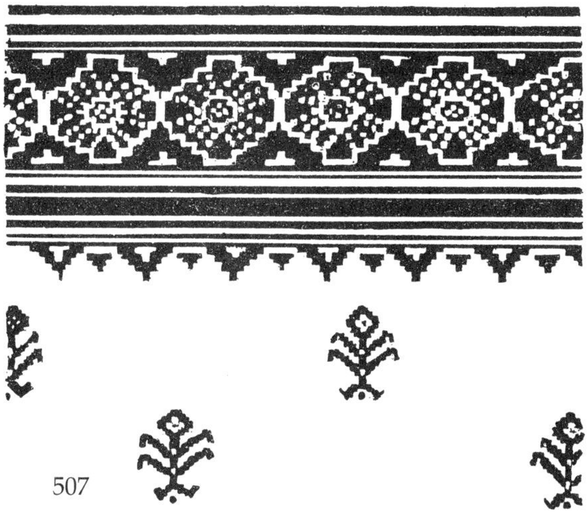

507

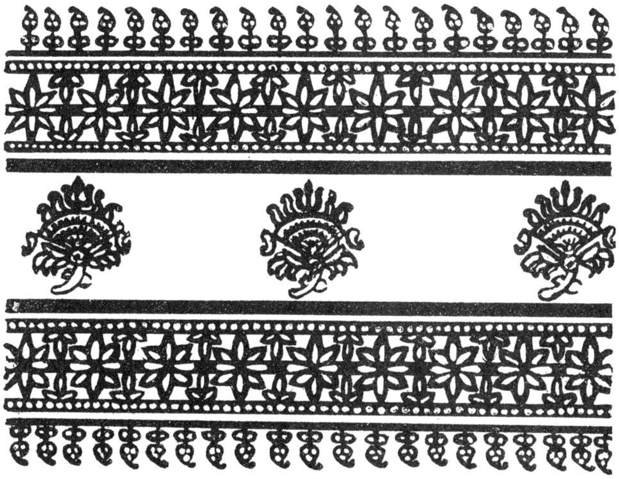

508

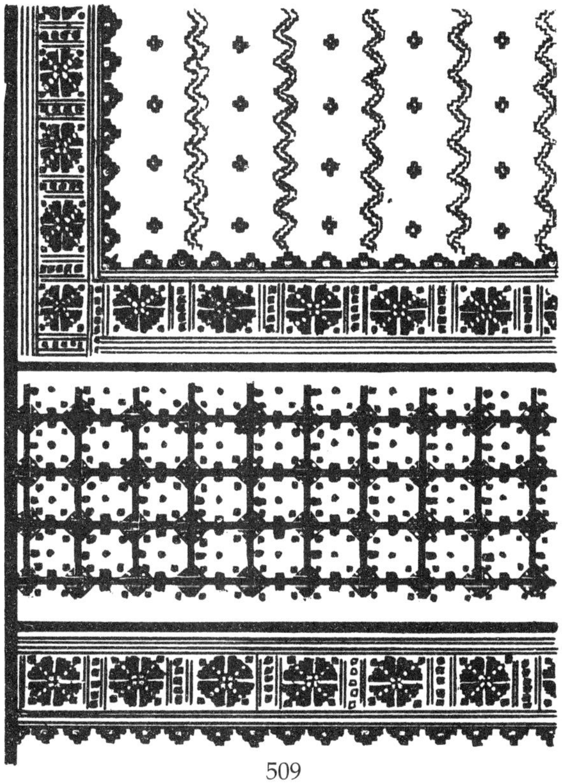

509

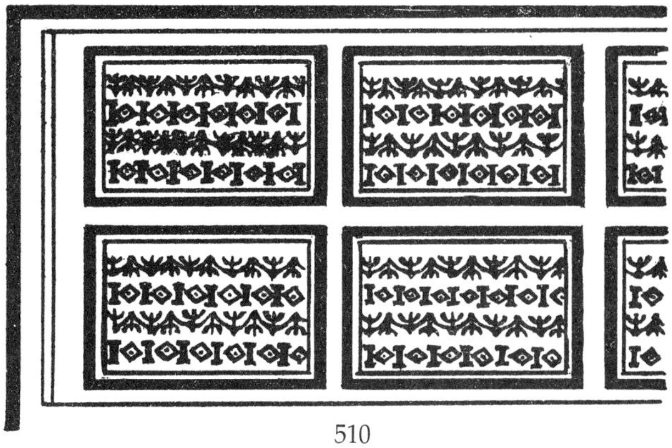

510

511

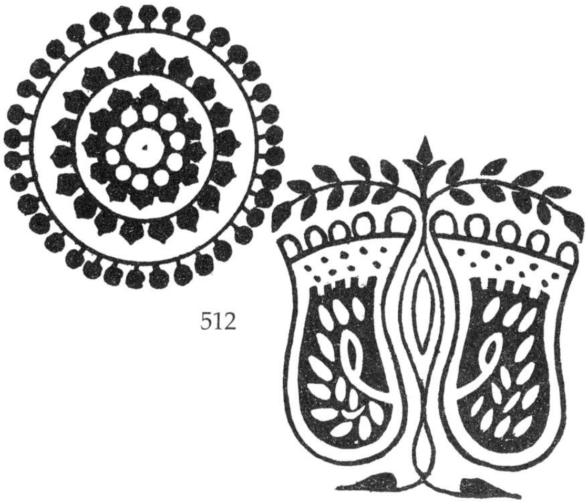

512

Wood Block Prints. **507.** Stylized floral motifs hand printed on a cotton textile, Bihar. **508.** Another cotton textile from Bihar hand printed with floral motifs. **509.** All over linear and geometrical patterns hand printed on a cotton textile, Bihar. **510–512.** Symbolic mystic motifs of the lotus and foot prints and finely worked central design in rectangles, from a hand-printed cotton textile, Bihar.

# Plate 60

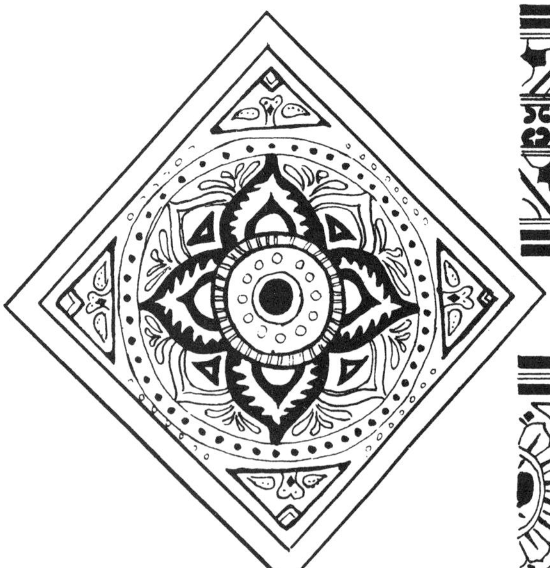

513

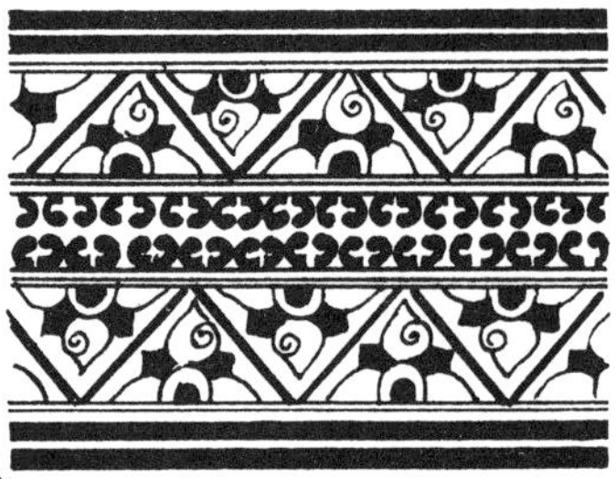

514

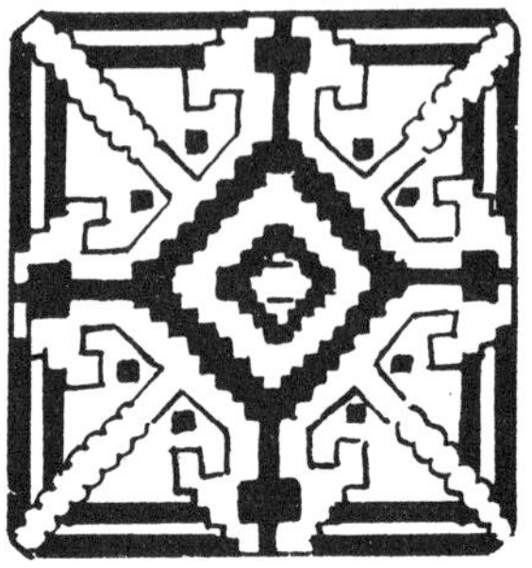

515

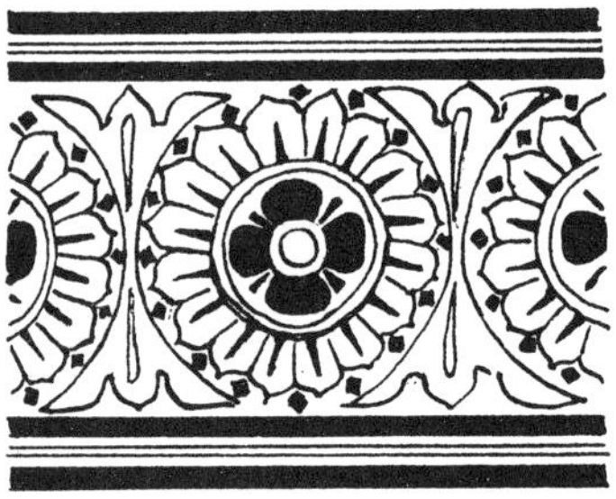

516

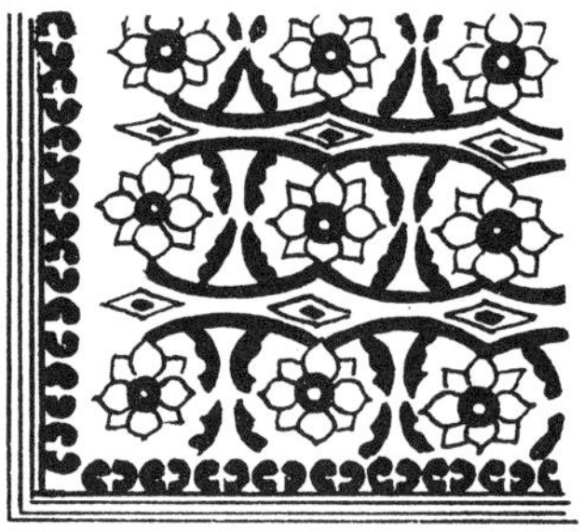

517

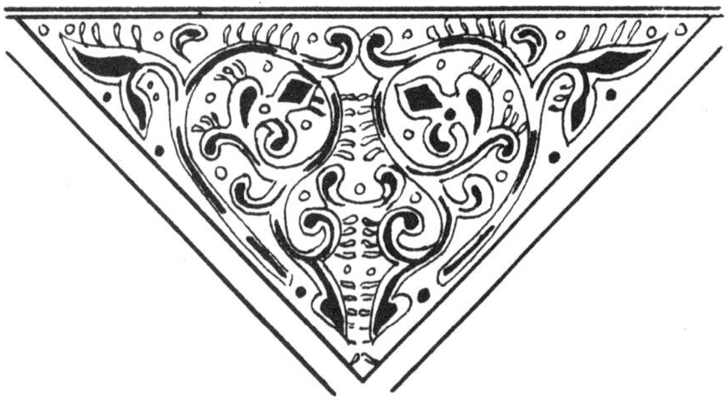

518

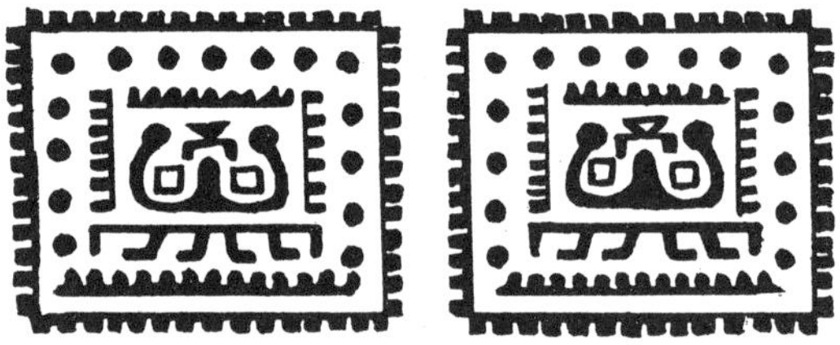

519

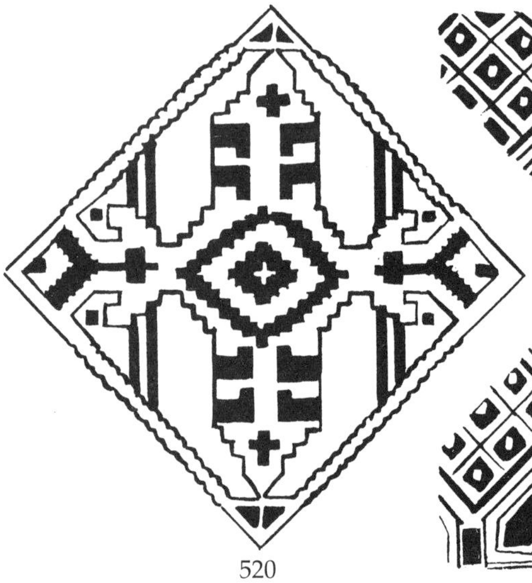

520

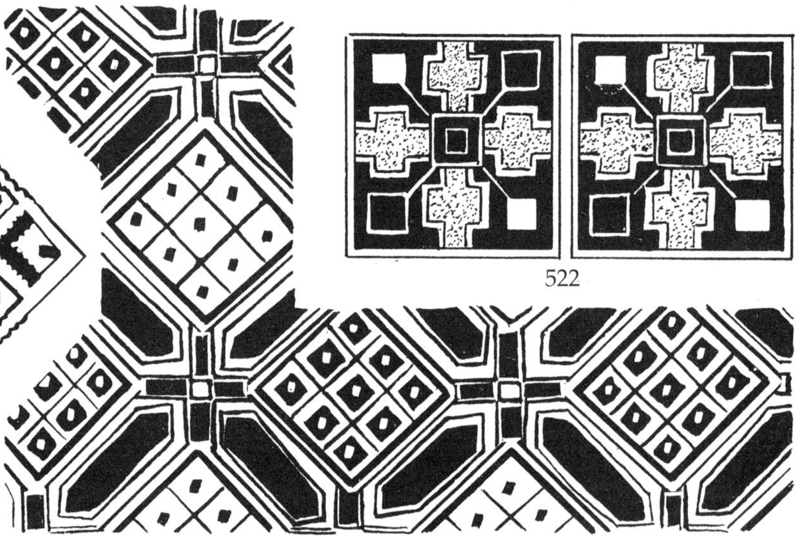

521

522

WOOD BLOCK PRINTS. **513, 518.** Geometrical motifs in the border of a hand-printed cotton textile, Bihar. **514, 516, 517.** Stylized floral and geometrical motifs in the borders and all over design of a hand-printed cotton Sari, Bihar. **515, 520.** Geometrical motifs in the all over hand-printed design of a cotton textile, Bihar. **519.** Abstract motifs in the all over hand-printed design of a silk fabric, West Bengal. **521, 522.** Geometrical motifs from the all over design and border of a hand-printed cotton Sari, Bihar.

# Plate 61

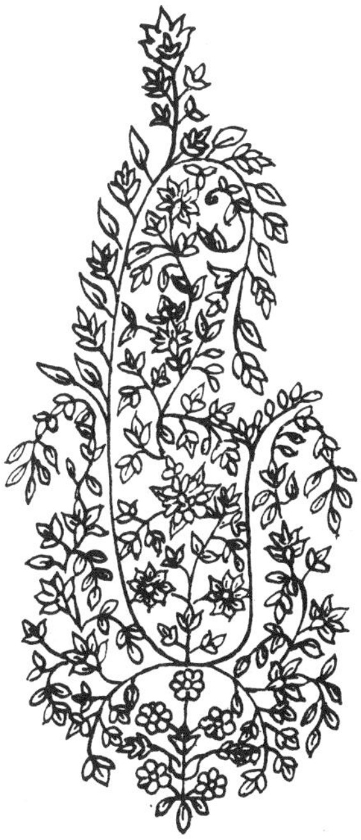

523

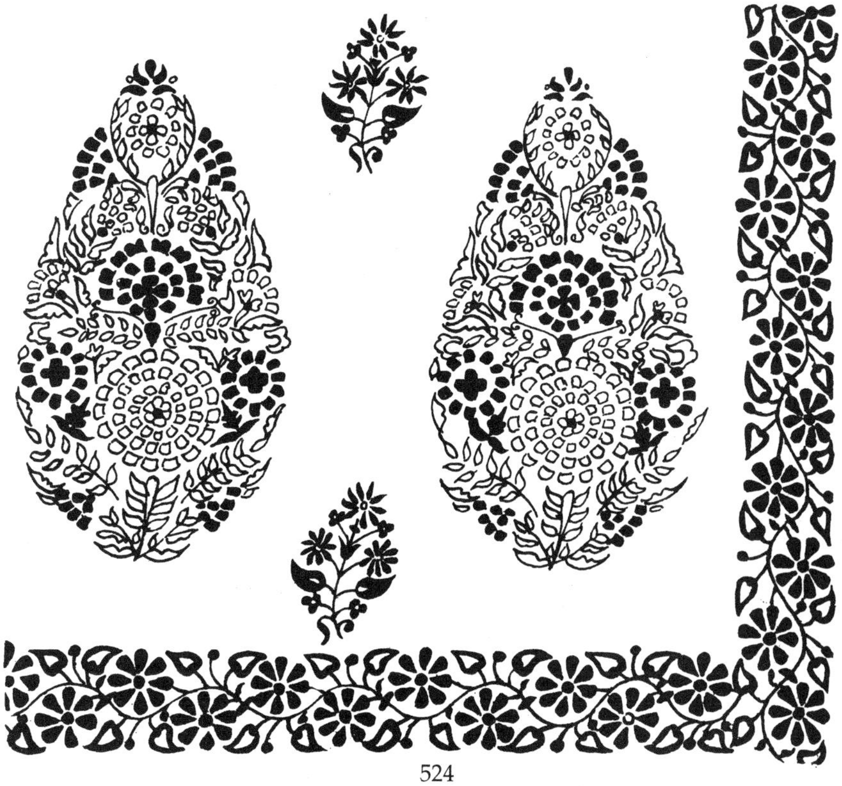

524

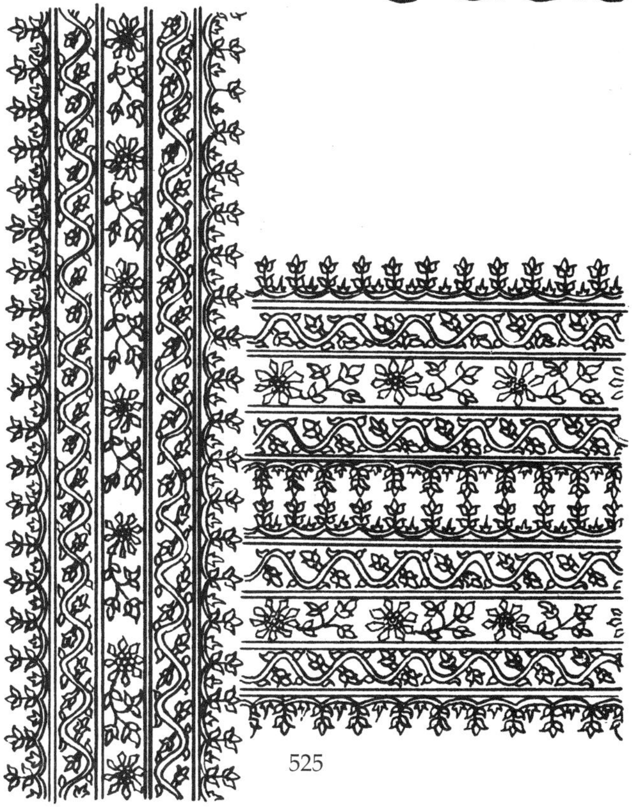

525

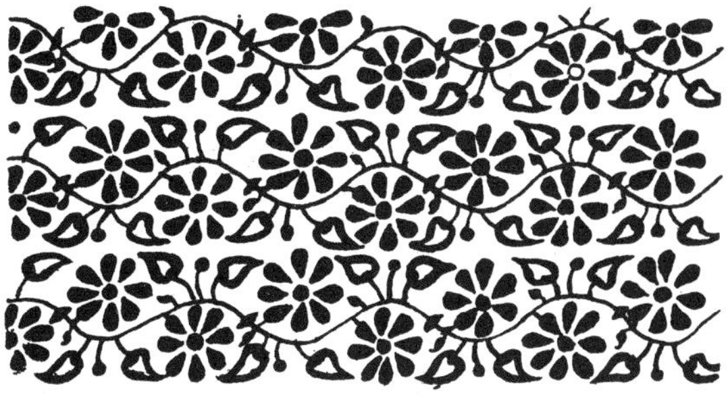

526

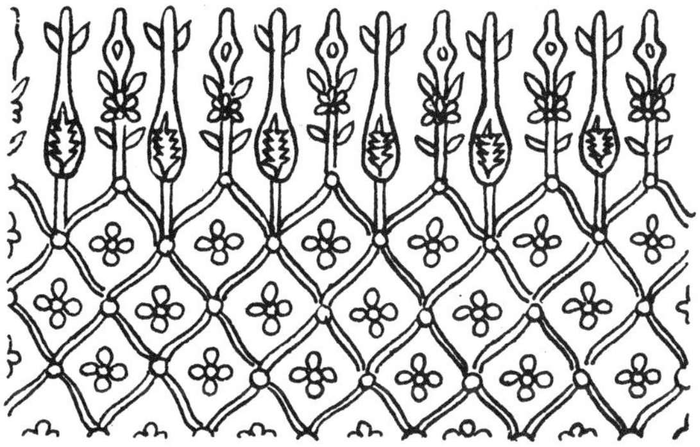

527

WOOD BLOCK PRINTS. **523.** Stylized Mango-floral motif hand printed on a cotton Sari, West Bengal. **524, 526.** Hand-printed stylized Mango-floral motifs and floral borders from a cotton Sari, West Bengal. **525, 527.** Details of stylized floral motifs on the Pallav and border of a hand-printed cotton Sari, West Bengal.

# Plate 62

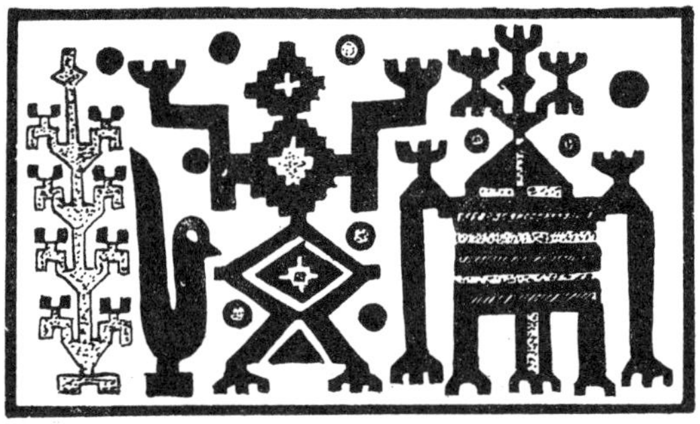

528

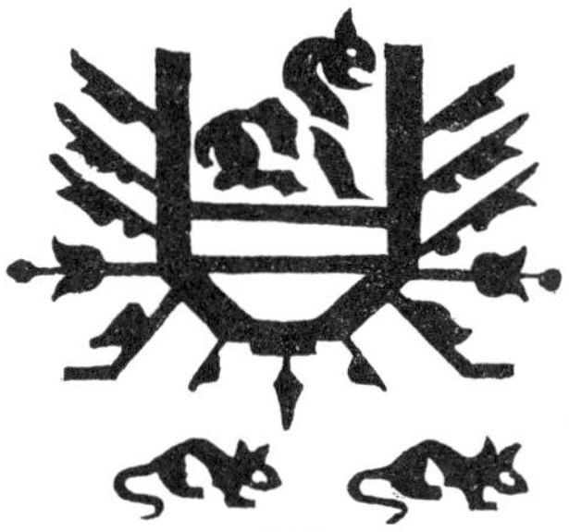

529

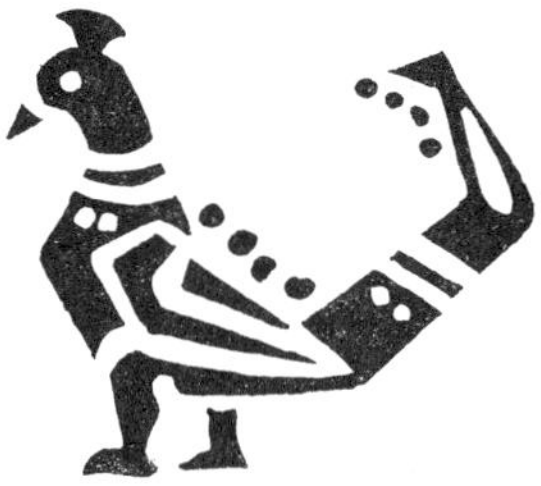

530

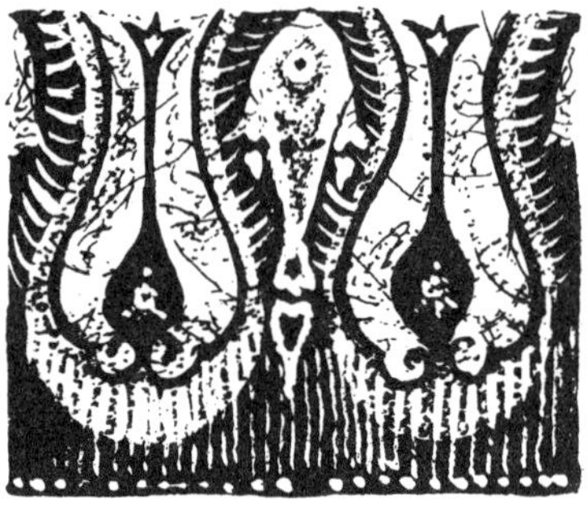

531

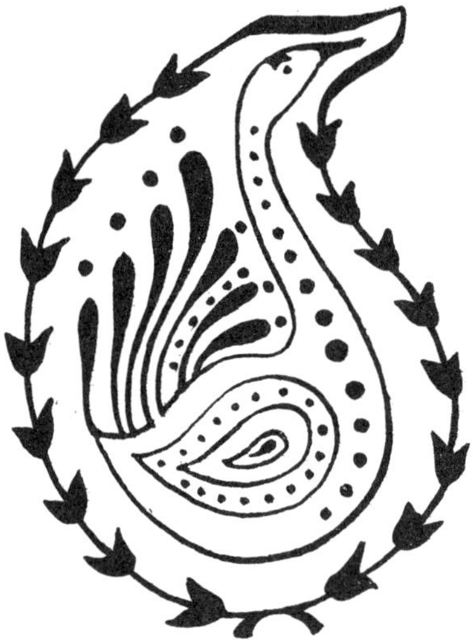

532

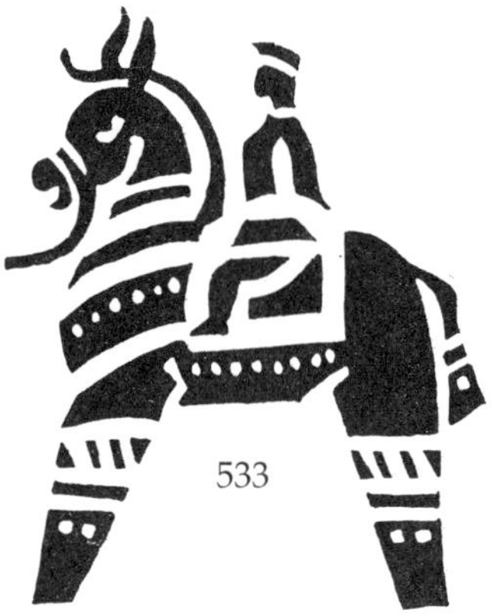

533

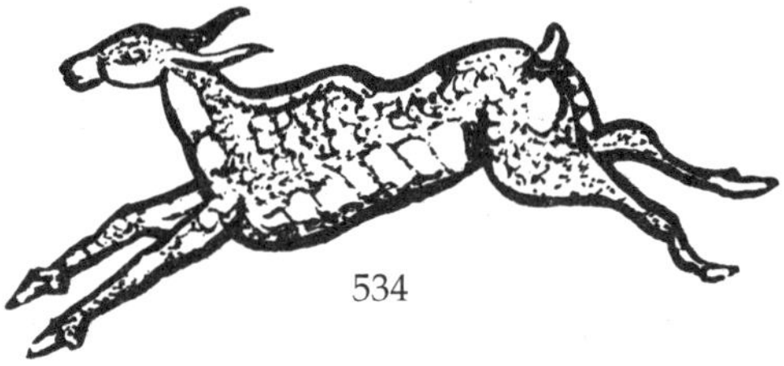

534

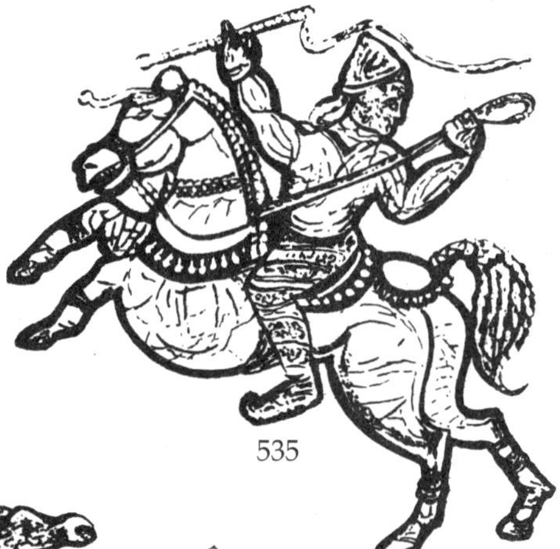

535

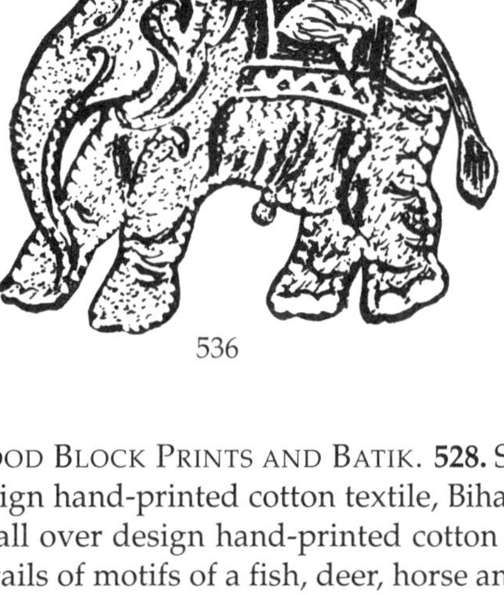

536

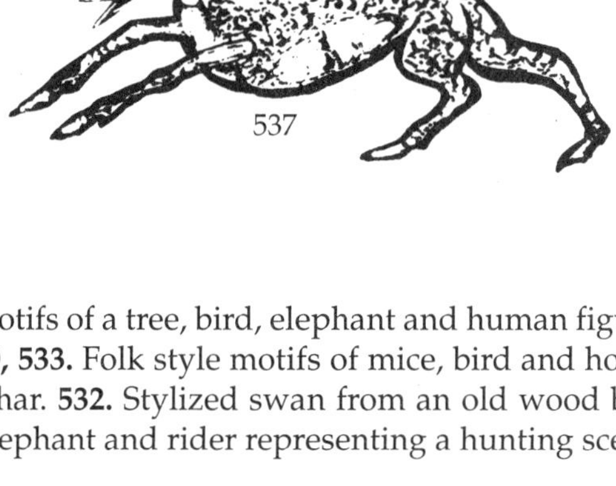

537

WOOD BLOCK PRINTS AND BATIK. **528.** Stylized motifs of a tree, bird, elephant and human figure from an all over design hand-printed cotton textile, Bihar. **529, 530, 533.** Folk style motifs of mice, bird and horse with rider from an all over design hand-printed cotton textile, Bihar. **532.** Stylized swan from an old wood block. **531, 534–537.** Details of motifs of a fish, deer, horse and rider, elephant and rider representing a hunting scene from the border of a screen-printed Batik Sari, Bihar.

# Plate 63

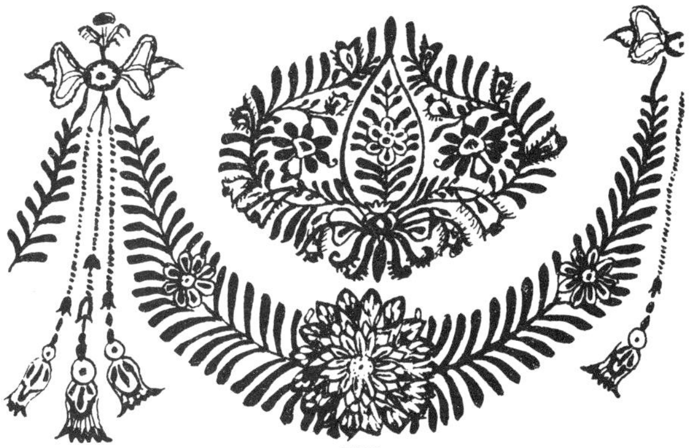

538

539

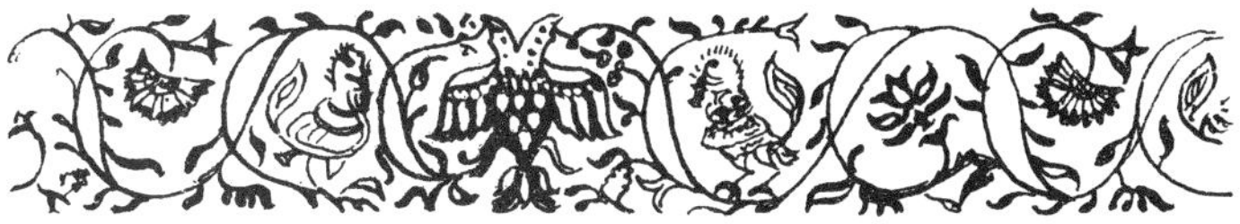

540

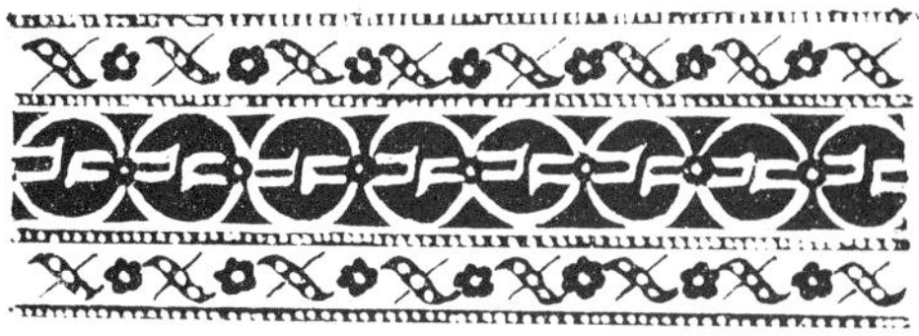

541

542

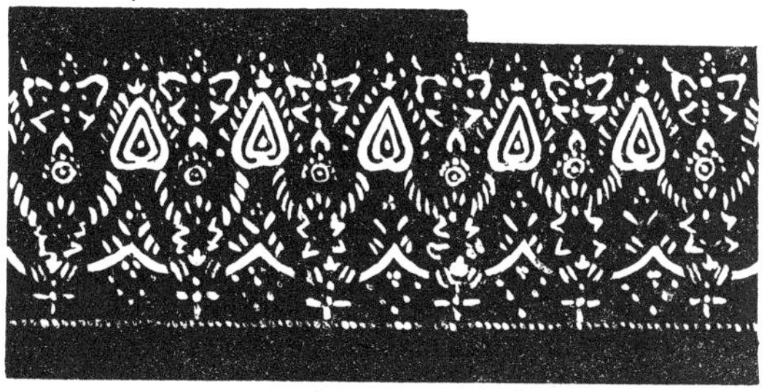

543

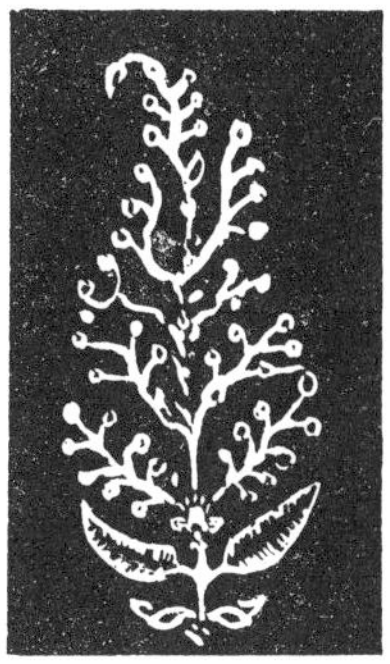

544

545

546

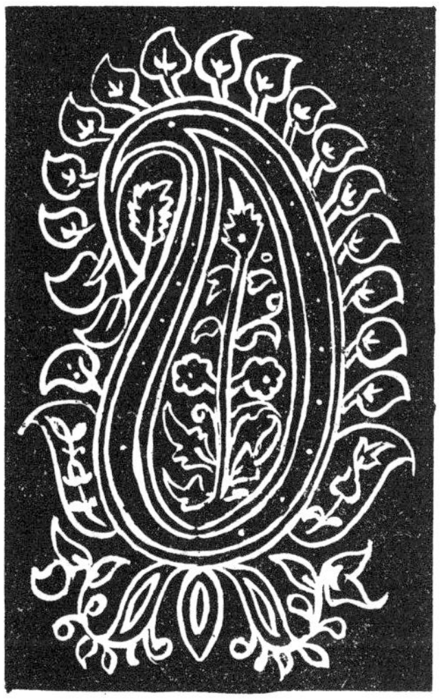

547

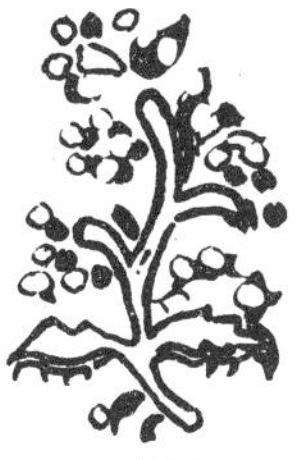

548

KALAMKARI. **538–540.** Details of stylized floral, geometrical and bird motifs from the borders of a Kalamkari, Andhra Pradesh. **541, 543.** Details of geometrical modes from a Kalamkari, Andhra Pradesh. **542, 544.** Details of floral forms from another Kalamkari, Andhra Pradesh. **545, 547.** Details of stylized bird and flower border and decorative mango from a traditional Kalamkari, Masulipatam, Andhra Pradesh. **546, 548.** Stylized floral and tree motifs from an old Kalamkari, Masulipatam, Andhra Pradesh.

# Plate 64

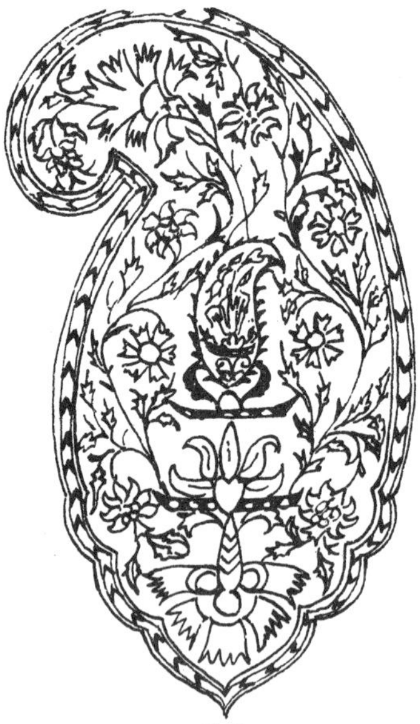

549

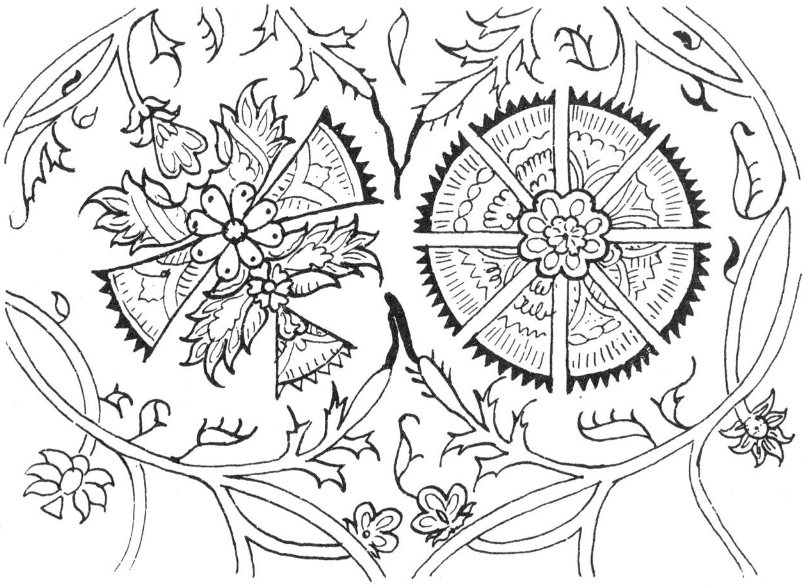

550

551

552

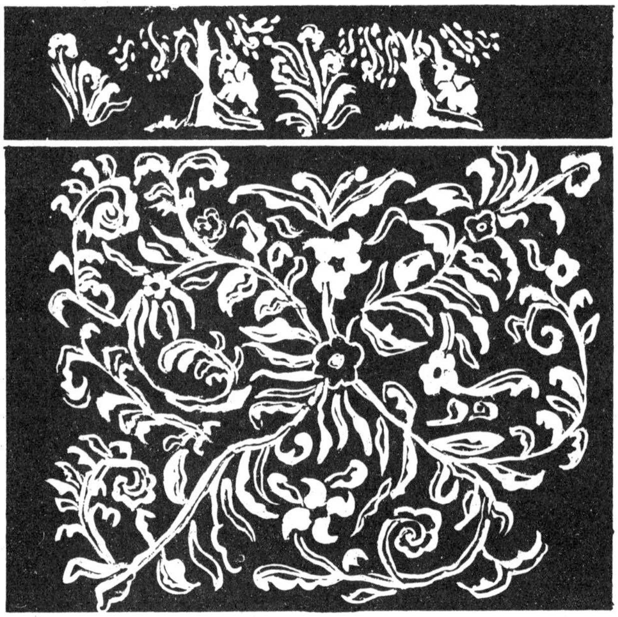

553

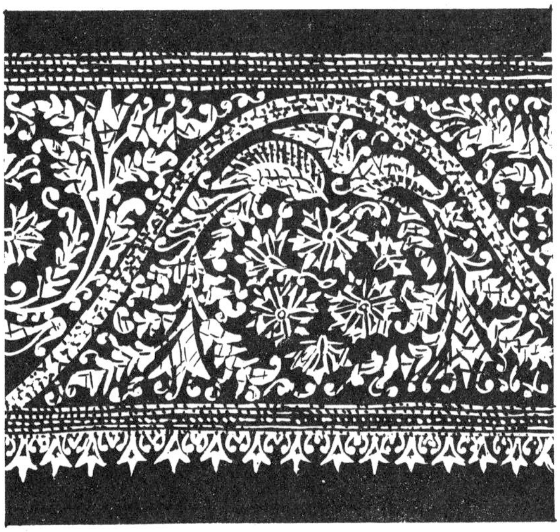

554

KALAMKARI, BATIK AND WOOD BLOCK PRINTS. **549–551.** Details of stylized mango, floral and geometrical motifs from the all over design of a traditional Kalamkari, Andhra Pradesh. **552.** Details of a stylized floral border motif from a hand-printed cotton textile, Madras. **553.** Floral ensemble with tree and elephant border from a Batik, West Bengal. **554.** Details of a hand-printed silk Sari border with floral and leaf ensembles, Uday Villa, West Bengal.

# Plate 65

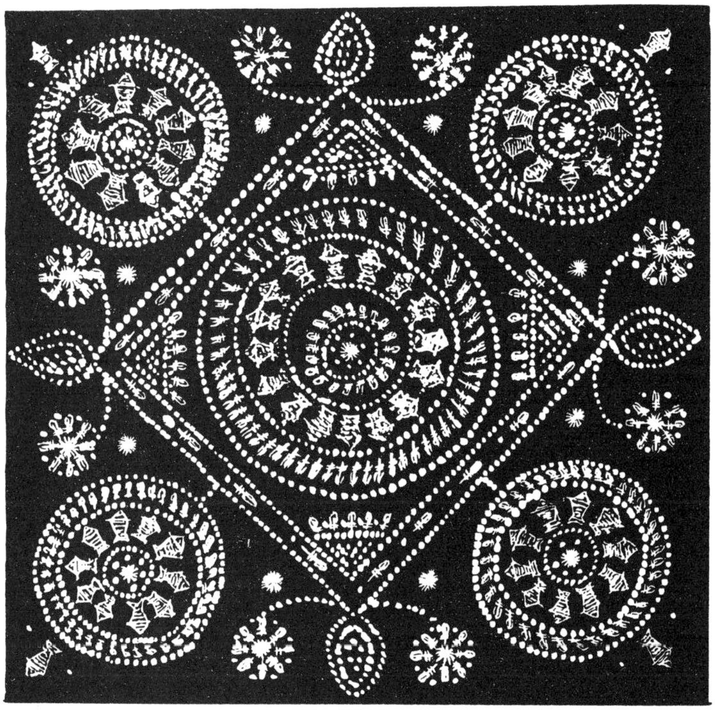

555

556

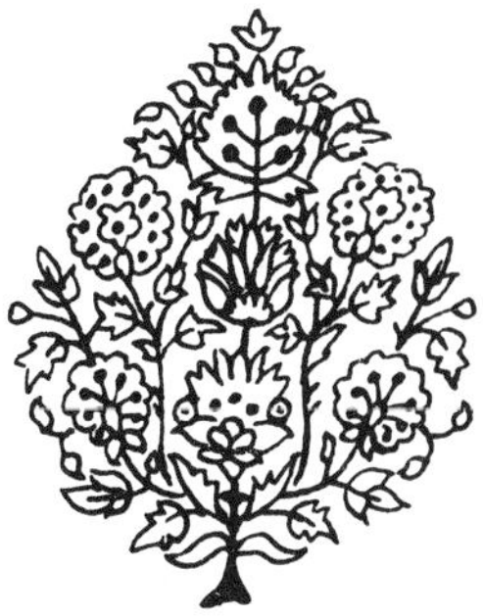

557

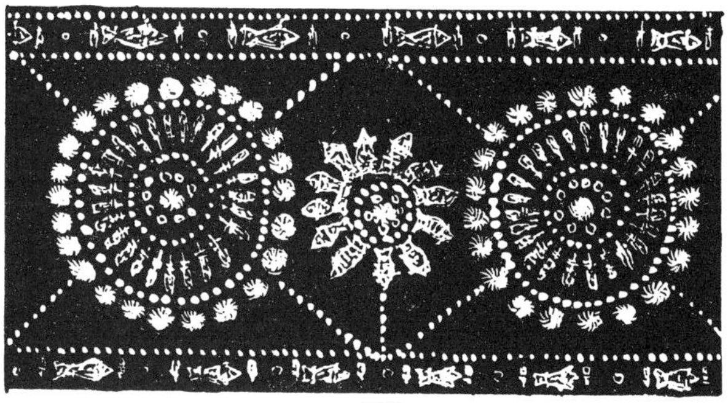

558

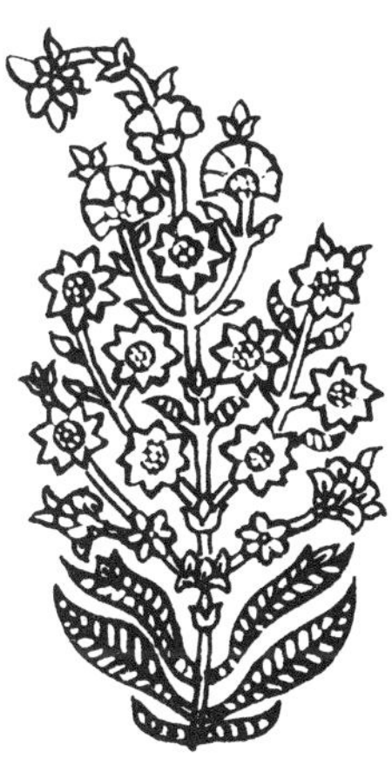

559

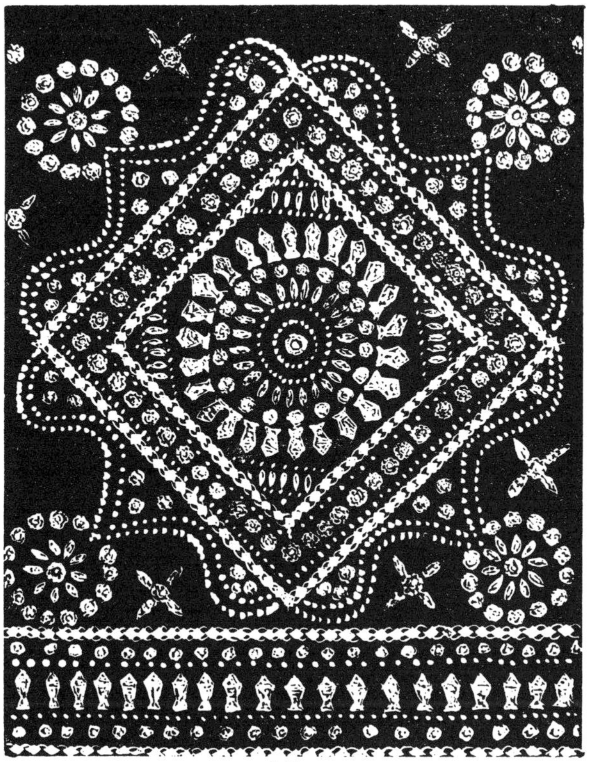

560

Tie and Dye with Hand Printing, and Wood Block Prints. **555, 558, 560.** Details of three unique stylized floral and geometrical motifs combining hand printing and tie and dye, Sursand, Bihar. **556.** Stylized flower from a hand-printed cotton textile, Bihar. **557, 559.** Stylized floral modes from two hand-printed cotton Saris, West Bengal.

# Plate 66

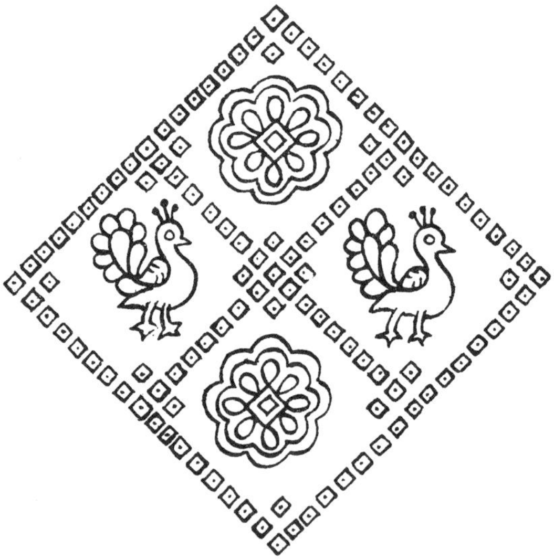

561

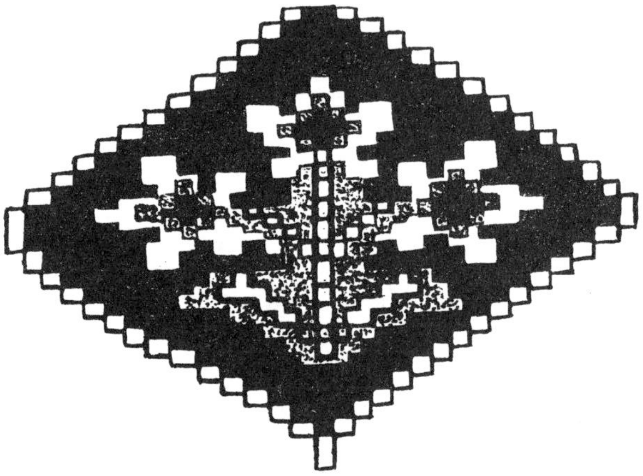

562

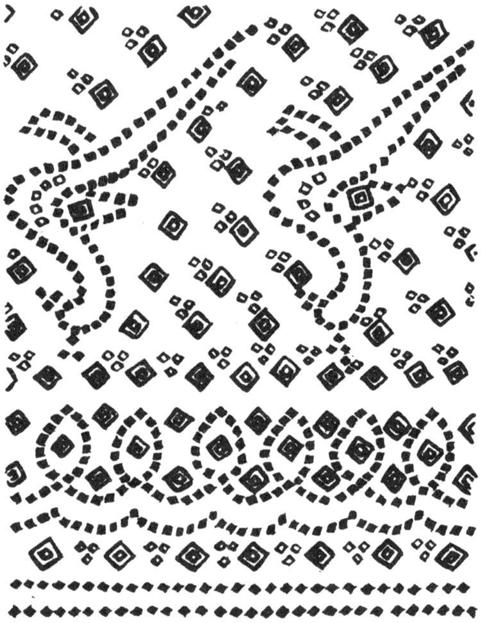

563

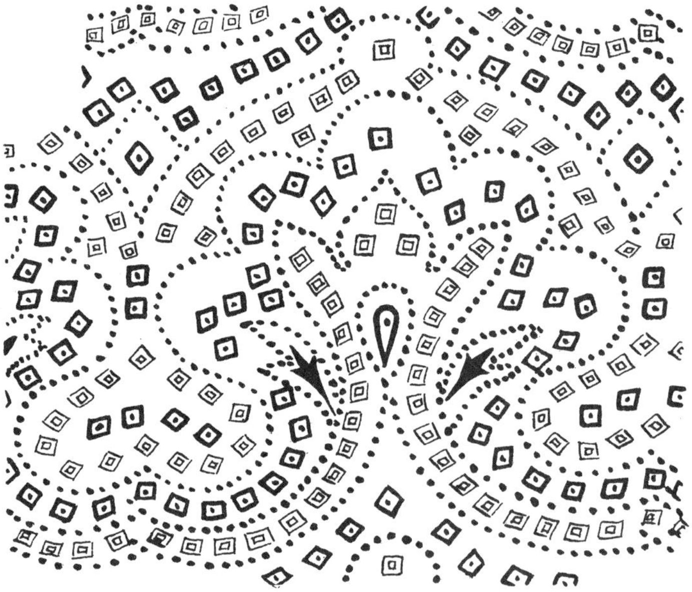

564

565

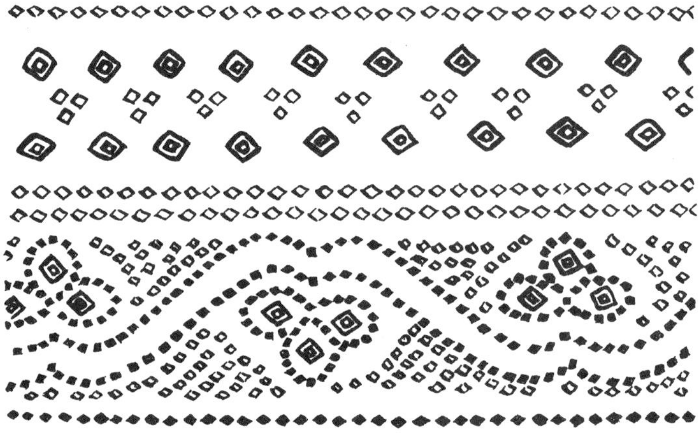

566

Wood Block Prints Based on Tie and Dye. **561.** Stylized floral, peacock and miniature squares hand printed in the tie and dye style on a cotton Sari, Gujarat. **562.** Stylized floral motifs hand printed (on the Patola mode of tie-dyeing the weft and warp before weaving), on a cotton Sari, Gujarat. **563.** Tie and dye mode with parrots hand printed on this fine cotton, Rajasthan. **564, 566.** Details of tie and dye modes hand printed on a fine cotton Sari, Gujarat. **565.** Detail of a hand-printed stylized lotus motif on the tie and dye style, Rajasthan.

# Plate 67

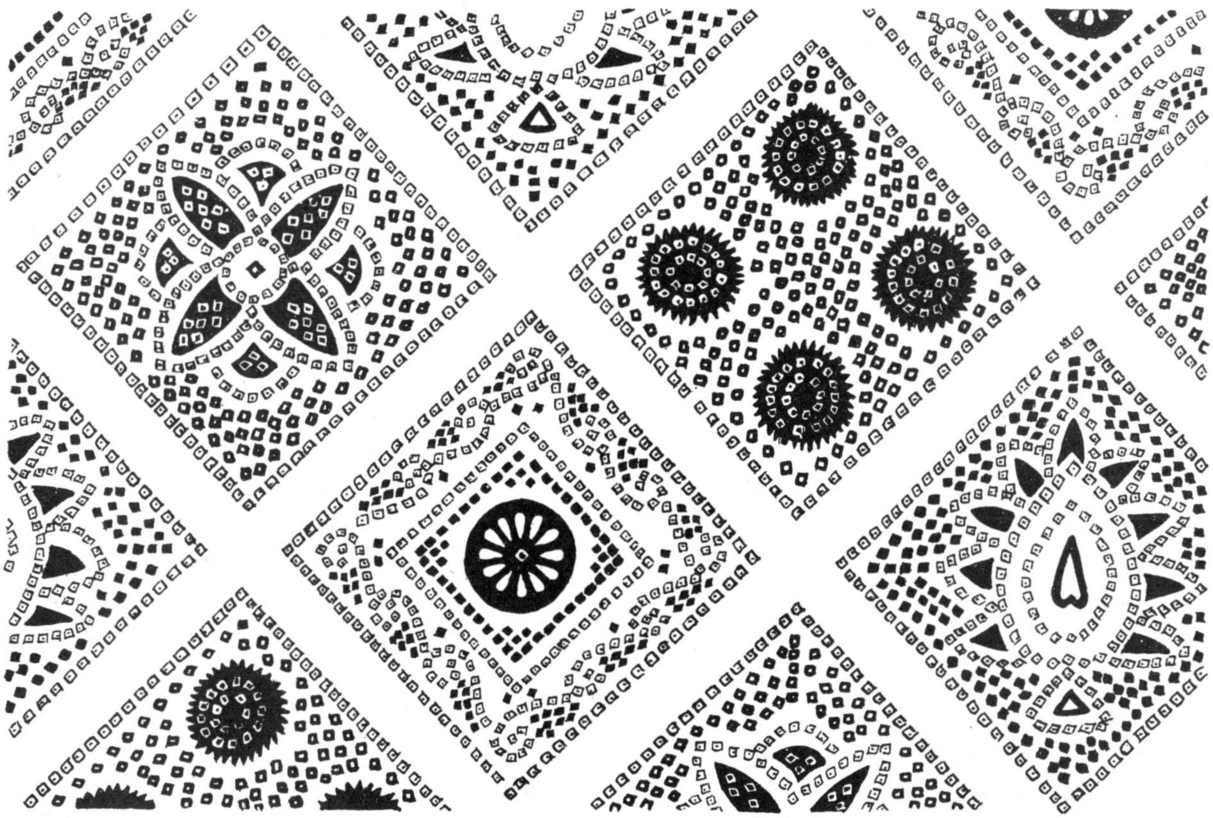

567

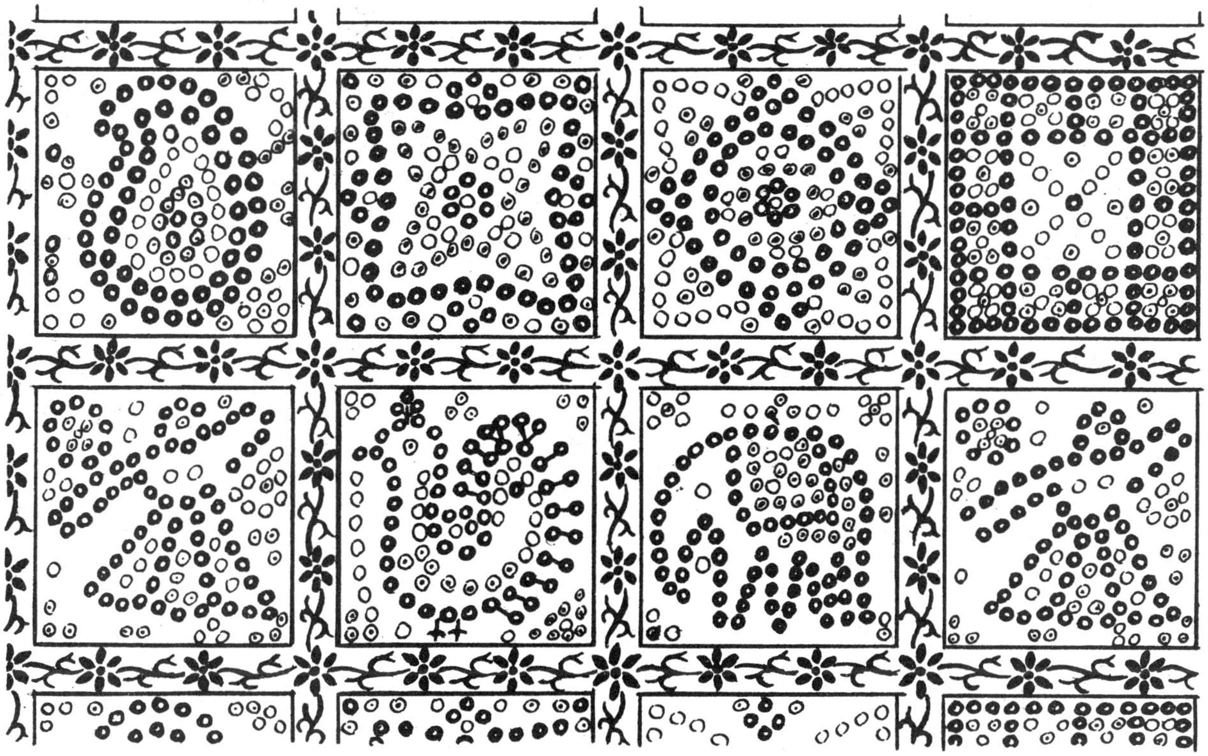

568

WOOD BLOCK PRINTS BASED ON TIE AND DYE. **567.** Multi-patterned motifs of geometrical shapes and dots hand printed all over a fine cotton Sari in the tie and dye mode, Saurashtra, Gujarat. **568.** Multi-patterned motifs of the mango, geometrical shapes, human figures, peacocks and elephants hand printed all over a cotton textile in the tie and dye mode, Gujarat.

# Plate 68

569

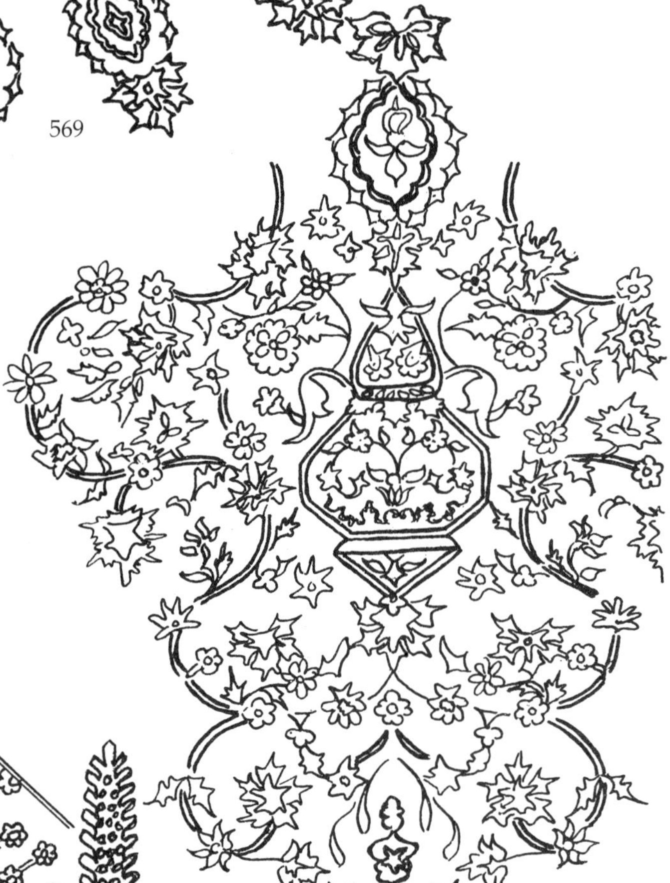

570

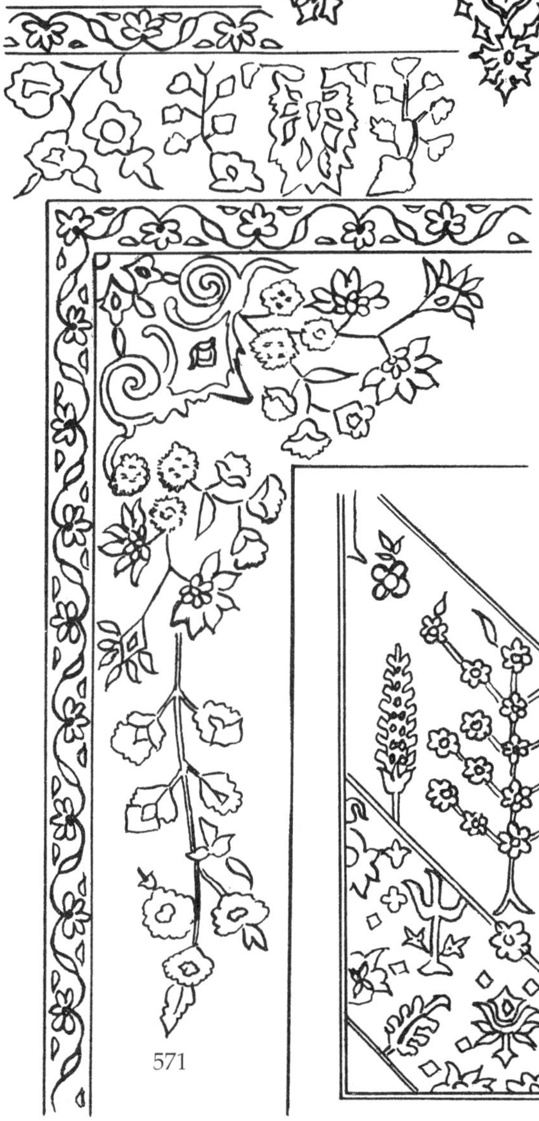

571

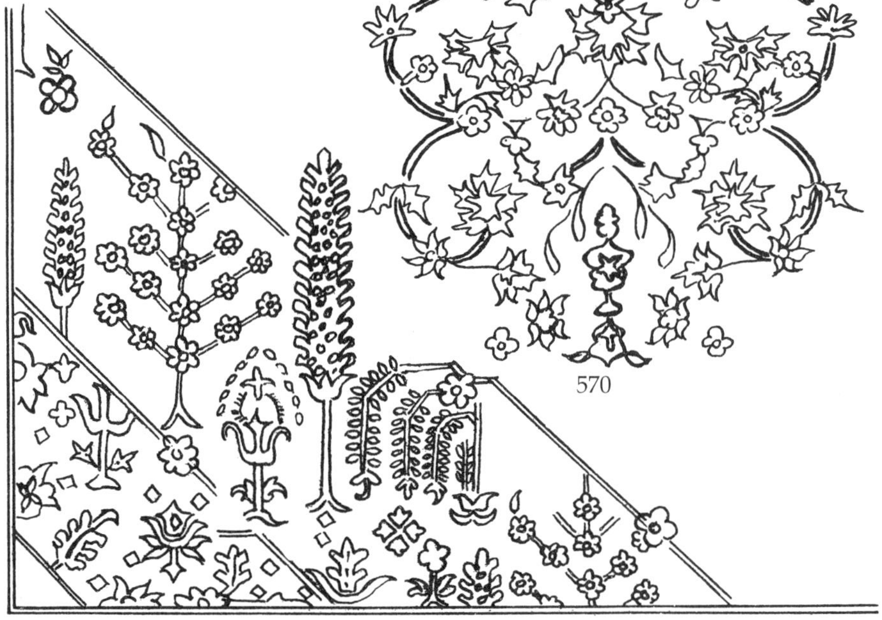

572

CARPETS. **569, 570.** Details of a section of the floral medallion representing the shadow cast by the lamp (**570** center), and floral arabesques around the entire surface of this fine Persian style carpet from Srinagar, Kashmir. **571.** Stylized flower spray motifs from the corner and section of the border of this Persian style carpet from Rajasthan. **572.** Details of a corner of a carpet with stylized motifs of the poplan, almond, Chenar (Plane) and willow trees, Srinagar, Kashmir.

# Plate 69

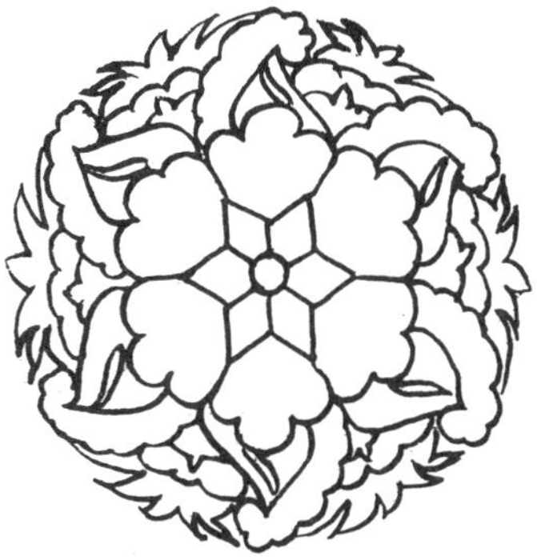

573

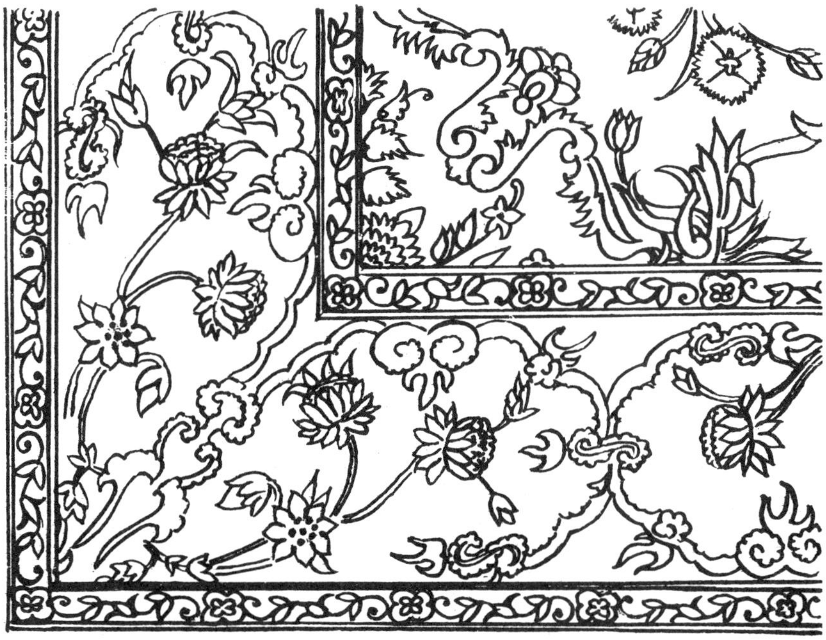

574

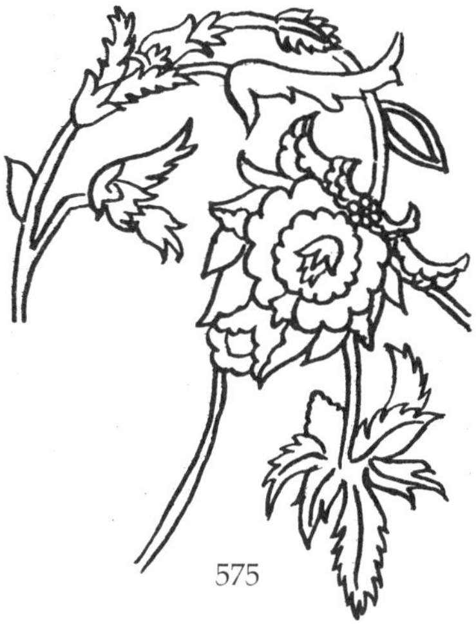

575

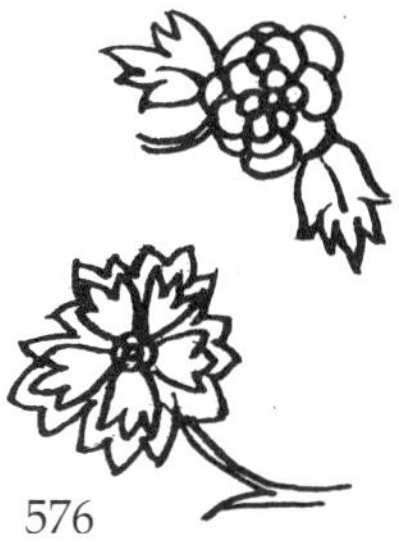

576

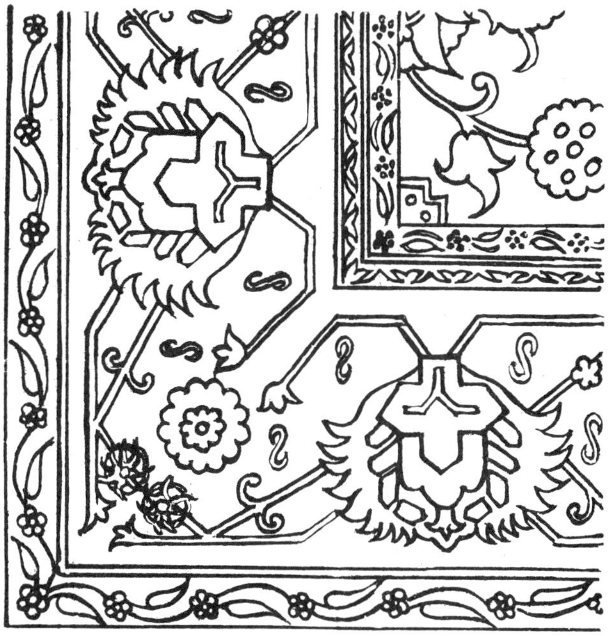

577

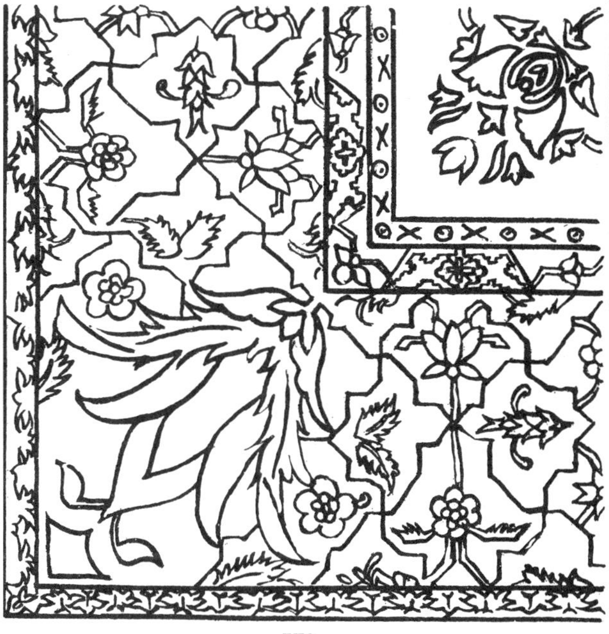

578

579

CARPETS. **573, 575, 578.** Details of stylized floral medallion and spray and foliated motifs from a section of the background and border of a carpet in the City Palace Museum, Jaipur, Rajasthan. **574, 576.** Dainty floral motifs from a corner and section of the border of a Persian carpet in the City Palace Museum, Jaipur, Rajasthan. **577, 579.** Details of stylized floral motifs from a section of the corner and border of a carpet in the City Palace Museum, Jaipur, Rajasthan.

# Plate 70

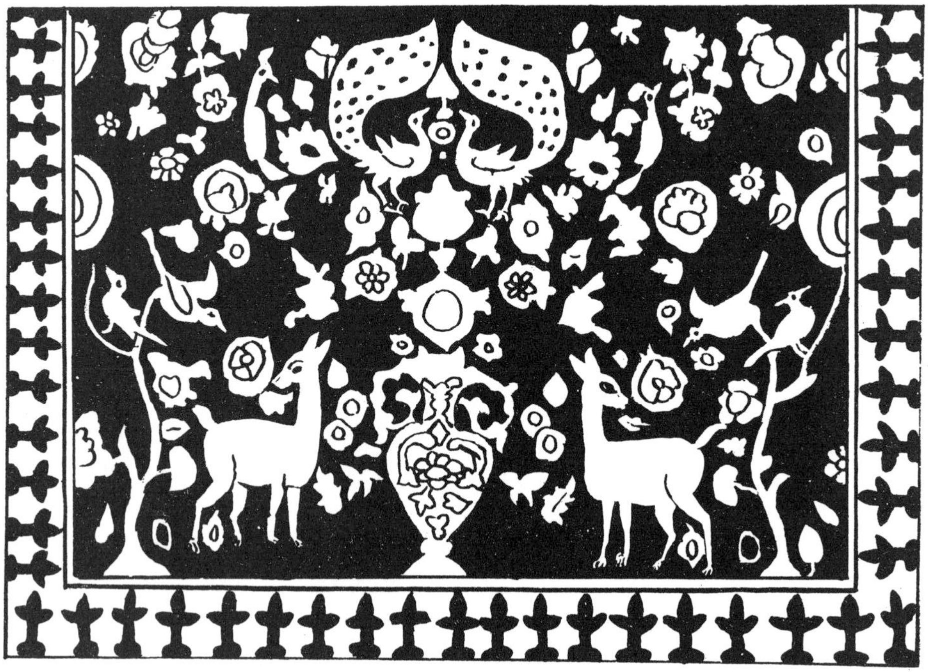

580

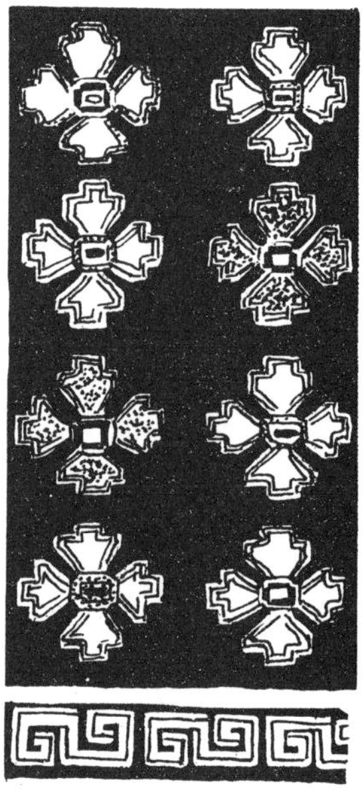

581

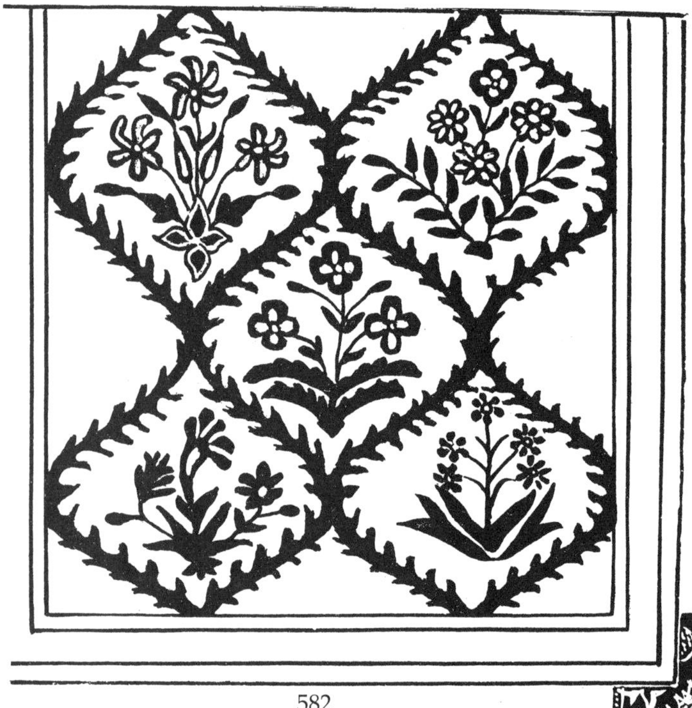

582

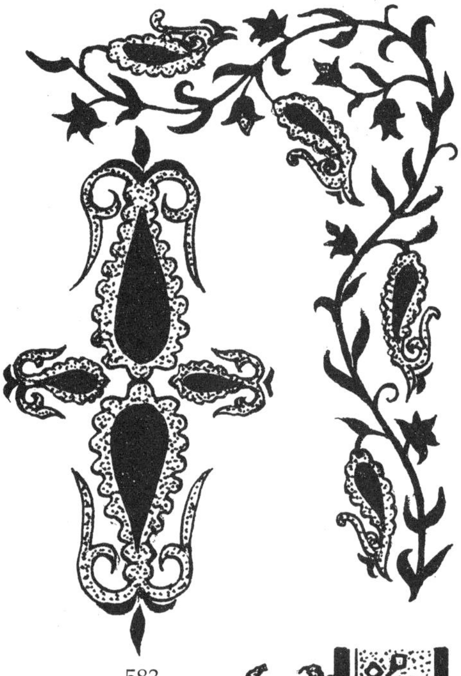

583

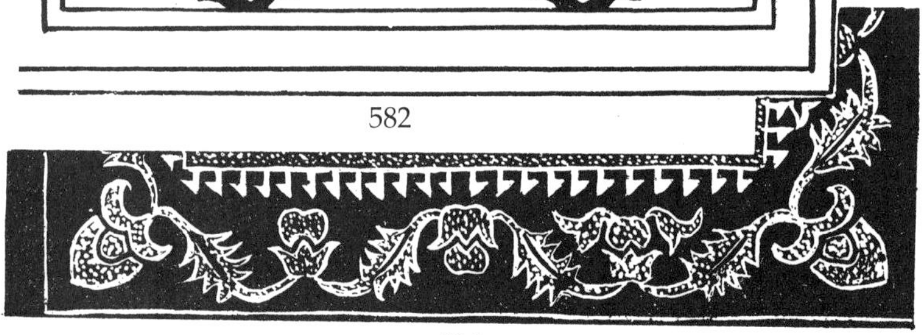

584

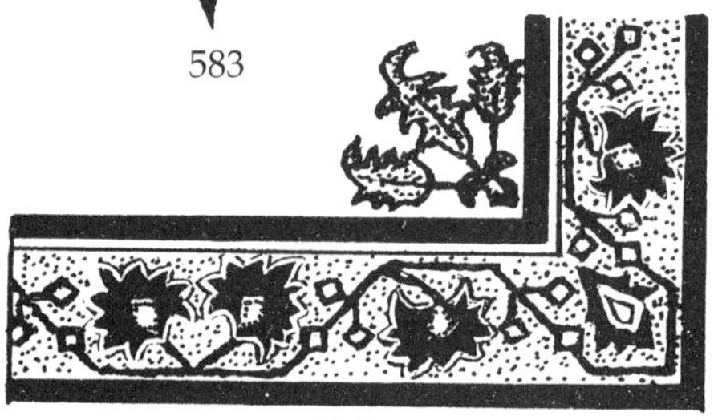

585

CARPETS. **580.** Details of a section of a woolen carpet from North India showing a scene with peacocks, flowers, birds, deer and a vase, 17th century. **581.** Four-petaled flowers from the main design with key pattern border in a Tibetan carpet from Kalimpong. **582.** Details of a section of a woolen carpet with motifs of flowering plants from North India, Royal Factory at Lahore, 17th century. **583.** Detail of main central motif of stylized mangoes and border in a carpet from Badhoi. **584, 585.** Details of sections of the borders of two carpets from Eluru and Warrangal.

# Plate 71

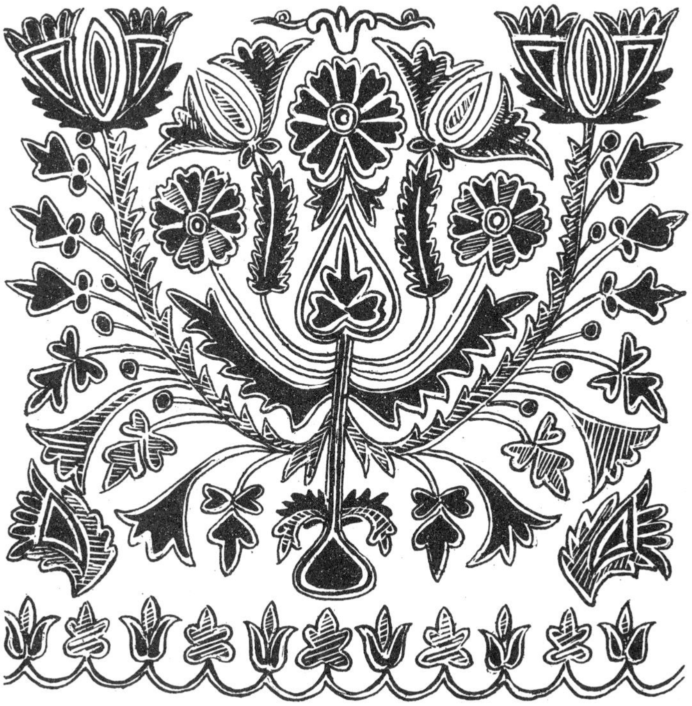

586

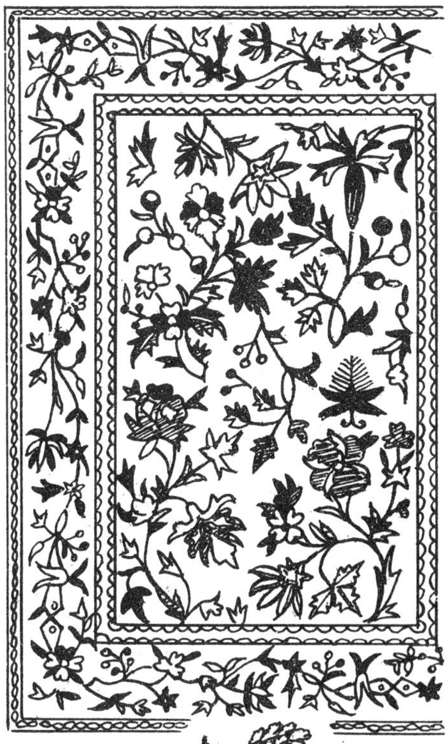

587

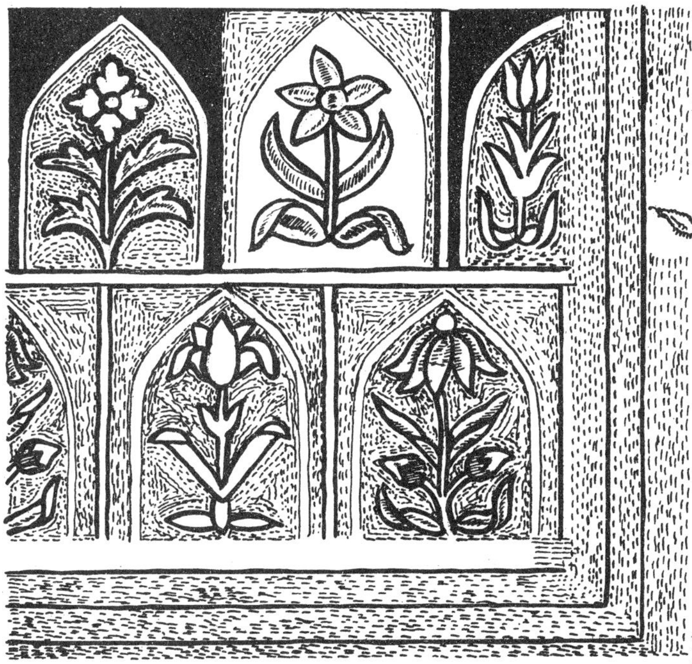

588

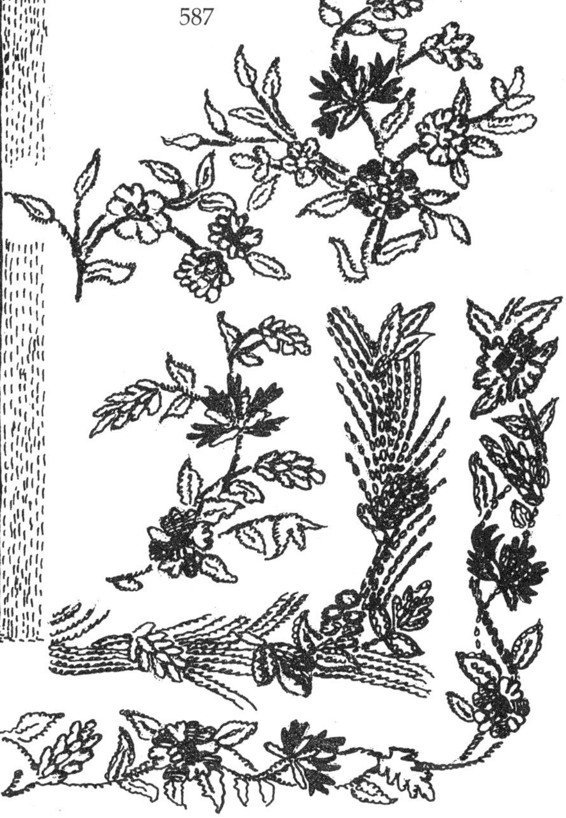

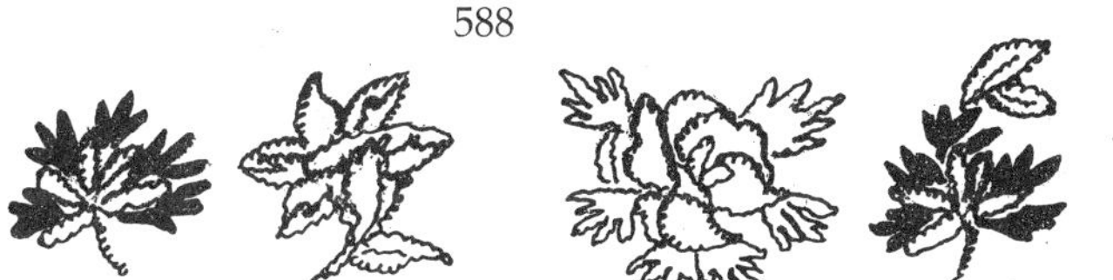

589

FLOOR RUGS. **586.** Stylized floral design from an embroidered Namdah (felt rug), Kashmir. **587.** Details of a typical embroidered Namdah with Nature emblems of the Chenar leaf, blossoms and flowers, Kashmir. **588.** Details of a section of an embroidered woolen floor rug with stylized Spring flowers—the narcissus, daffodil, tulip and primula, Kashmir. **589.** Details of an embroidered Namdah (felt rug) with Spring flowers and floral sprays, Srinagar, Kashmir.

# Plate 72

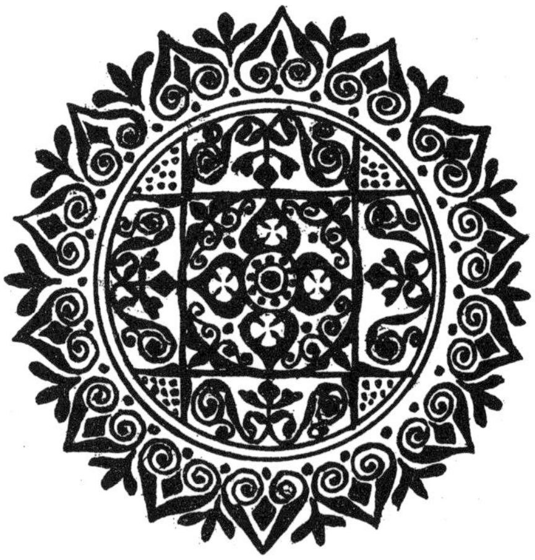

590

591

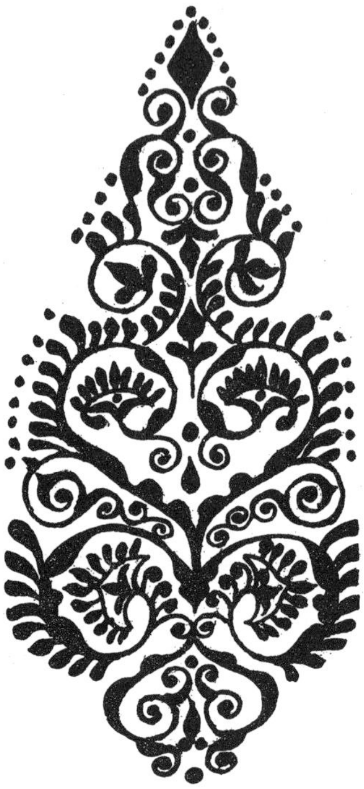

592

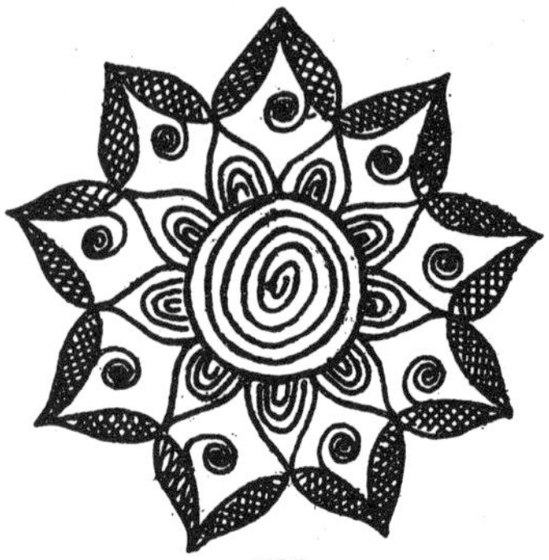

593

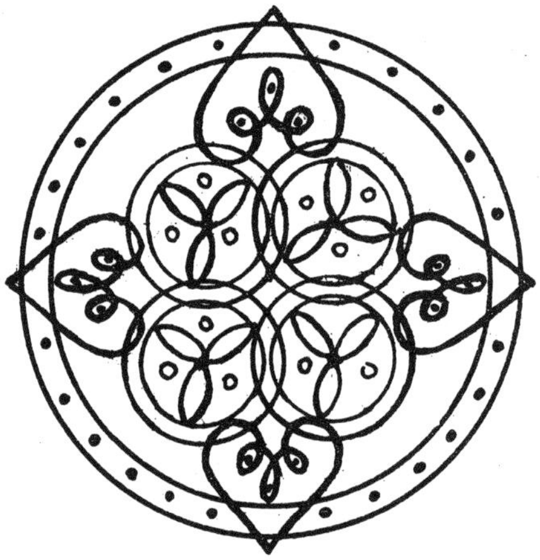

594

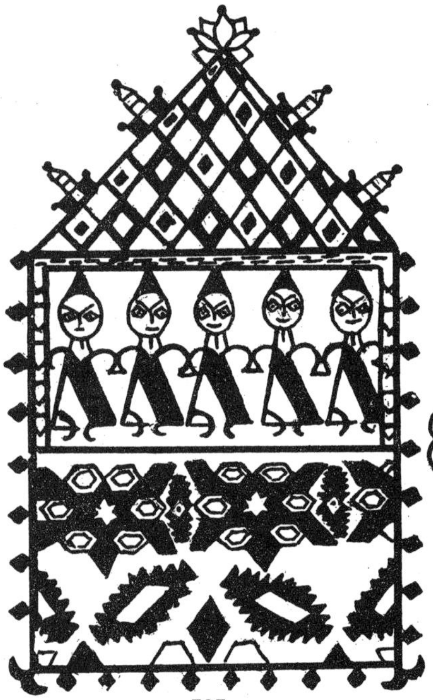

595

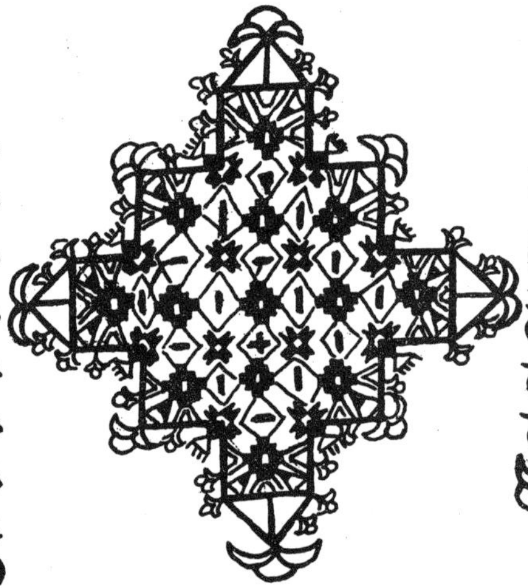

596

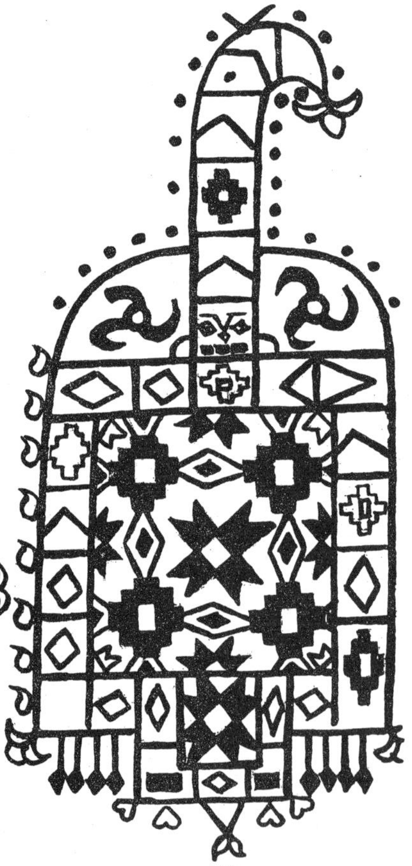

597

FLOOR AND WALL DECORATION. **590–592.** Alpana (Floor decoration)—modern adaptations of stylized floral forms at Shantiniketan, West Bengal. **593.** Traditional stylized star motif in Alpana, Faridpur, Bengal. **594.** Kolam (Floor decoration) with geometrical motifs, Madras, South India. **595–597.** Madana (Decorative Wall paintings), folk style designs, Rajasthan.

# Plate 73

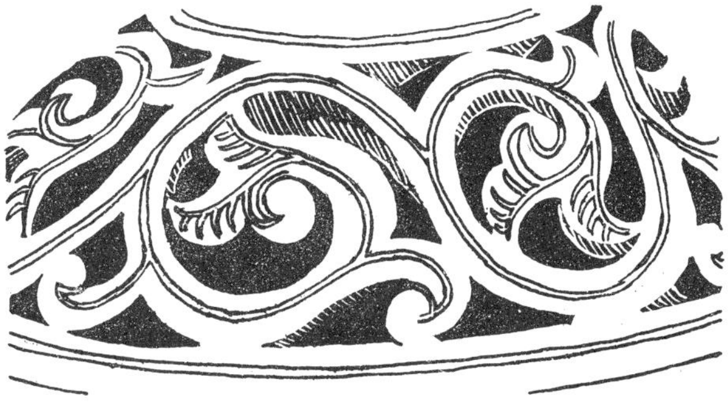

598

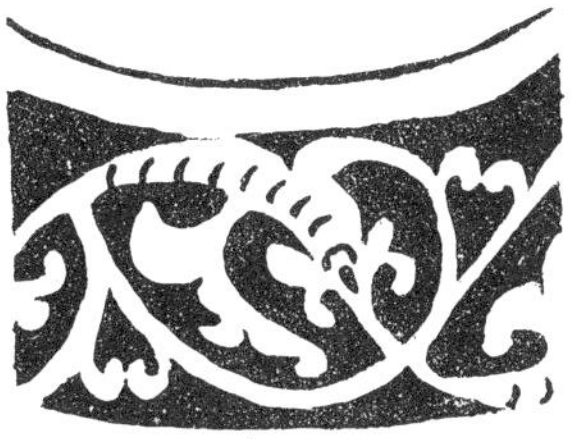

599

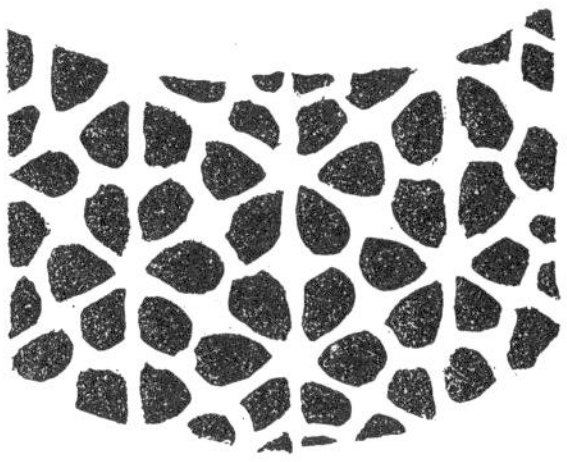

600

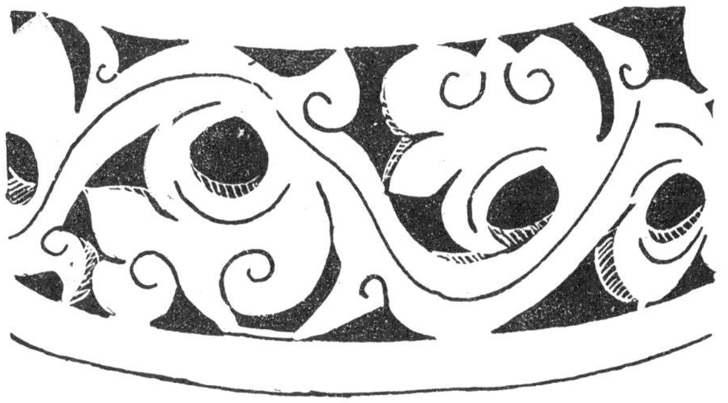

601

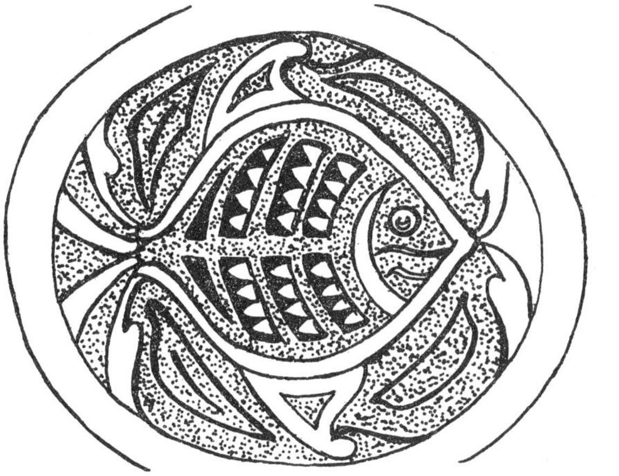

602

603

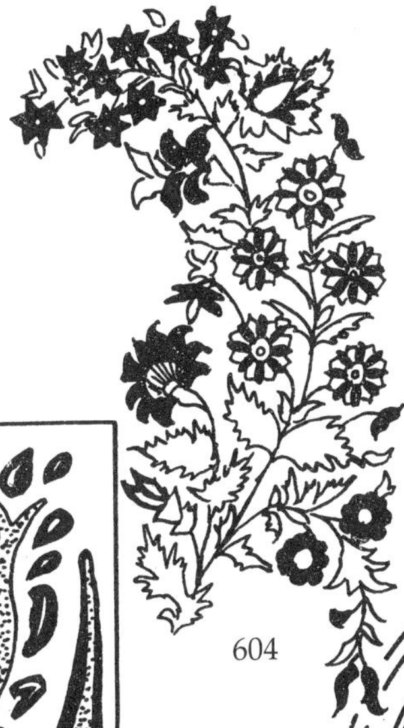

604

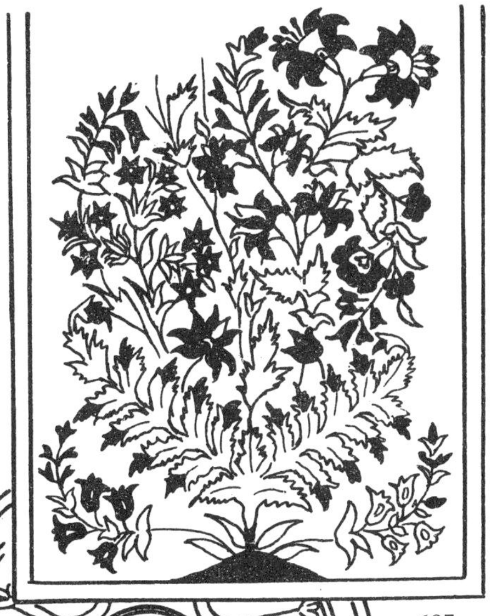

605

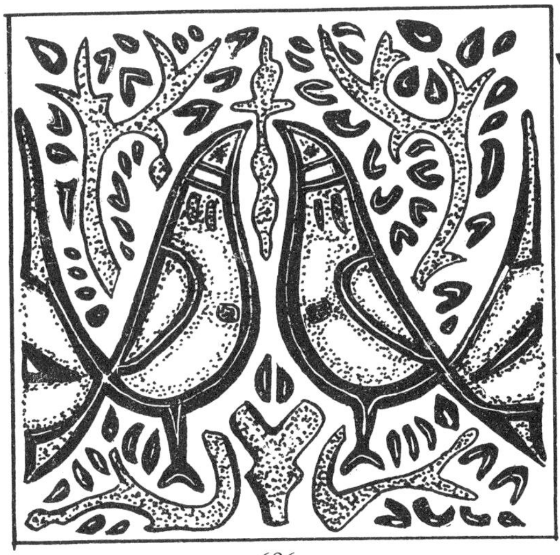

606

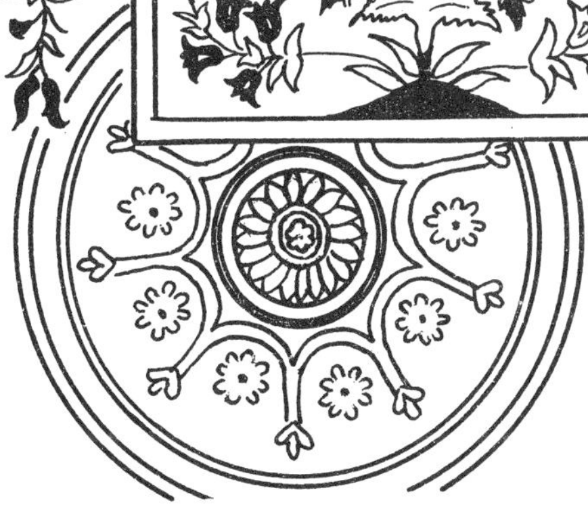

607

CERAMICS AND POTTERY. **598.** Painted motif of stylized leaves on a black unglazed clay pot, West Bengal. **599, 600.** Unglazed pottery from South India fretted with geometrical patterns. **601.** Double wall perforated work on a North Indian traditional clay goblet (Surai) with stylized leaves on curving stems. **602, 606.** Details of glazed tiles with folk style fish, and birds with trees, Uday Villa, West Bengal. **603–605.** Encaustic tile with details showing floral and flowering tree motifs in dark blue and pale green, Multan, Punjab. **607.** Detail of embossed central motif of a stylized lotus and stars on a dark blue glazed pottery plate, Kaligiri, South India.

# Plate 74

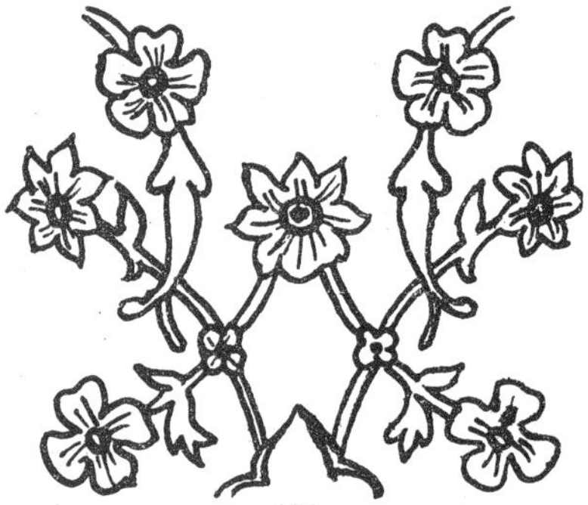
608

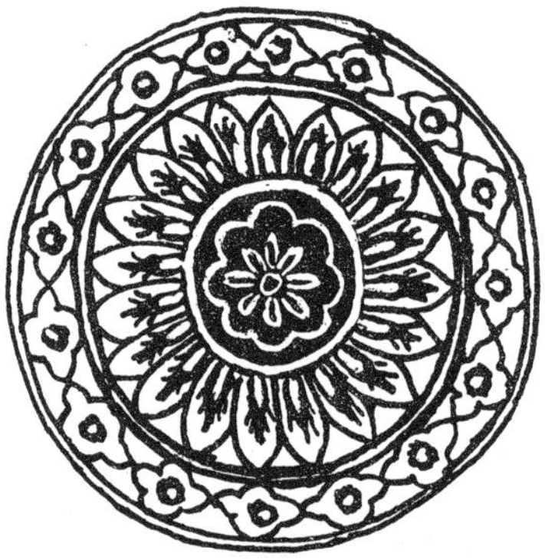
609

610

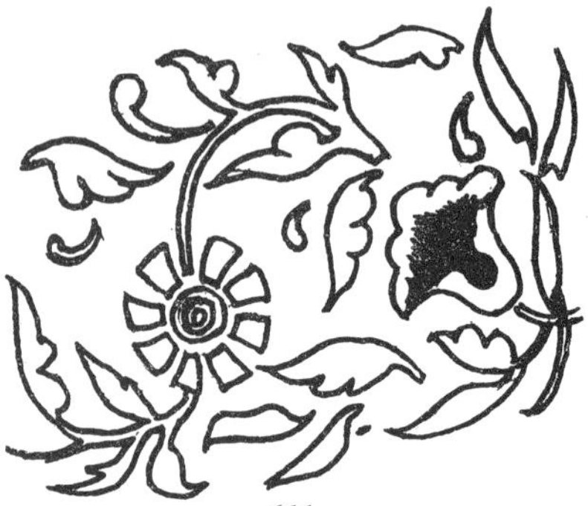
611

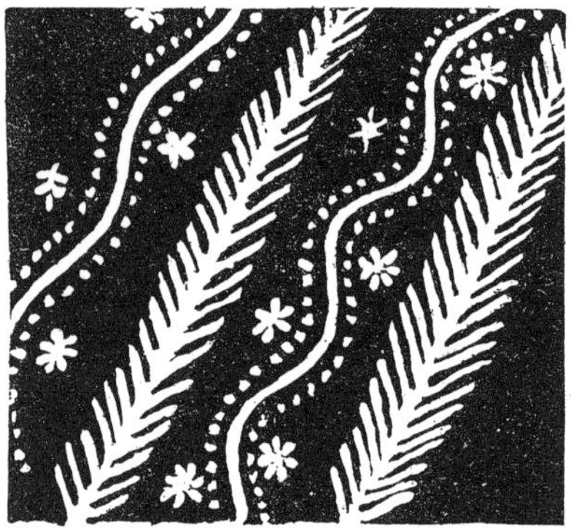
612

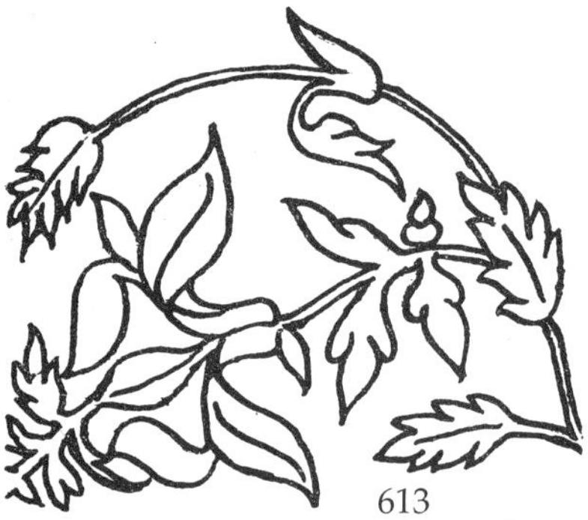
613

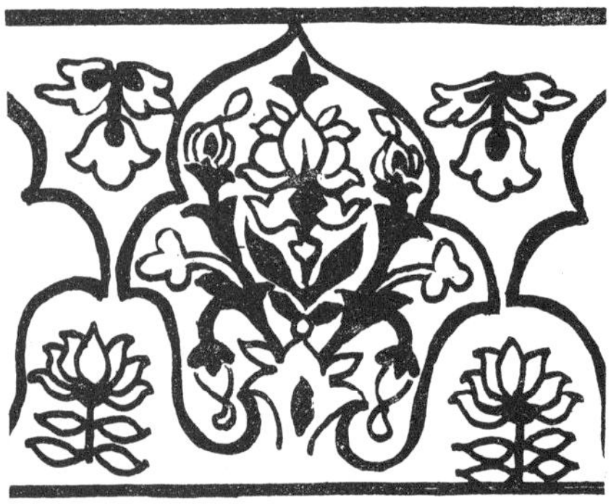
614

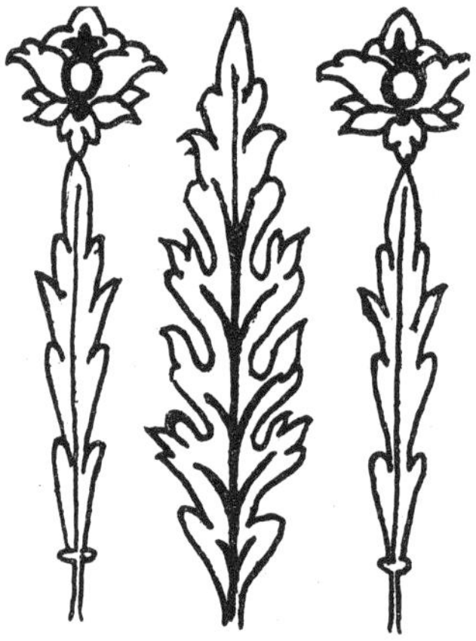
615

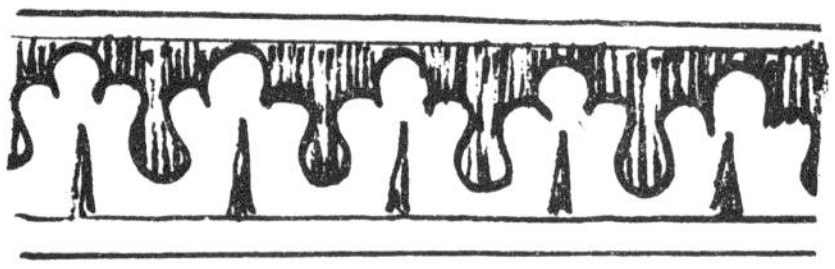
616

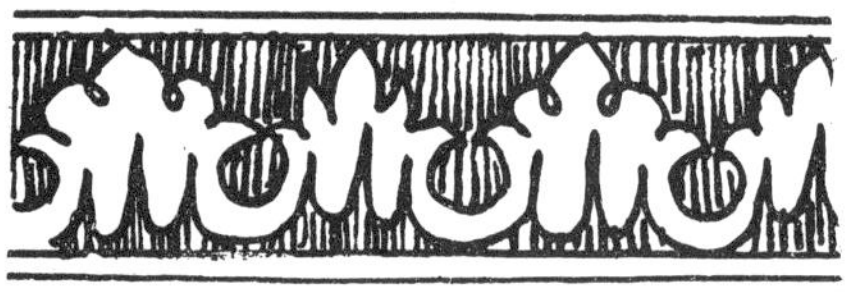
617

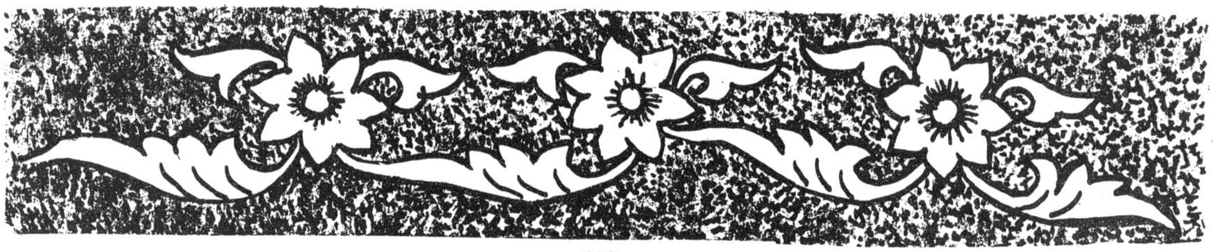
618

CERAMICS AND POTTERY. **608–618.** Details of stylized floral-motifs such as the jasmine, lotus, iris, cornflower and lily on curving stems with leaves in white and deep blue on the cobalt blue glazed pottery of Jaipur, found on vases, bowls, plates and decorative pieces, Rajasthan.

# Plate 75

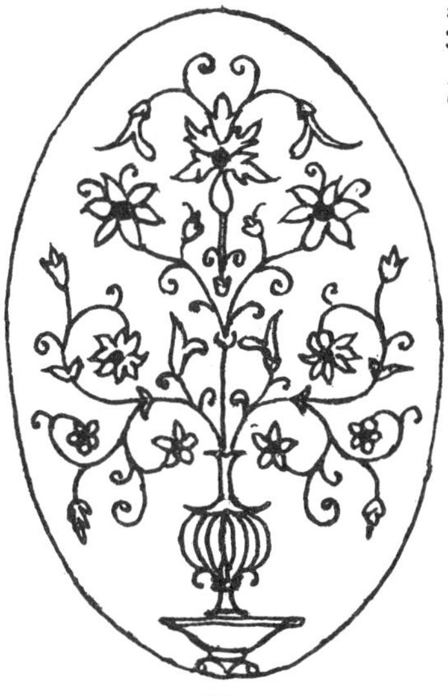

619

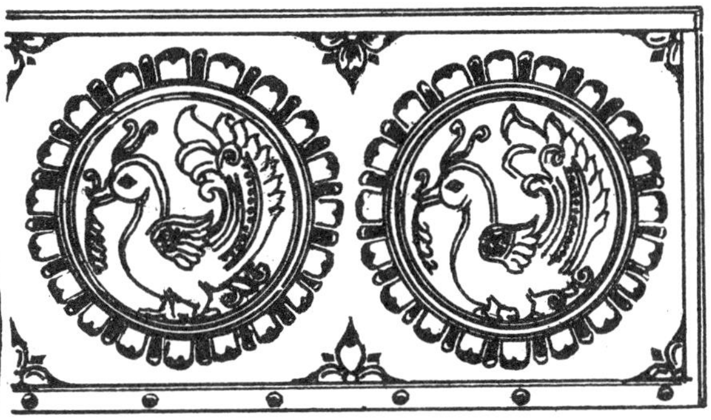


620

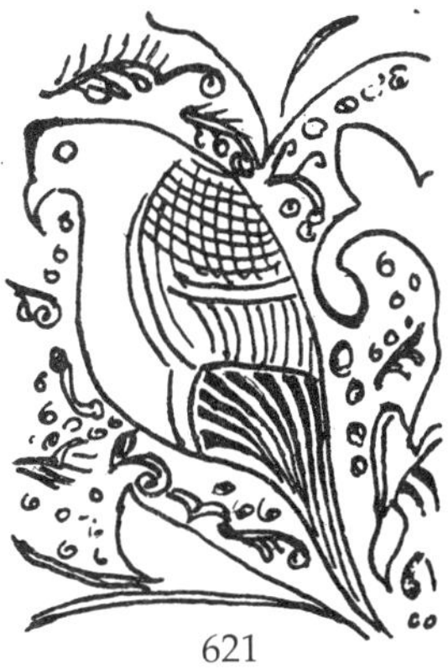

621

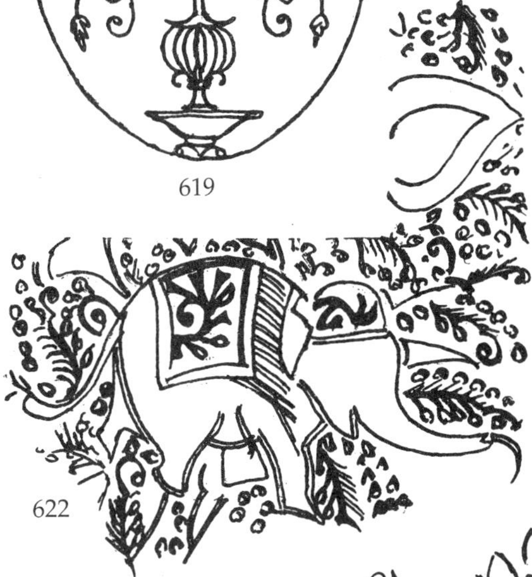

622

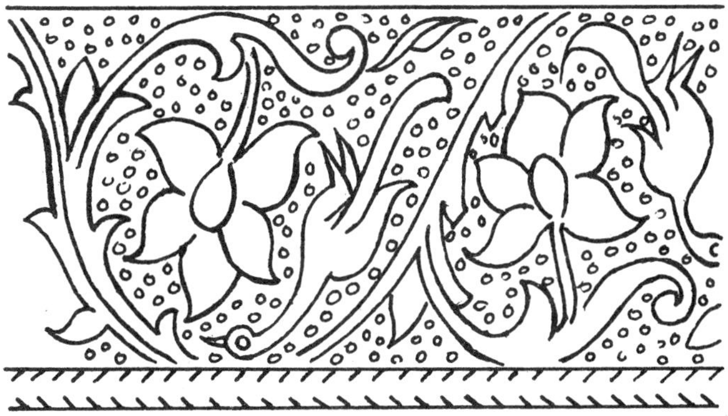

623

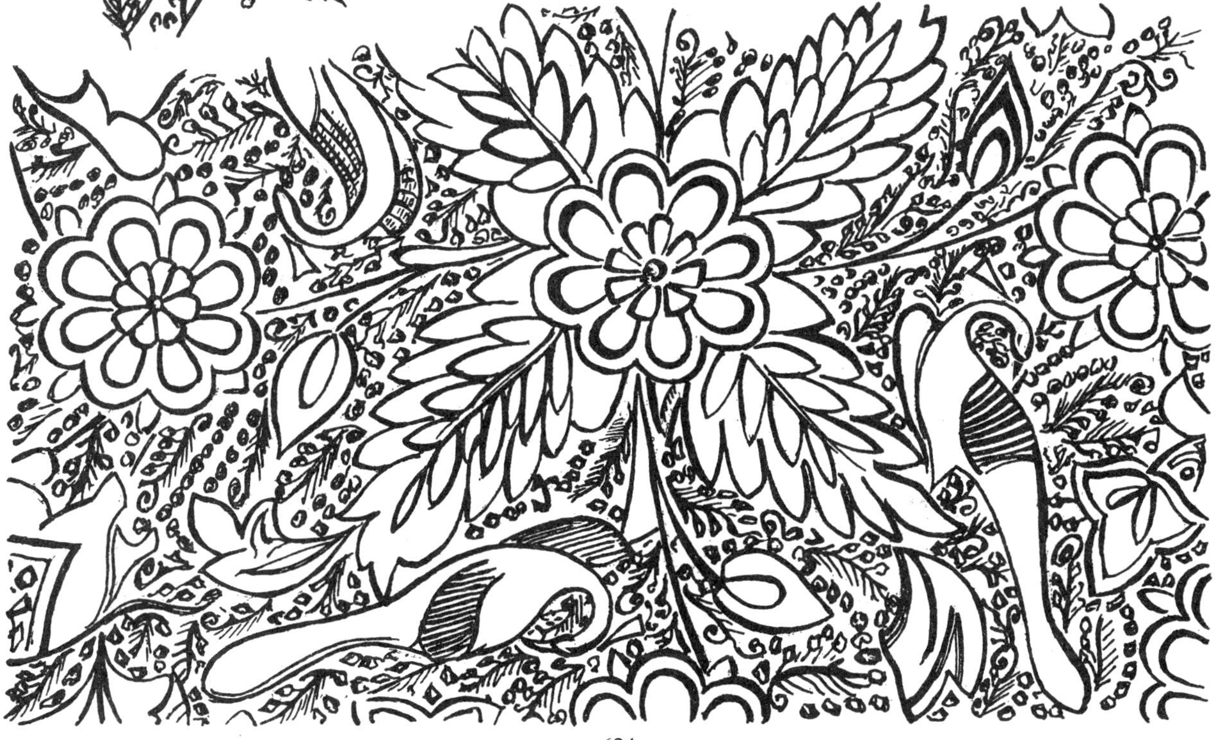

624

METALWARE. **619.** Details of brass inlay on a panel with Persian style flower arrangement in vase, Chiniot, North India. **620.** Brass embossed work with motifs of stylized swans on a wooden cushion seat, Bangalore, Mysore State. **621, 622, 624.** Intricate brass embossed work with motifs of birds, elephants, flowers and peacocks, Rajasthan. **623.** Details of embossed metalware with flowers and flying geese, Rajasthan.

# Plate 76

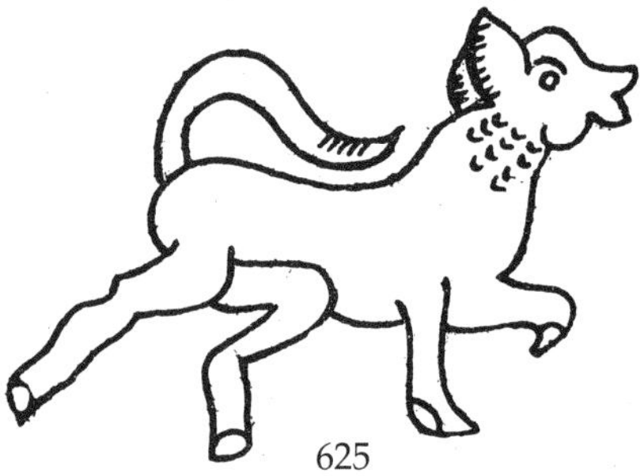
625

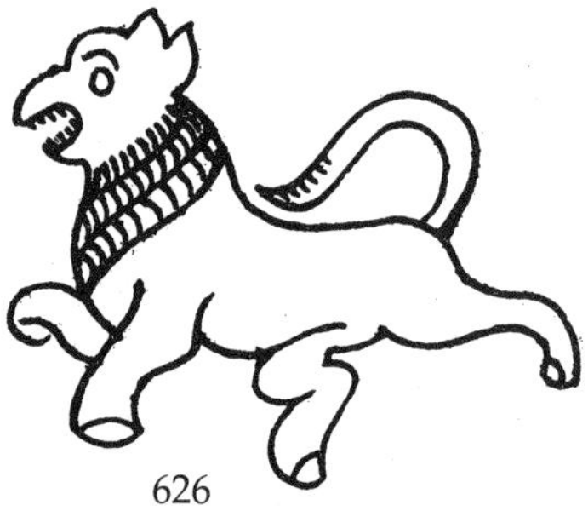
626

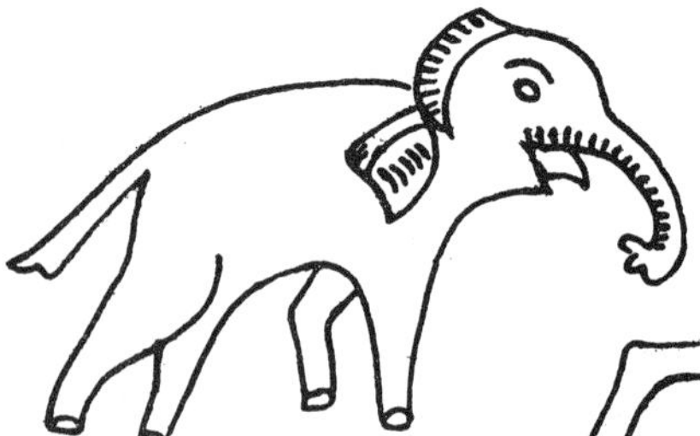
627

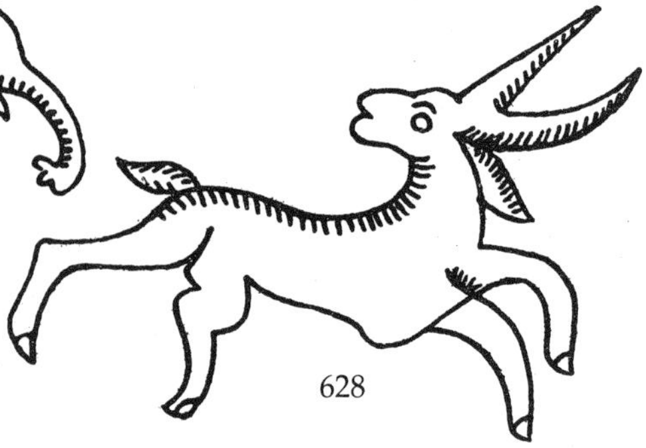
628

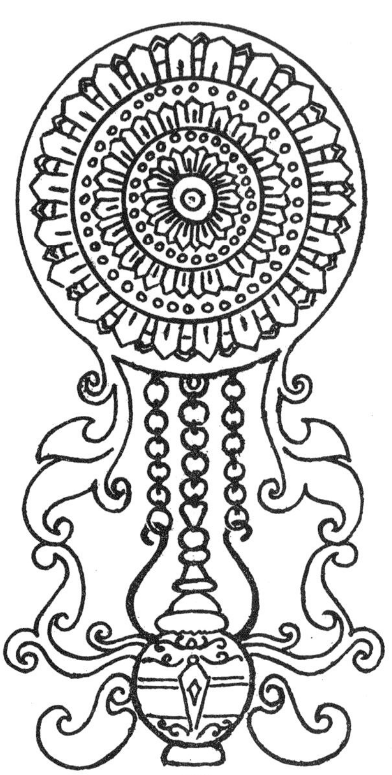
629

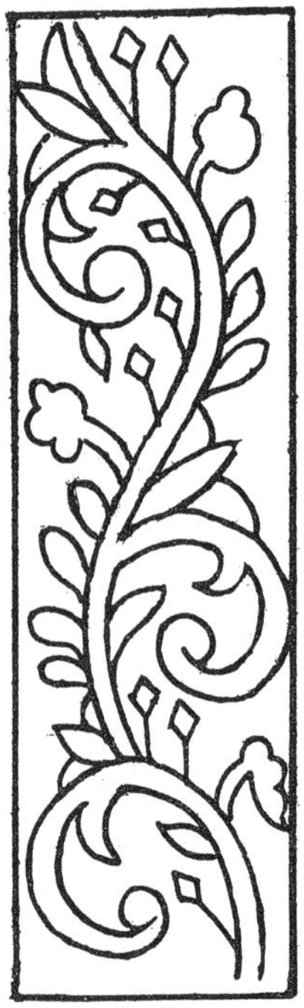
630

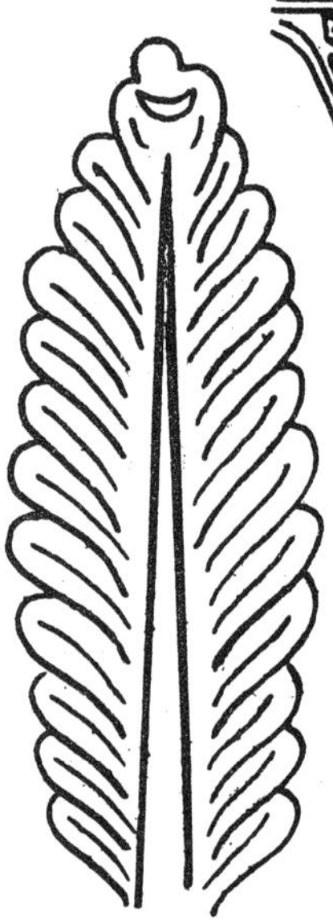
631

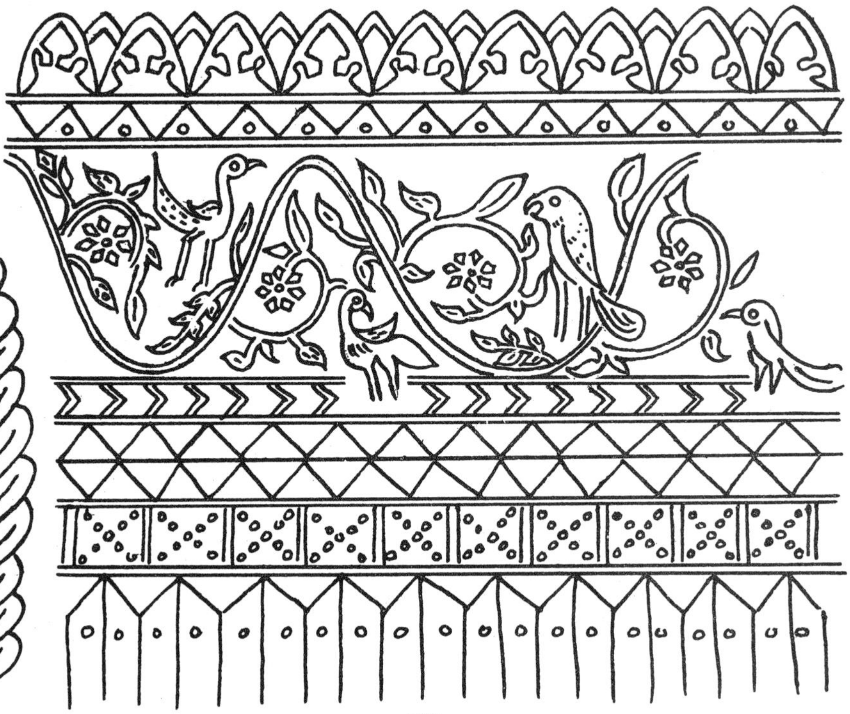
632

METALWARE. **625–628.** Examples of stylized legendary animals, elephant and deer embossed on metal articles, Rajasthan. **629.** Details of an embossed metal lotus medallion with trailing leaves and jar from a temple, Rajasthan. **630, 631.** Examples of embossed motifs of floral and palm leaf designs on metalware, Rajasthan. **632.** Details of embossed birds, flowers and leaves on curving stems with geometrical pattern on metalware, Rajasthan.

## Plate 77

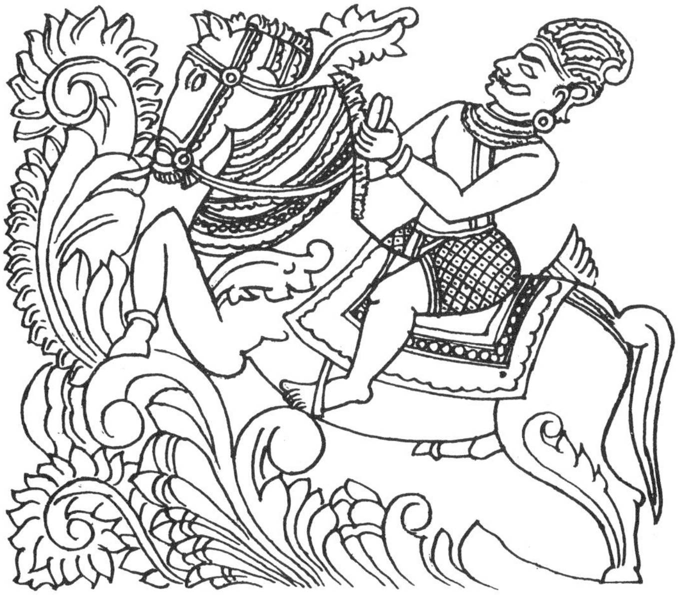

633

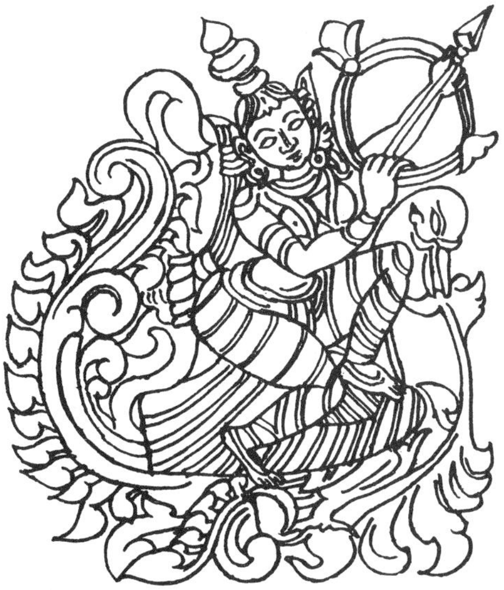

634

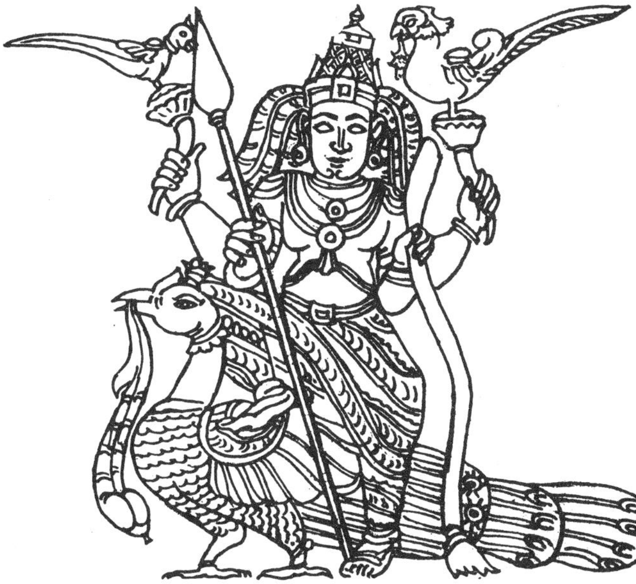

635

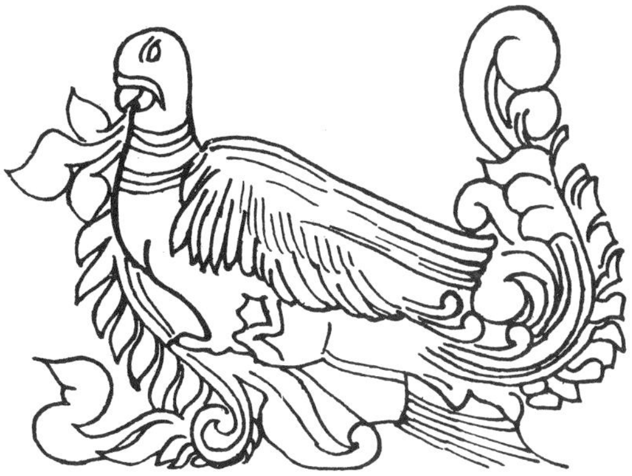

636

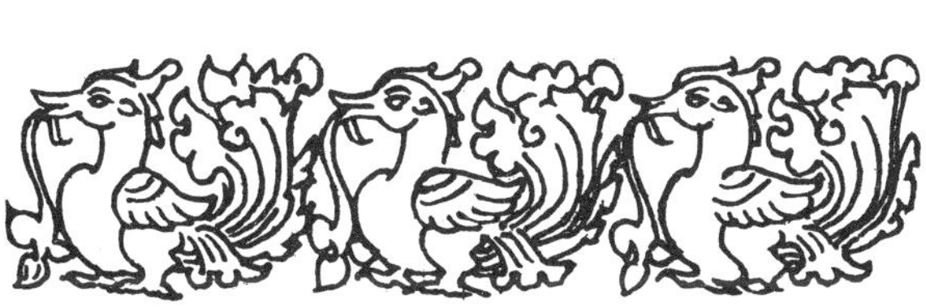

637

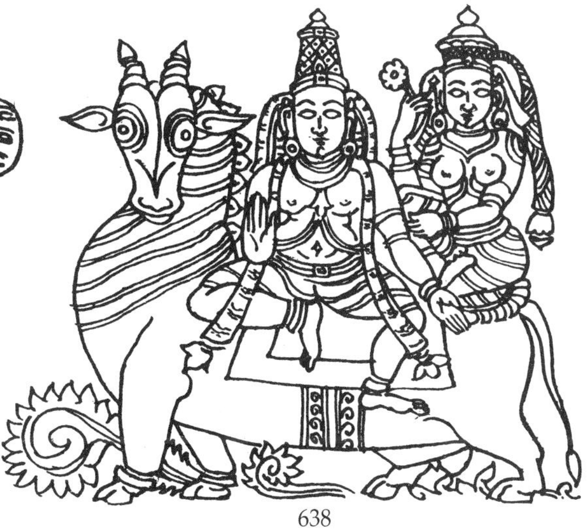

638

WOOD CARVING. **633.** Rider on horseback and floral motif. **634.** God Shiva as Maha Yogi. **635.** God Subramanya and peacock. **636.** Stylized swan and leaves. **637.** Stylized swans, drawing from a section of an old wood carving on a Ratha (temple chariot). **638.** God Shiva and consort goddess Parvathi in procession after marriage. All motifs **633–638** are from old wood carvings in South India.

# Plate 78

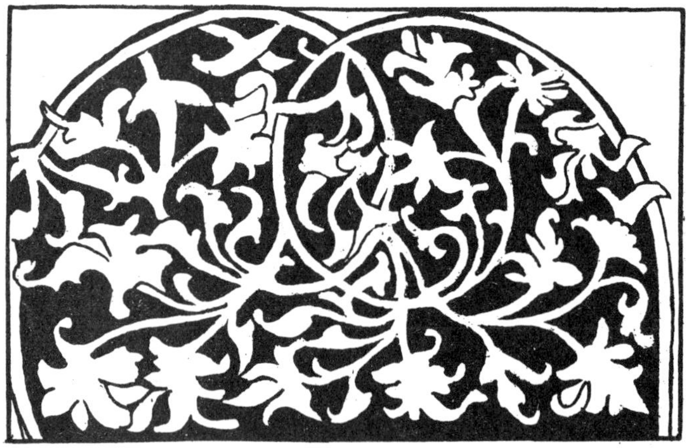

639

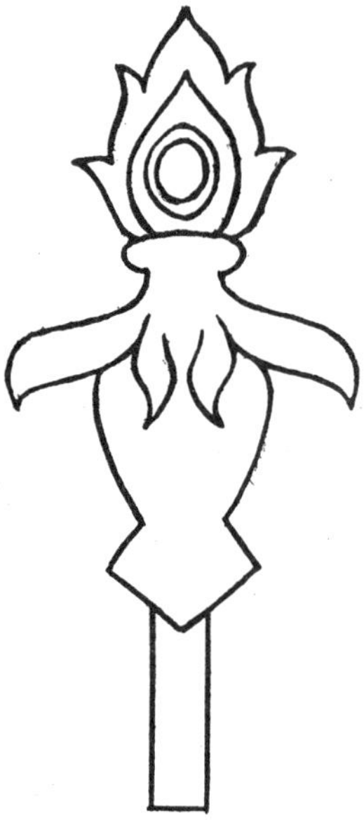

640

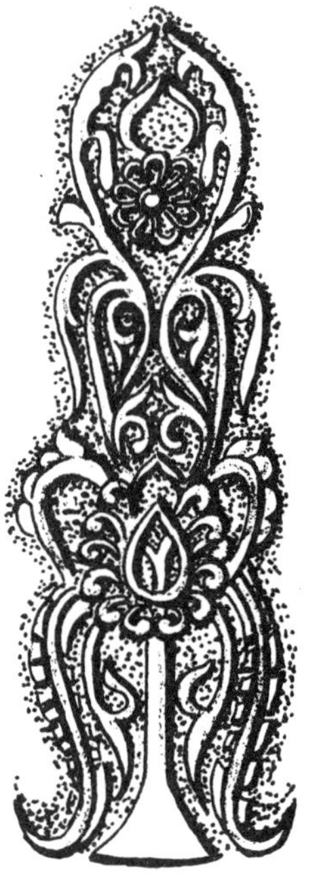

641

642

643

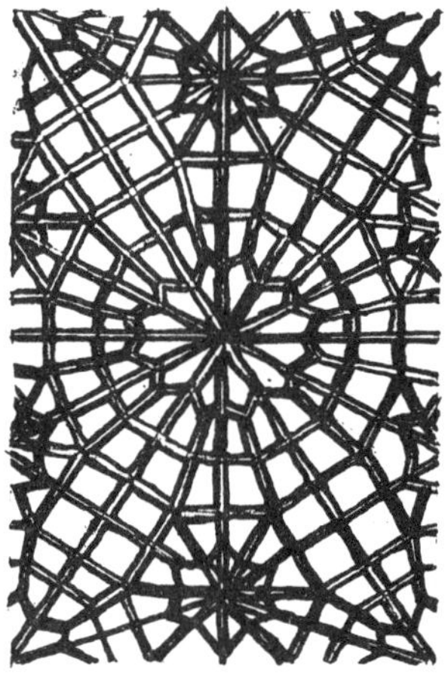

644

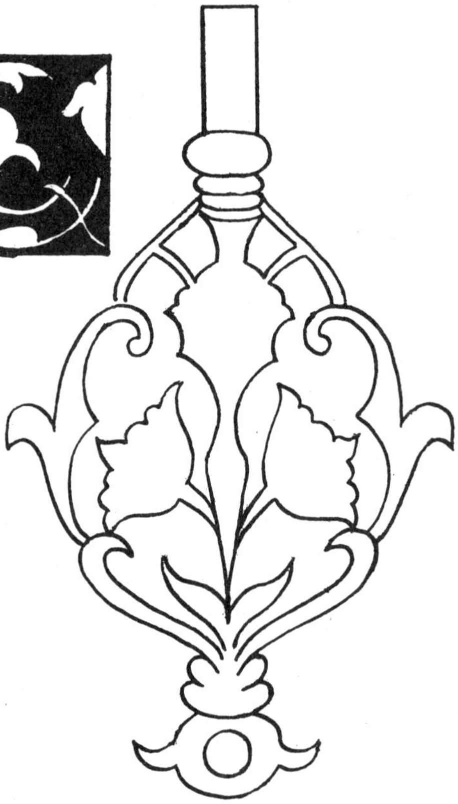

645

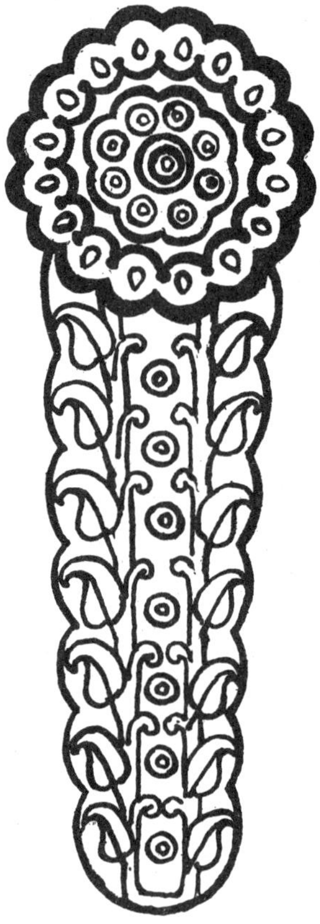

646

WOOD CARVING. **639.** Details of section of carved wood panel after a famous perforated window at Ahmadabad, Gujarat. **640, 645, 646.** Stylized floral and foliated motifs from wood carvings, Rajasthan. **641.** Floral ensemble from a carved candlestick in rosewood, Bombay, Maharashtra. **642, 643.** Details of examples of traditional wood carving with leaf motifs, North India. **644.** Details of a section of a carved wooden screen, Punjab.

# Plate 79

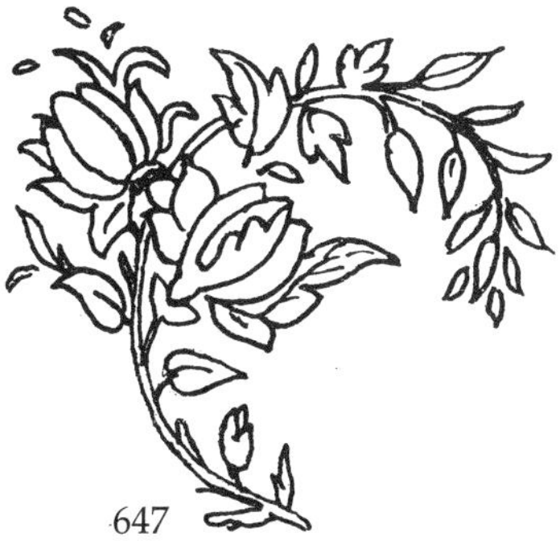
647

648

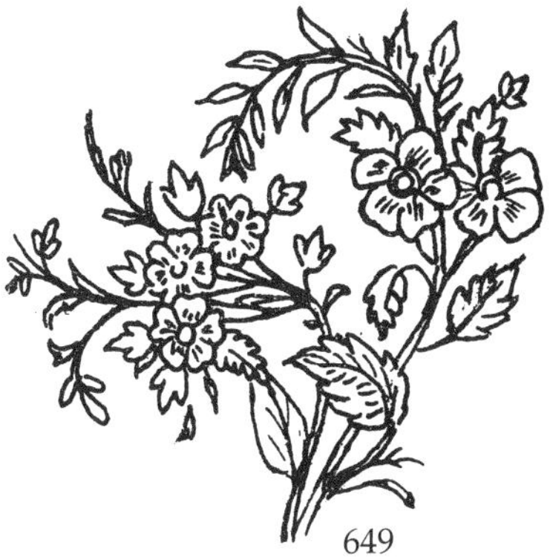
649

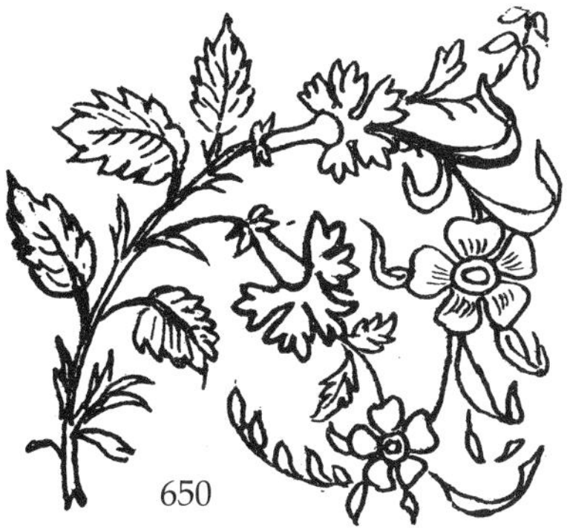
650

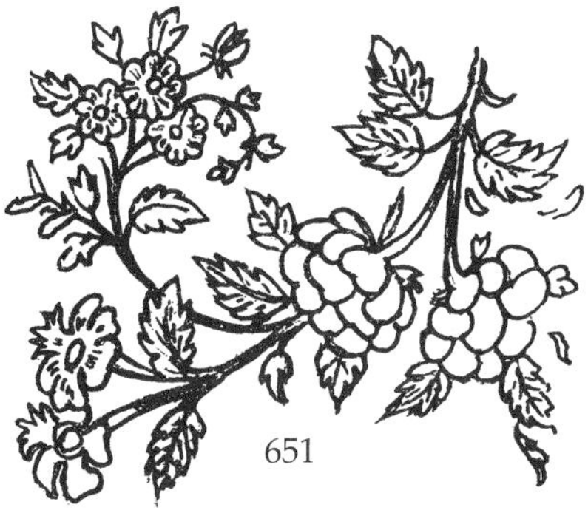
651

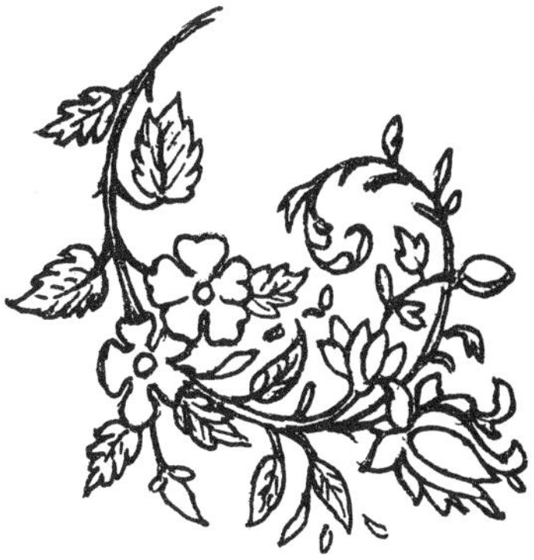
652

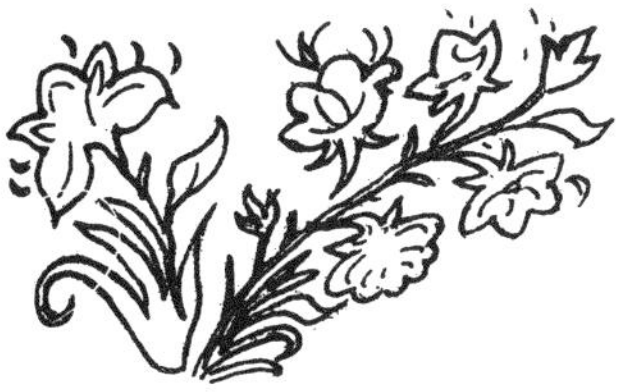
653

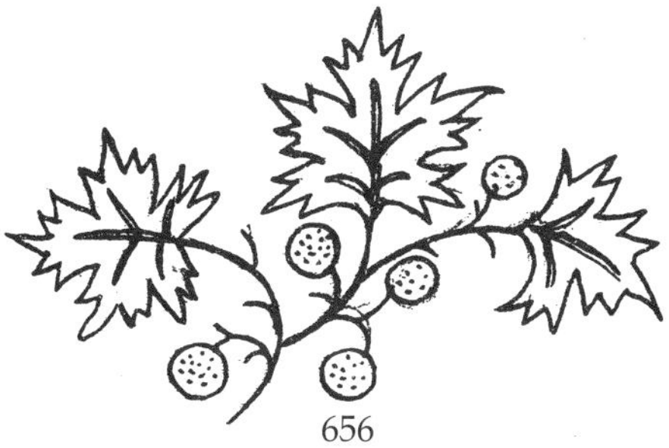
656

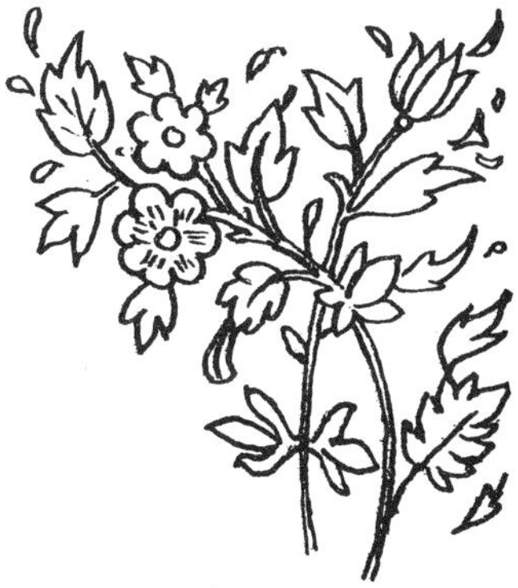
657

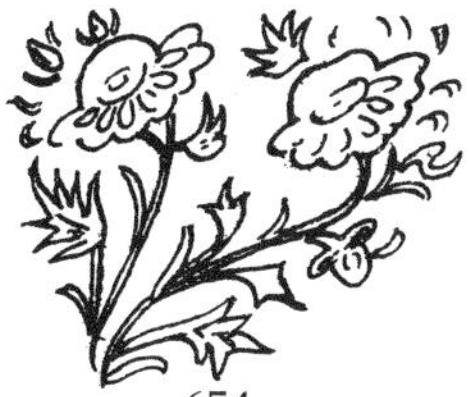
654

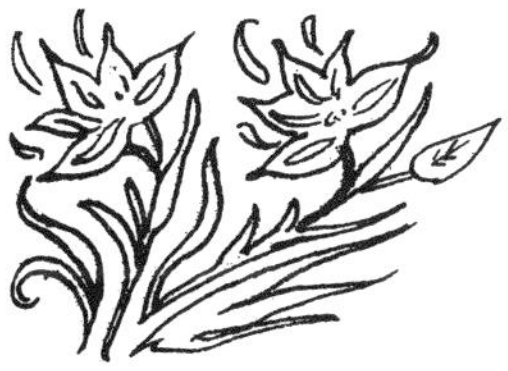
655

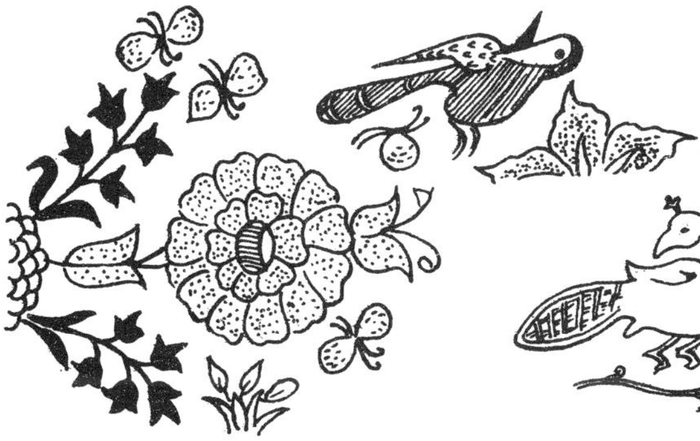
658

659

LACQUERWARE. **647–652, 657.** Various floral sprays in these motifs from the top of a lacquered box with golden design on a black background, 18th century. **653–655, 656, 658, 659.** Floral, Chenar leaf, stylized rose, butterflies, and birds from various papier-mâché hand-painted and lacquered articles, Kashmir.

# Plate 80

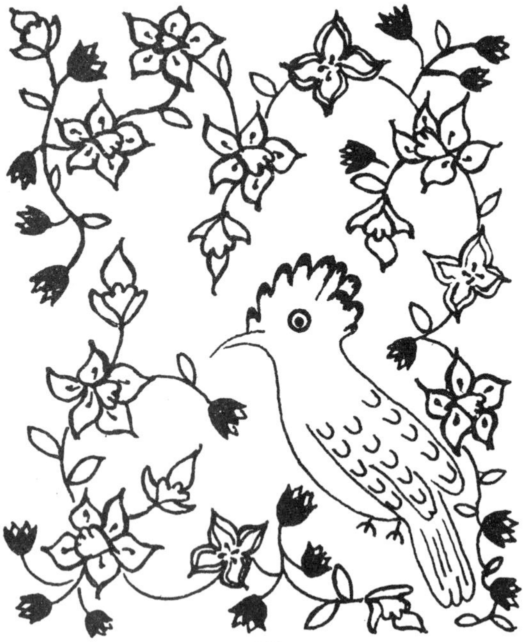

660

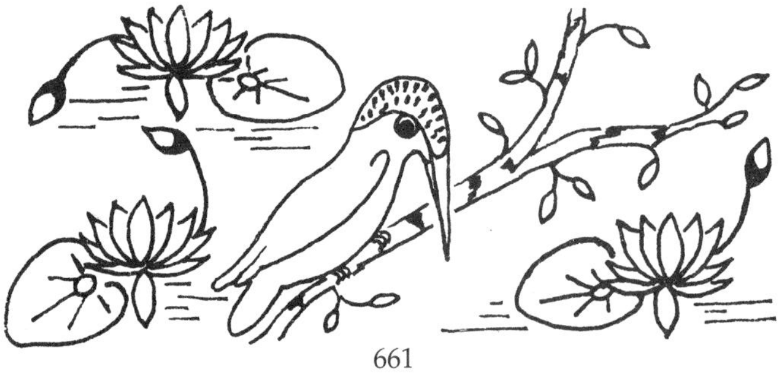

661

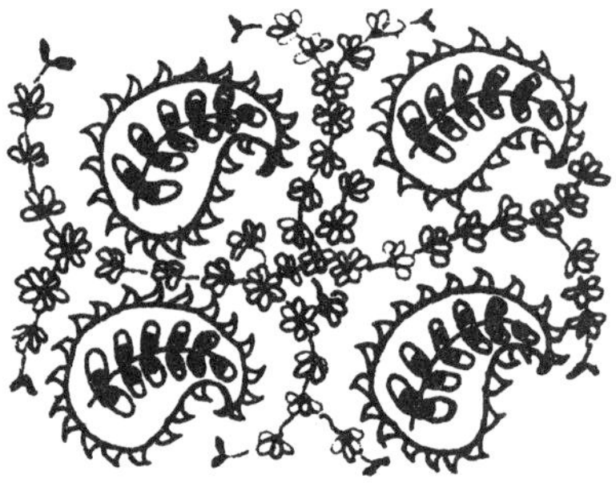

662

663

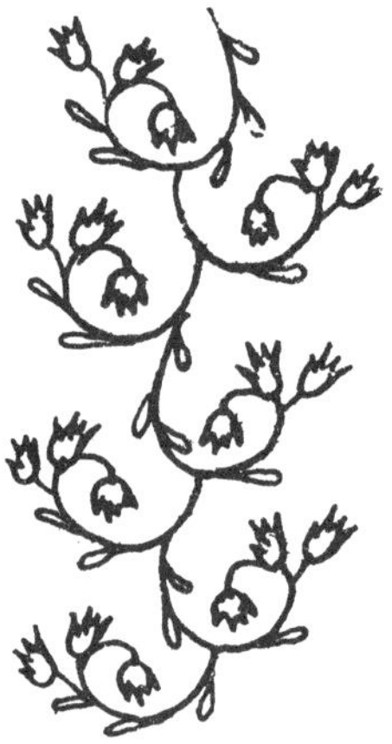

664

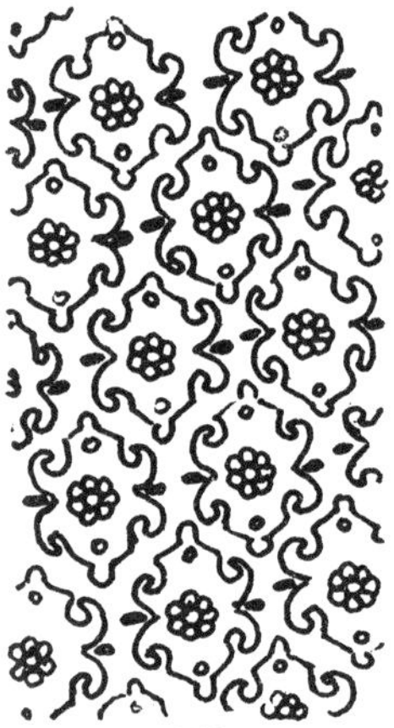

665

666

667

668

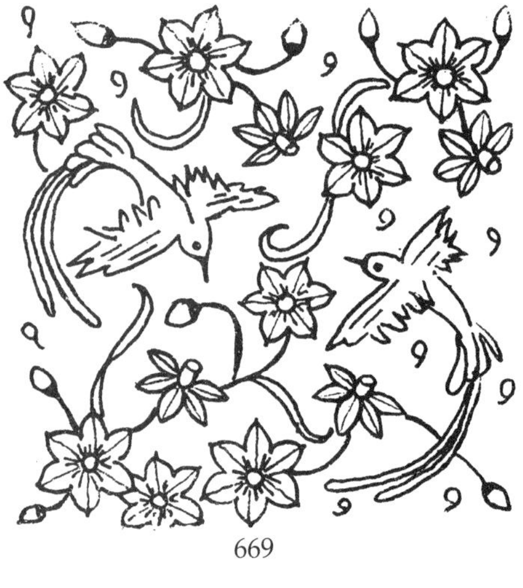

669

670

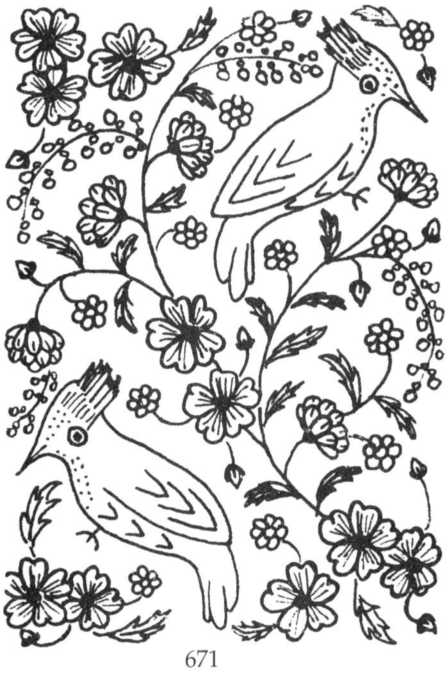

671

LACQUERWARE. **660–671.** Stylized daffodils, lotuses, almonds, lily of the valley, narcissi and other spring flowers and the hoopoo, kingfisher, bird of paradise, flycatcher and woodpecker are some of the motifs from various papier-mâché hand-painted and lacquered articles, Kashmir.

# Plate 81

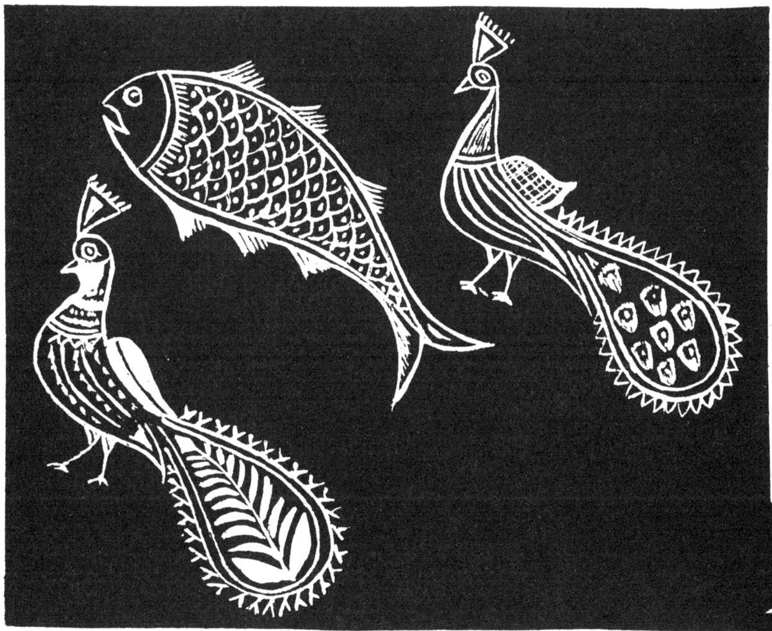

672

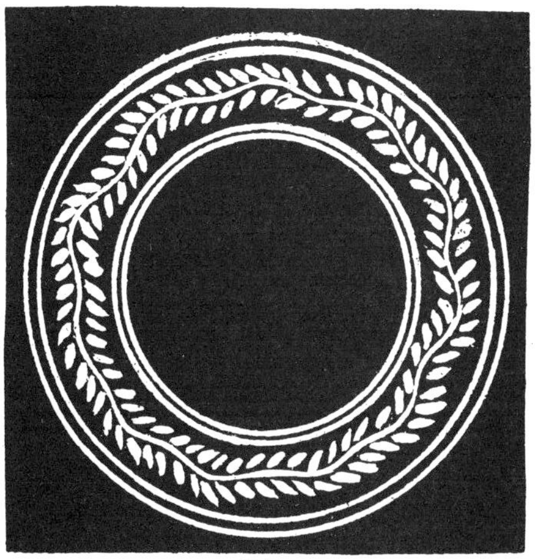

673

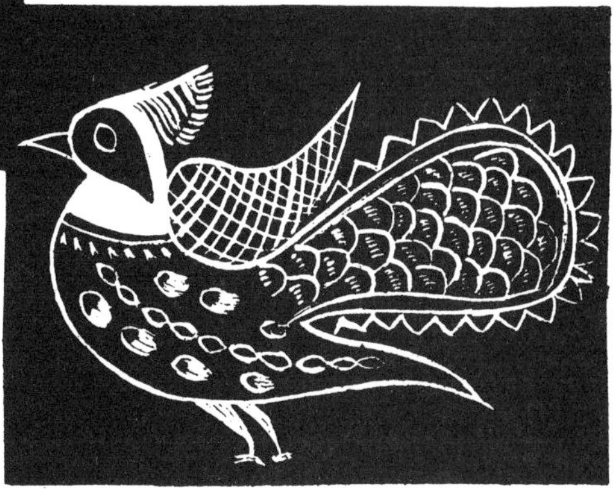

675

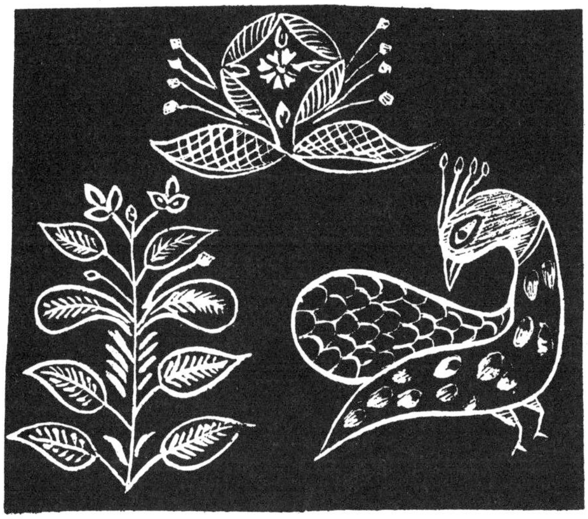

674

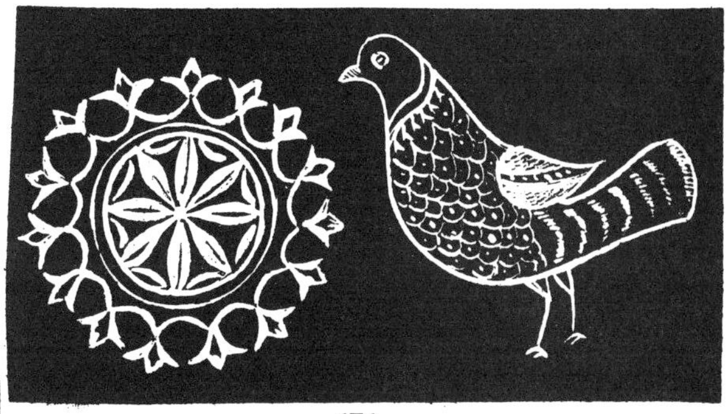

676

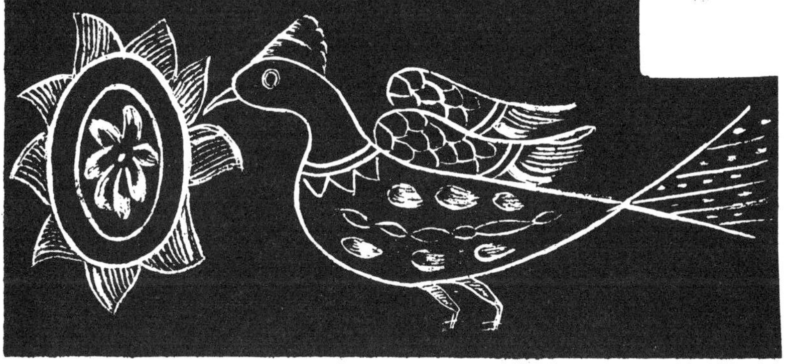

677

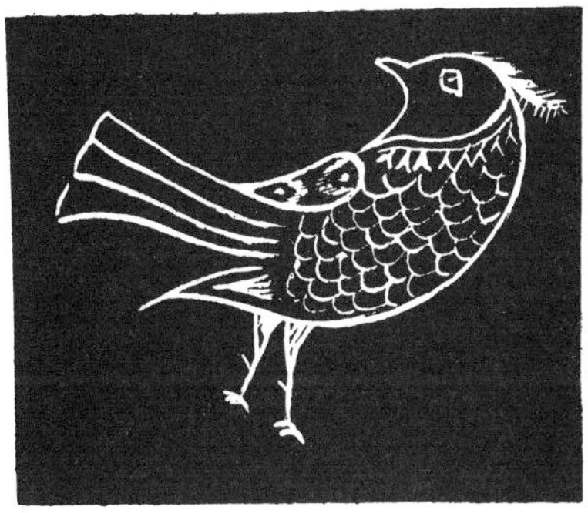

678

LACQUERWARE. **672–678.** Details of stylized peacocks, fish, foliated pattern, flowers, birds and geometrical shapes hand-painted and lacquered on various wooden bowls, boxes, vases and containers from Bihar.

# Plate 82

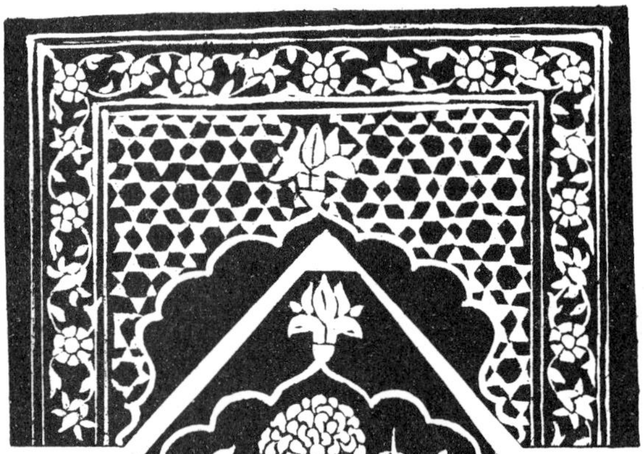

679

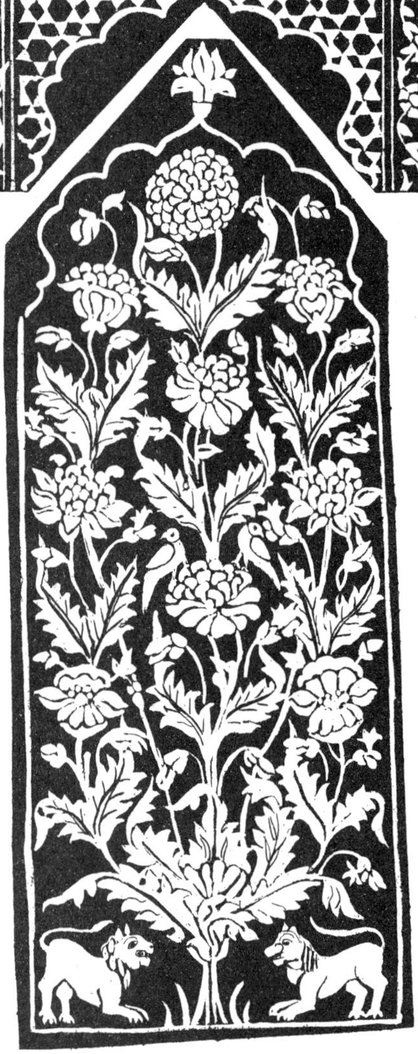

680

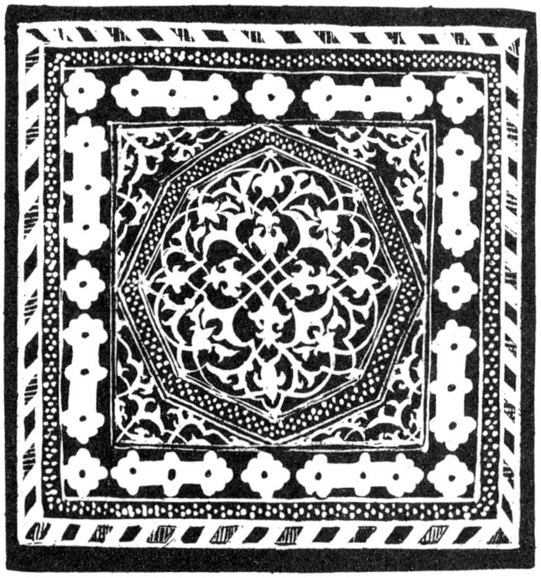

681

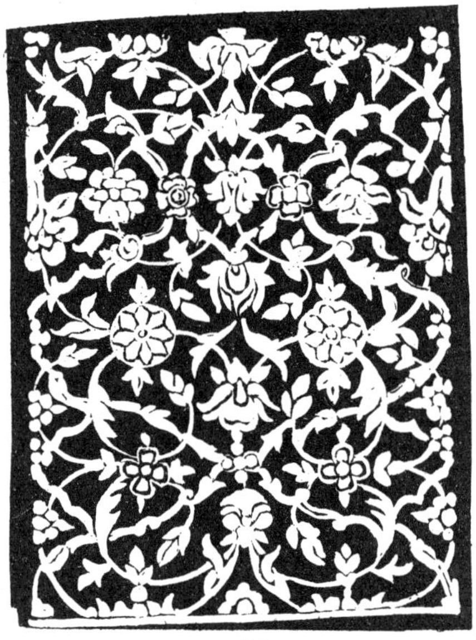

682

683

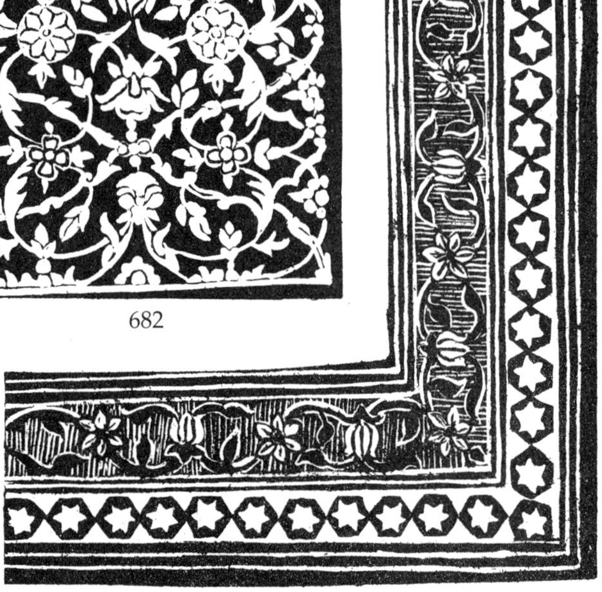

684

IVORY INLAY. **679, 680.** Details of the top and central floral designs with birds and lions from a panel of ivory inlay on wood in the Golden Temple, Amritsar, Punjab. **681, 683.** Details of ivory inlay of floral and geometrical ensembles on a wooden door in the palace at Amber, old capital of Jaipur State, Rajasthan. **682, 684.** Details of the central and border floral and star ensembles from another panel of ivory inlay on wood in the Golden Temple at Amritsar, Punjab.

# Plate 83

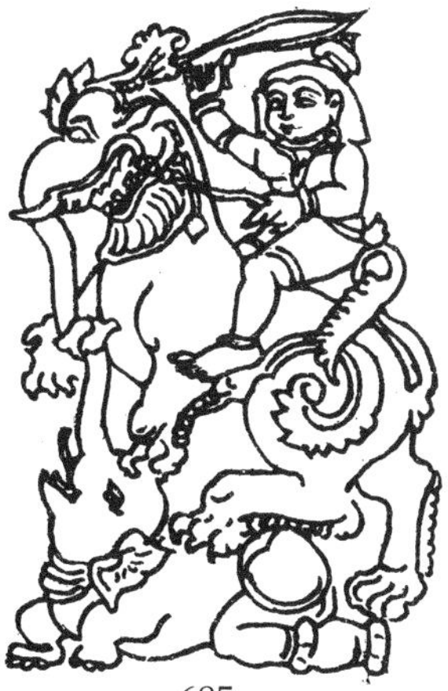

685

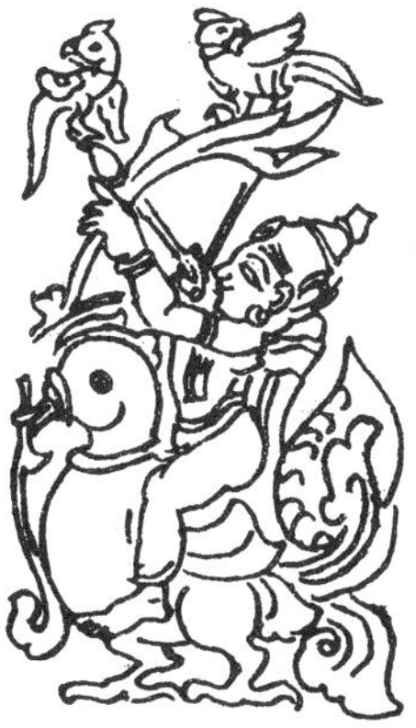

686

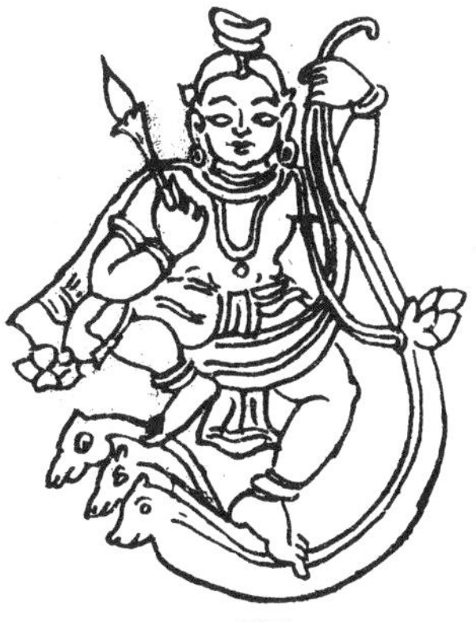

687

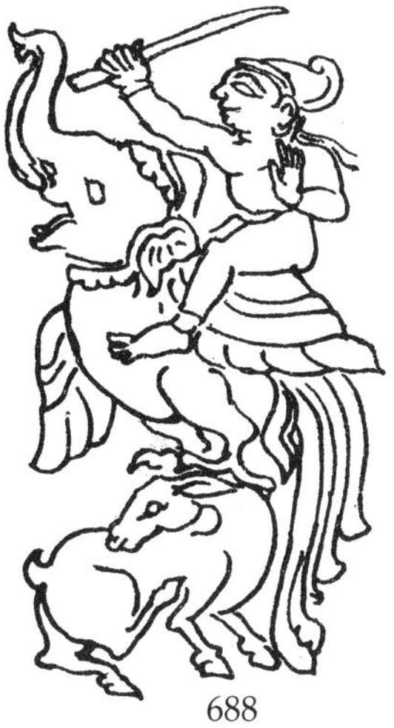

688

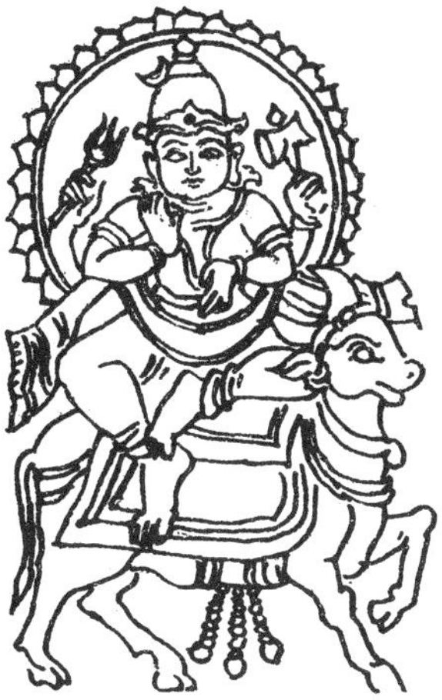

689

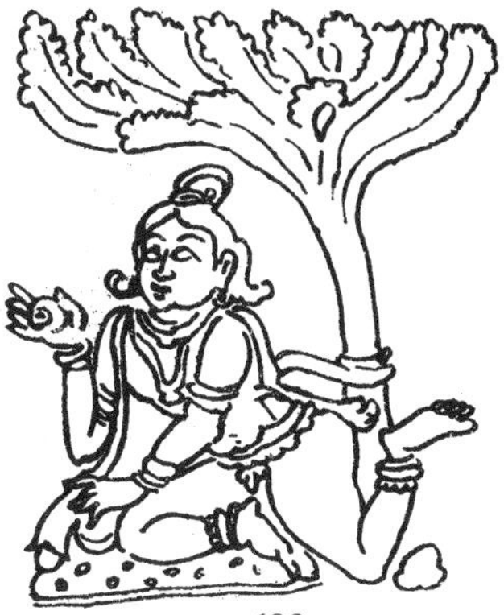

690

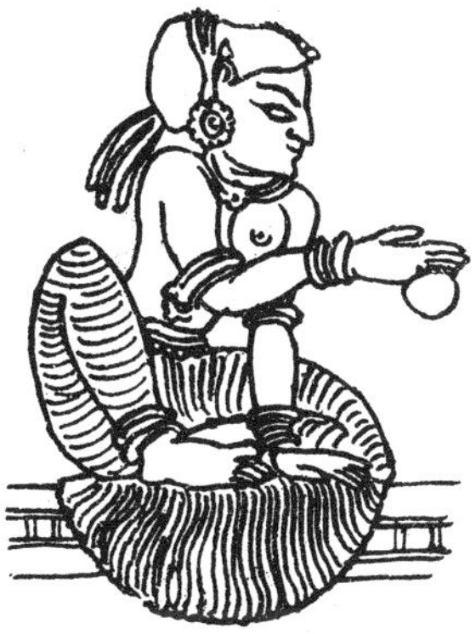

691

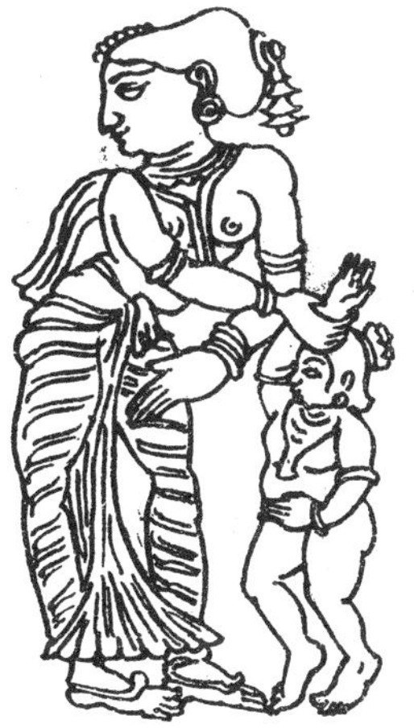

692

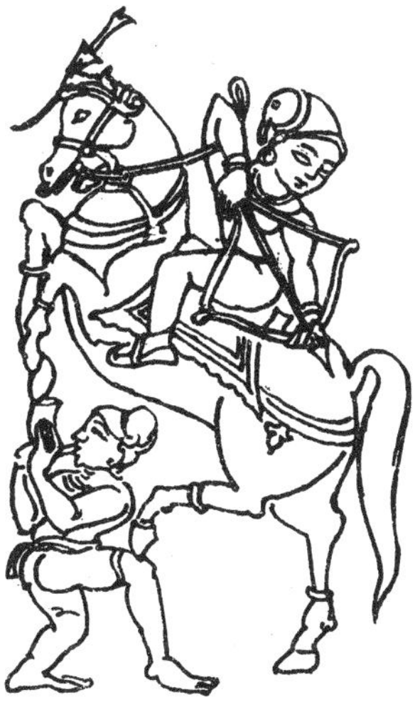

693

Ivory Carving. **685–693.** Drawings of ivory carving from a door in the Mysore palace, showing through picture motifs various characters, stylized and mythological birds and animals from myth and legend, Mysore State.

# Plate 84

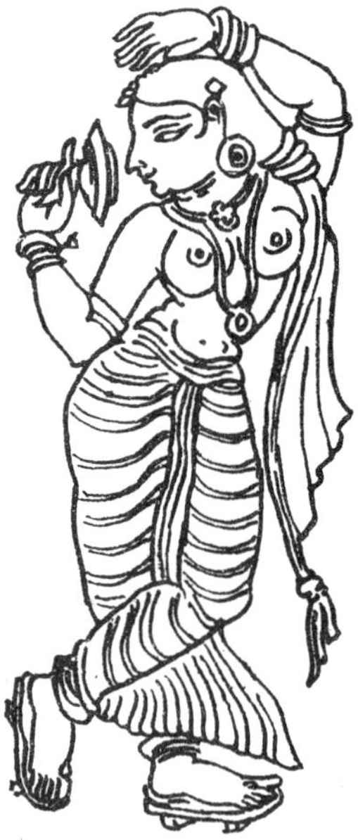

694

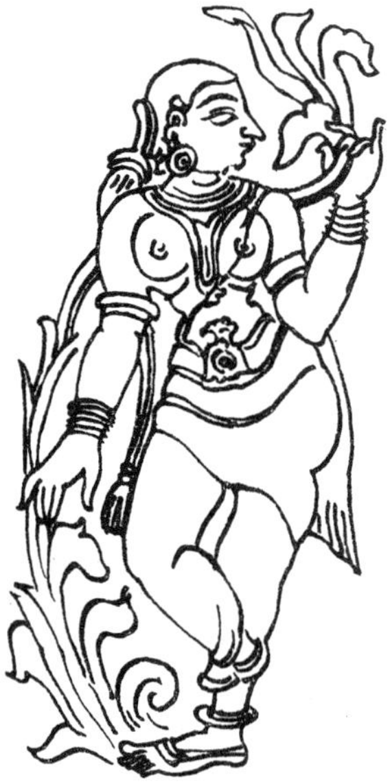

695

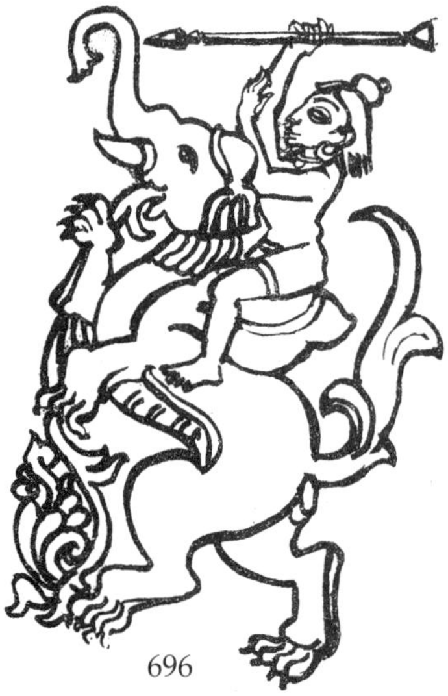

696

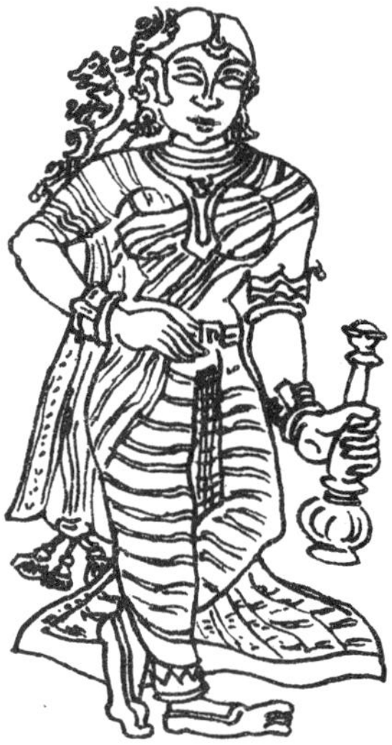

697

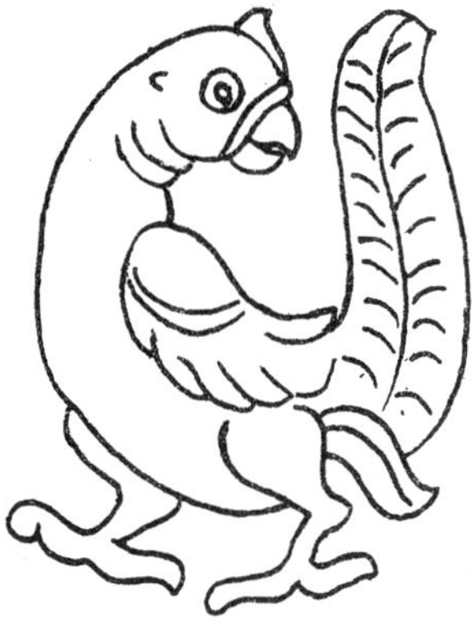

698

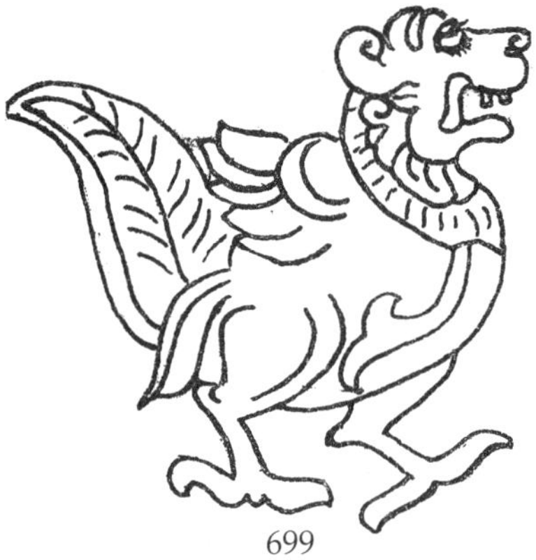

699

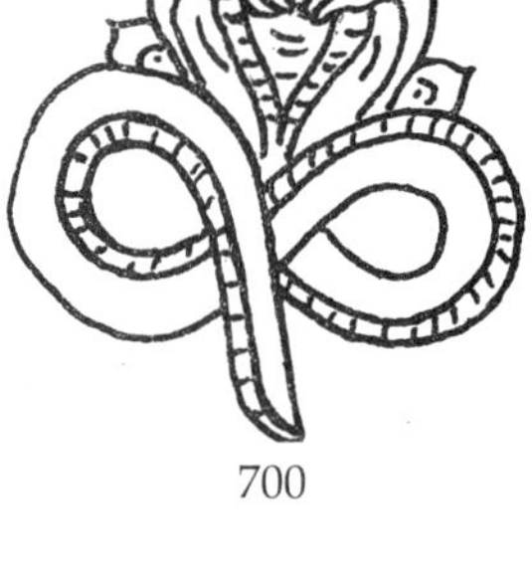

700

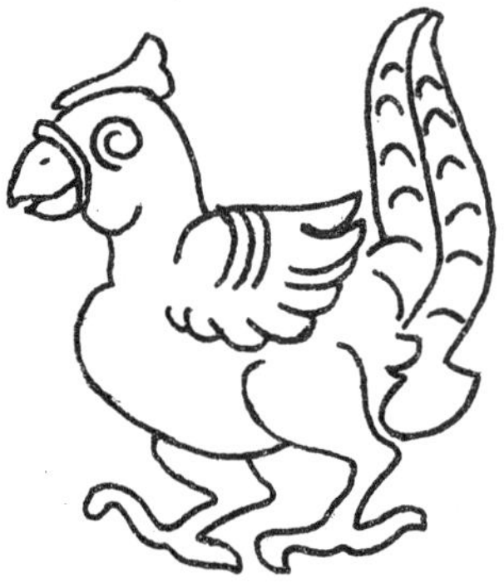

701

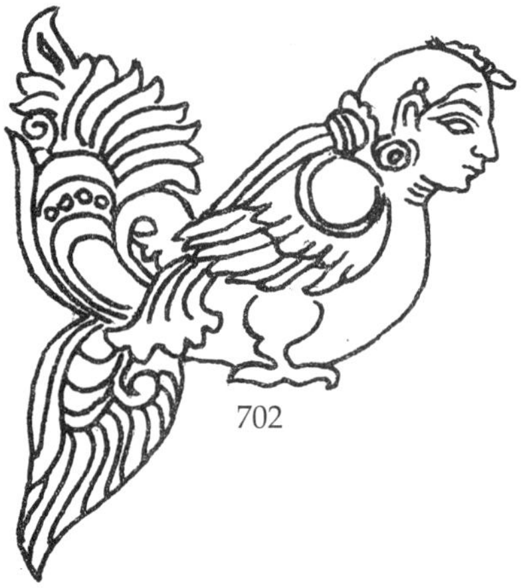

702

IVORY CARVING. **694–702.** Drawings of ivory carving from a door in the Mysore palace, showing through picture motifs various characters, stylized and mythological birds and animals from myth and legend.

# Plate 85

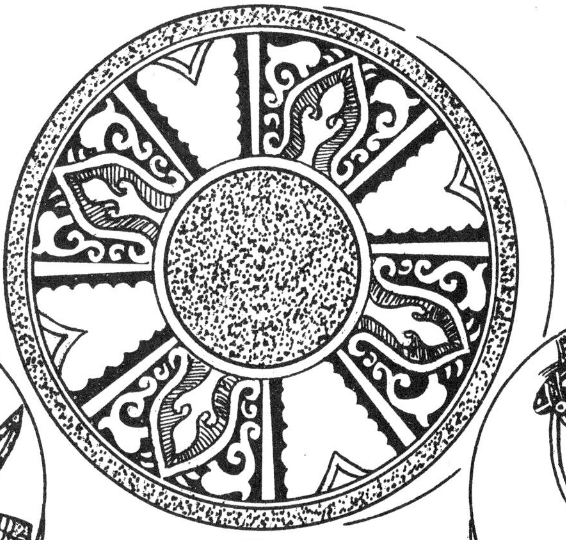

704

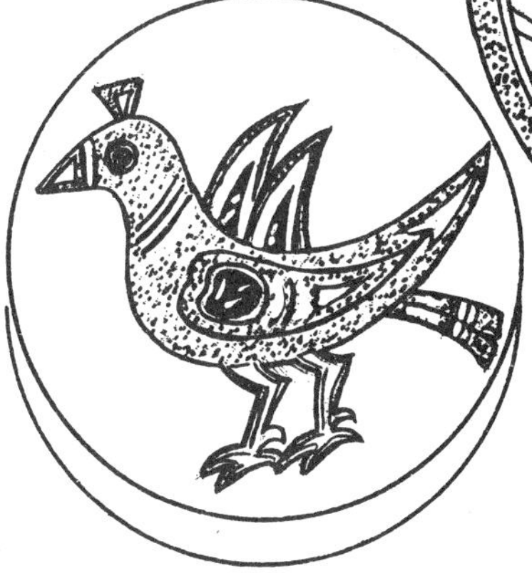

703

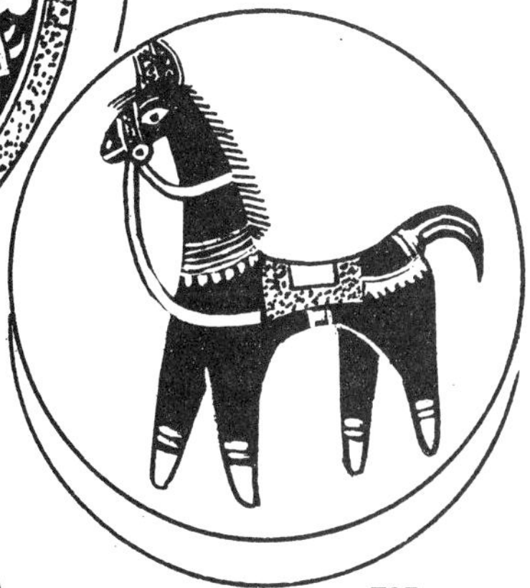

705

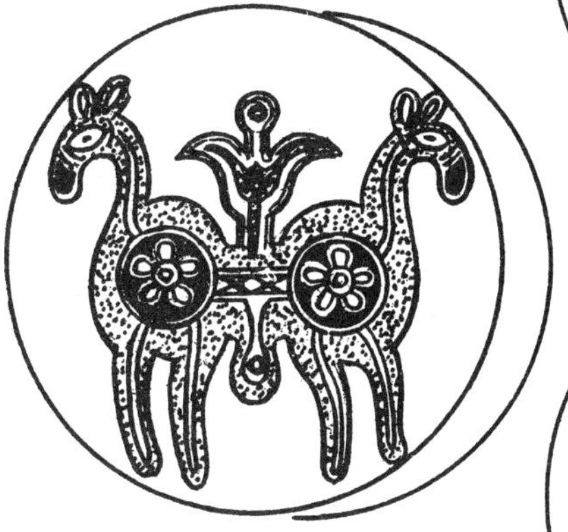

707

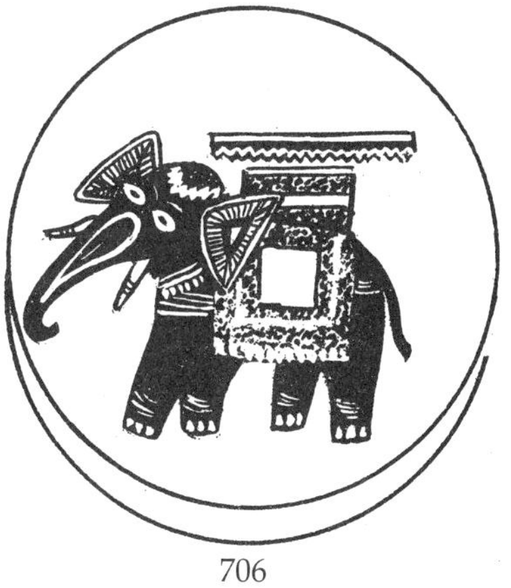

706

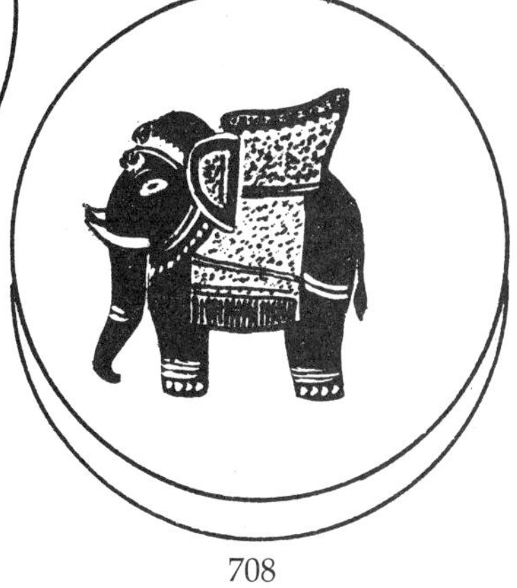

708

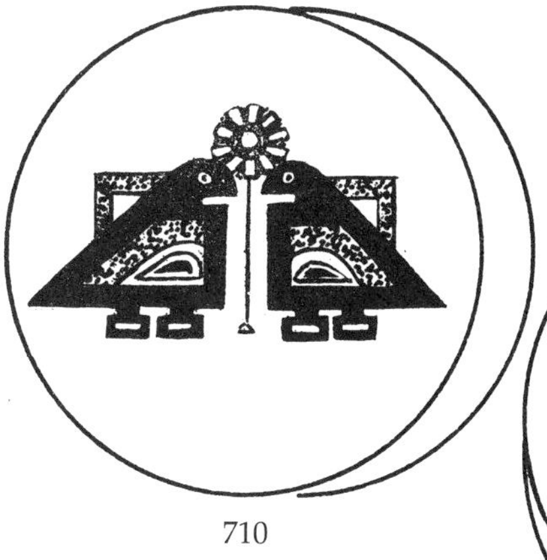

710

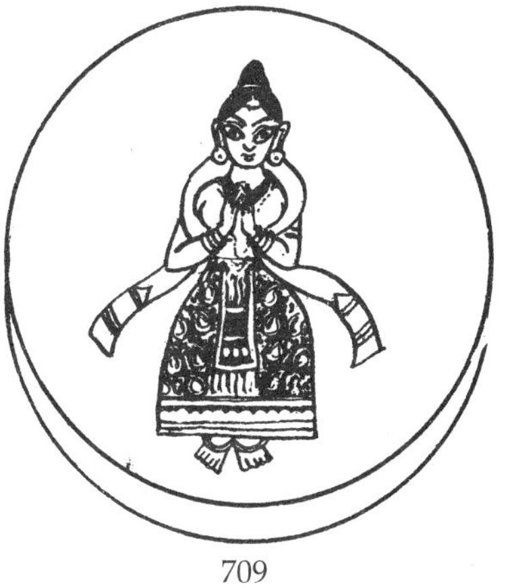

709

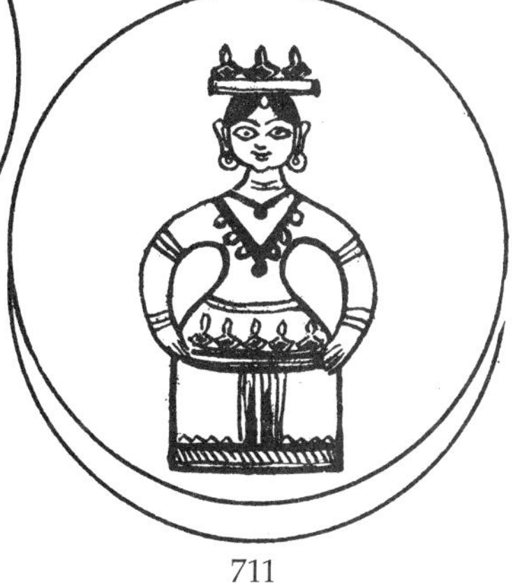

711

TAKULI WORK. **703–711.** Details of place mats made out of motifs with folk motifs of birds, elephants, the camel, geometrical pattern and human figures, based on the ancient art of Takuli ornamental work done on fine glass with "Tabaque" (gold or silver leaf), and used by women as an ornament for the center of the forehead, Bihar.

# Plate 86

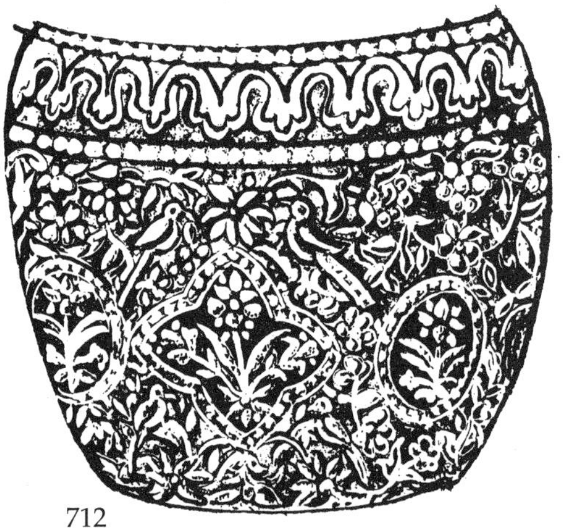

712

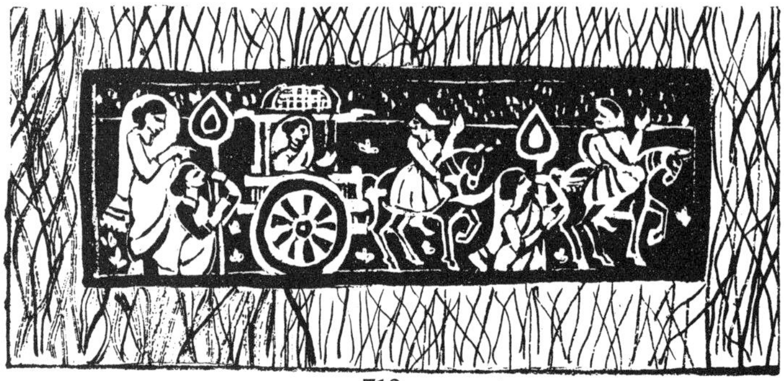

713

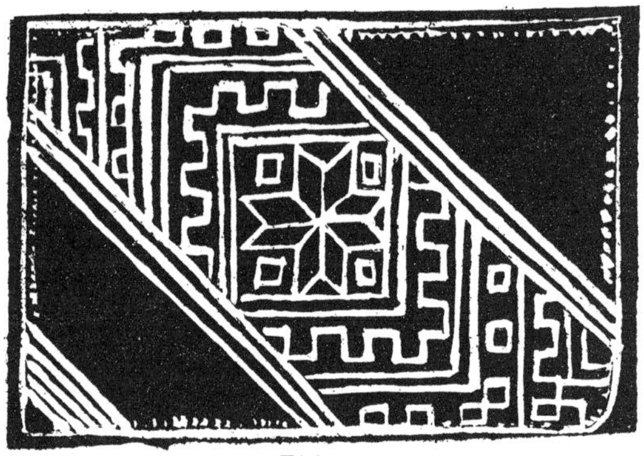

714

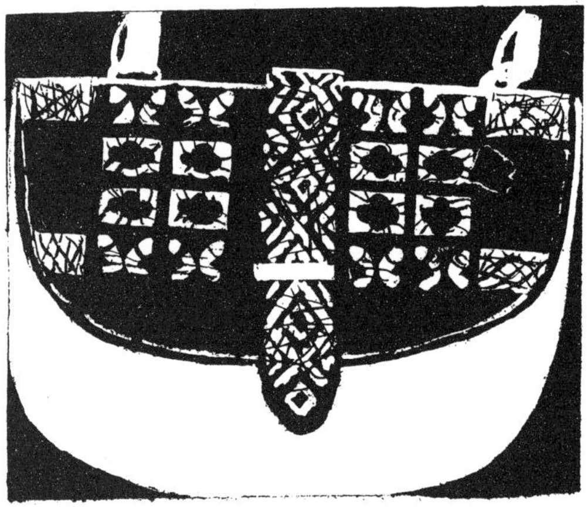

715

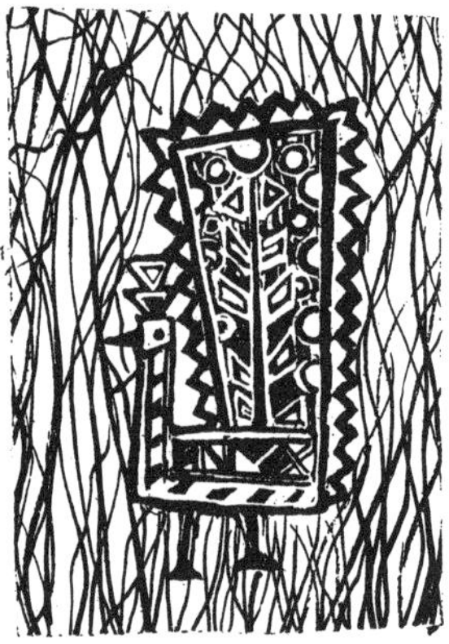

716

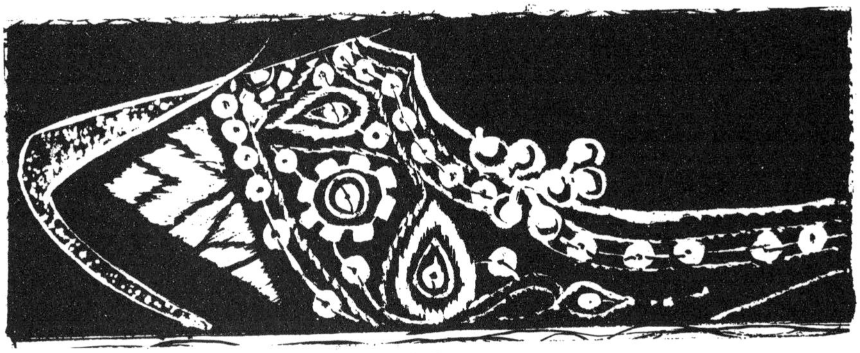

717

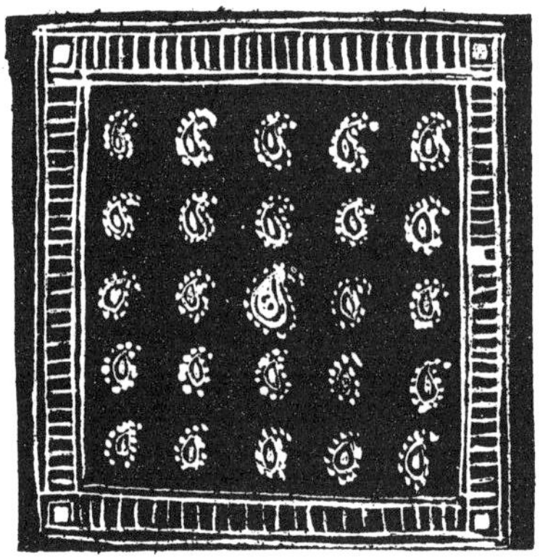

718

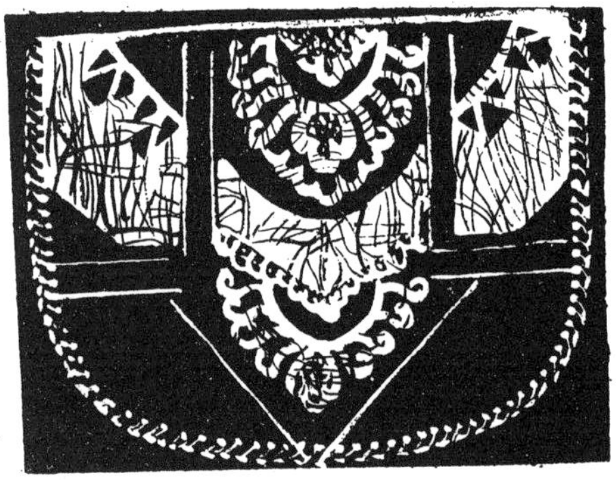

719

LEATHER WORK. **712.** Details of gold embossed work with delicate floral and bird ensembles worked on camel skin (the art of Monabathi), Bikanir, Rajasthan. **713–719.** Embossed and painted motifs of geometrical pattern, stylized peacock and mangoes and procession, from various leather articles for purses and handbags, West Bengal and gold embroidered shoe from Jaiselmer (Rajasthan).

# Plate 87

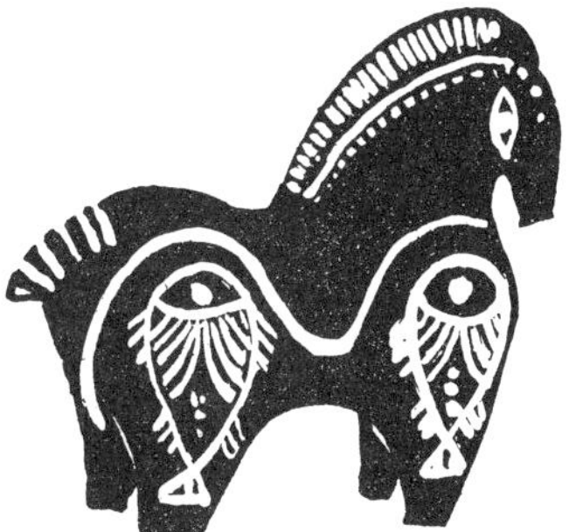
720

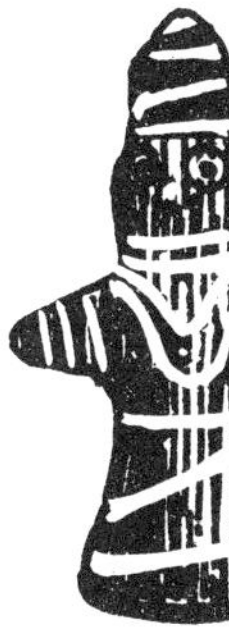
721

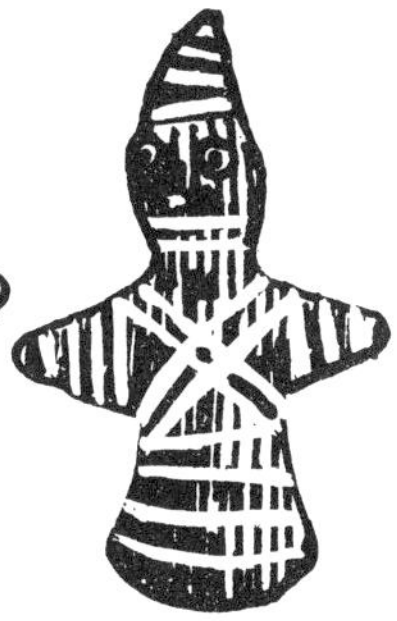
722

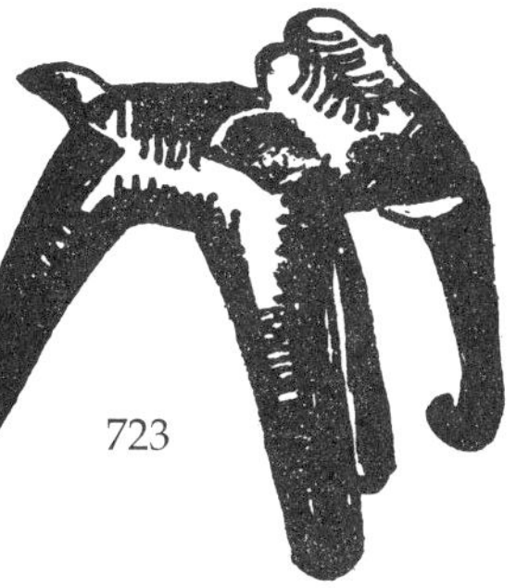
723

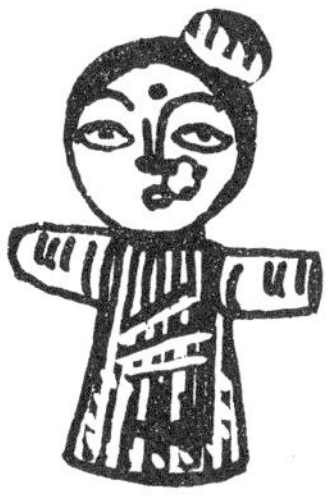
724

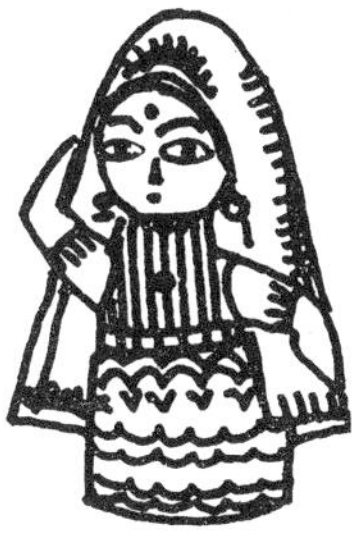
725

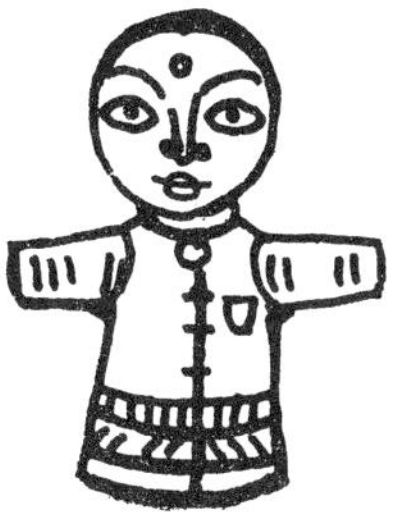
726

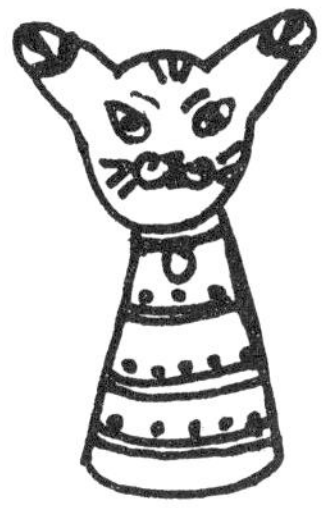
727

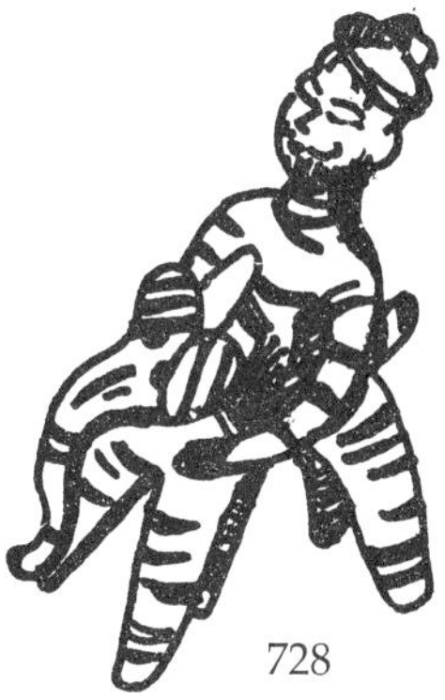
728

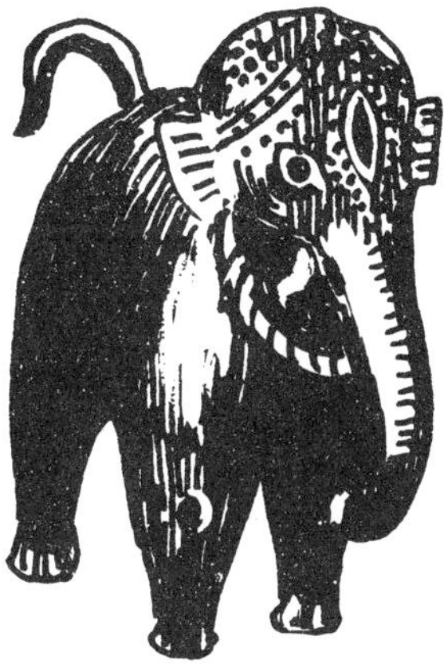
729

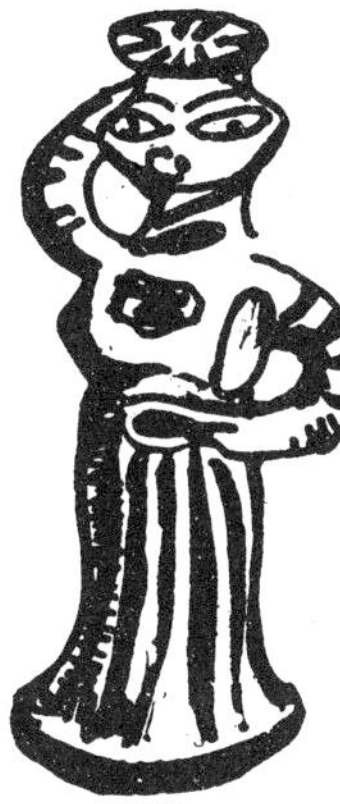
730

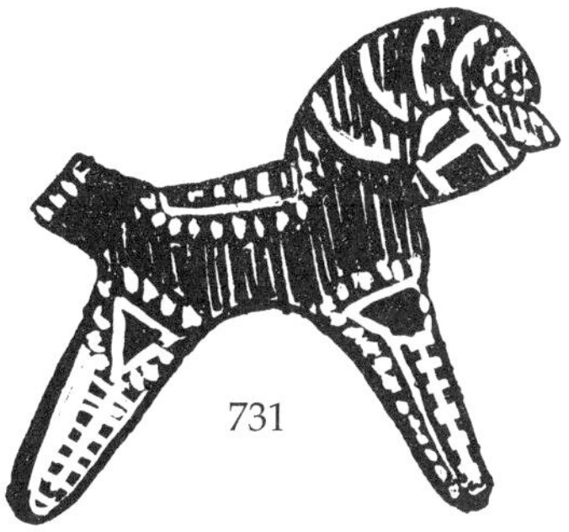
731

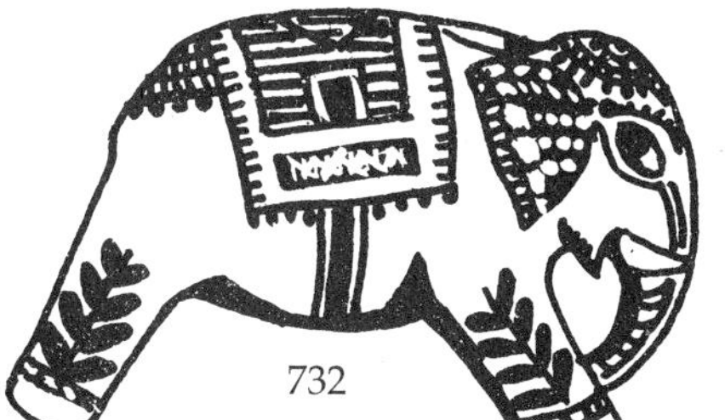
732

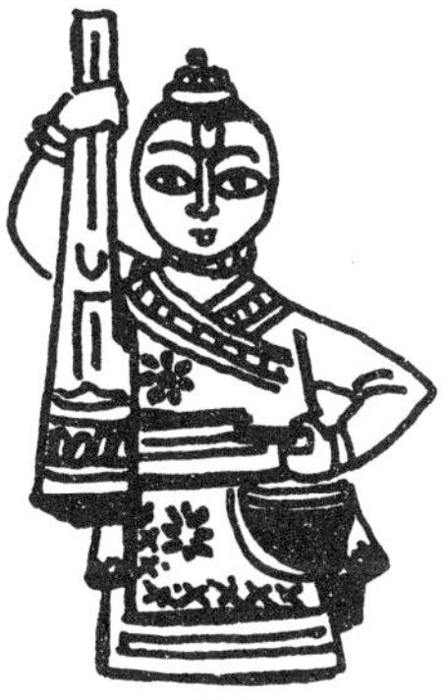
733

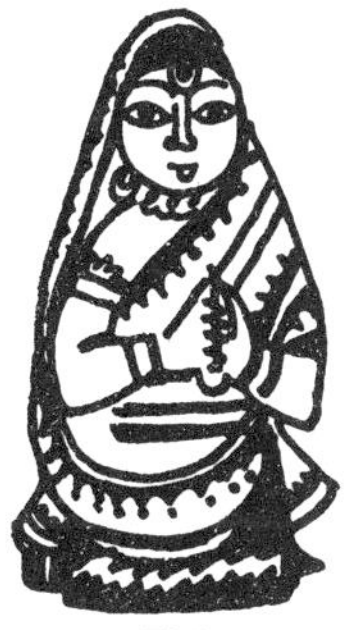
734

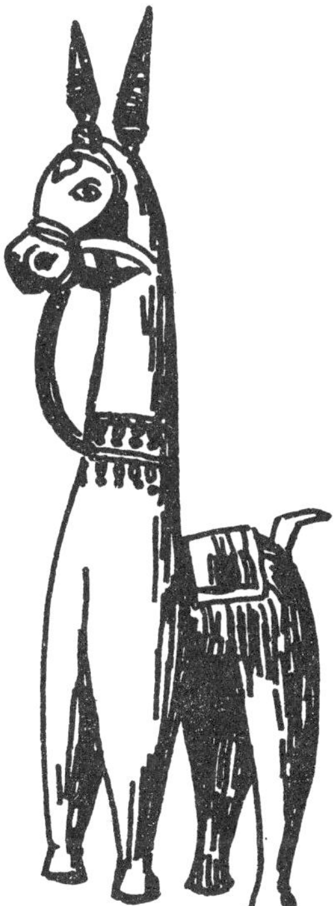
735

TOYS, DOLLS AND DECORATIVE PIECES—CLAY. **720–735.** Painted clay folk toys, dolls and decorative pieces from West Bengal, comprising stylized horses, elephants, dolls, and a cat. **720** is a clay horse typical of the Bankura village product, of West Bengal.

# Plate 88

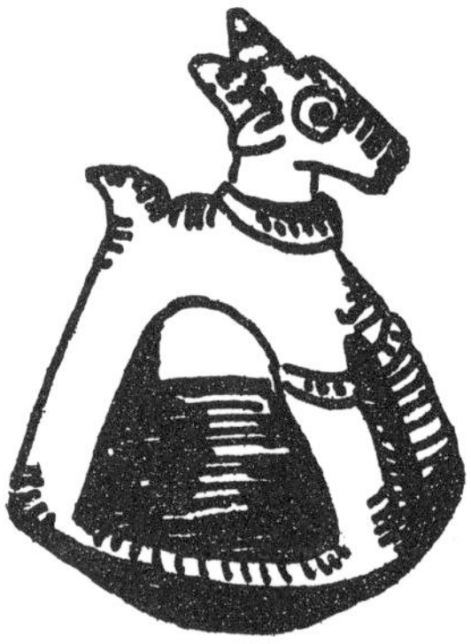
736

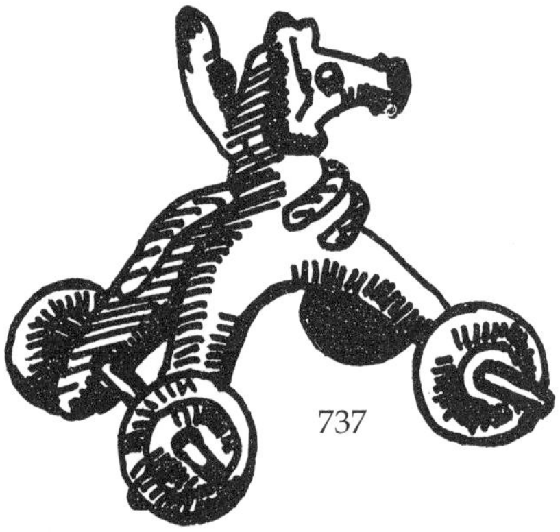
737

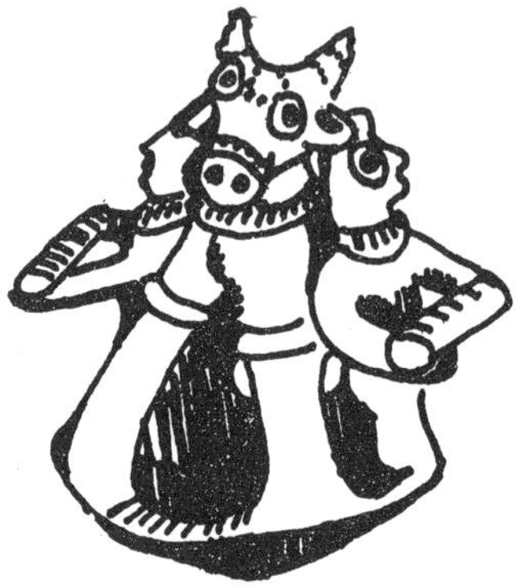
738

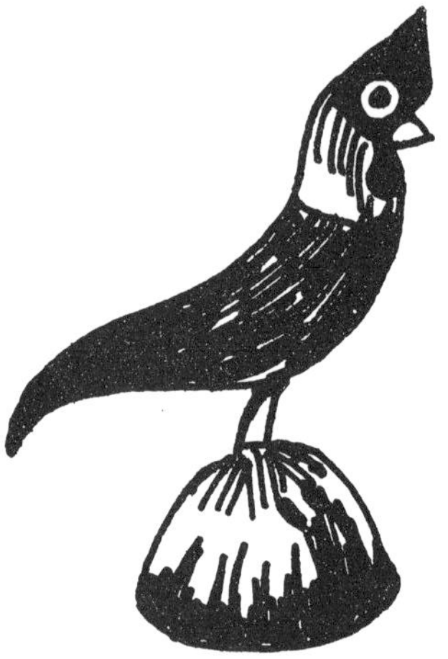
739

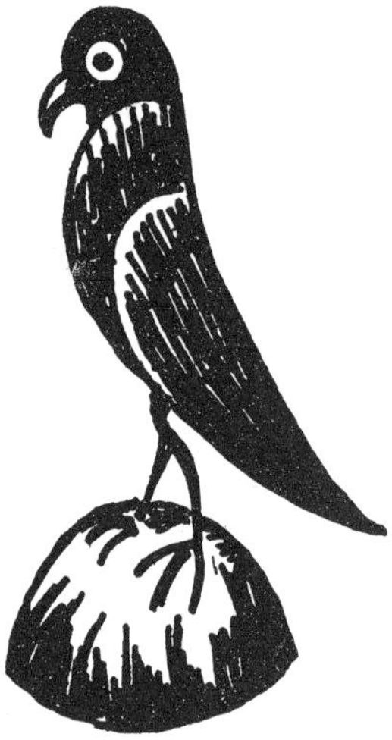
740

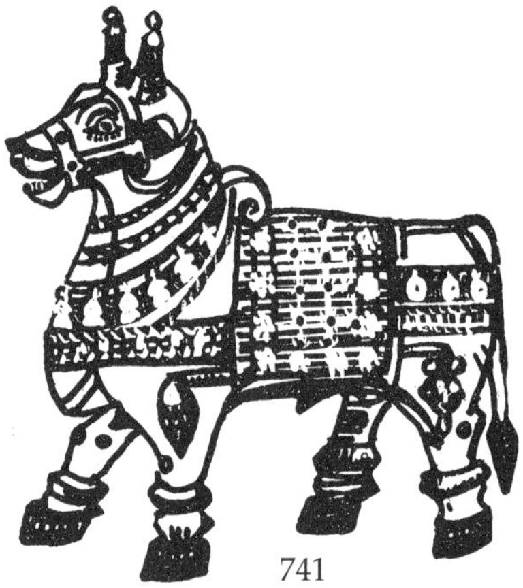
741

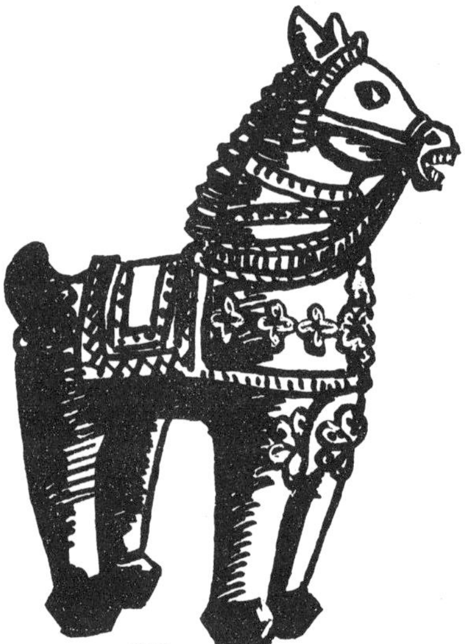
742

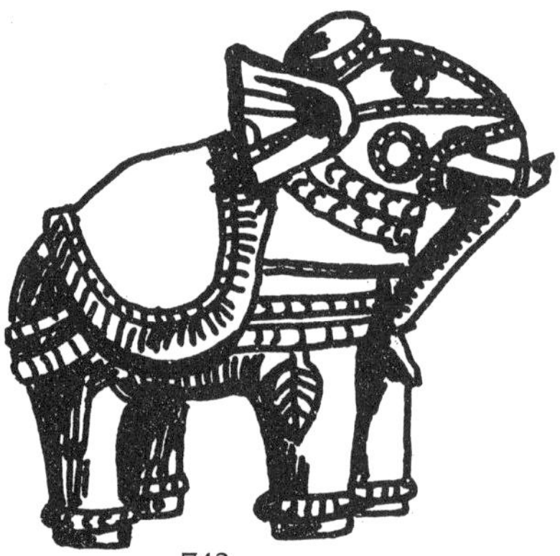
743

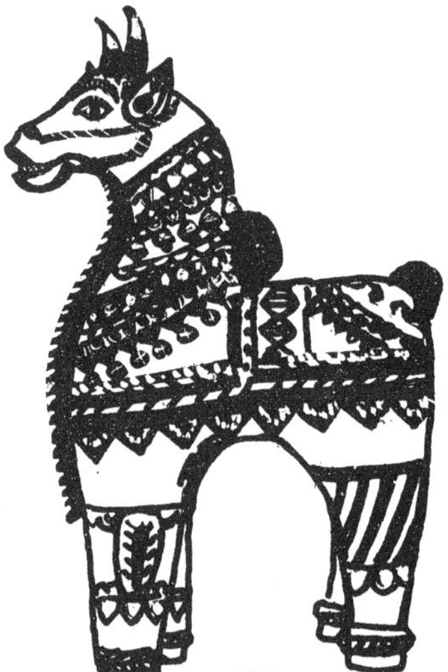
744

Toys, Dolls and Decorative Pieces—Clay. **736–738.** Painted clay folk horses from Orissa. **739, 740.** Ornamental clay birds hand painted from Uttar Pradesh. **741, 744.** Large ornamental hand-painted clay cows seen frequently in rural settings, traditionally South India. **742–743.** Folk style unpainted red clay horse and elephant from Mysore State.

# Plate 89

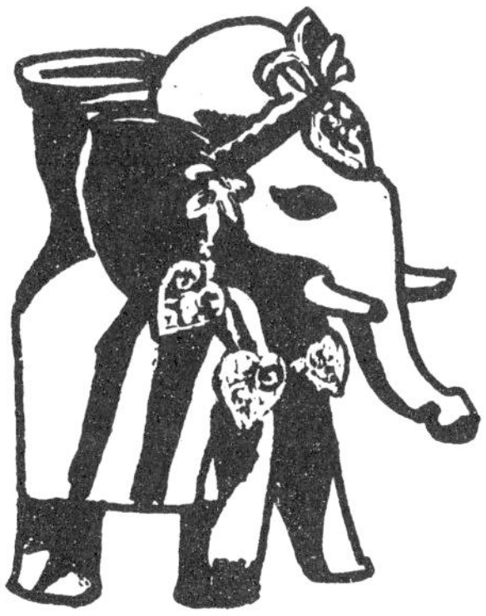
745

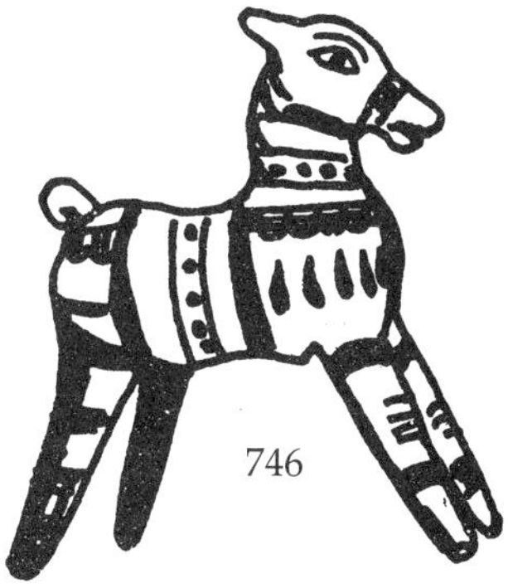
746

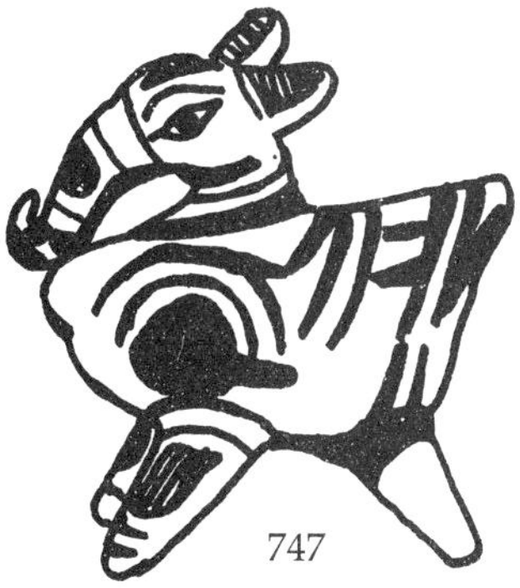
747

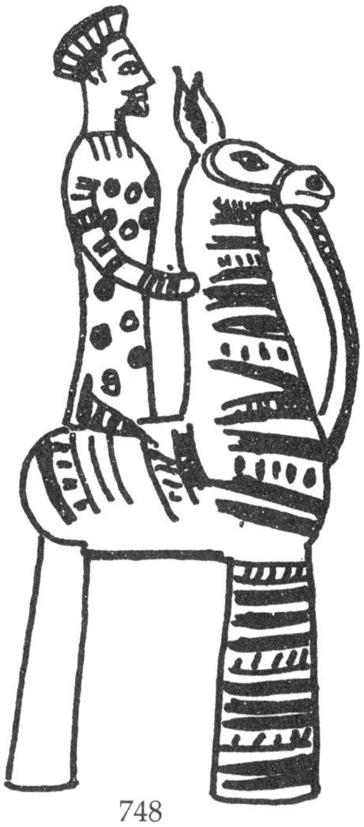
748

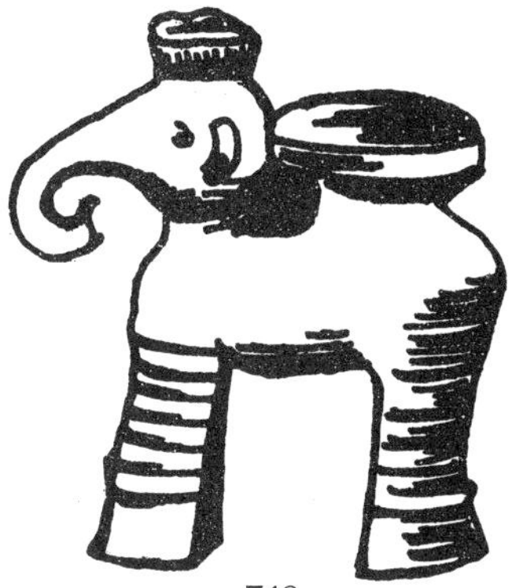
749

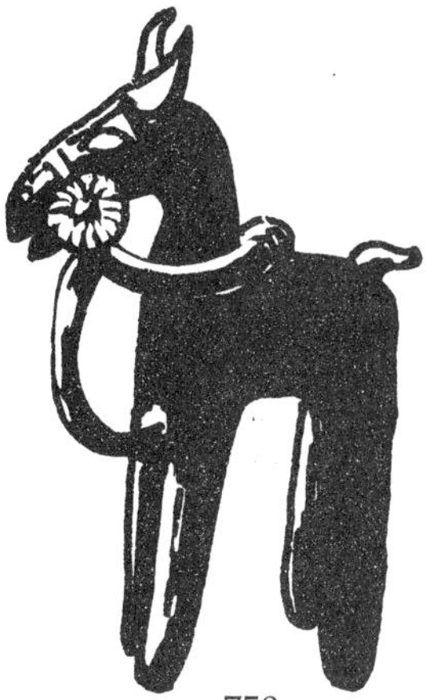
750

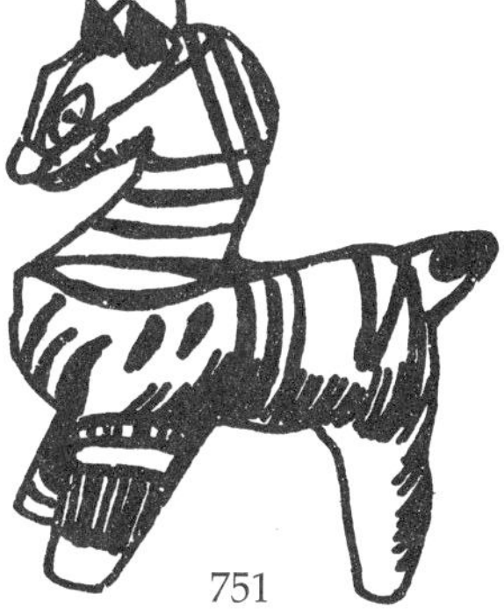
751

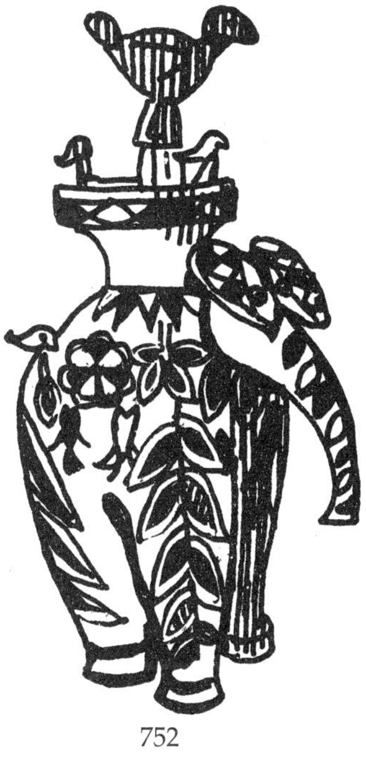
752

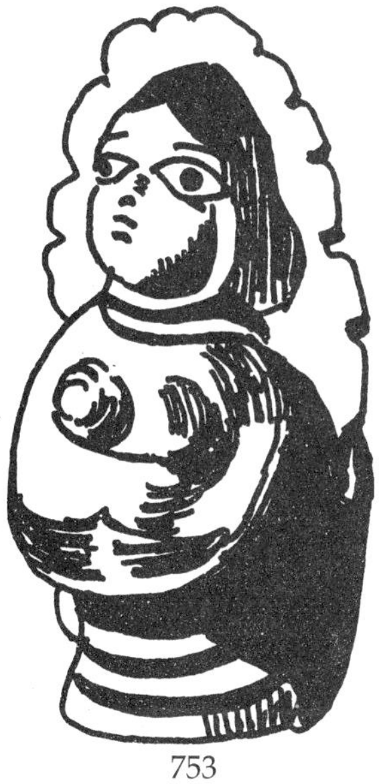
753

Toys, Dolls and Decorative Pieces—Clay. **745–753.** Hand-painted clay folk toys of Bihar, comprising elephants, horses and human figures.

# Plate 90

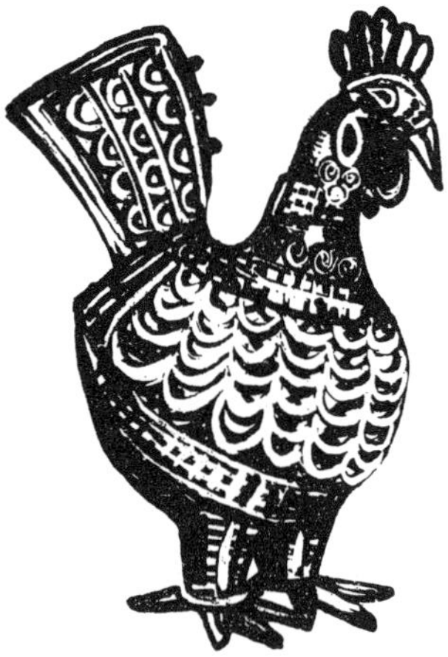

754

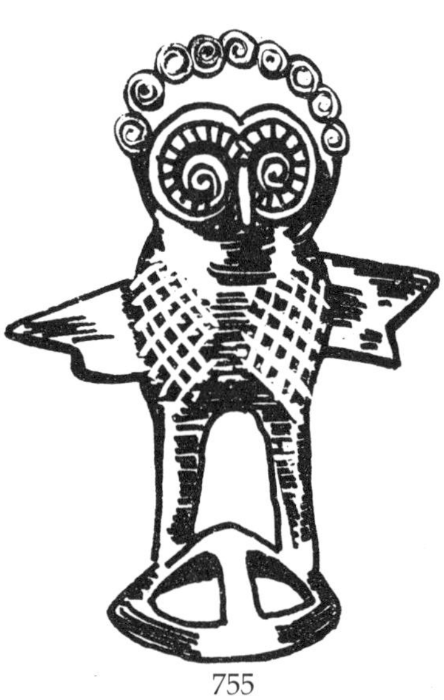

755

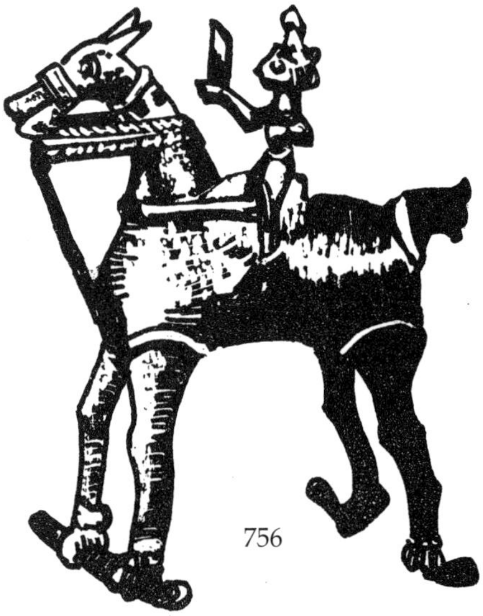

756

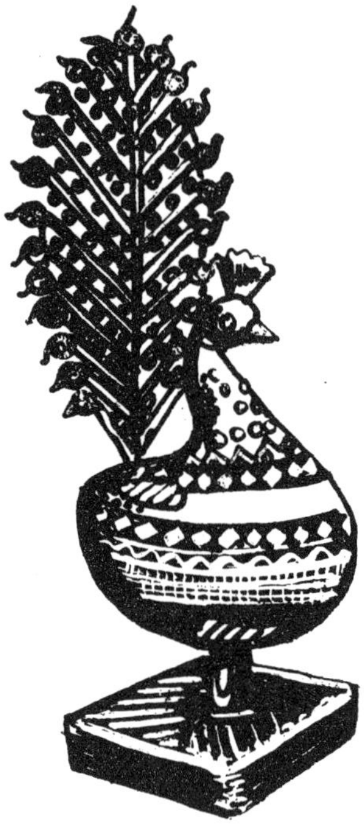

757

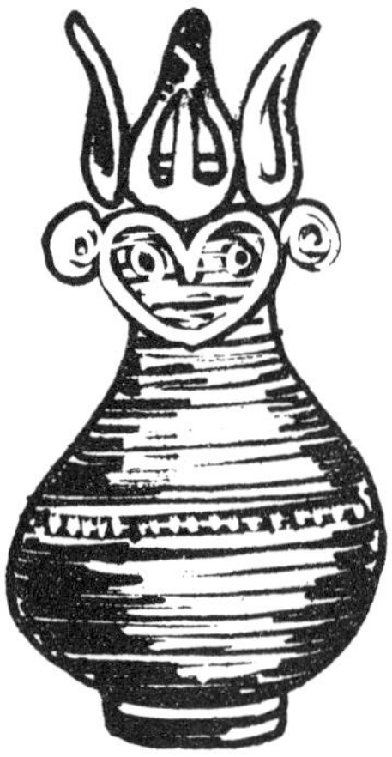

758

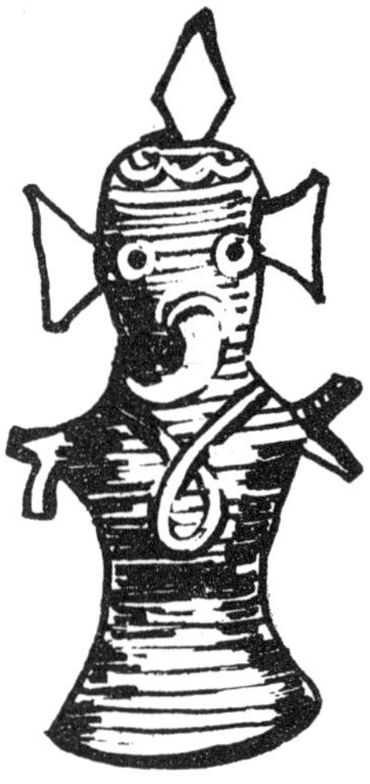

759

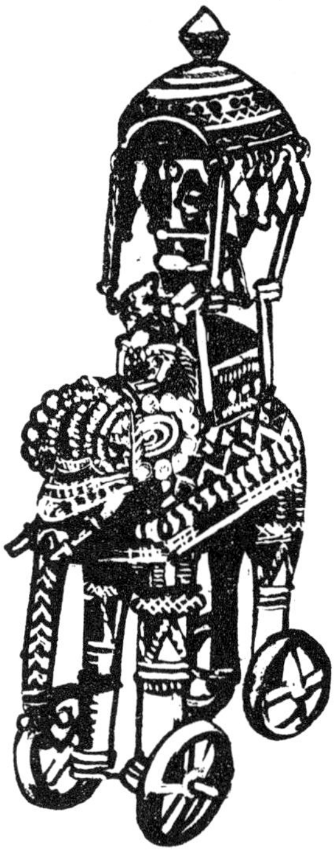

760

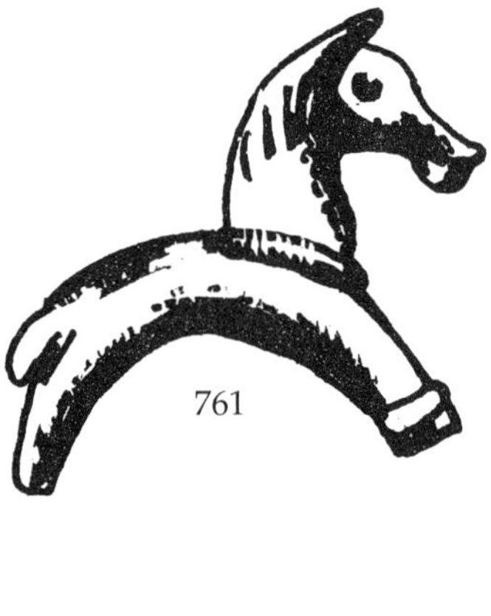

761

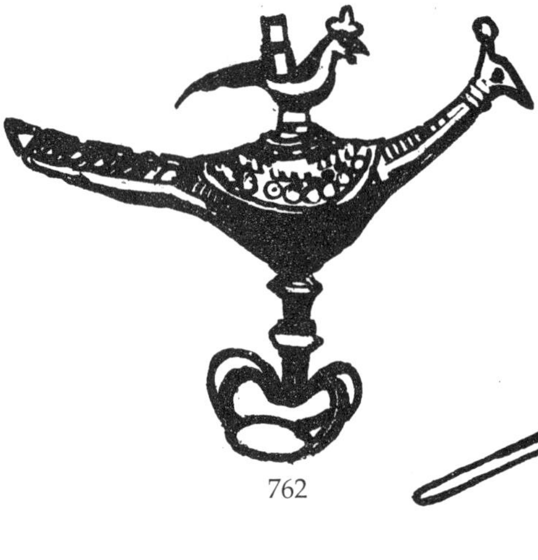

762

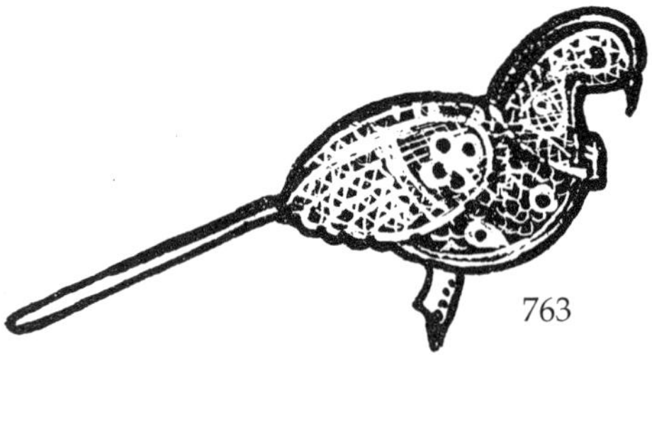

763

TOYS, DOLLS AND DECORATIVE PIECES—METAL. **754, 755.** Dokhra metal, tribal ornamental hen and owl, West Bengal. **756–759, 761, 762.** Dokhra metal, tribal ornamental stylized peacock, elephants, birds and horse from Bihar. **760.** Ornamental Dokhra metal, tribal decorative piece of an elephant with rider; Madhya Pradesh. **763.** Ornamental bird in silver, Andhra Pradesh.

# Plate 91

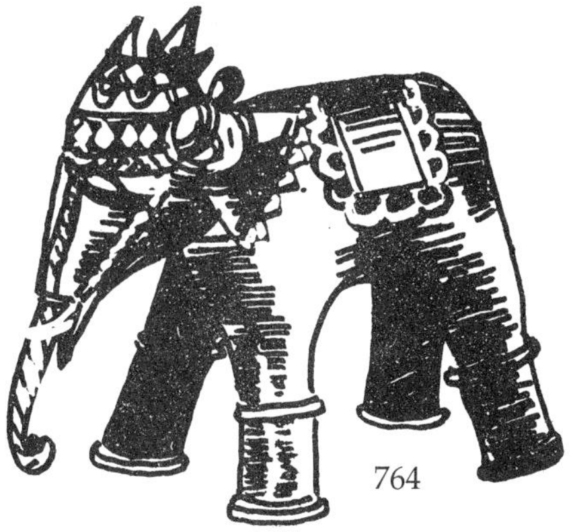

764

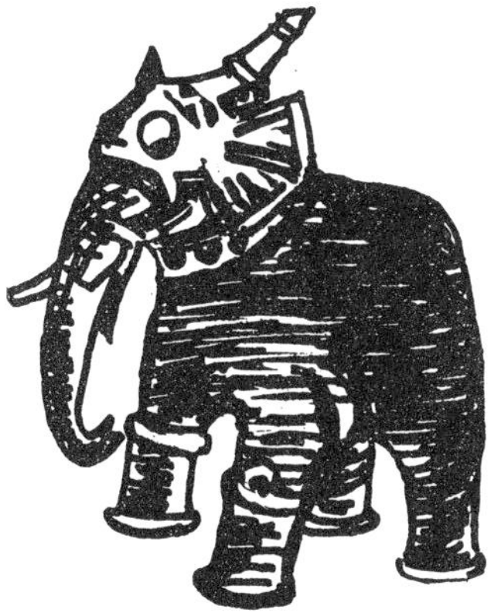

765

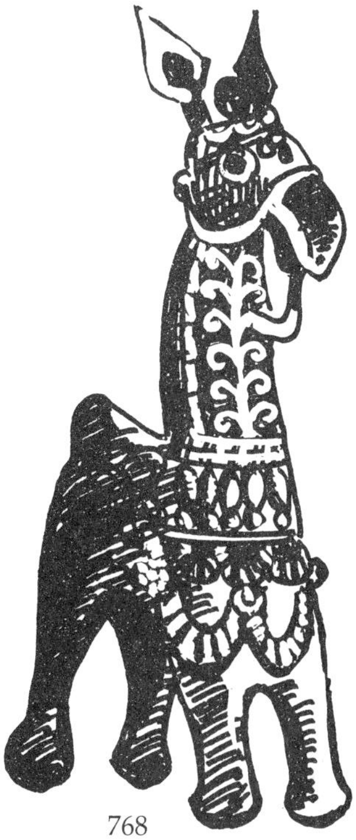

768

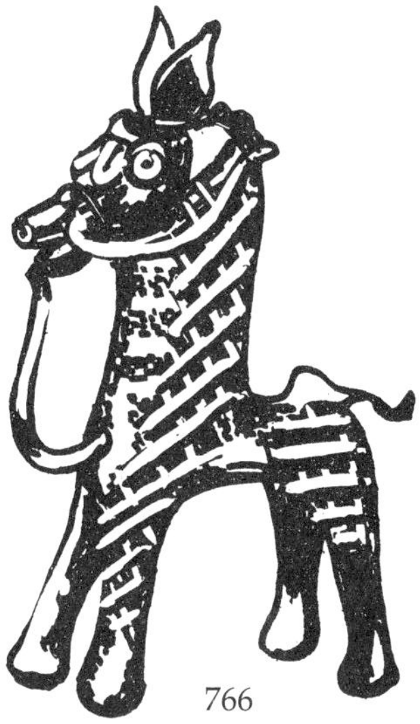

766

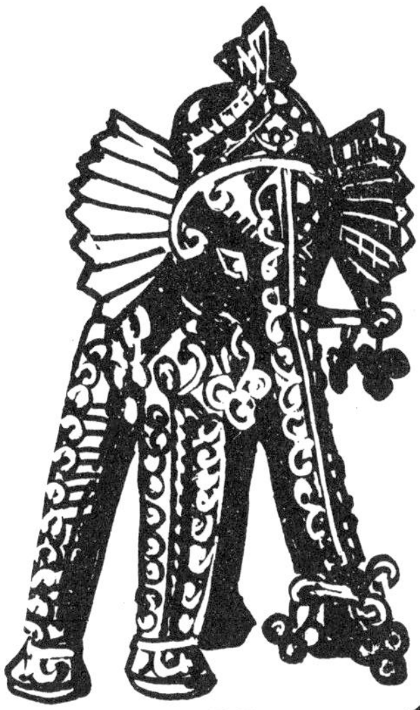

767

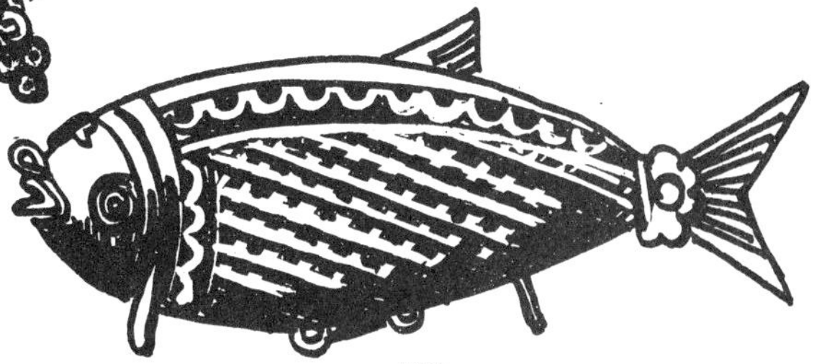

769

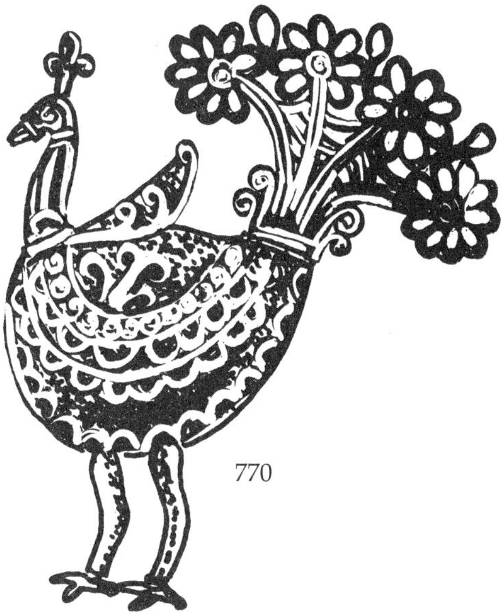

770

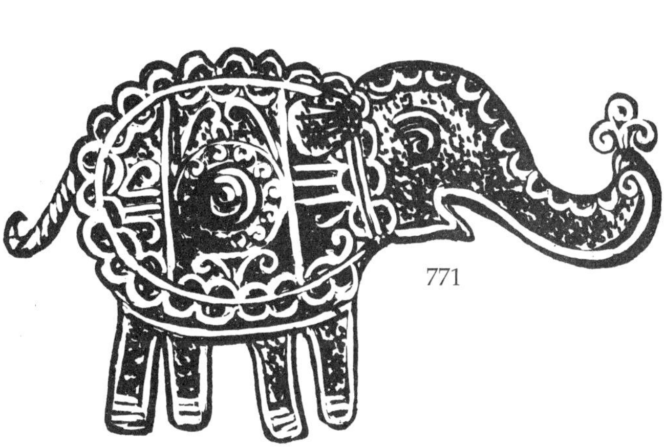

771

TOYS, DOLLS AND DECORATIVE PIECES—METAL. **764, 765.** Dokhra metal, tribal ornamental elephants, Orissa. **766–771.** Dokhra metal, tribal decorative elephants, horses, fish and peacock, West Bengal.

# Plate 92

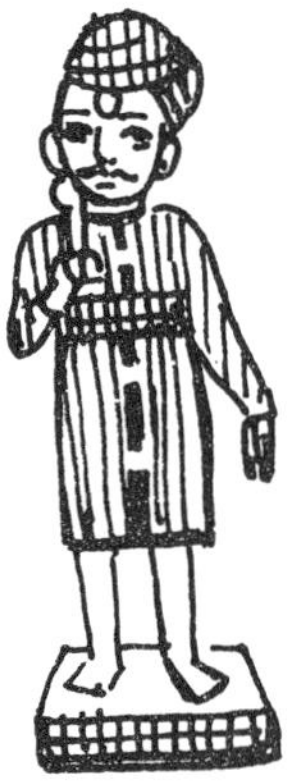
772

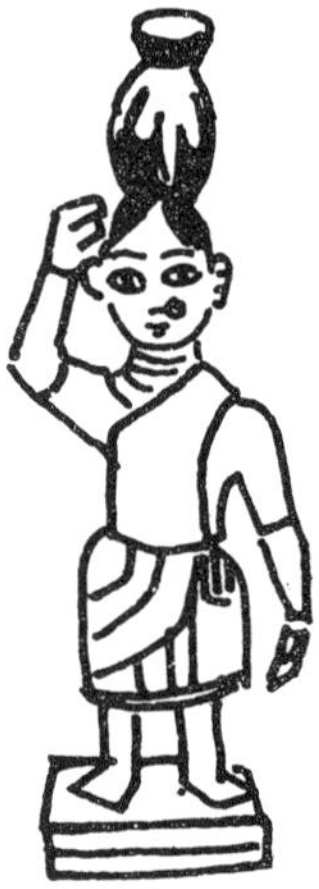
773

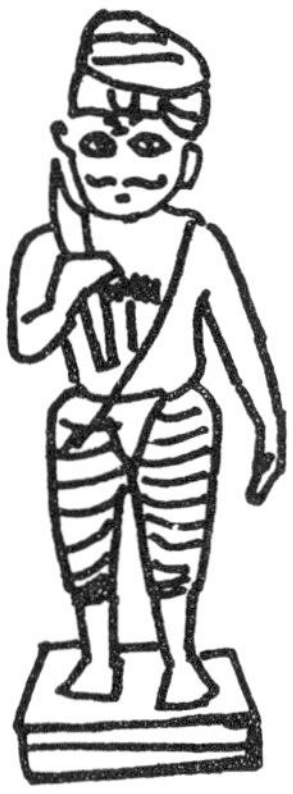
774

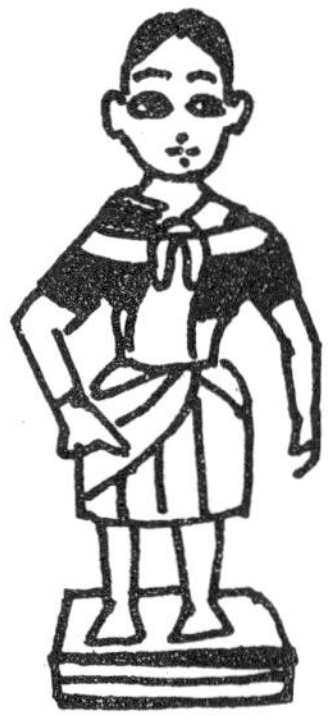
775

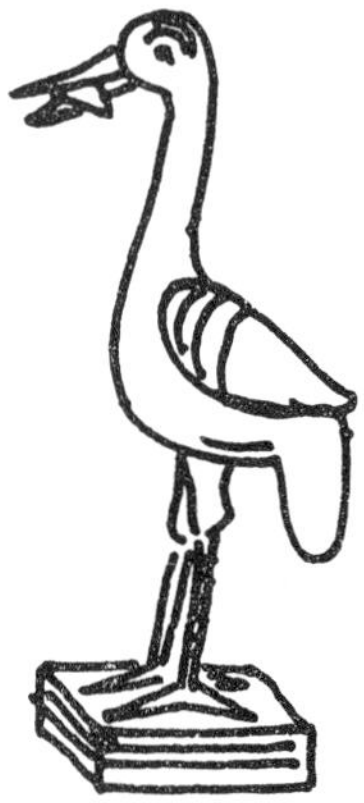
776

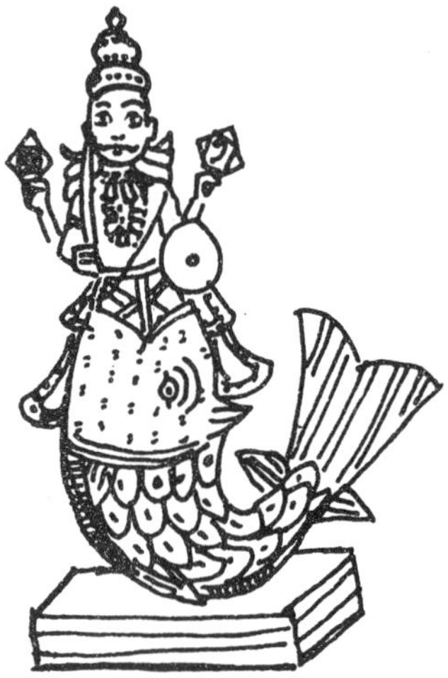
777

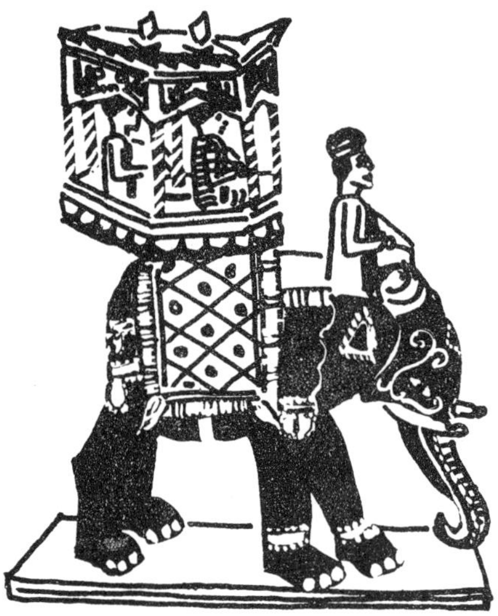
778

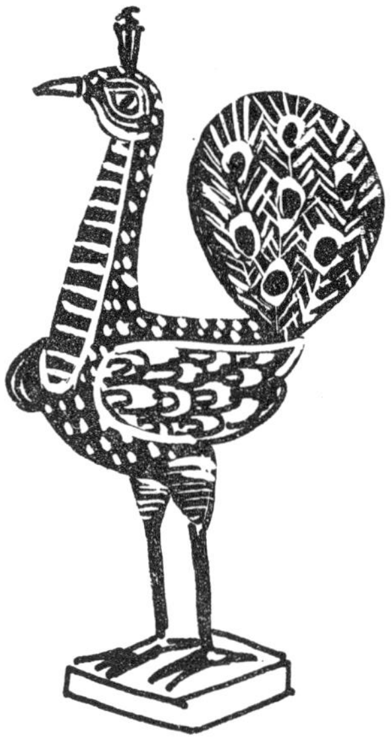
779

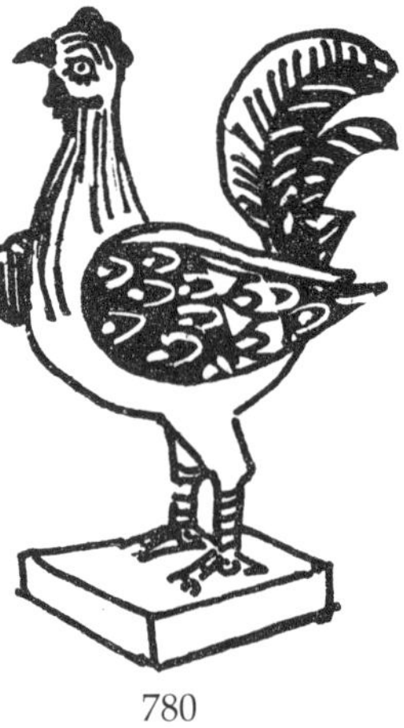
780

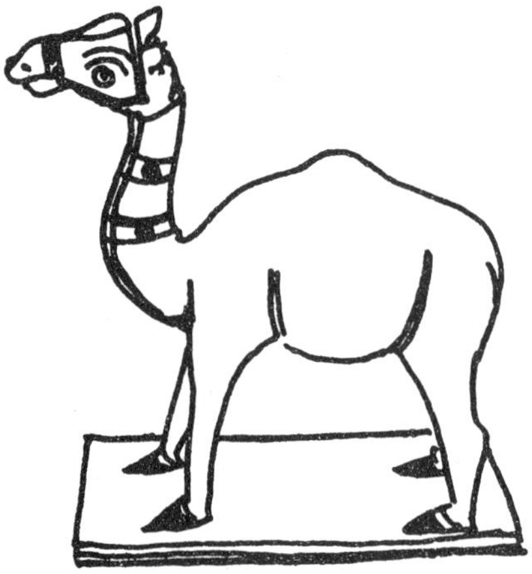
781

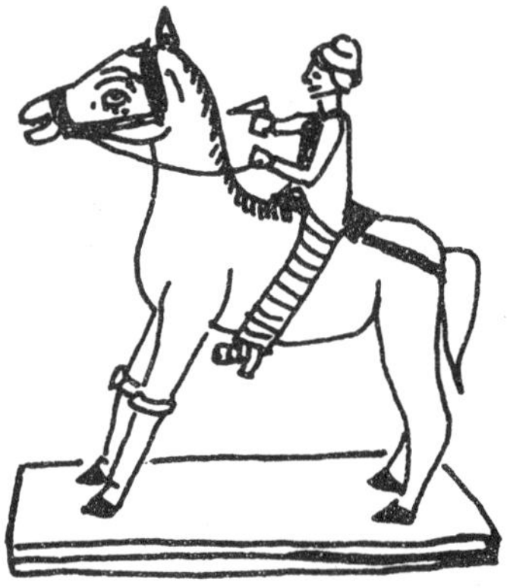
782

Toys, Dolls and Decorative Pieces—Wood. **772–782.** Decorative lacquered toys of Kondapalli, Andhra Pradesh, comprising village people, fish, elephant with rider and howdah, peacock, cock, camel and horse with rider.

Plate 93

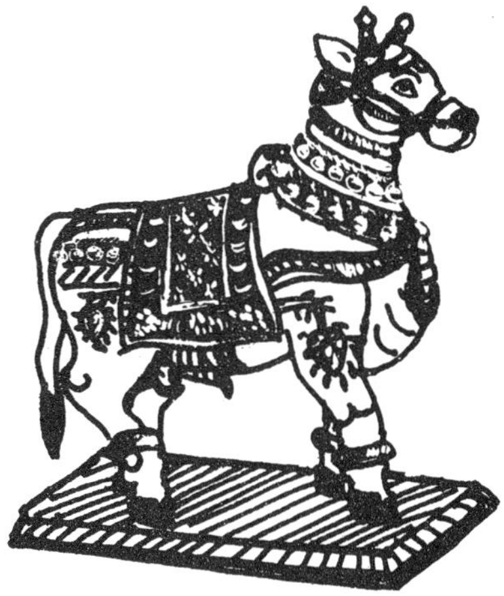

783

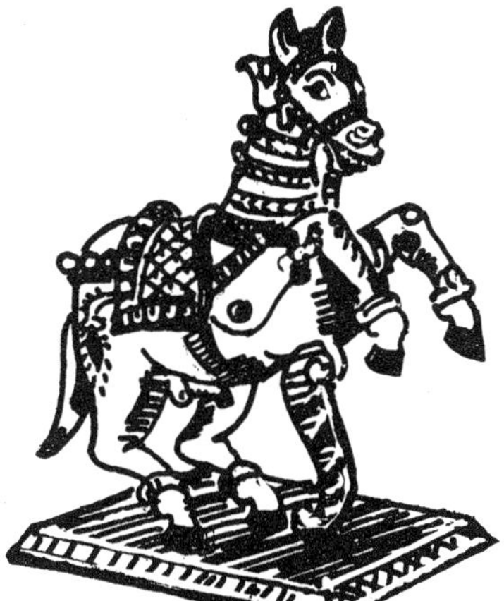

784

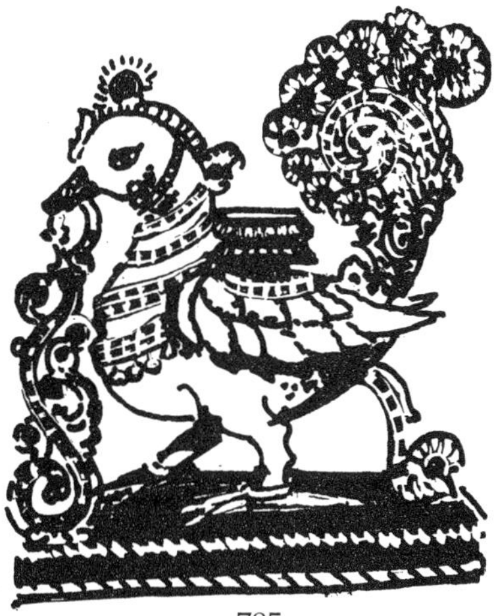

785

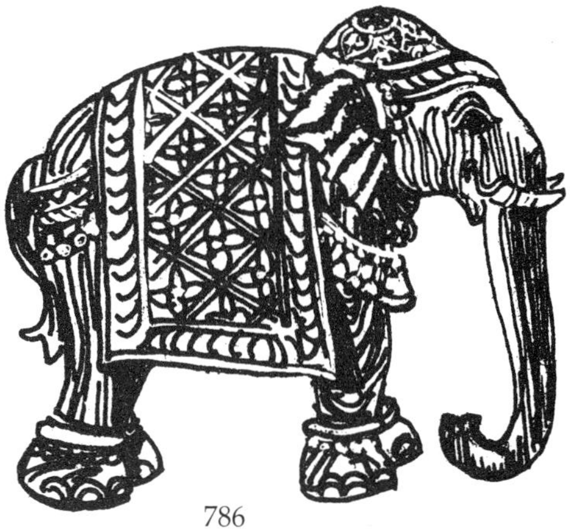

786

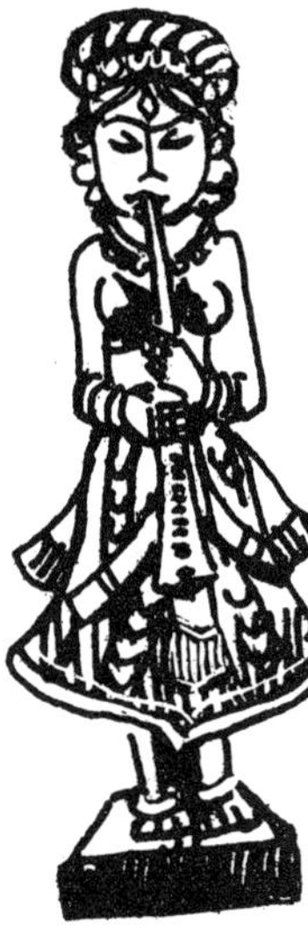

787

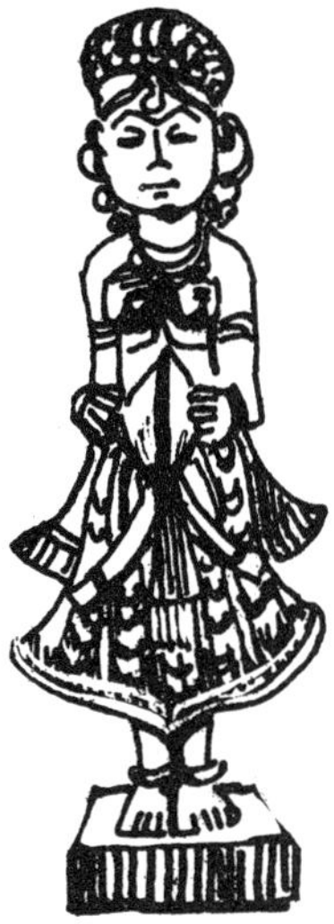

788

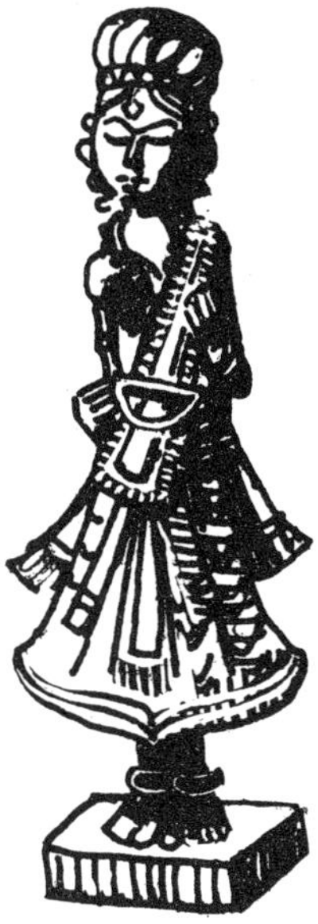

789

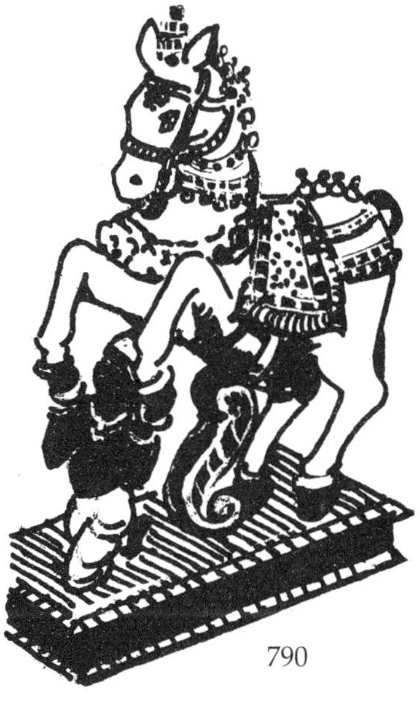

790

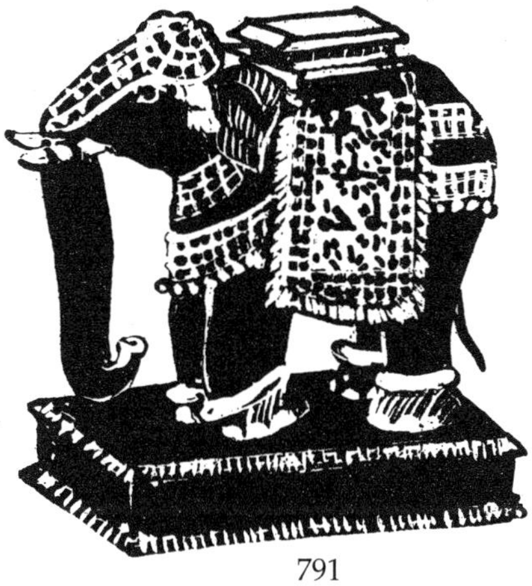

791

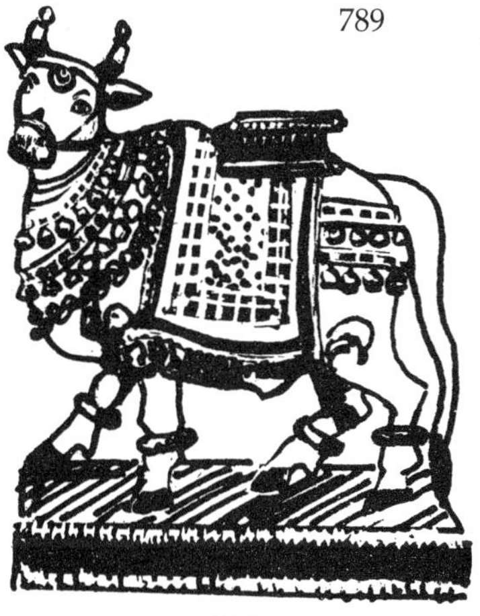

792

TOYS, DOLLS AND DECORATIVE PIECES—WOOD. **783–785, 790–792.** Decorative Tanjore wood work with glass inlay, comprising cow, horses (Aswavahana), swan (Hamsavahana), elephant (Gajavahana) and bull (Rushavahana), Madras State. **786.** Decorative elephant carved from rosewood, Bangalore, Mysore State. **787–789.** Wooden figurines from old Saurashtra carvings representing flutist, cymbal player and instrumentalist, Bombay, Maharashtra.

# Plate 94

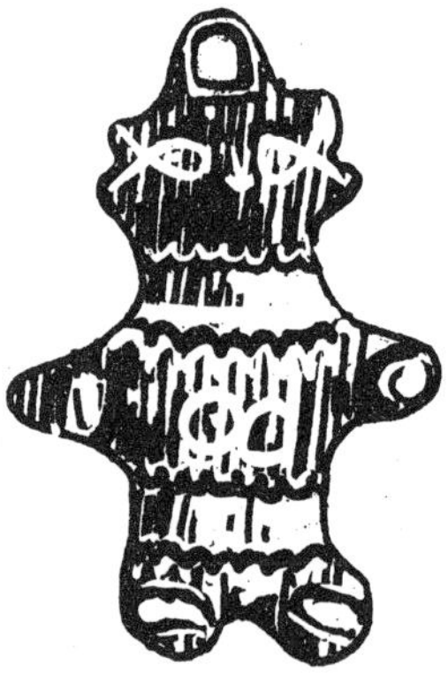
793

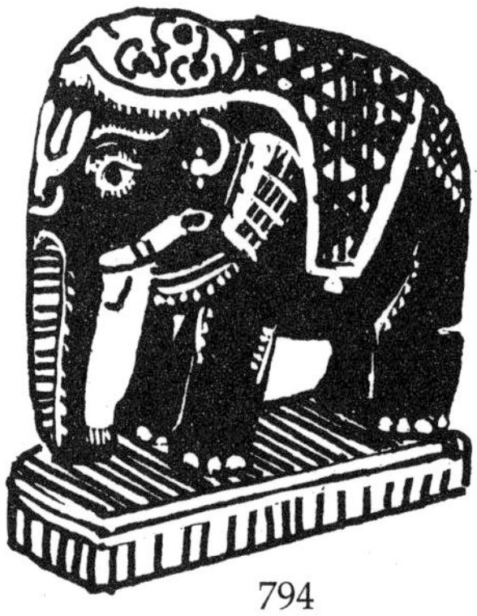
794

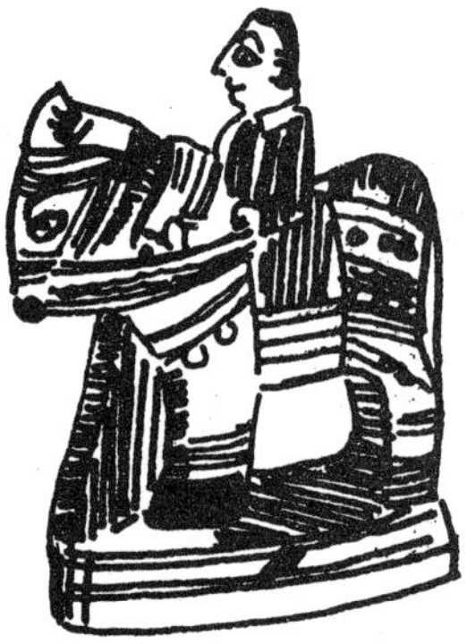
795

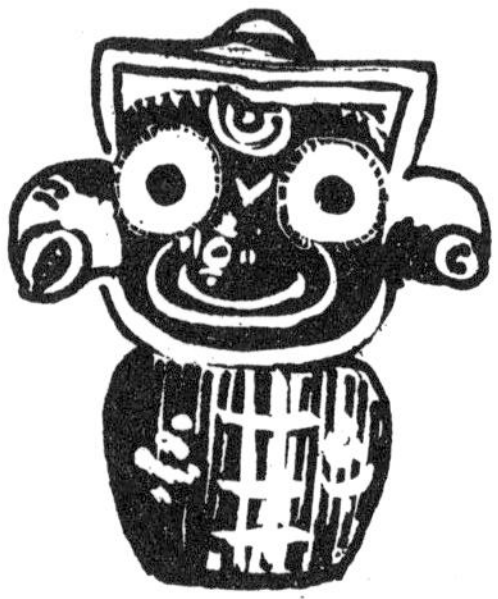
796

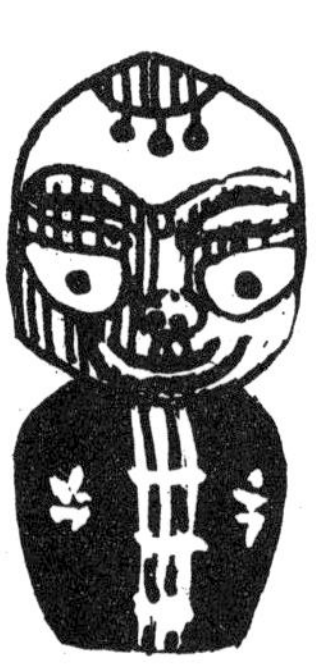
797

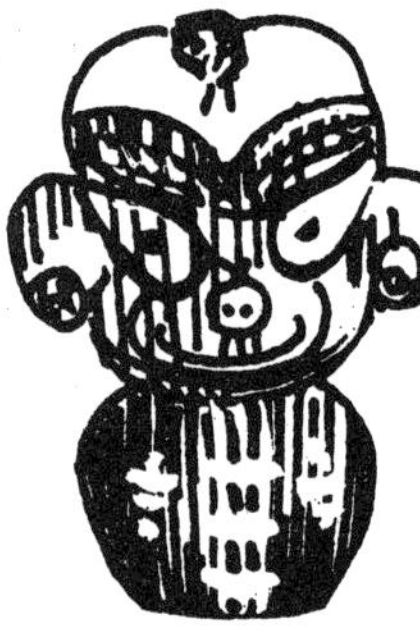
798

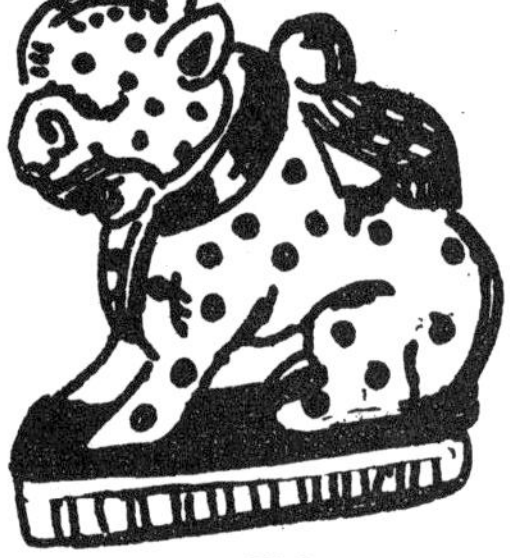
799

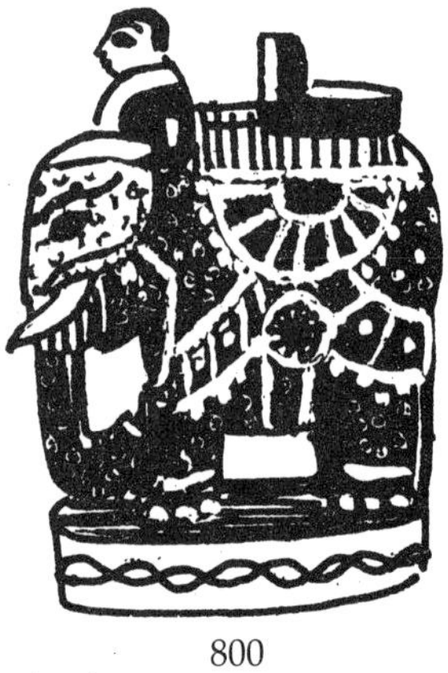
800

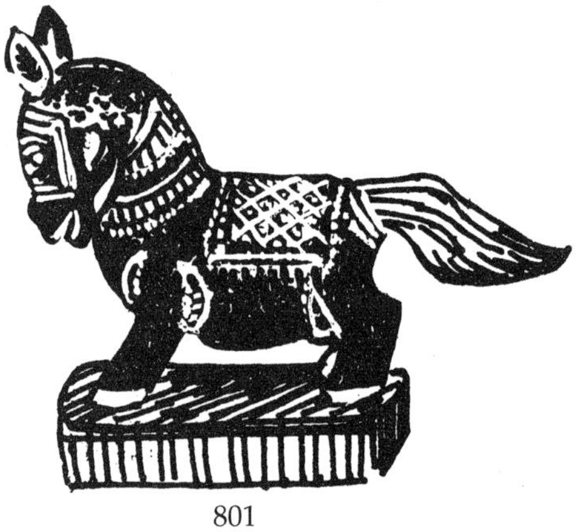
801

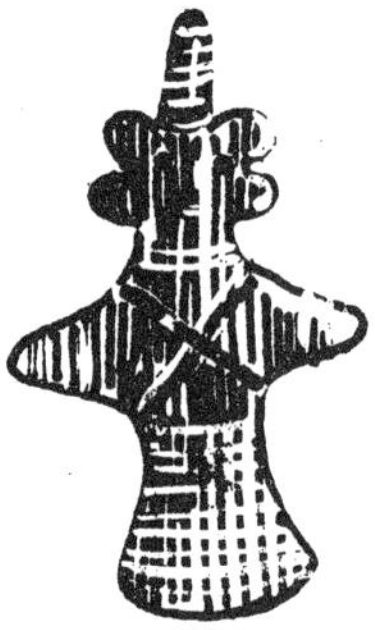
802

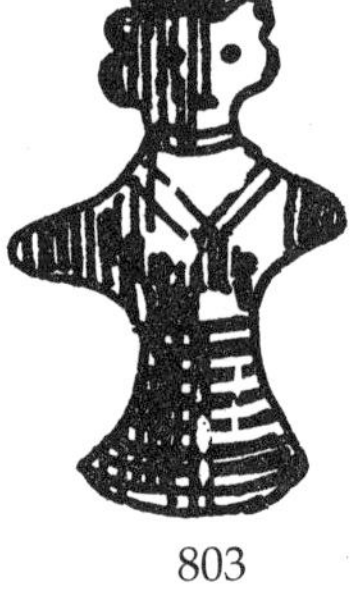
803

Toys, Dolls and Decorative Pieces—Wood. **793–803.** Decorative painted wooden dolls, elephants, horses and votive figures from Orissa. (**796, 797, 798** are the Jagannath Set, Bara Thakur, Subudra and Jagannath respectively).

# Plate 95

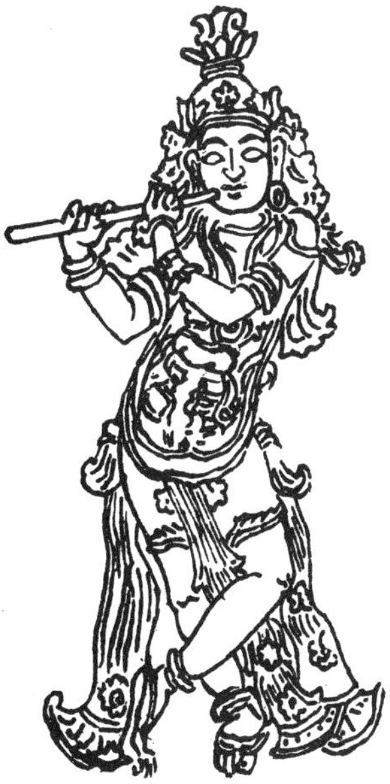
804

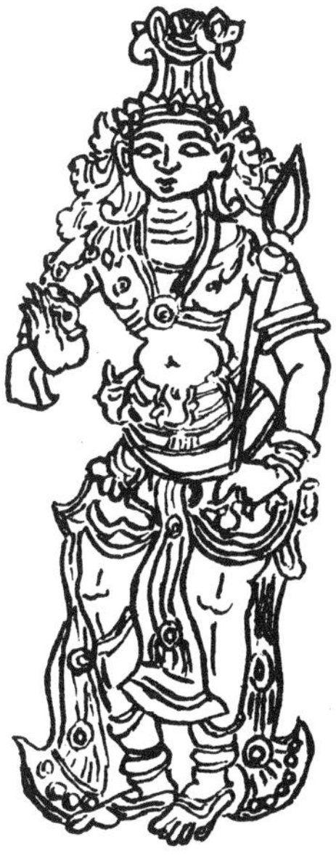
805

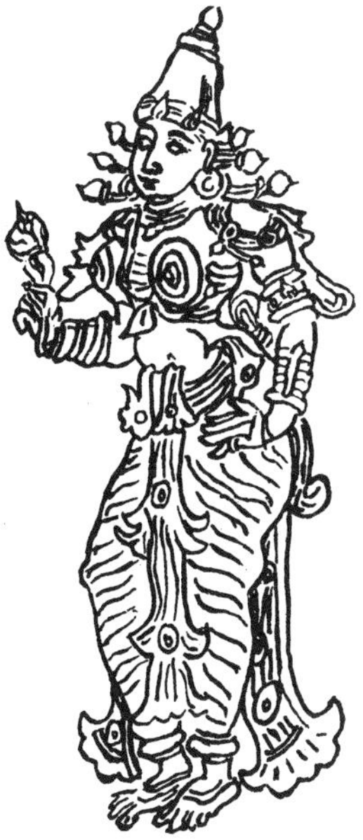
806

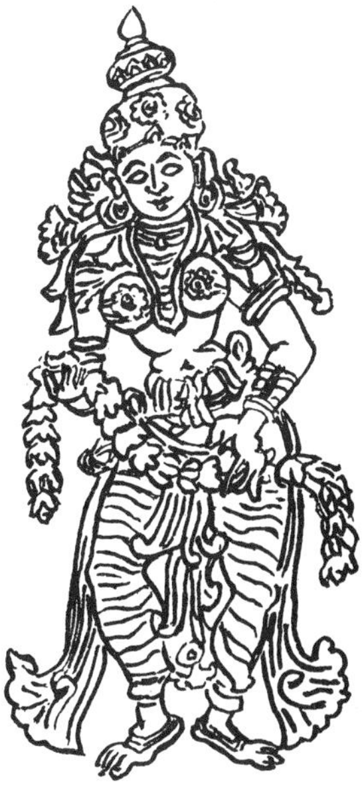
807

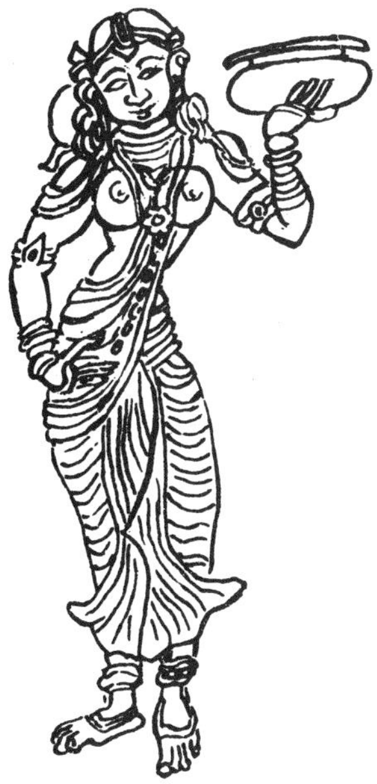
808

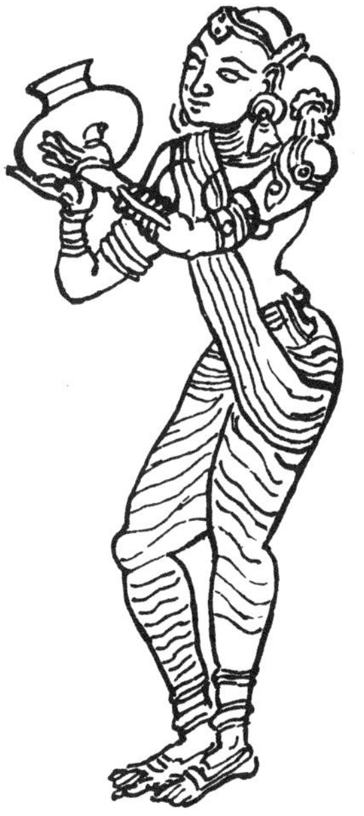
809

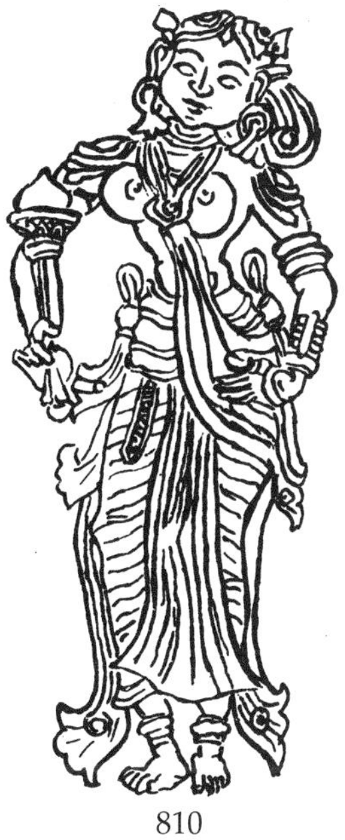
810

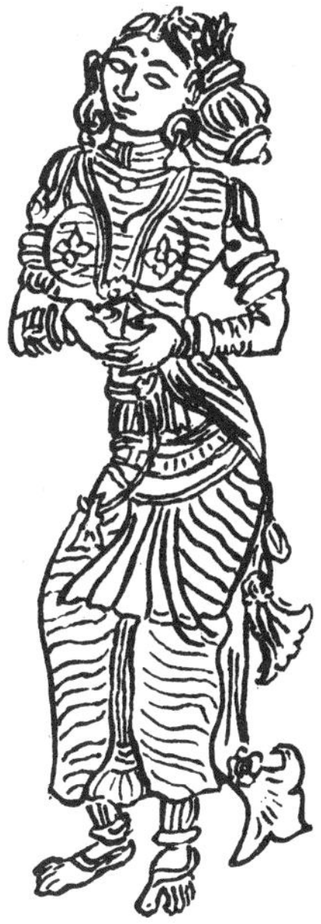
811

JEWELRY AND ORNAMENT. **804–807.** Drawings from sculptures in the Padmanabhaswamy temple, Trivandrum, Kerala, 10th century A.D., showing Shri Krishna, Vishnu and other deities with their special crowns and ornaments. **808–811.** Drawings from sculptures in the Padmanabhaswamy temple, Trivandrum, Kerala, 10th century A.D., showing various hairstyles and ornaments for women.

# Plate 96

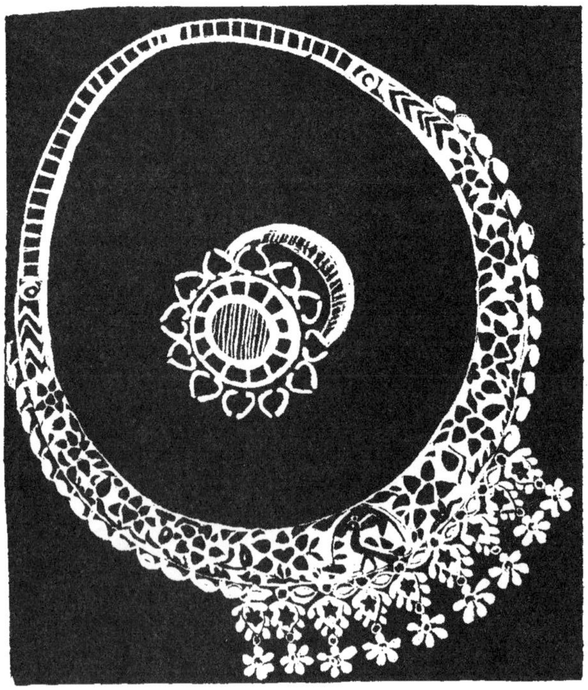

812 813

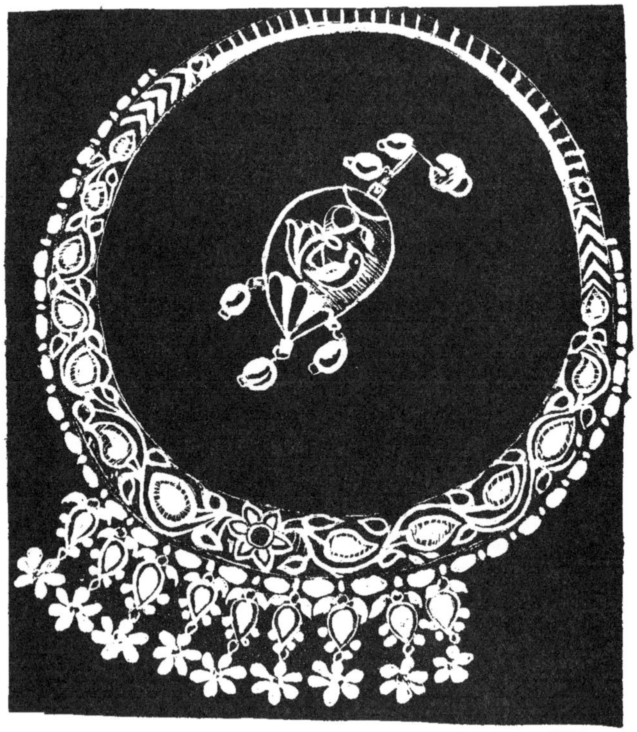

814 815

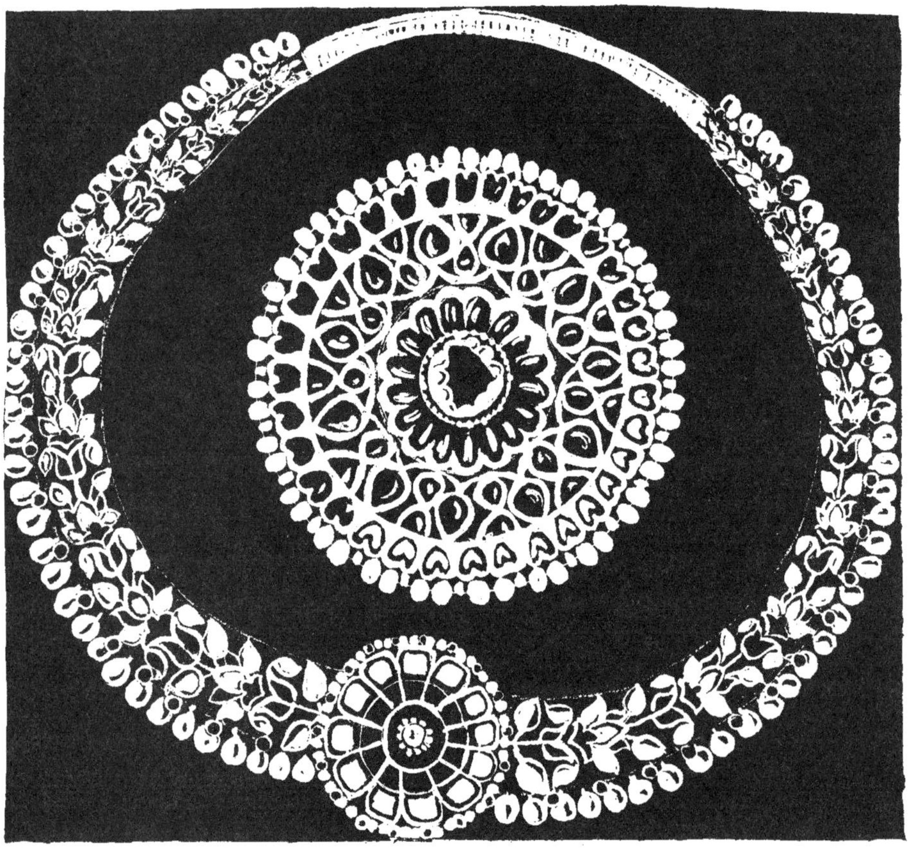

816 817

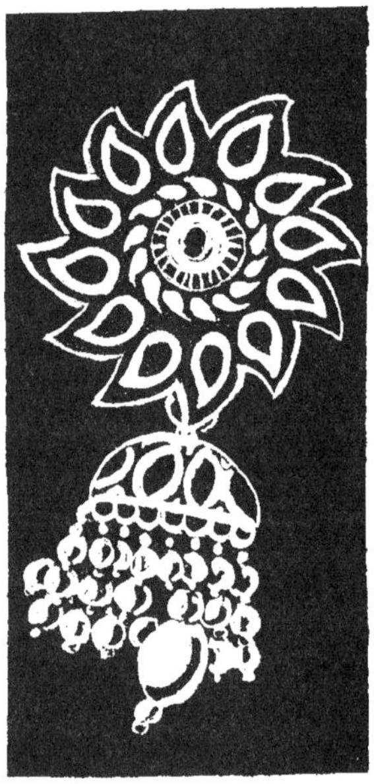

818

Jewelry and Ornament. **812, 814.** Two views of the traditional "Hasli" necklace in gold, enameled in motifs of jasmine flowers and leaves (left) and (right) set with precious stones in the shapes of jasmine flowers and buds on curving stems. **813.** A heavy jeweled gold ring, with enamel work behind the setting. **815.** An earring with enameled bird motif and pearl pendants. **816, 817.** Another traditional "Hasli" necklace studded with precious stones to form motifs of flowers and leaves. The reverse side is enameled with floral motifs. (Inset, **817**) a gem-studded, stylized lotus-shaped head ornament to match. **818.** A Jhumki (bell-shaped) earring with stylized star top set with precious stones in mango motif; the fringe and pendant consist of pearls.

# Plate 97

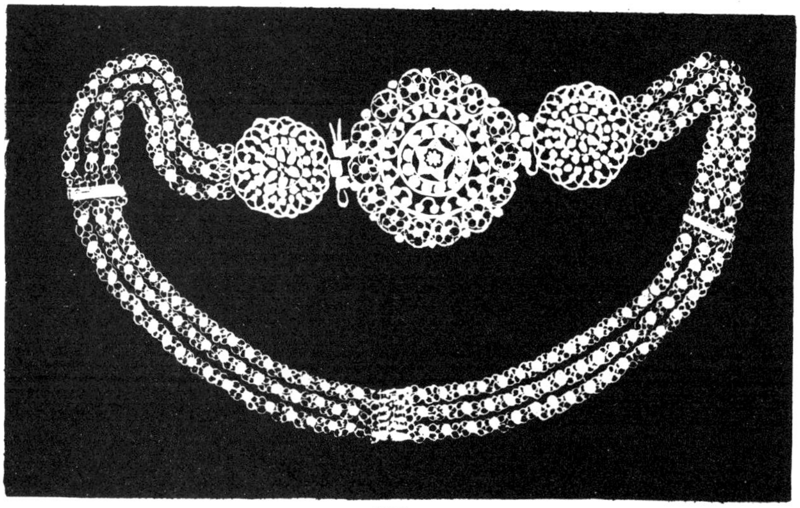

819

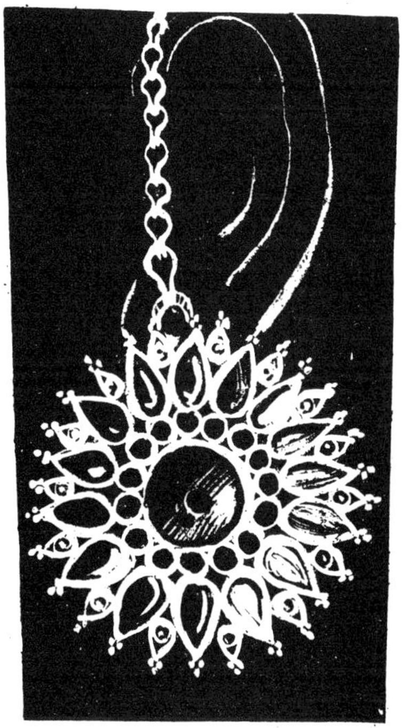

820

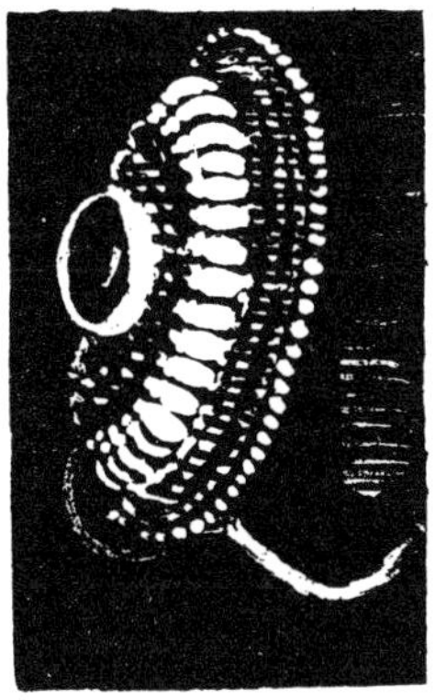

821

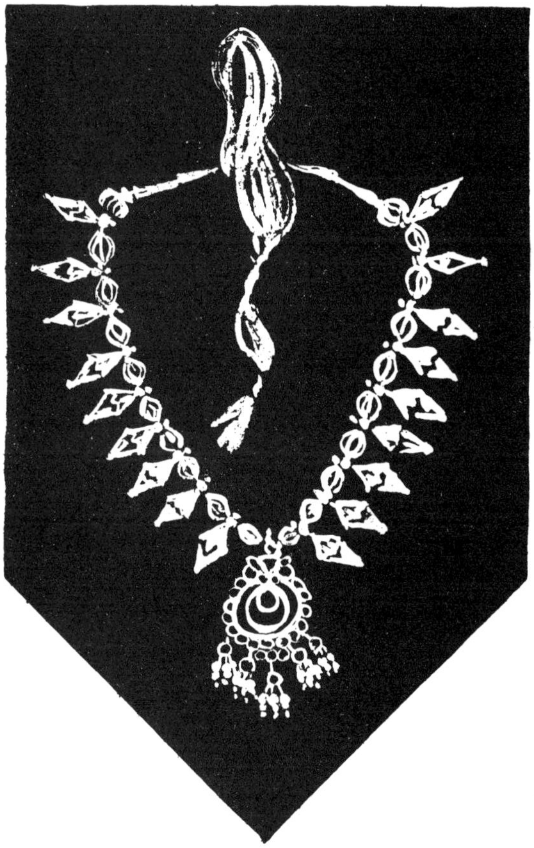

822

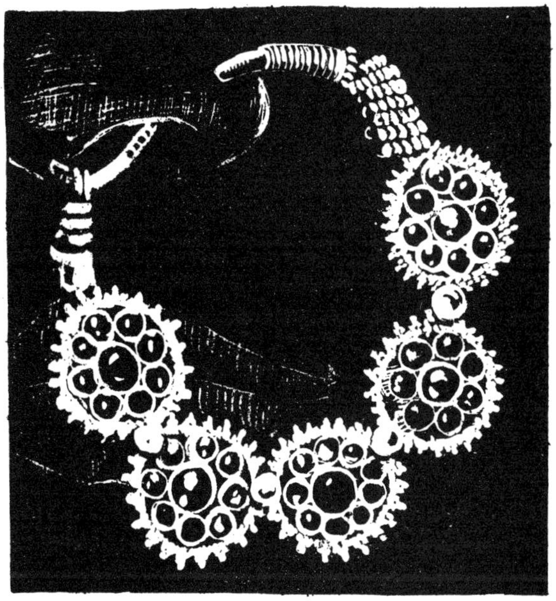

823

JEWELRY AND ORNAMENT. **819.** A filigree silver Sadhav flower-shaped waist belt (Kamarbandhi) with floral medallion clasp, worn by women in Bihar. **820.** Star-shaped earring set with colored stones from Kangra Valley (Himachal Pradesh). **821, 823.** Two sets of nose ornaments from Kulu Valley, Himachal Pradesh; the top one (**821**) called the Nat, worn on the right side of the nose, and the one below, a circlet of jeweled flowers is worn on the left side of the nose. **822.** The Champakali Har, a necklace with musk melon seeds and buds of silver strung together with a floral filigree pendant.

# Plate 98

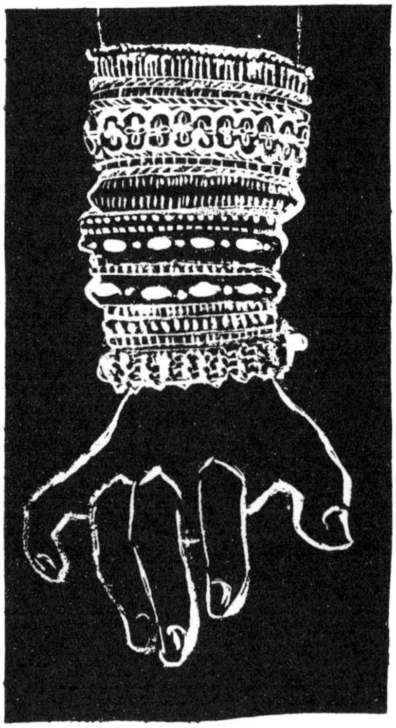

824

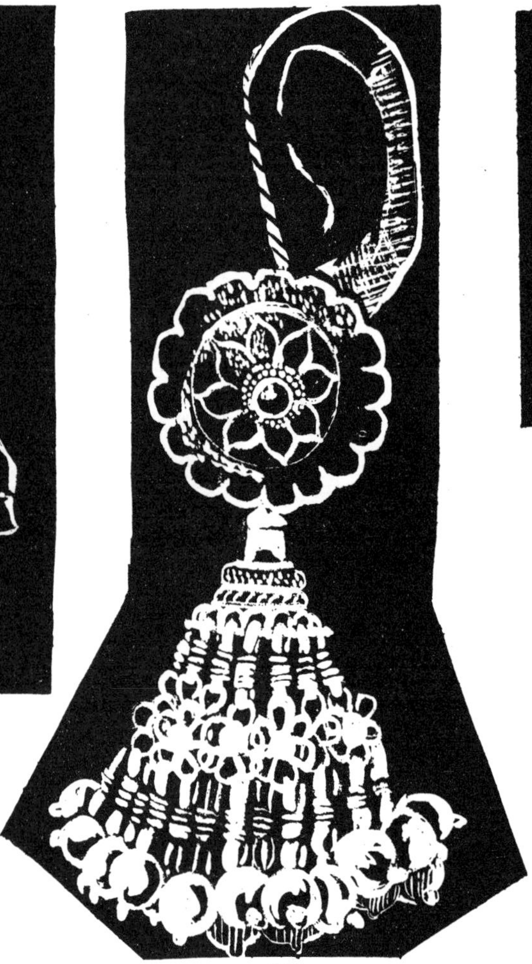

825

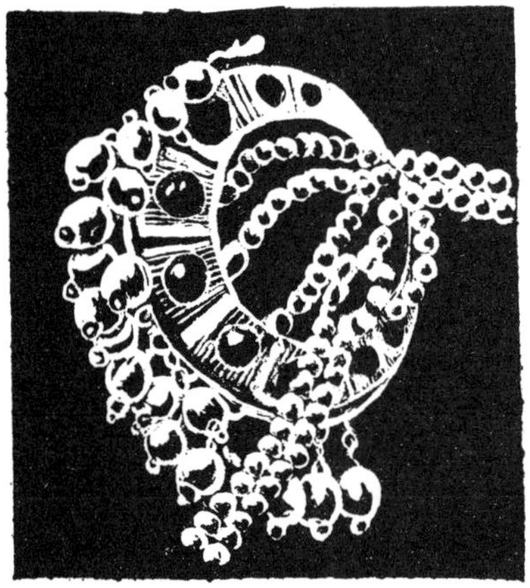

826

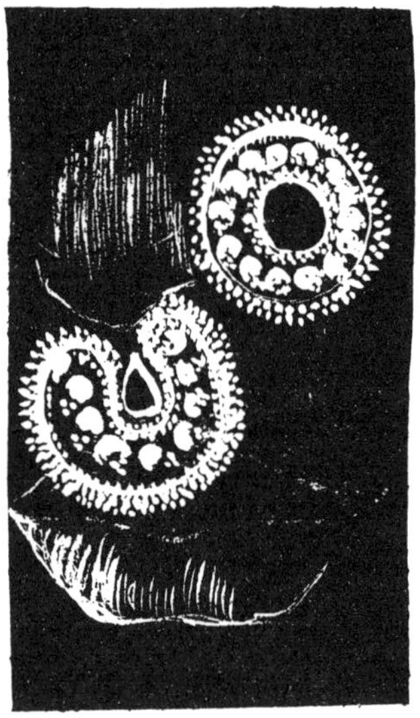

827

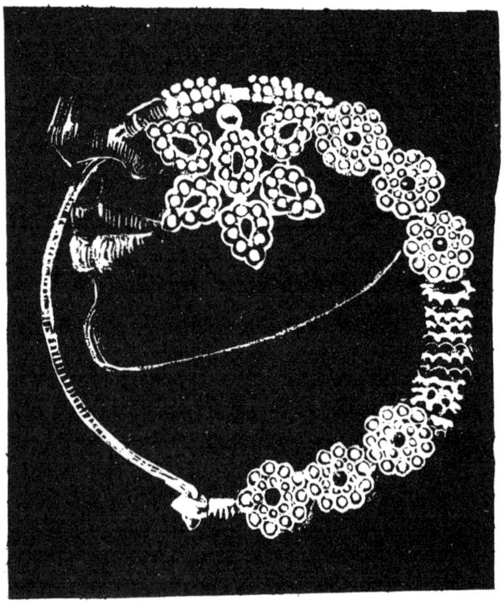

828

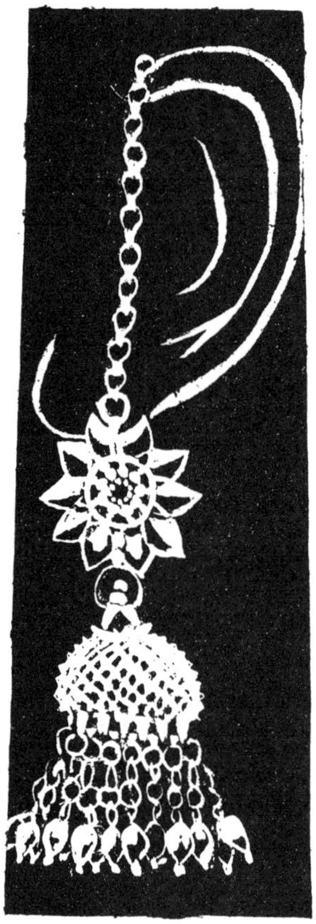

829

JEWELRY AND ORNAMENT. **824.** A variety of silver bracelets with floral and geometrical motifs worn by peasant women in the mountain areas of India. **825.** A silver earring with enameled lotus top and strands of silver decorated with flowers and buds from Kulu Valley, Himachal Pradesh. **826.** A stone-studded head jewel with bud pendants worn near the ear is attached by silver beads to **828,** the embossed flower and star nose jewel which hangs beside **829,** the star and tasseled earring with melon seed-shaped pendants, from Chamba, Himachal Pradesh. **827.** Two more nose ornaments worn by some women in the Kulu Valley, Himachal Pradesh.

# Plate 99

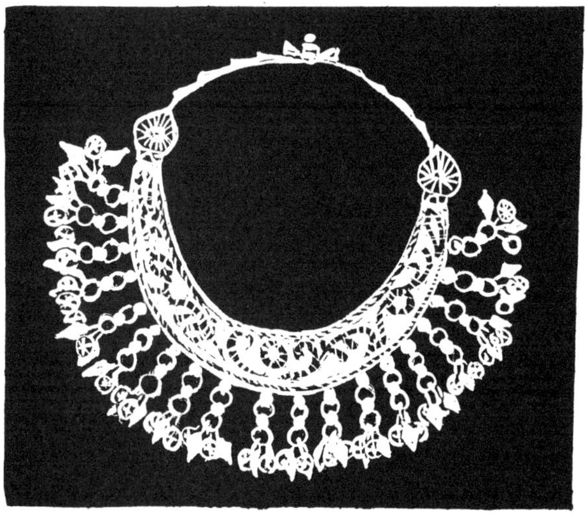

830

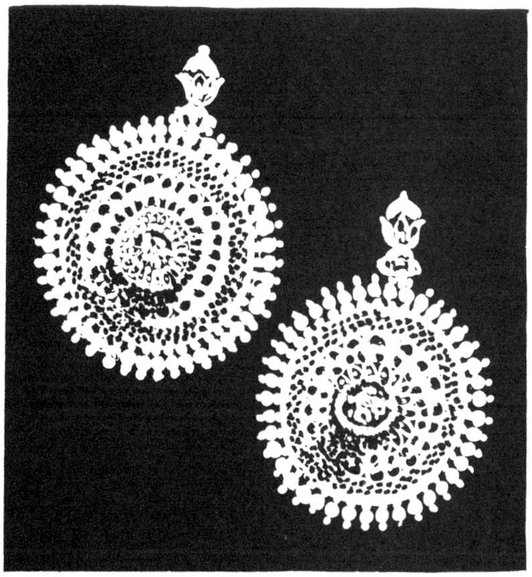

831

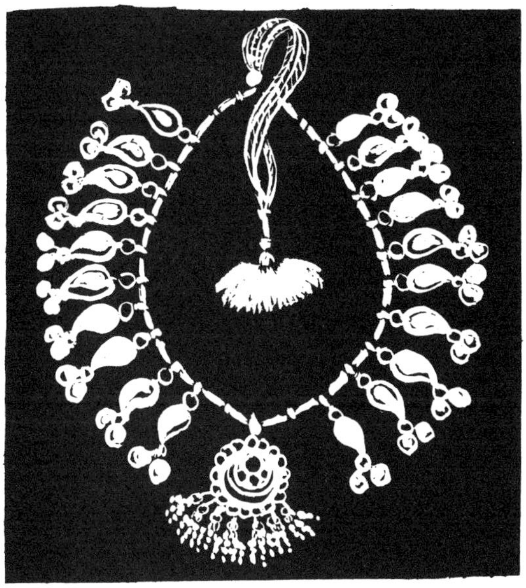

832

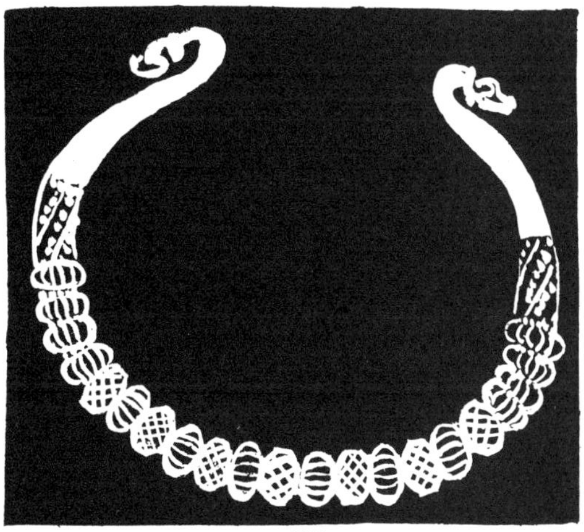

833

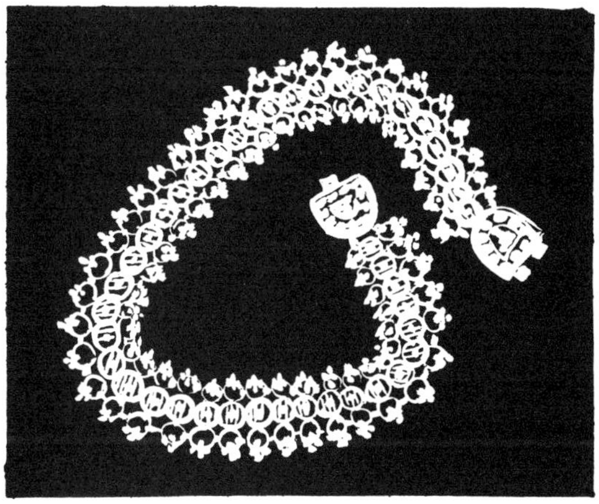

834

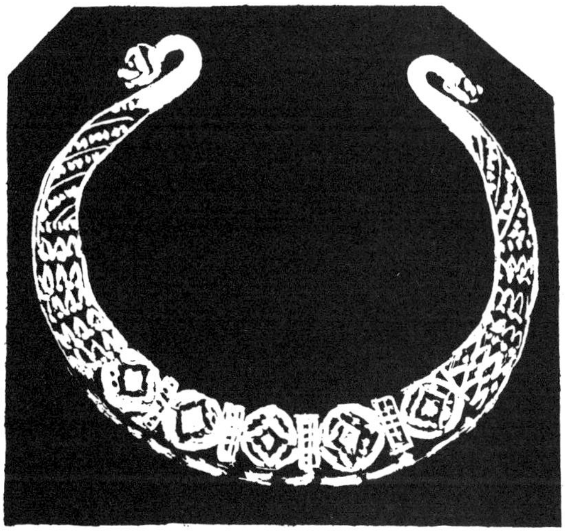

835

JEWELRY AND ORNAMENT. **830.** A Chamel Tauk, Jasmine flower silver necklace. **831.** Lotus type Tarki earrings in silver. **832.** Another Champakali Har silver contemporary design necklace with musk melon seed-shaped pendants and silver filigree pendant. **833, 835.** Two silver Kanthedar Hansuli silver chokers with stylized floral motifs. **834.** A waist belt (Kamarcandhi) in silver with flower motifs. All these jewels **830–835** are from Bihar.

# Plate 100

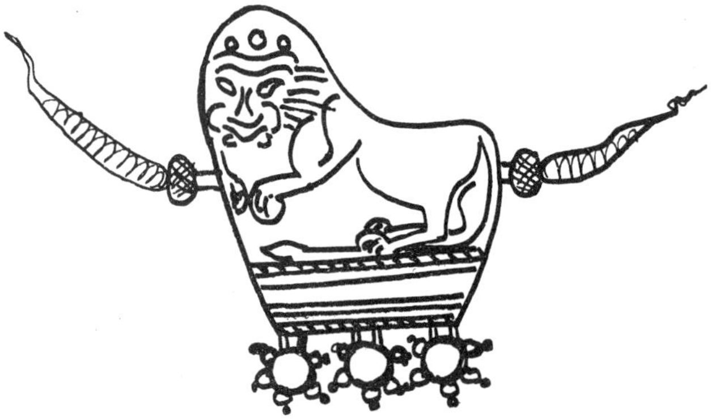
836

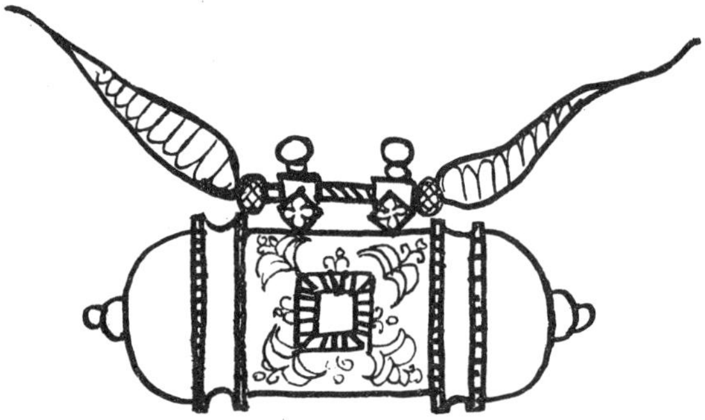
837

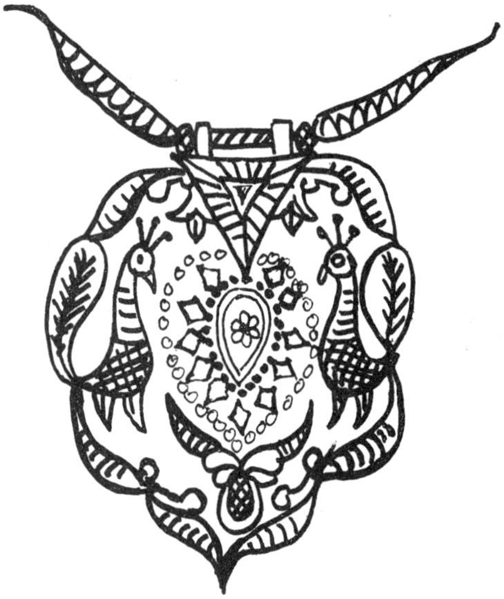
838

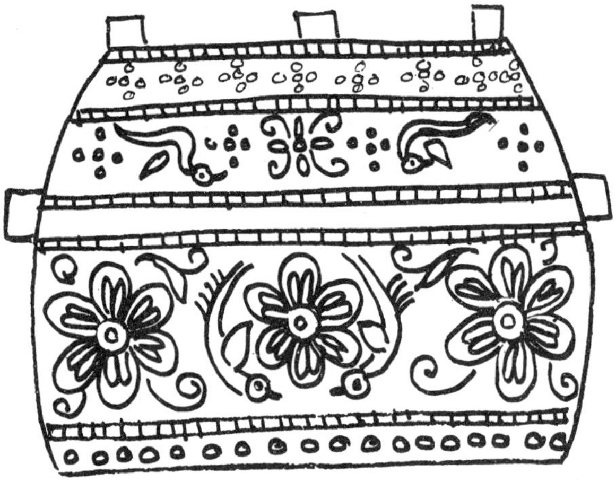
839

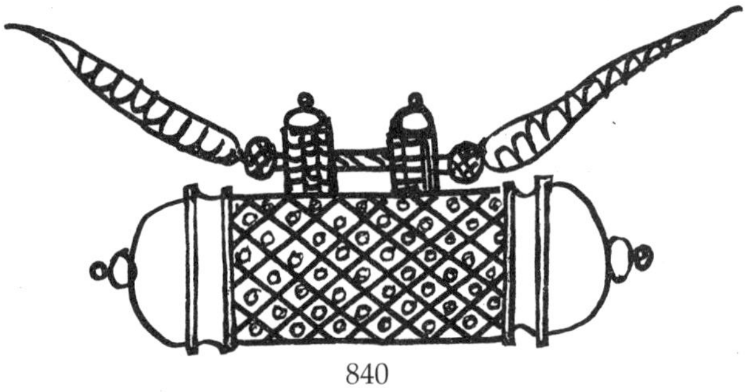
840

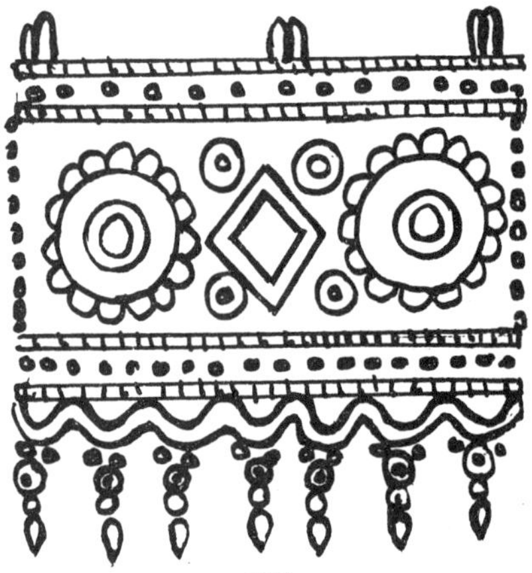
841

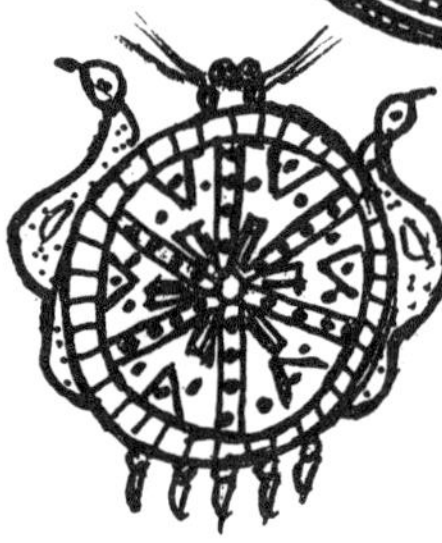
842

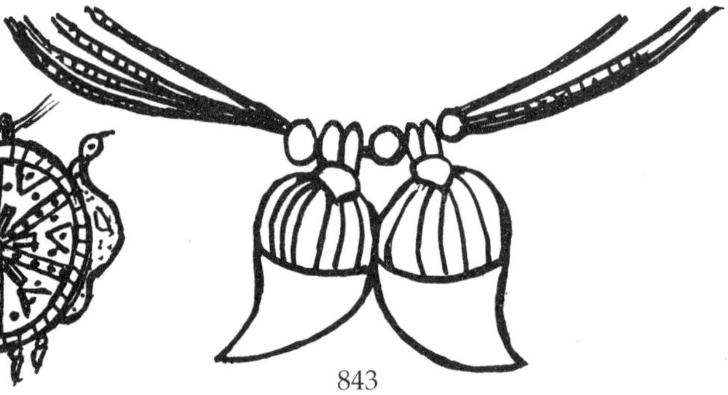
843

JEWELRY AND ORNAMENT. **836–843.** Different types of silver necklace pendants worn by the Bhil tribal women of Rajasthan, employing motifs of a lion, peacocks, birds, flowers, geometrical shapes and mangoes.

# Plate 101

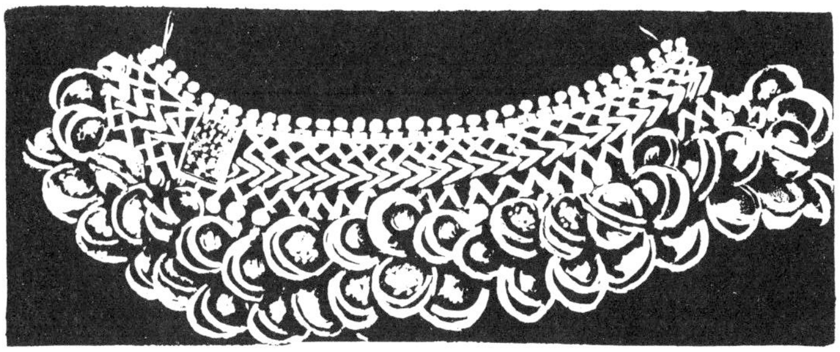

844

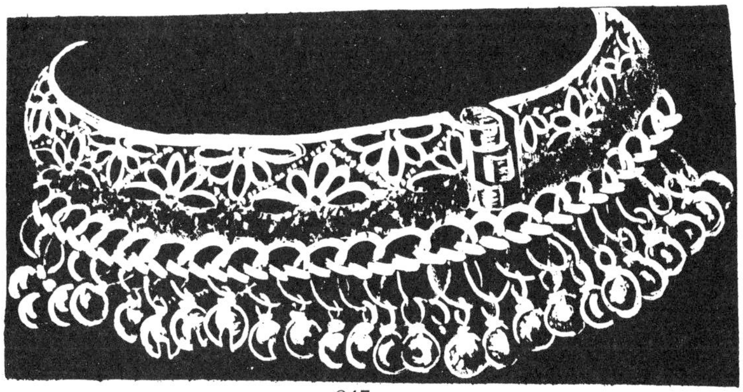

845

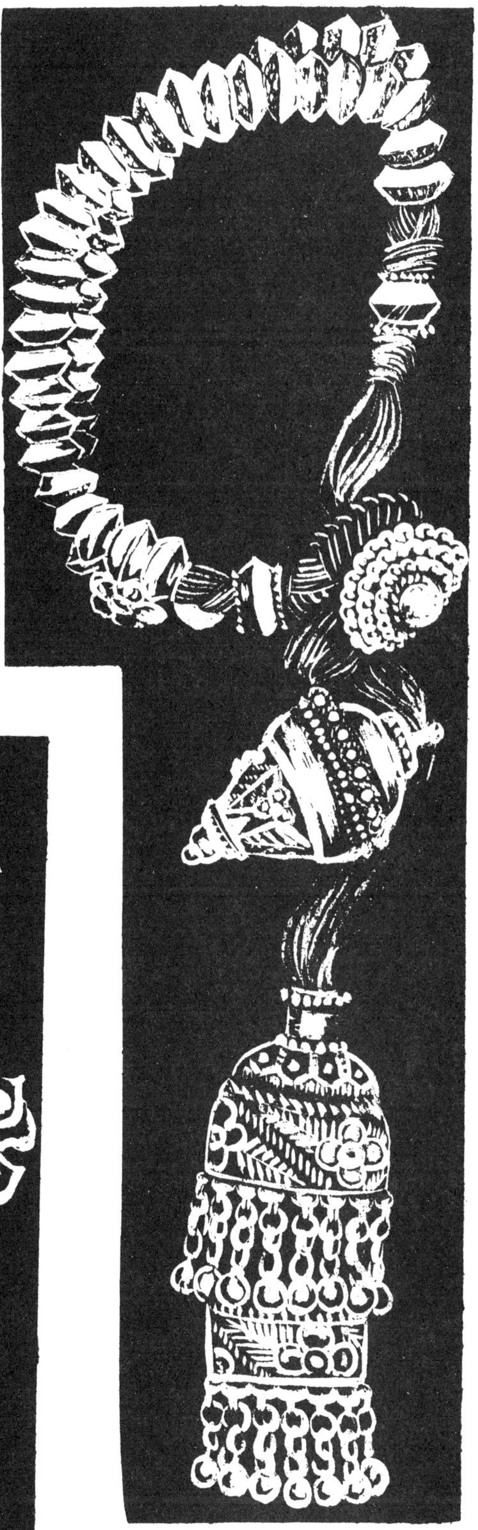

847

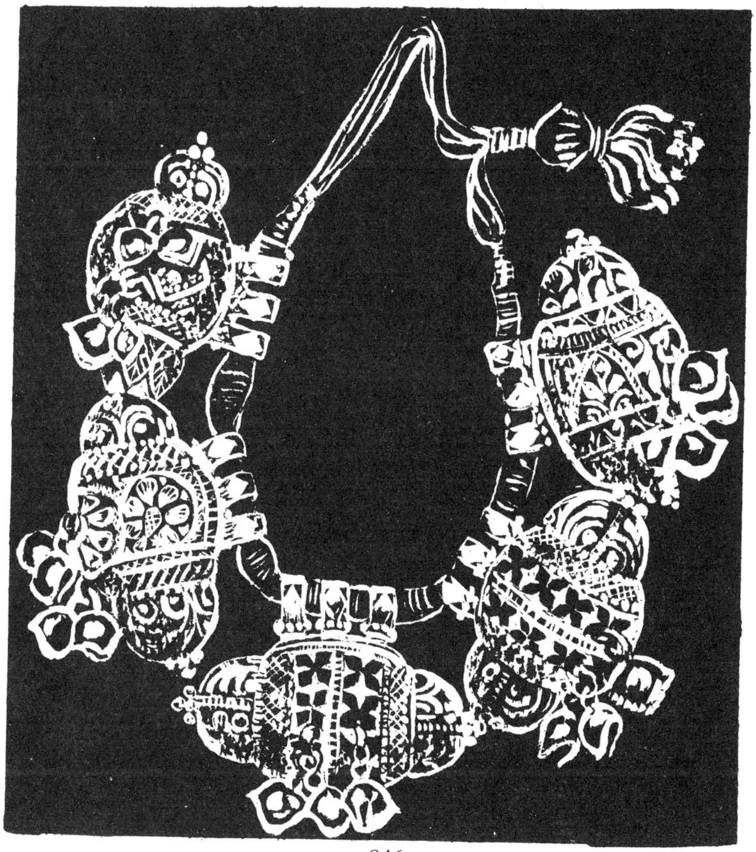

846

JEWELRY AND ORNAMENT. **844.** Silver anklet (Paje) from Chamba, Himachal Pradesh. **845.** Silver embossed anklet from Jaisalmer, Rajasthan. **846.** An armlet composed of pendants embossed with floral and star motifs (Bijoutha) from Bihar. **847.** Another picturesque embossed armlet with bell-shaped pendants (Baju-band) from Bihar.

## Plate 102

848

849

850

851

852

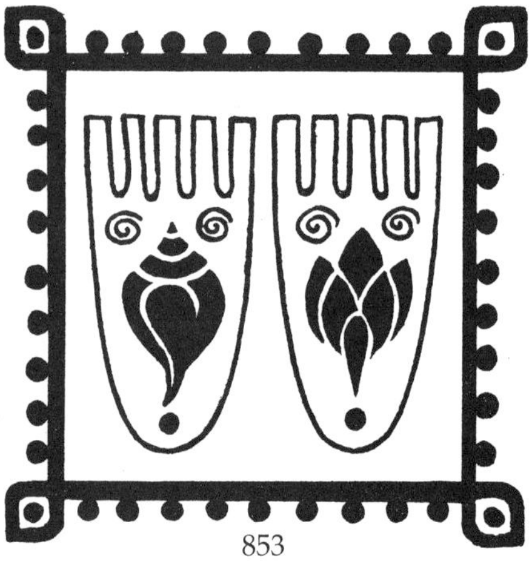

853

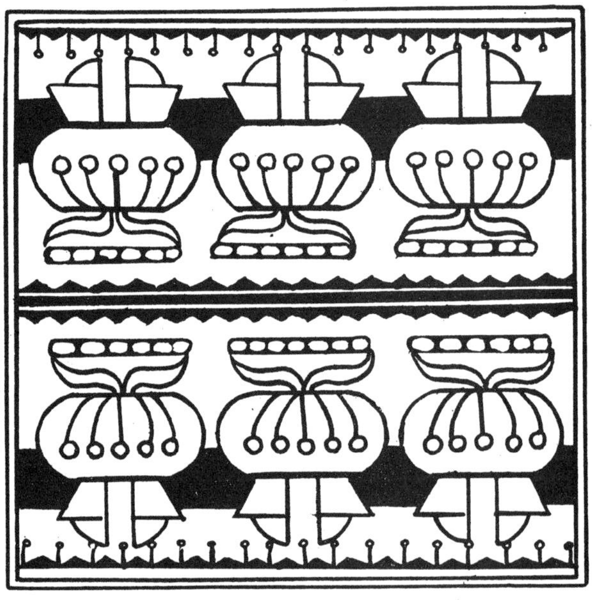

854

CREATIVE DESIGNS. **848–1000.** Stylized floral, bird, animal, tree and mango motifs, geometrical forms, sacred symbols and human figures created and inspired by traditional pattern modes of India. These designs and motifs are adaptable for any craft.

# Plate 103

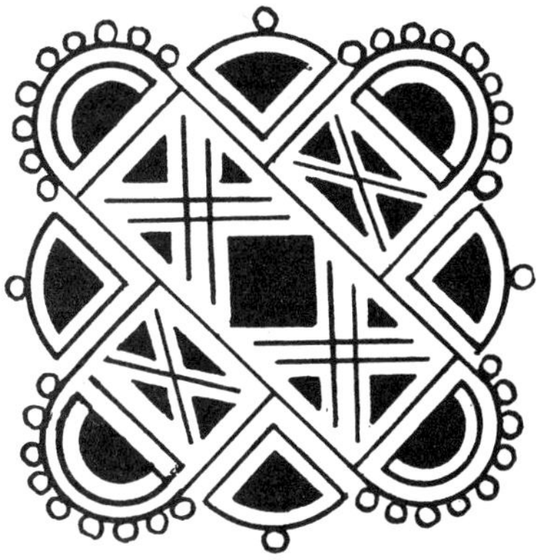
855

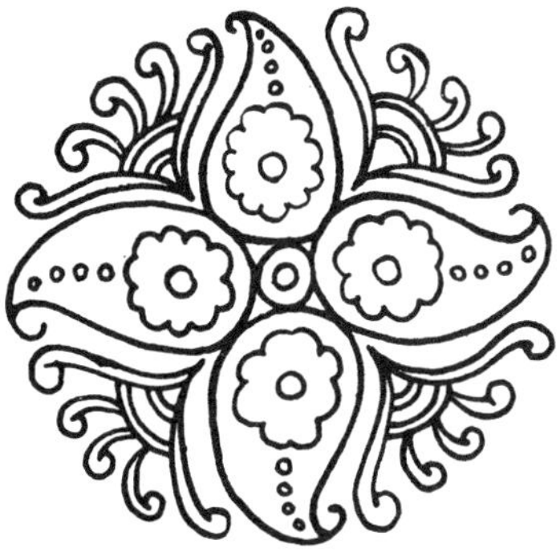
856

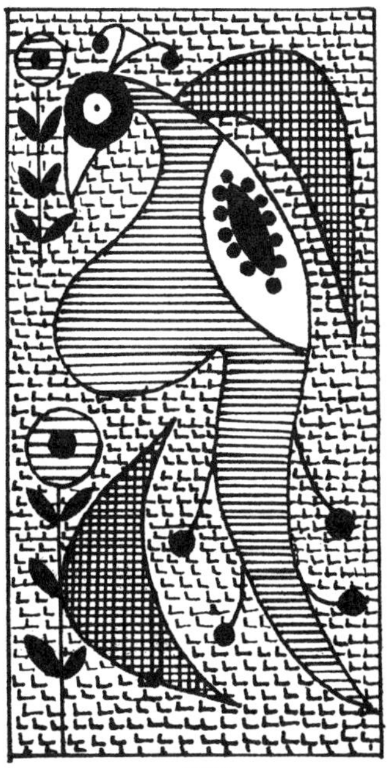
857

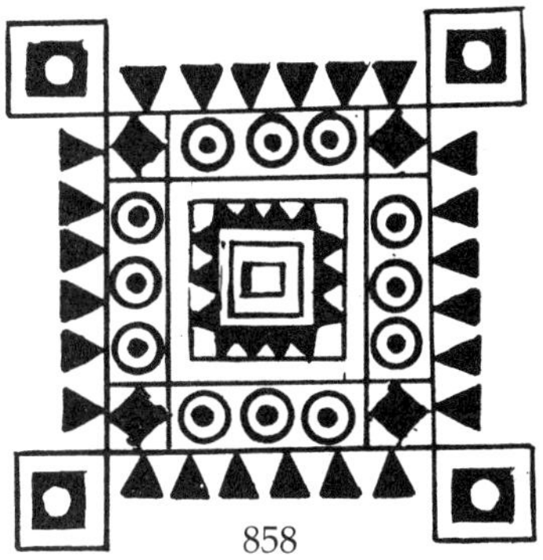
858

859

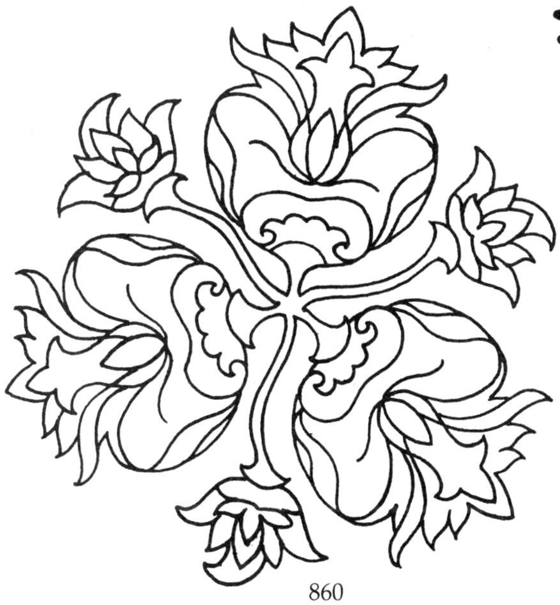
860

861

# Plate 104

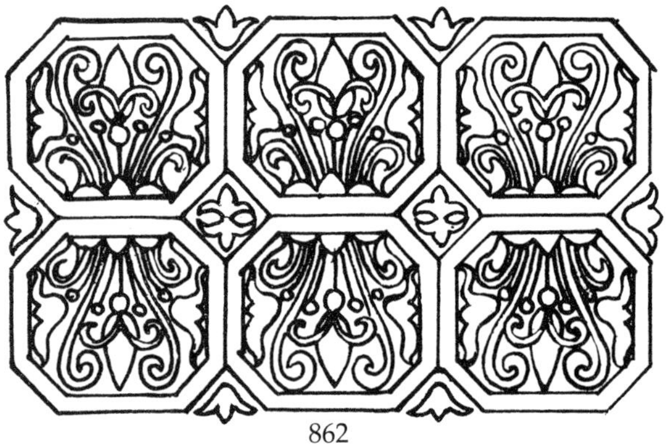

862

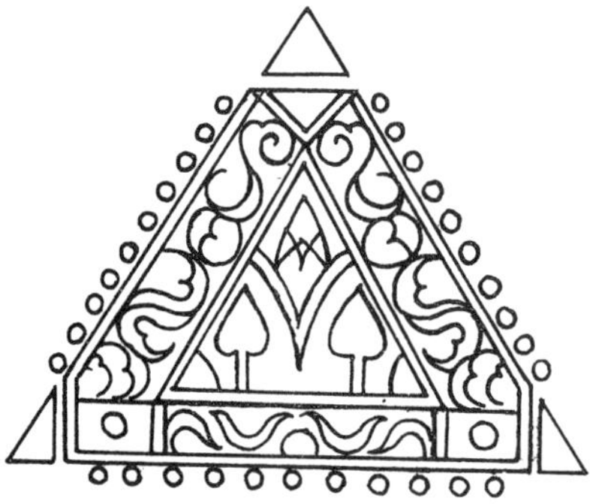

863

864

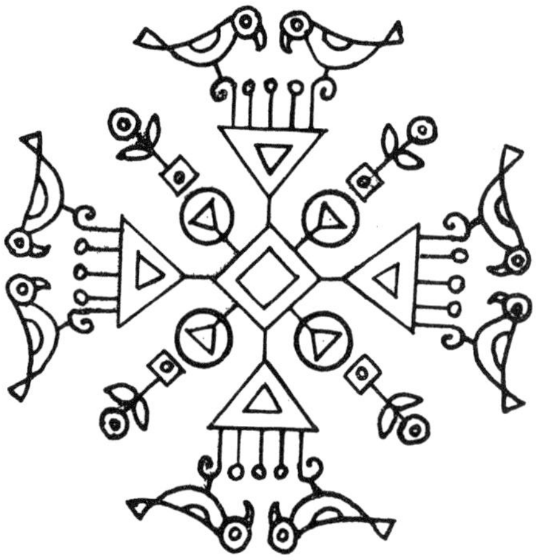

865

866

867

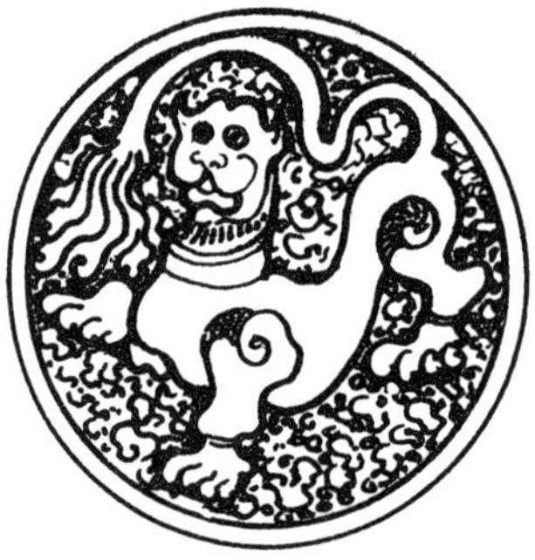

868

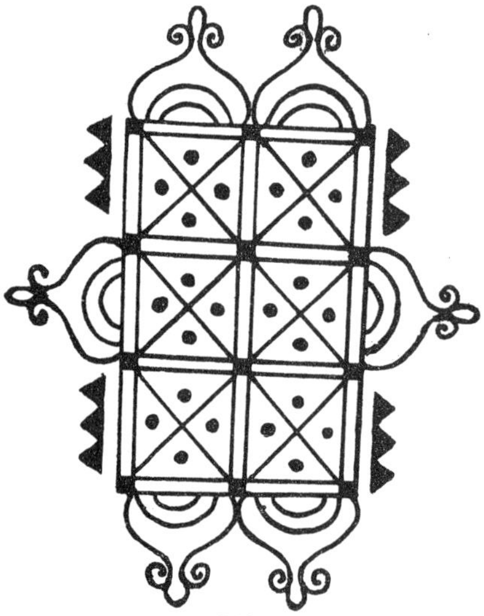

869

# Plate 105

870

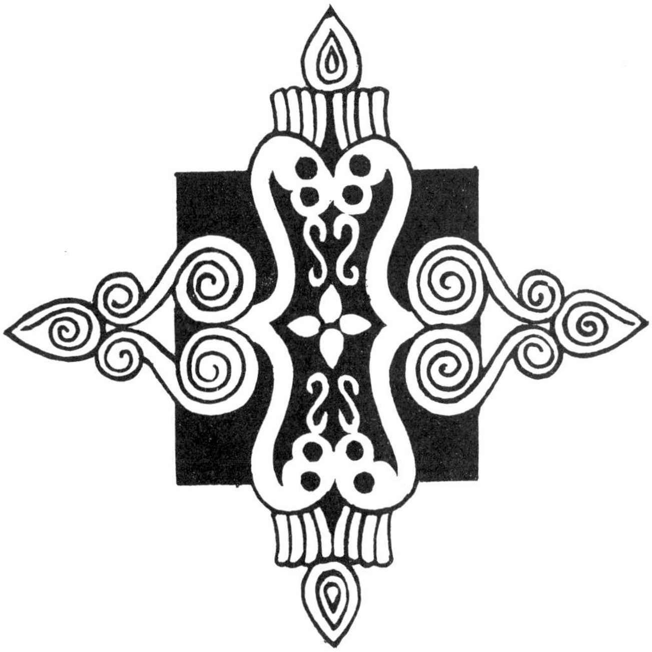

871

872

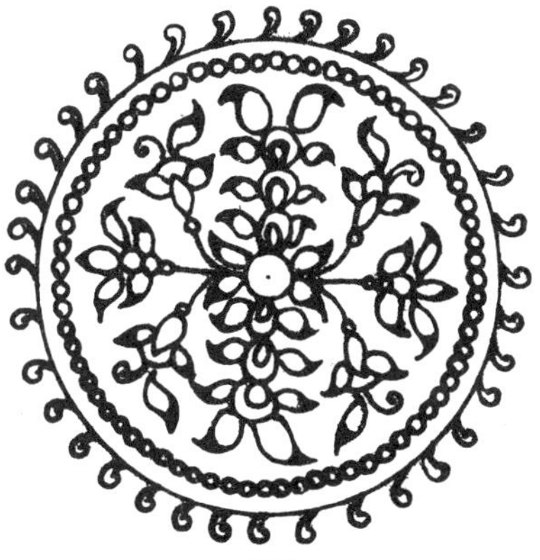

873

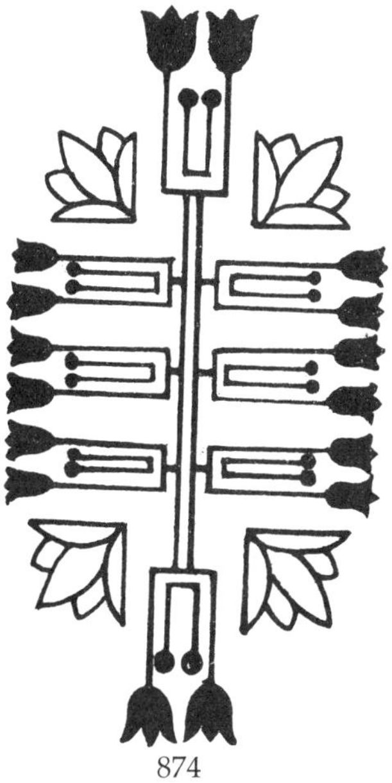

874

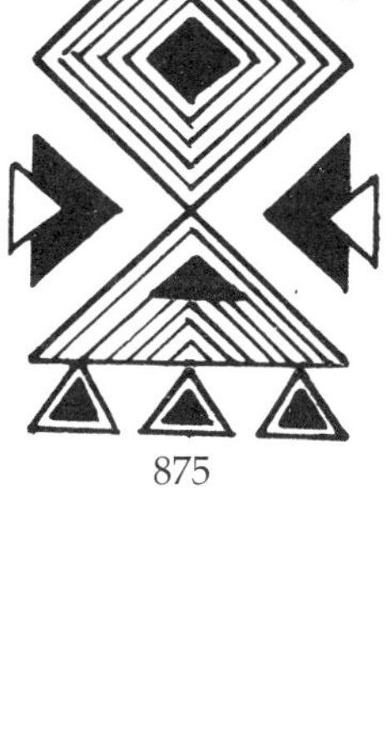

875

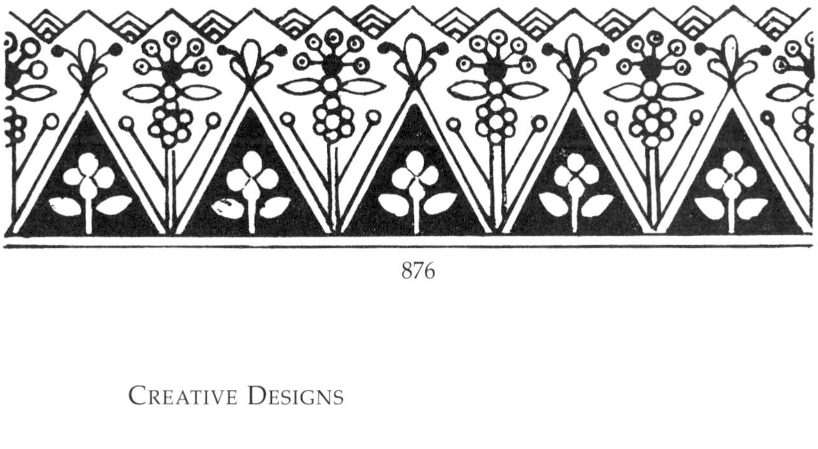

876

# Plate 106

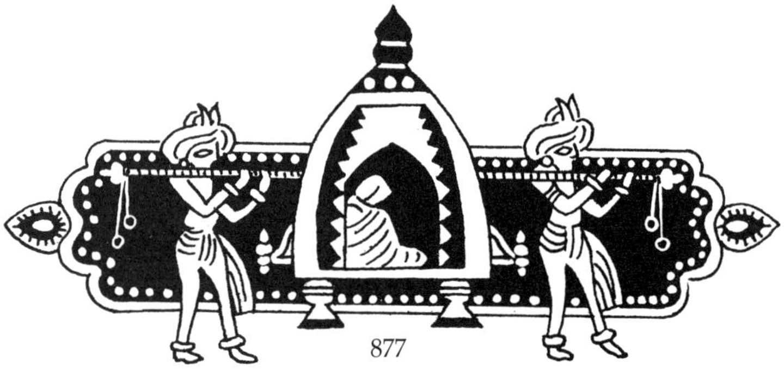

877

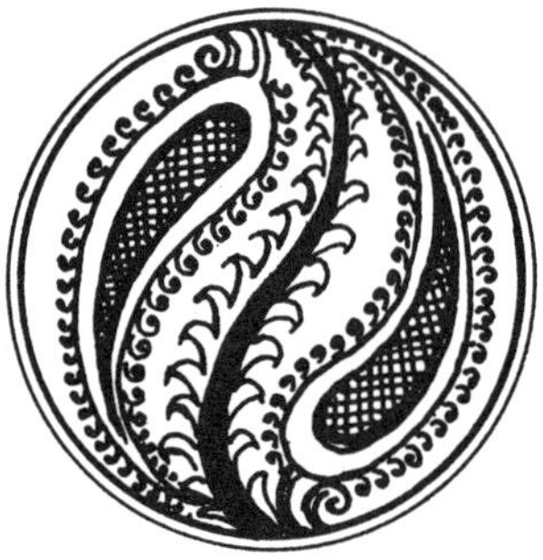

878

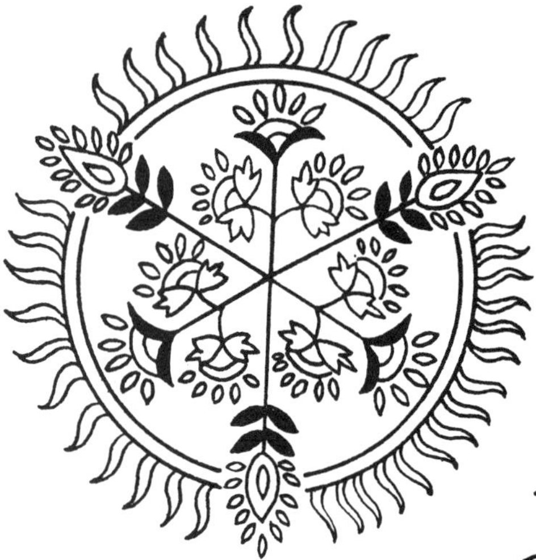

879

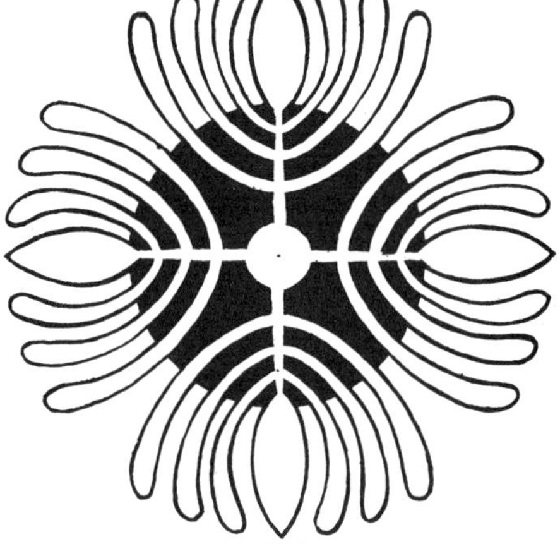

880

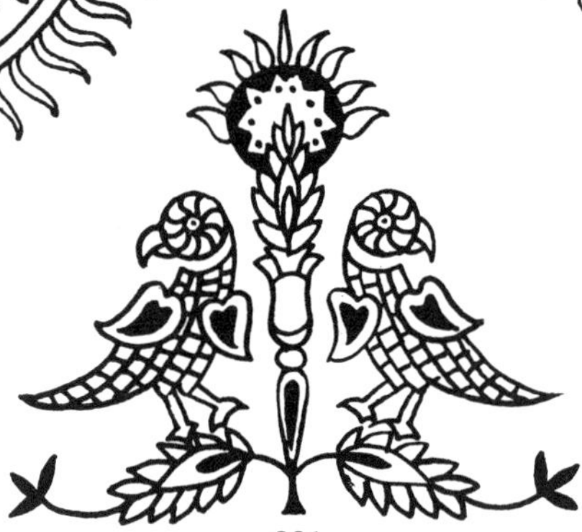

881

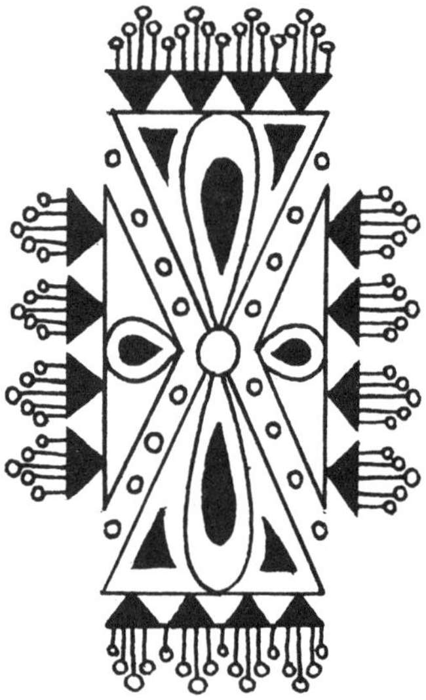

882

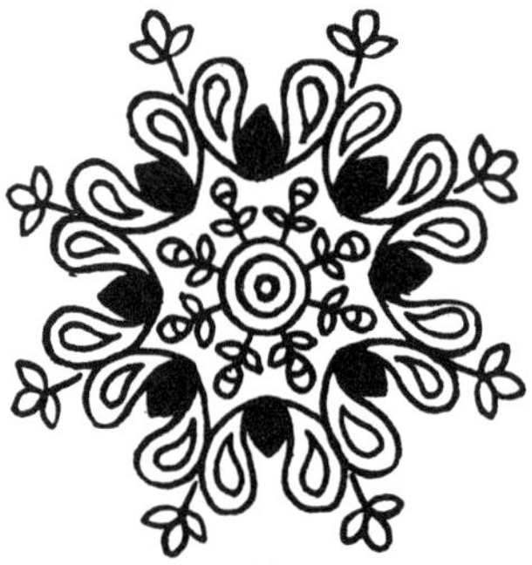

883

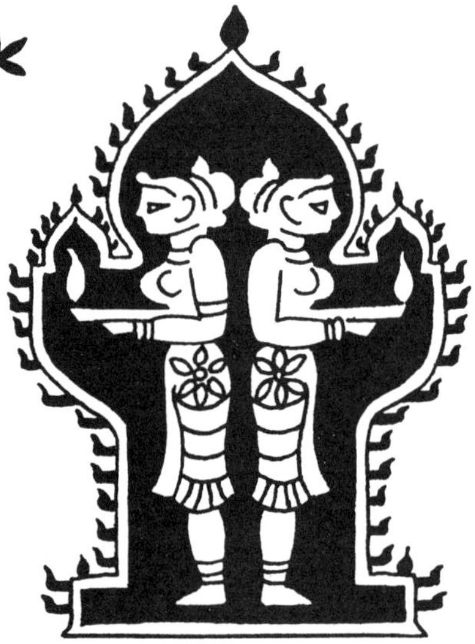

884

# Plate 107

885

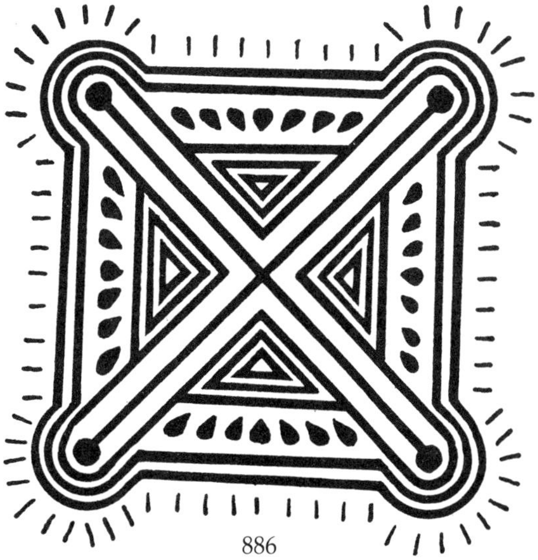

886

887

888

889

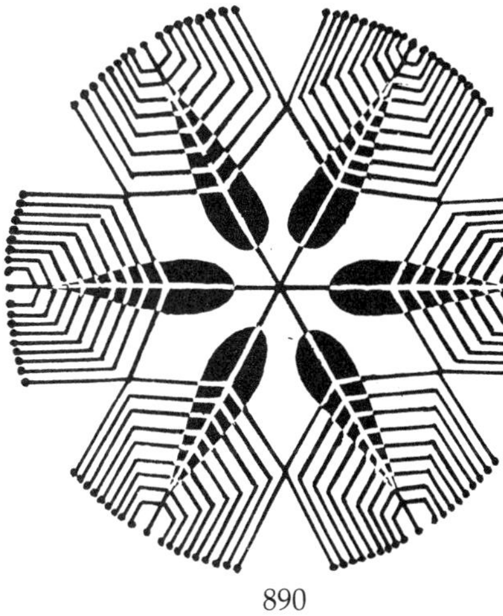

890

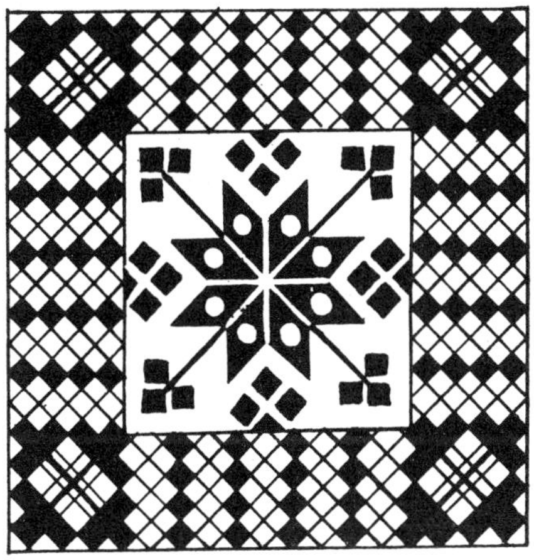

891

892

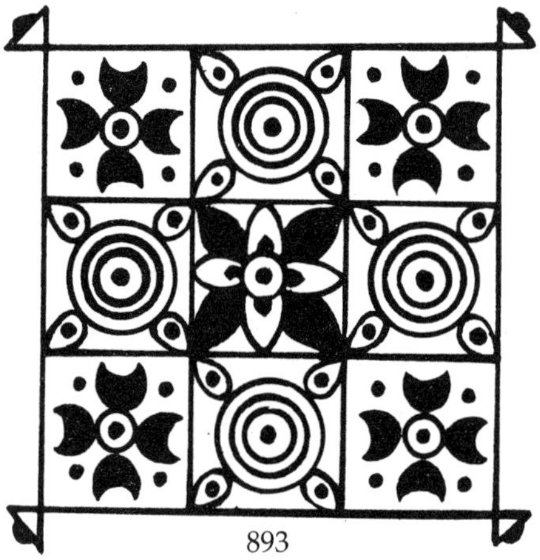

893

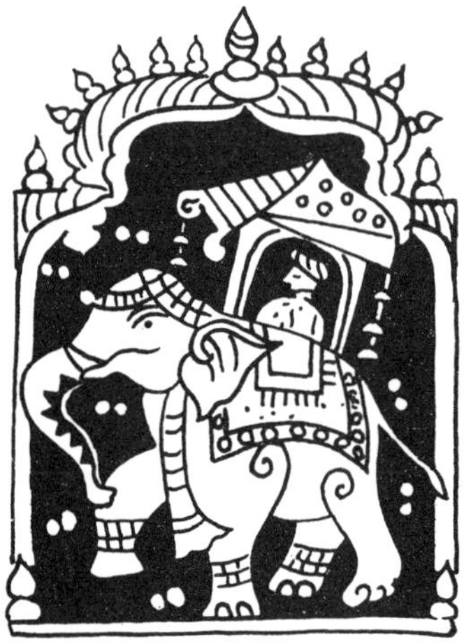

894

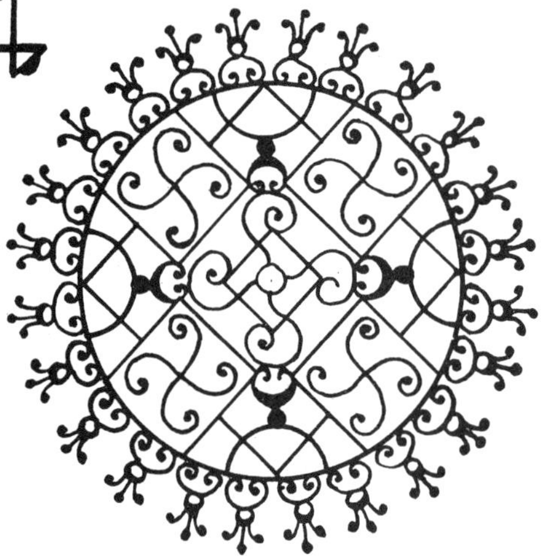

895

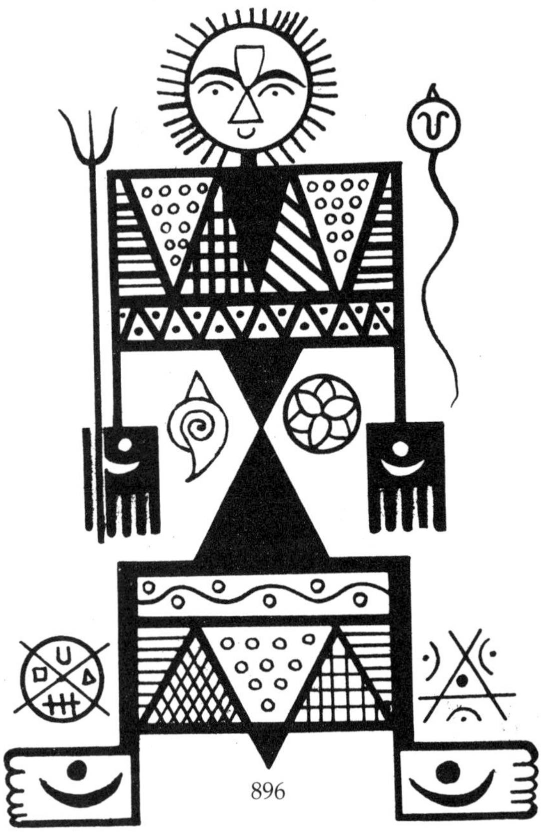

896

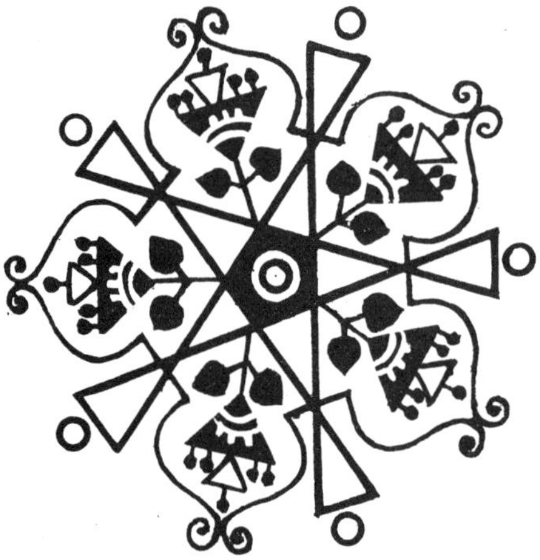

897

# Plate 109

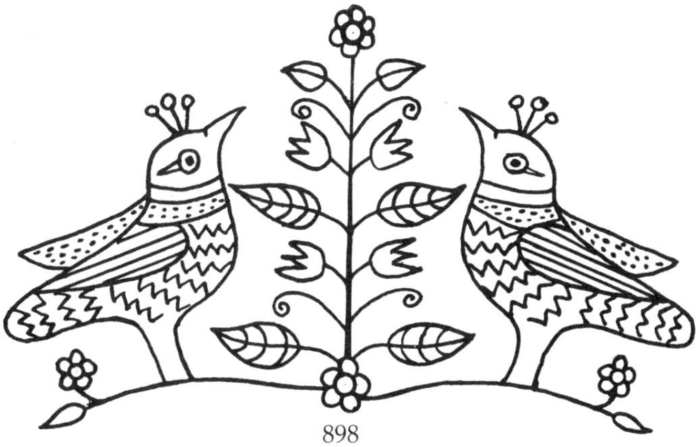

898

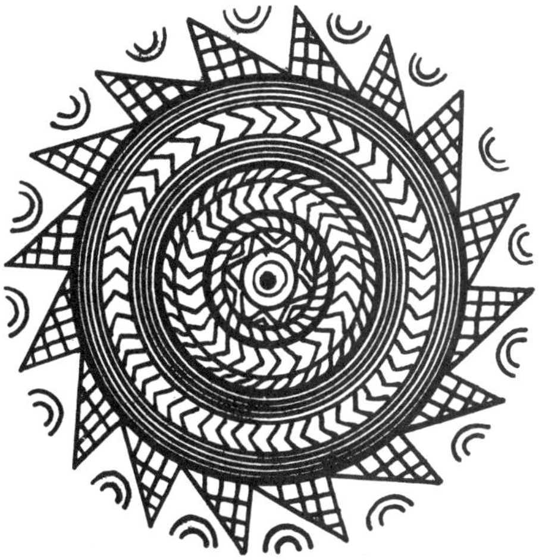

899

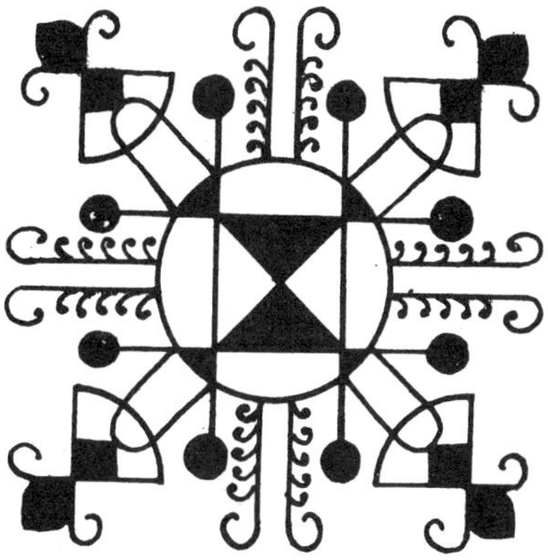

900

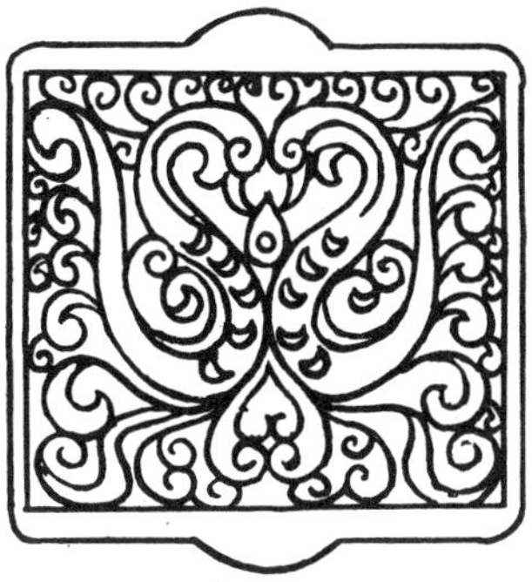

901

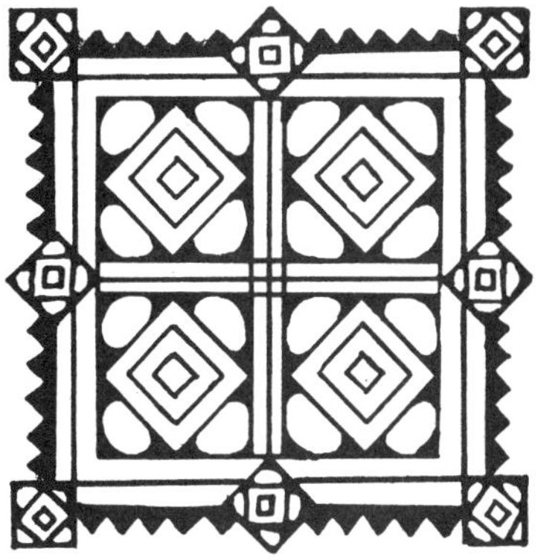

902

903

904

# Plate 110

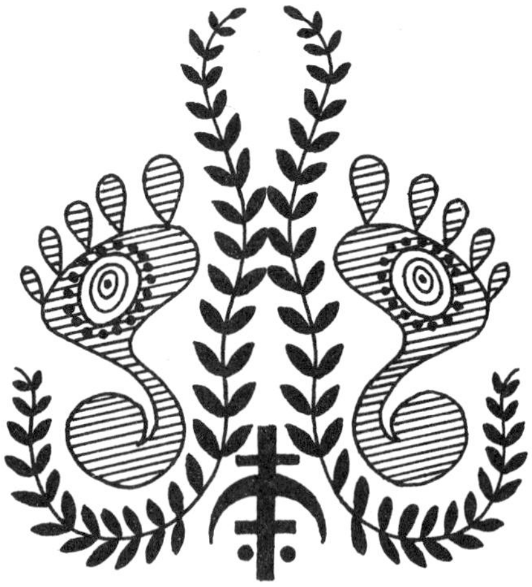

905

906

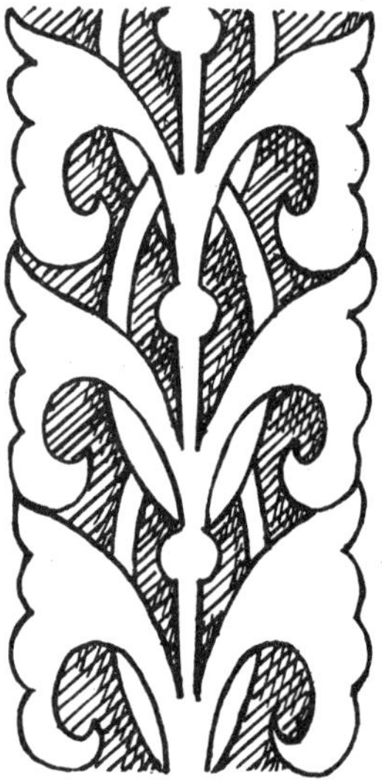

907

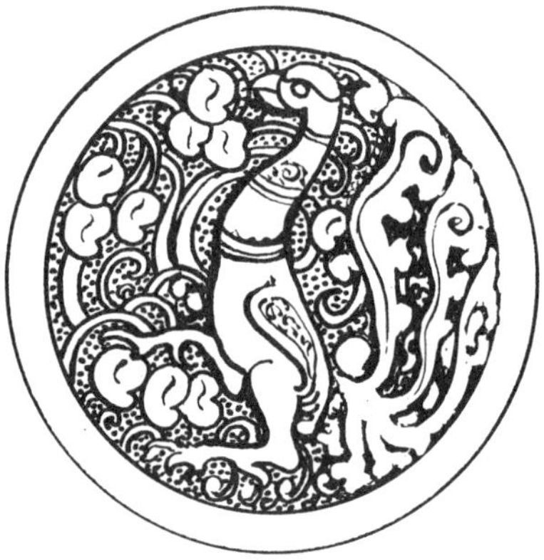

908

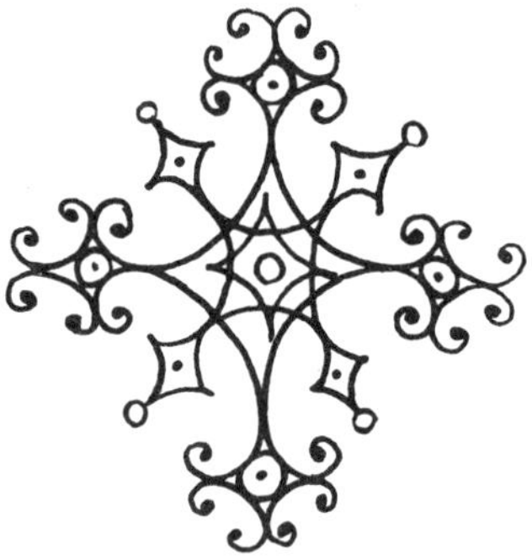

909

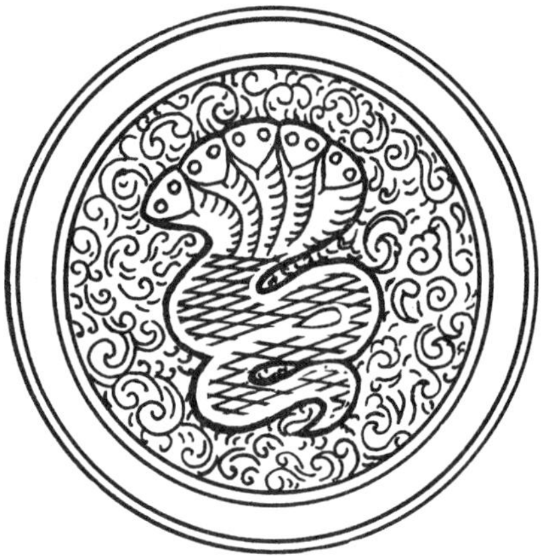

910

911

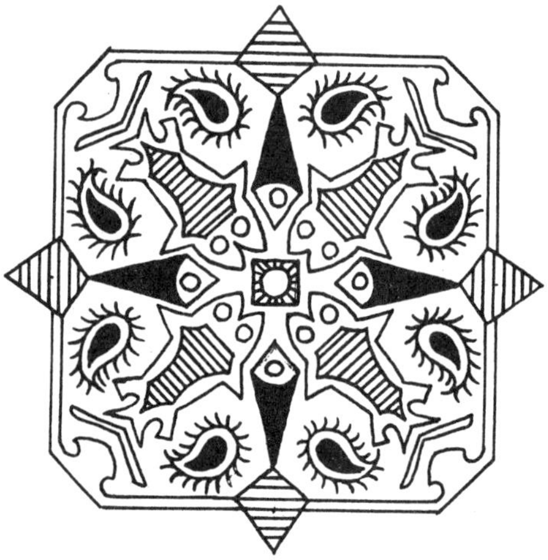

912

# Plate 111

913

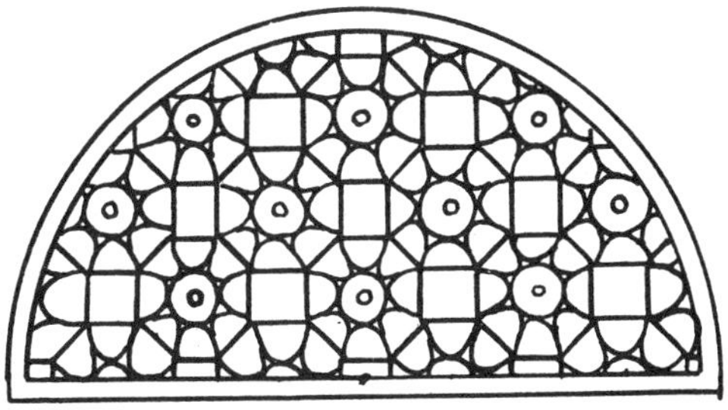

914

915

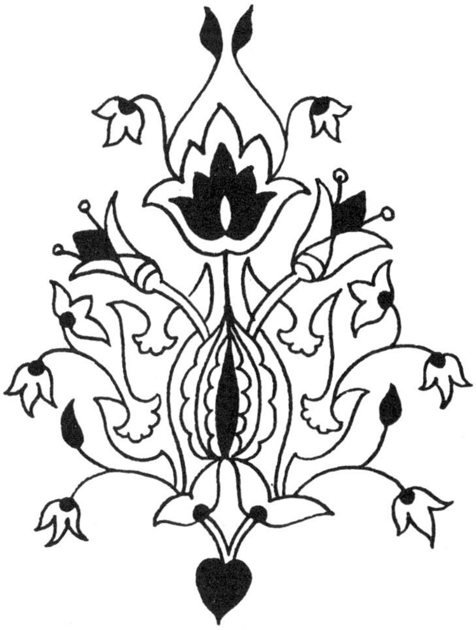

917

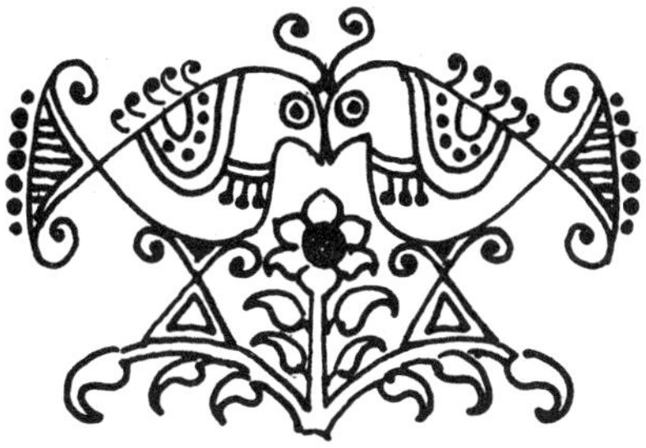

916

918

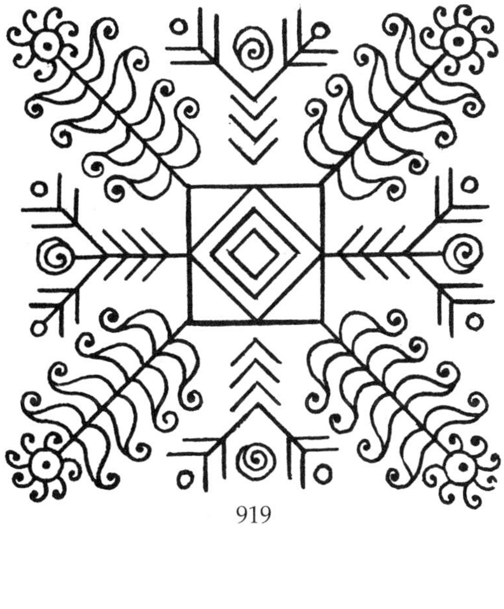

919

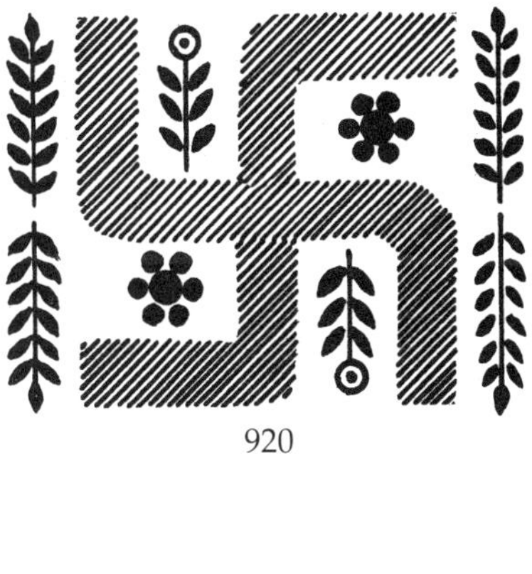

920

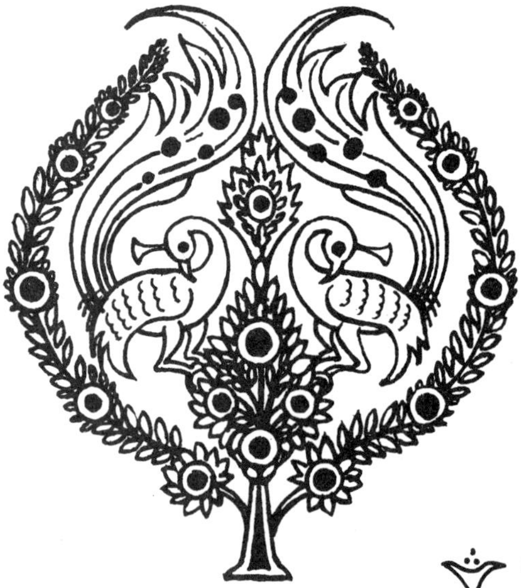

921

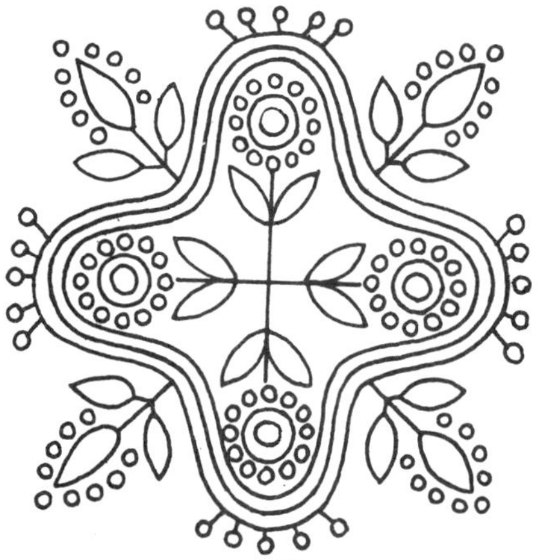

922

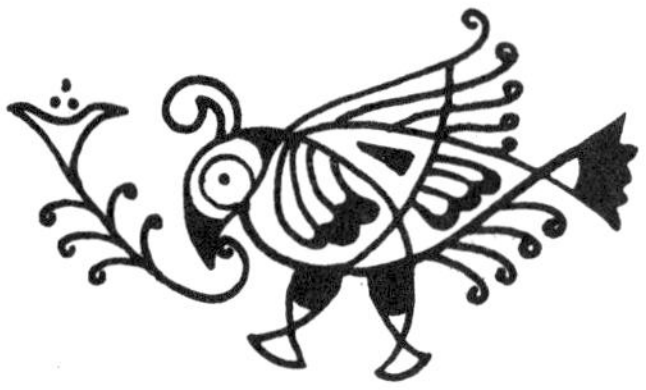

923

924

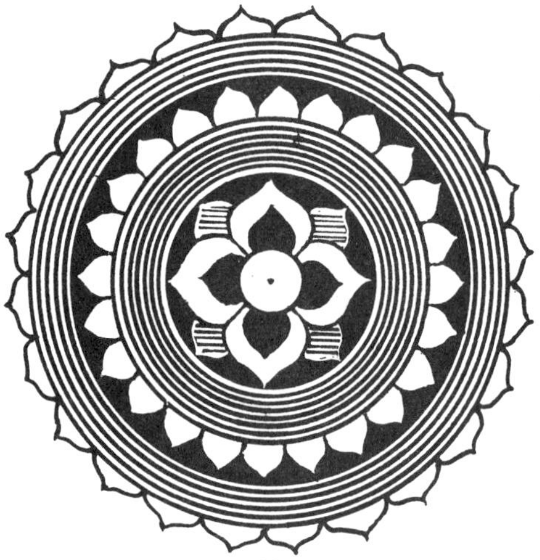

925

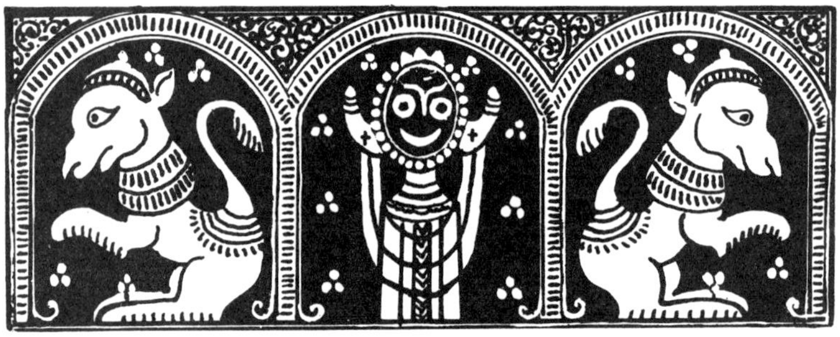

926

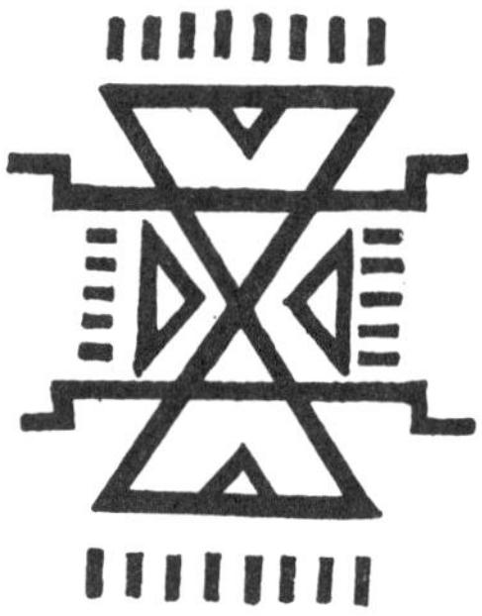

927

# Plate 113

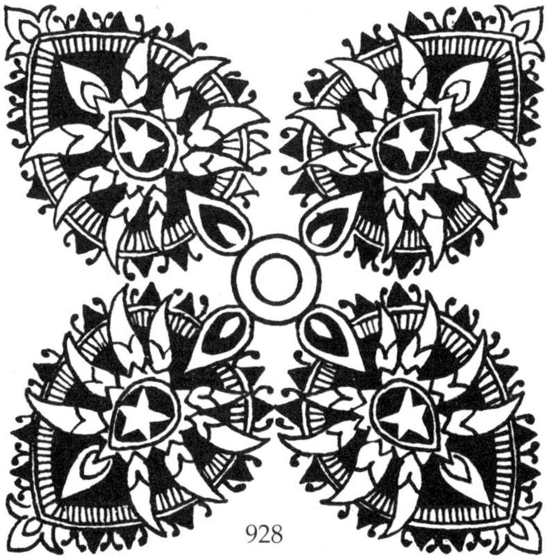
928

929

930

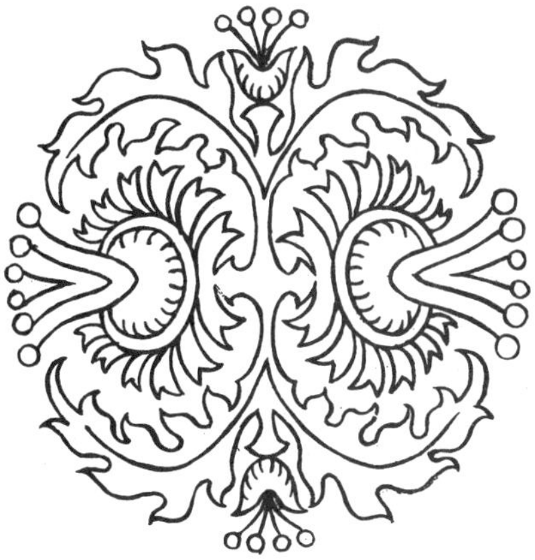
931

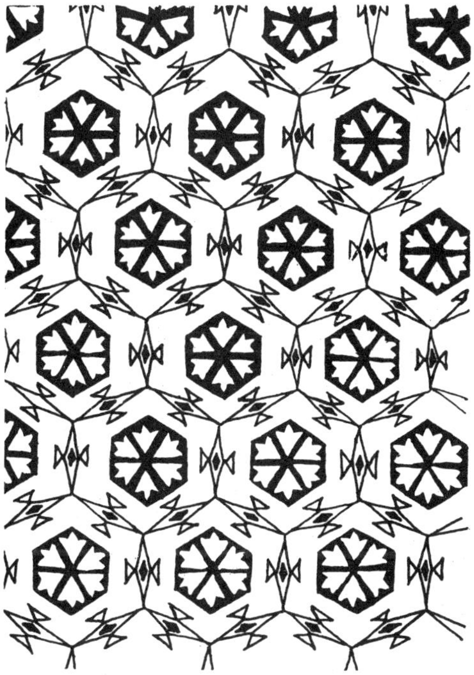
932

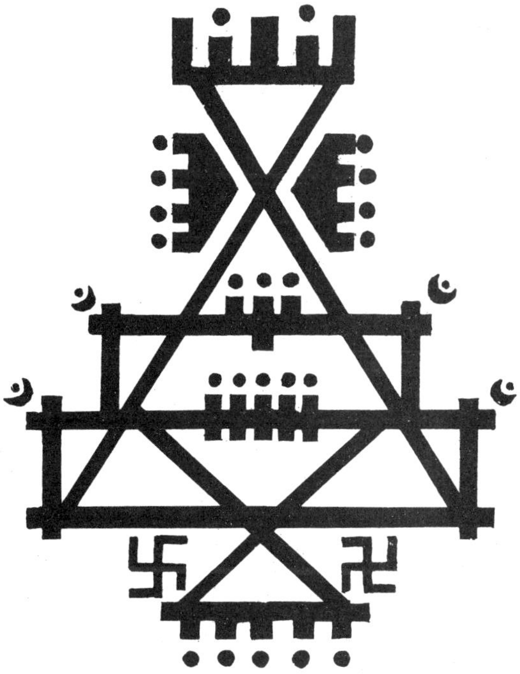
933

934

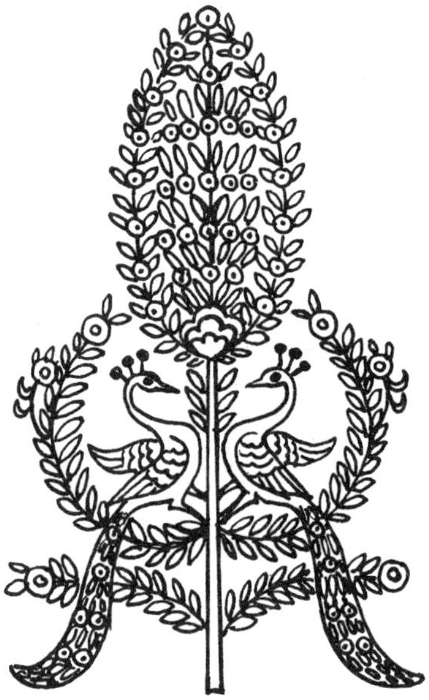

935

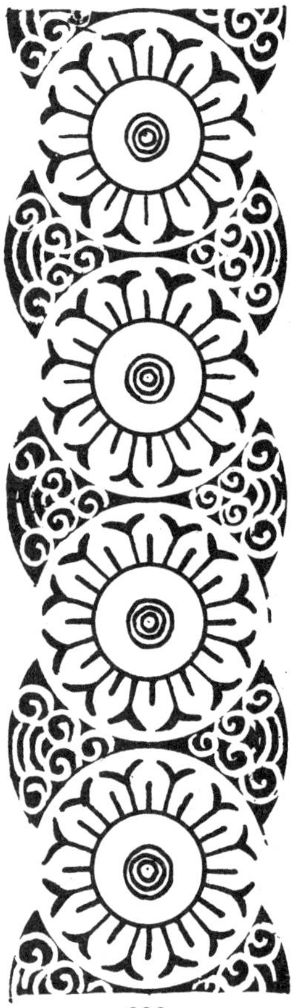

938

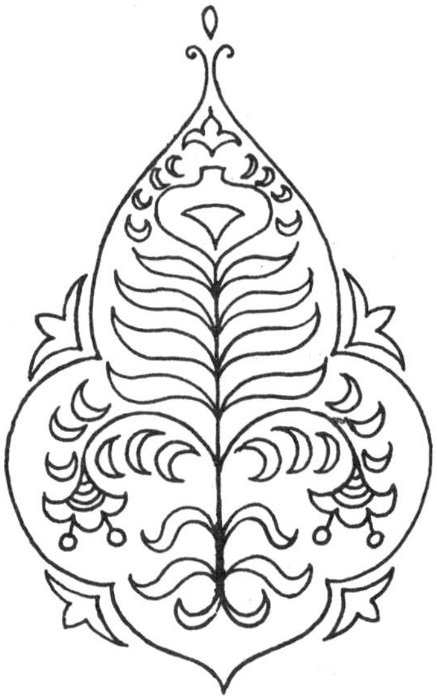

936

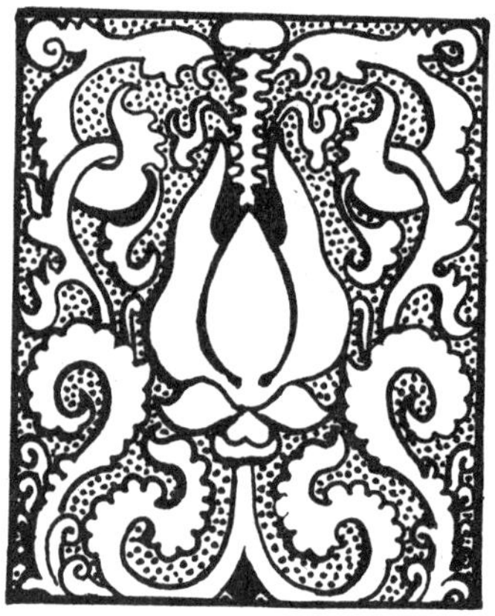

937

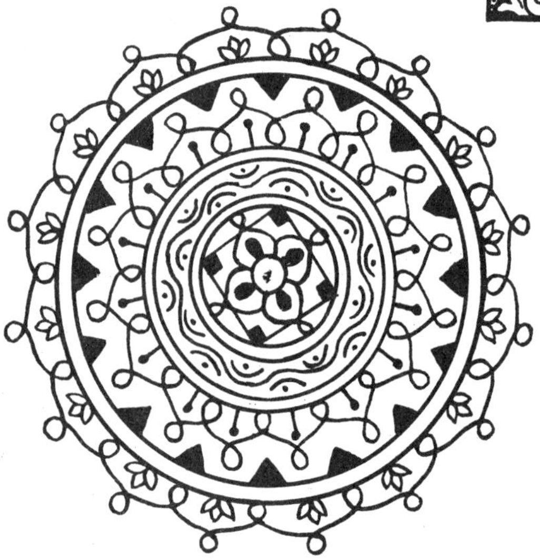

939

940

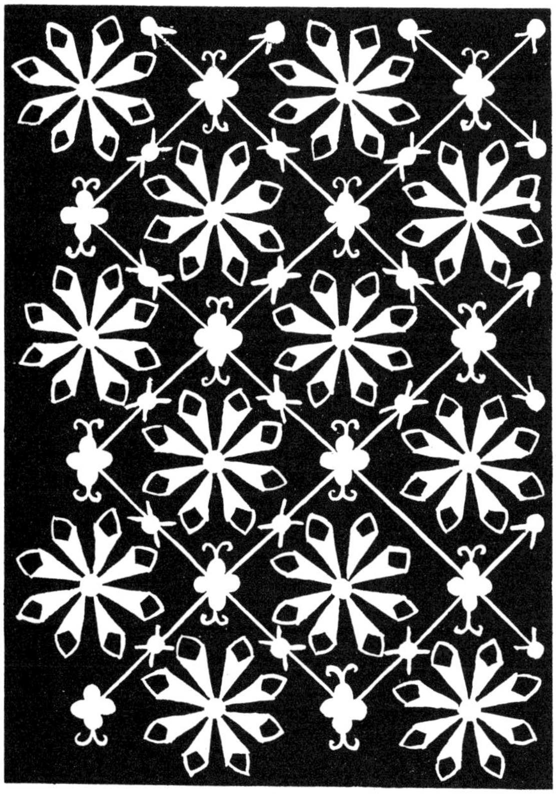

941

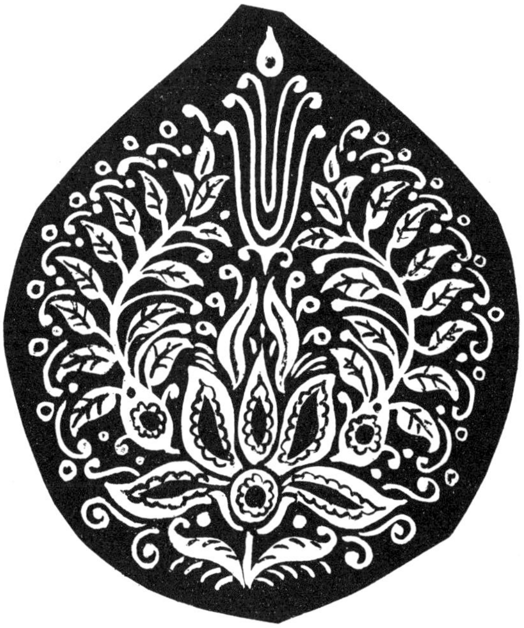

942

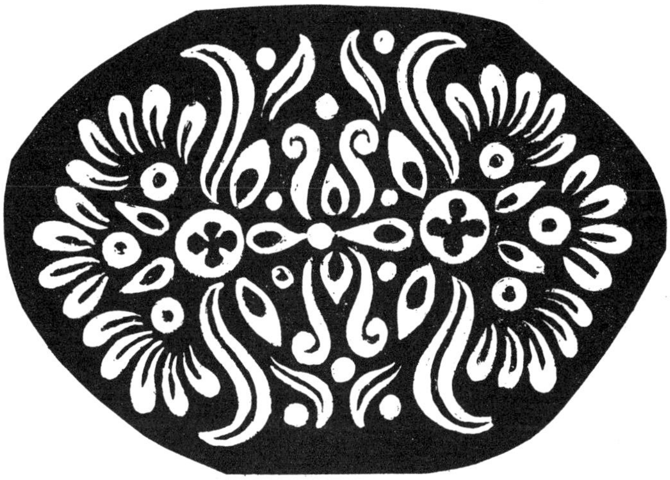

943

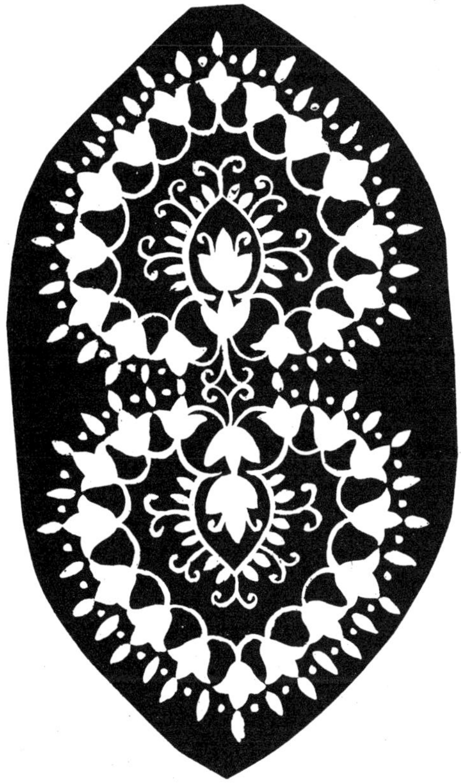

944

945

946

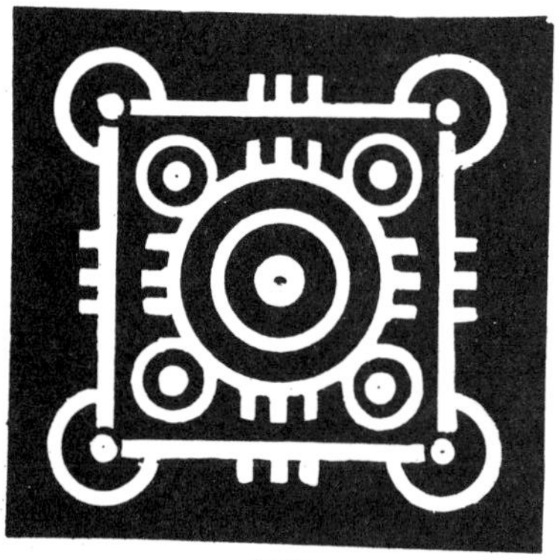

947

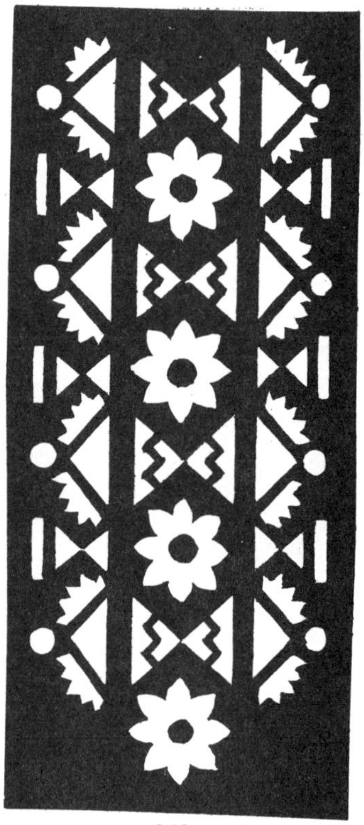

949

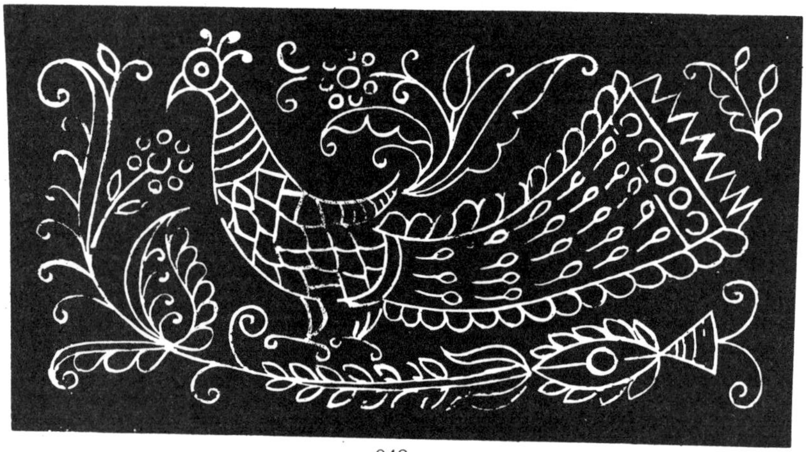

948

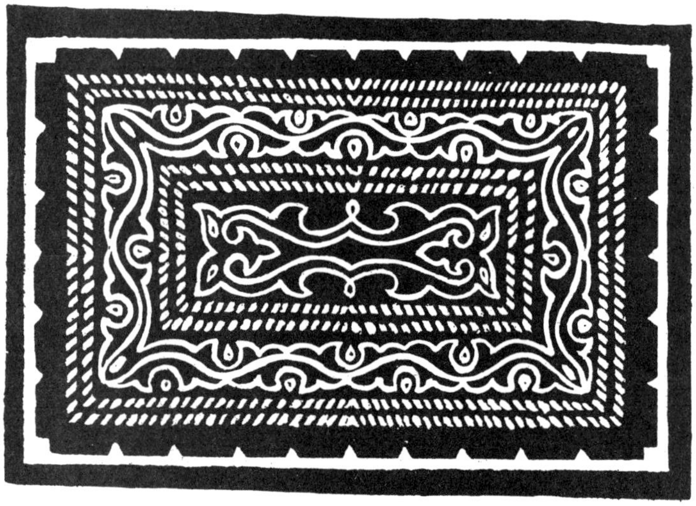

950

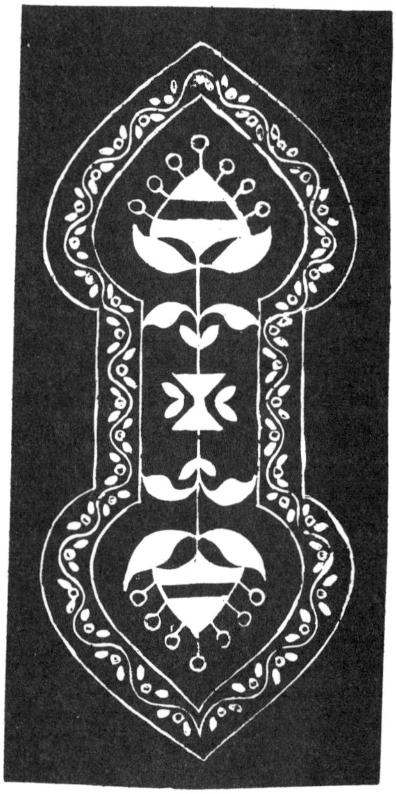

951

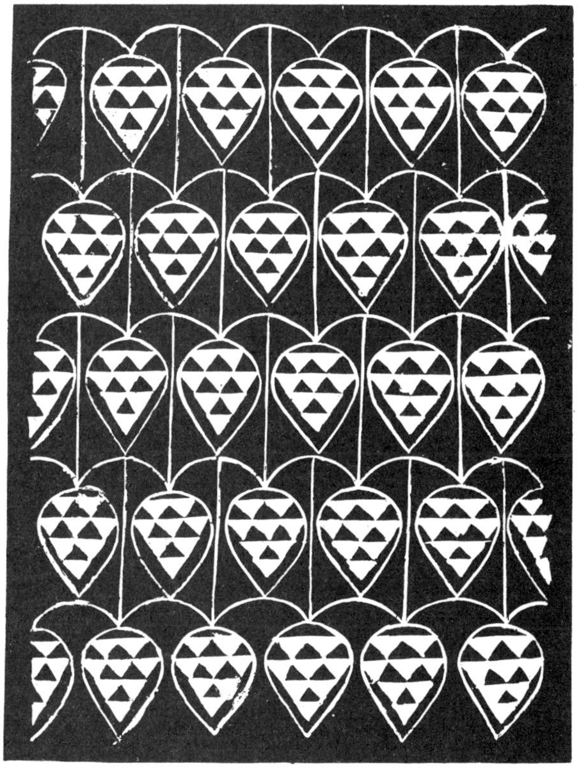

952

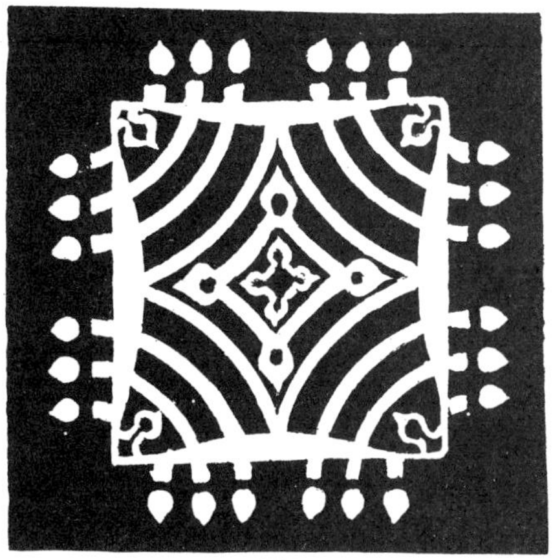

953

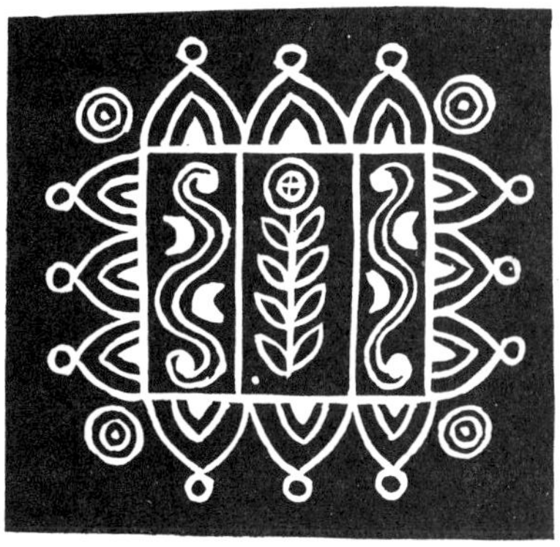

954

955

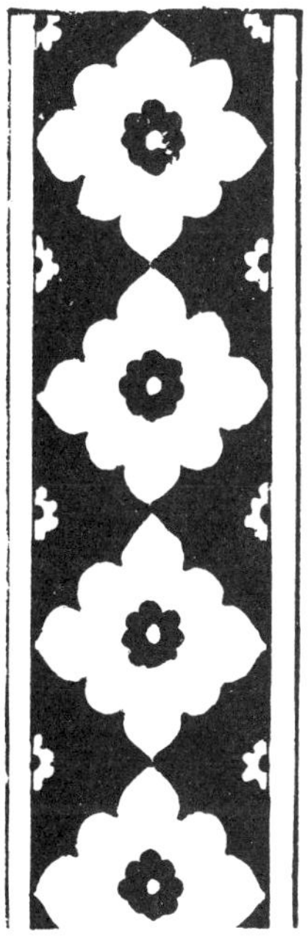

956

# Plate 118

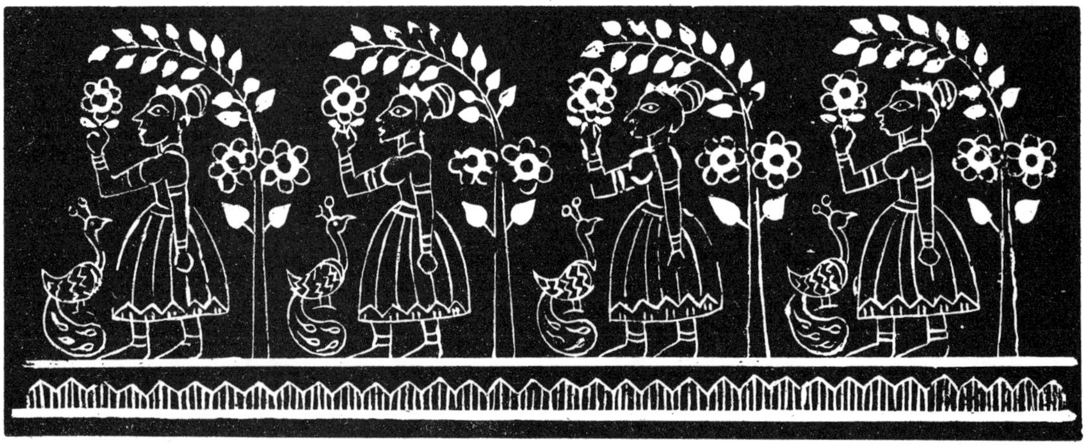

957

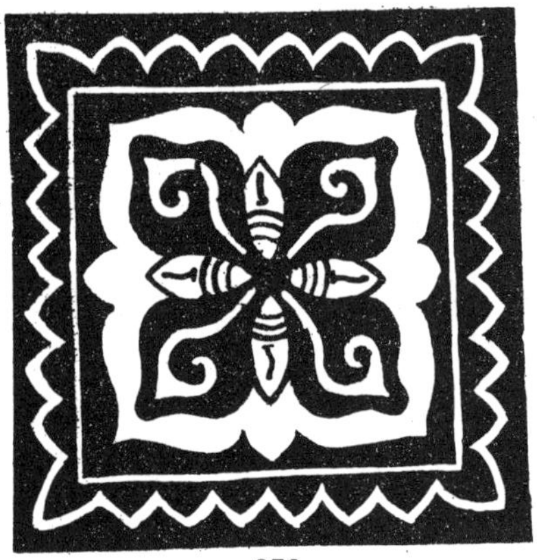

958

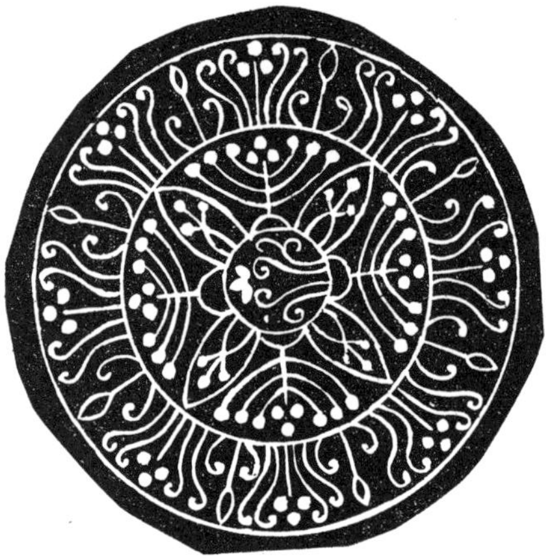

959

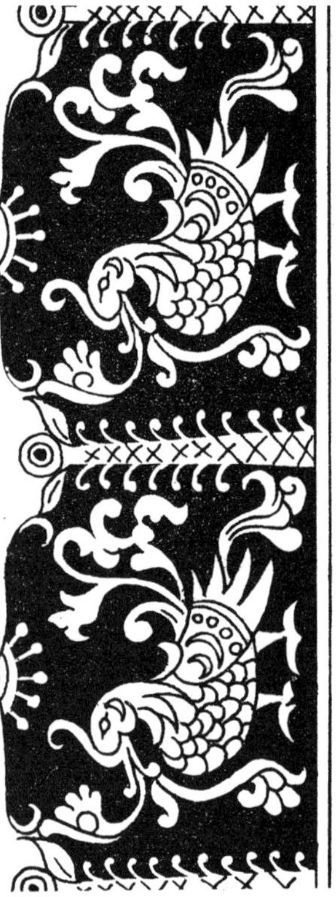

960

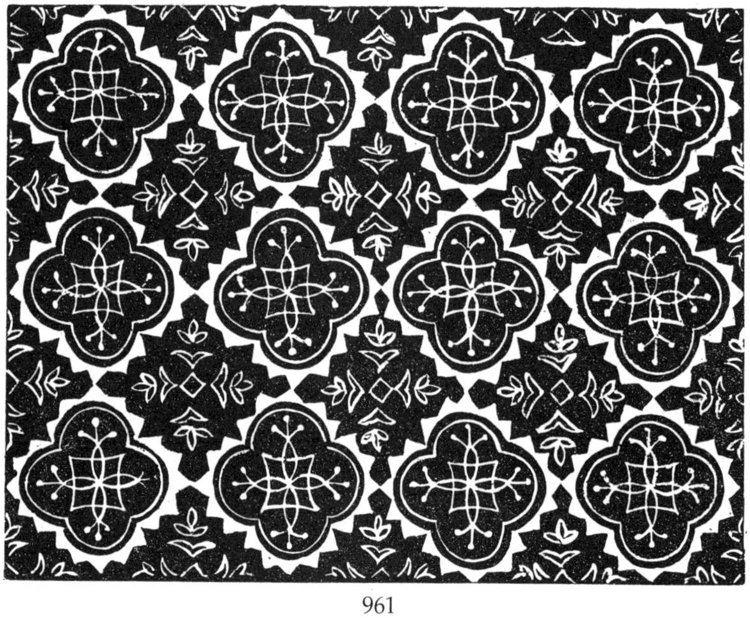

961

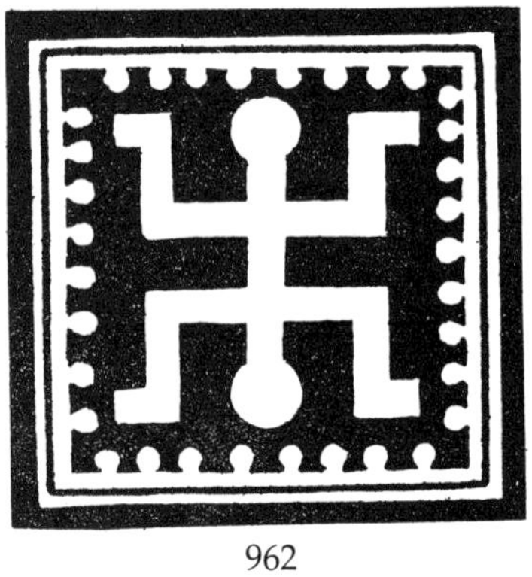

962

# Plate 119

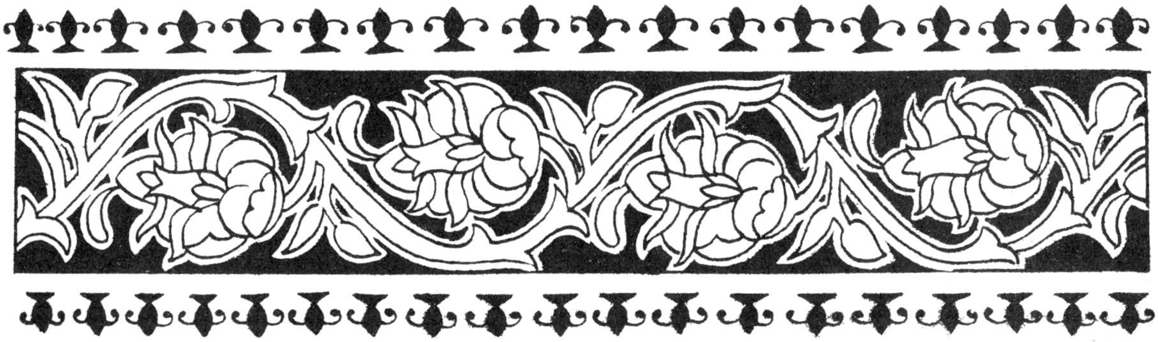

963

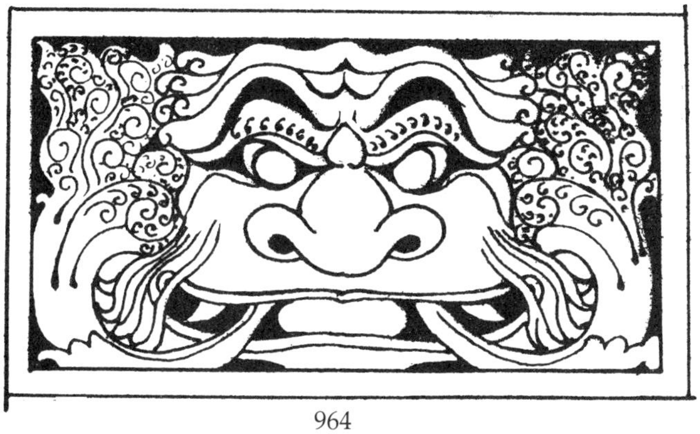

964

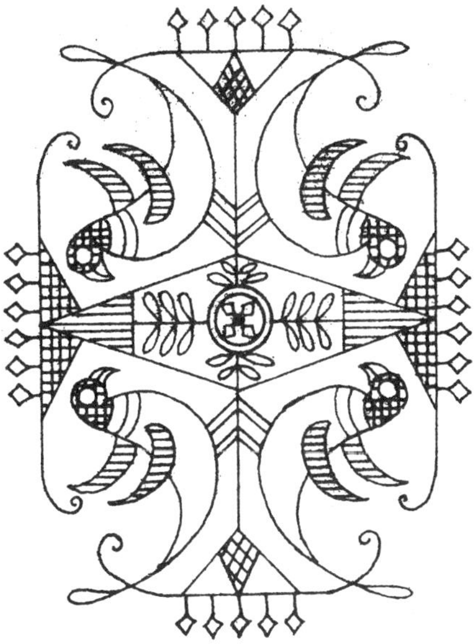

965

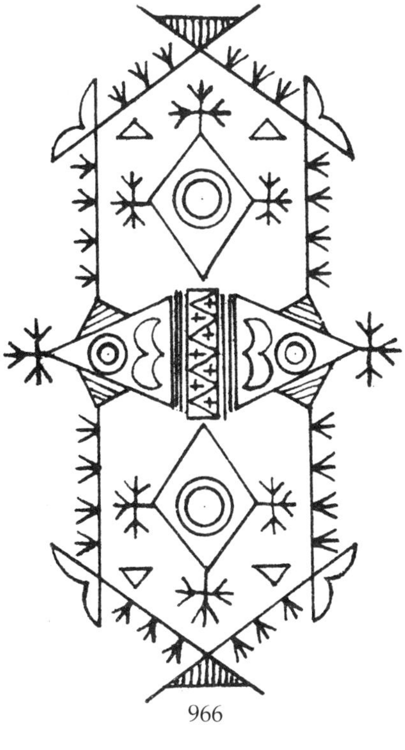

966

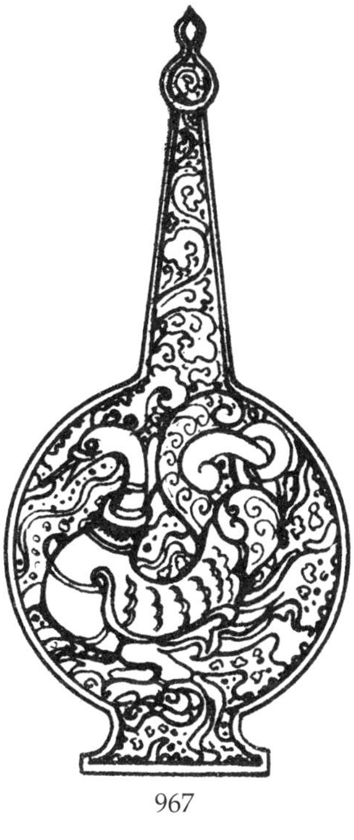

967

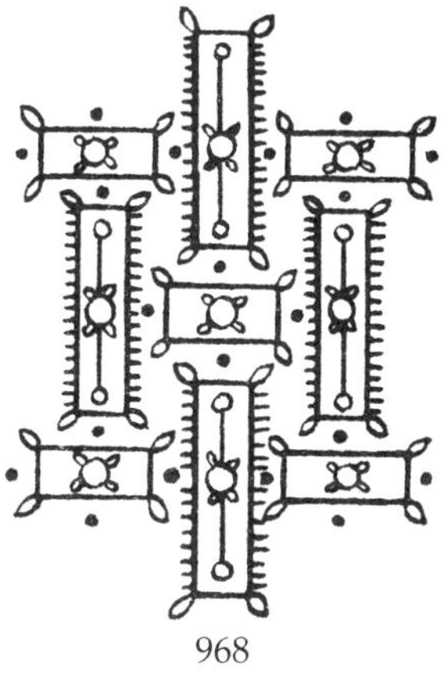

968

# Plate 120

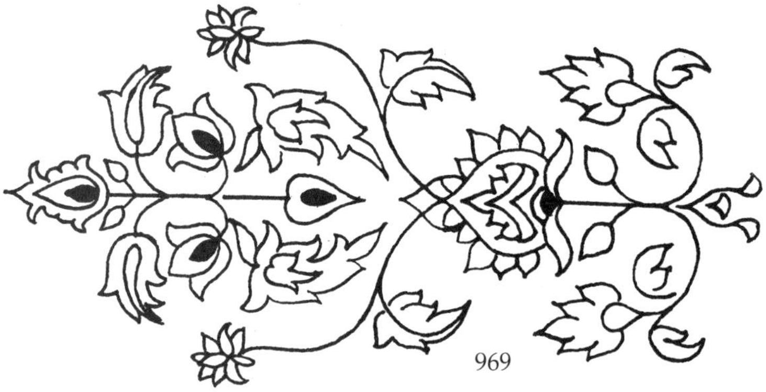

969

972

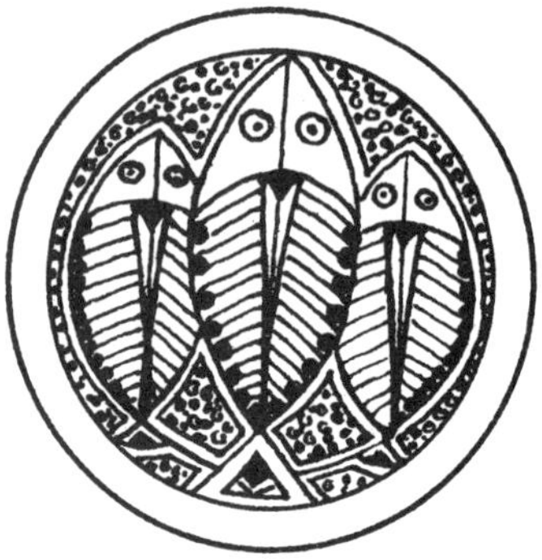

970

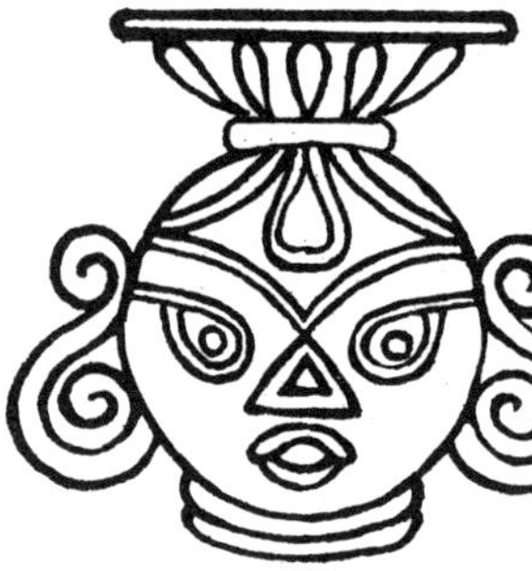

971

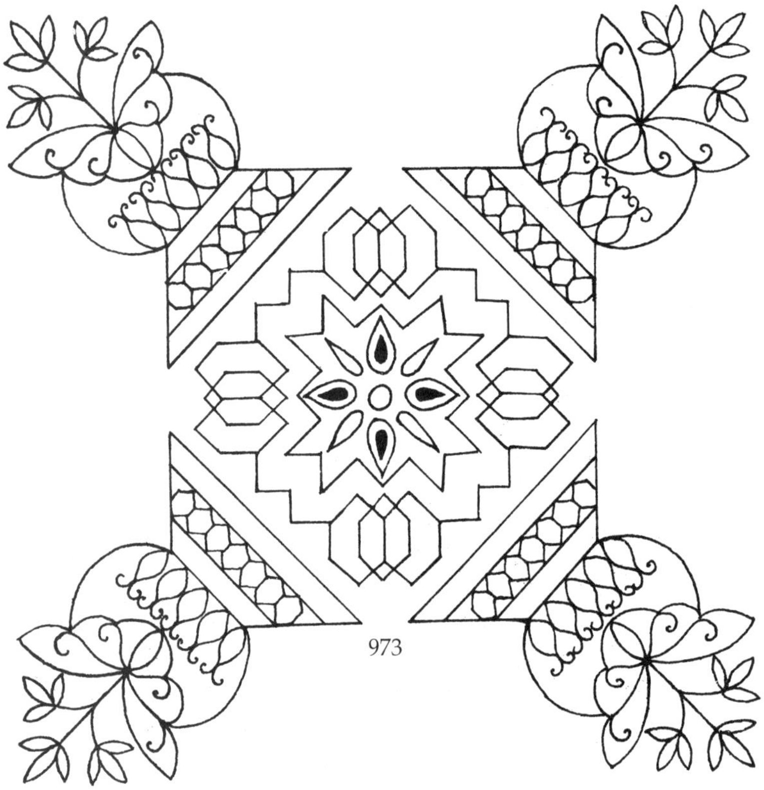

973

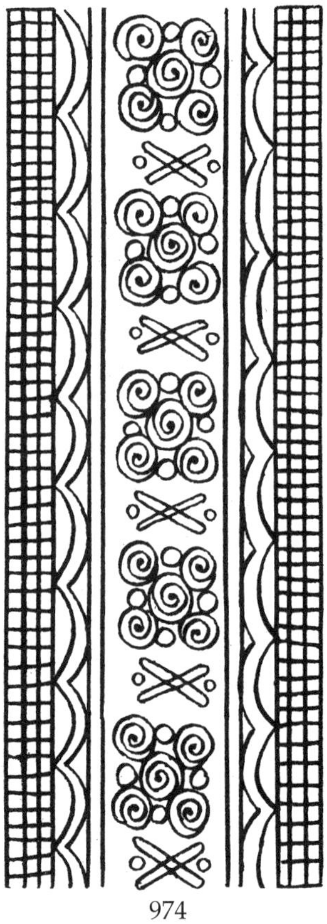

974

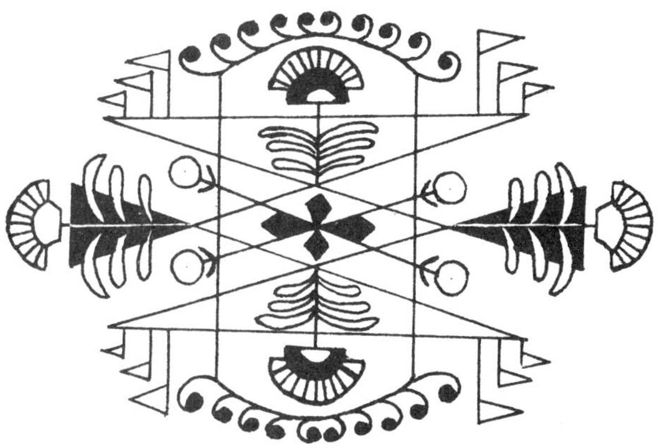

975

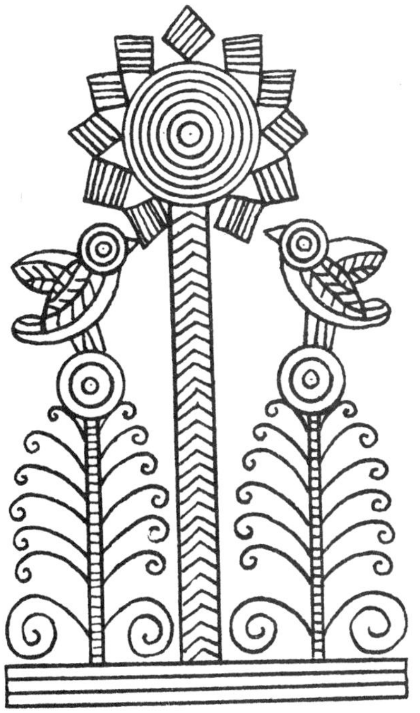

977

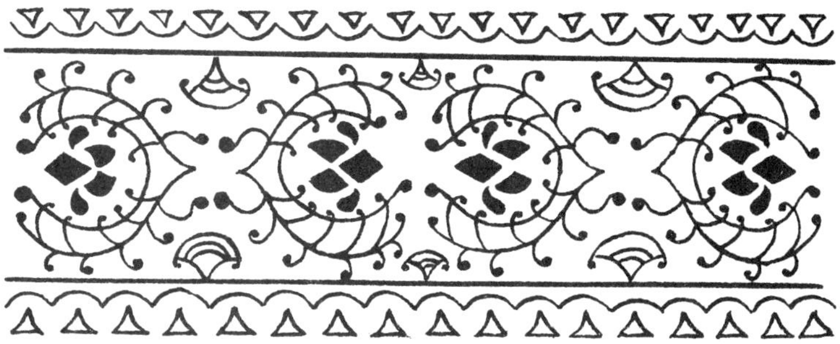

976

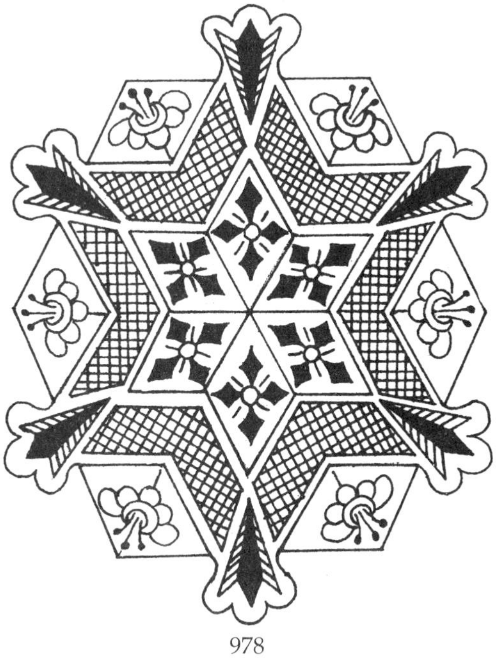

978

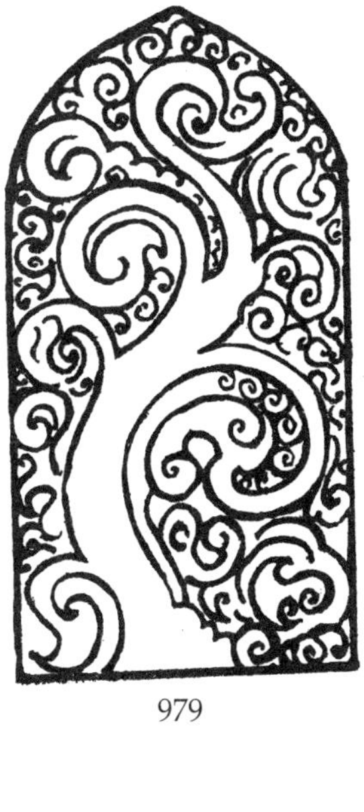

979

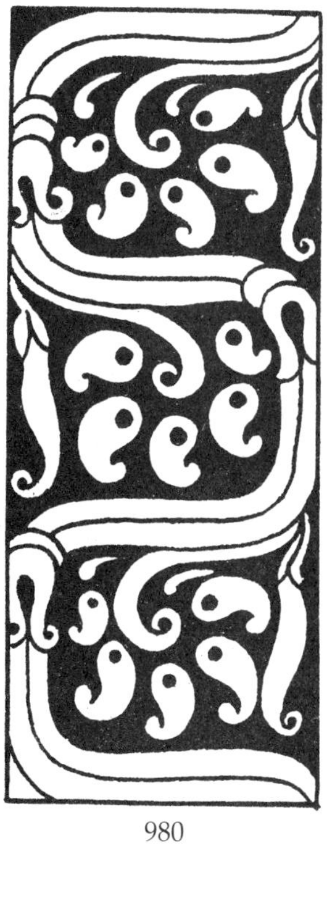

980

# Plate 122

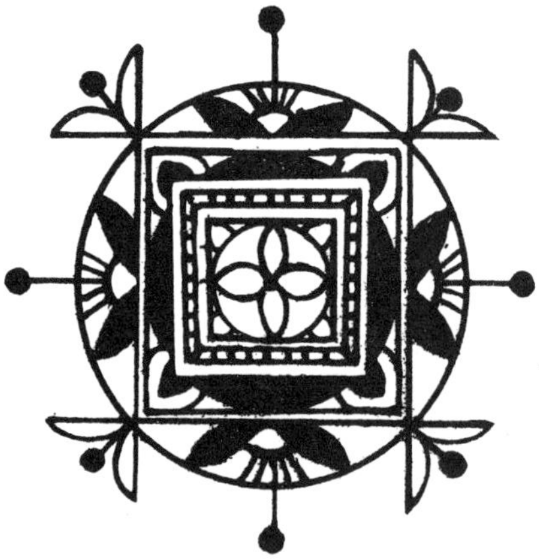

981

982

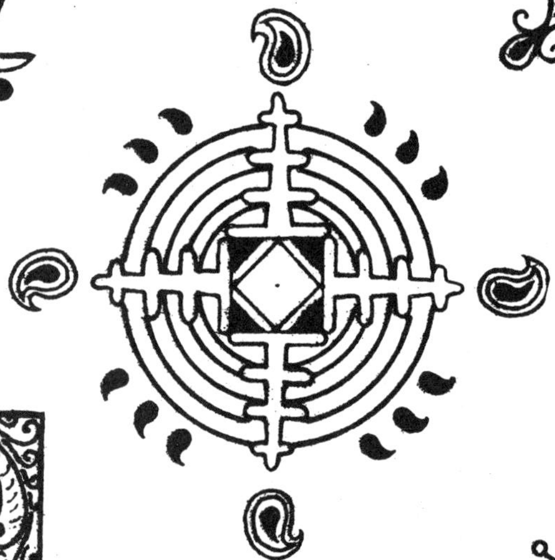

983

984

985

986

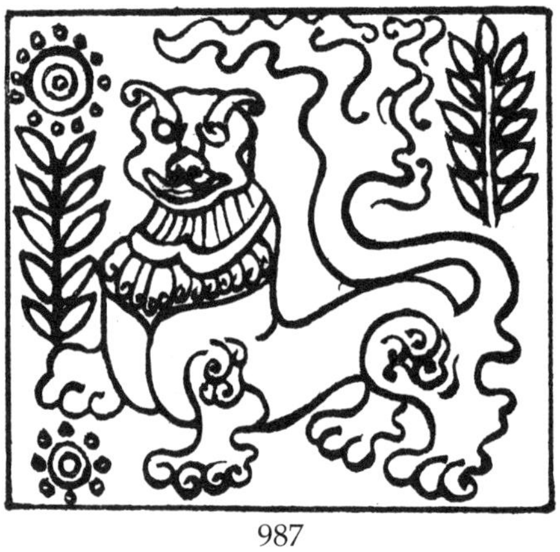

987

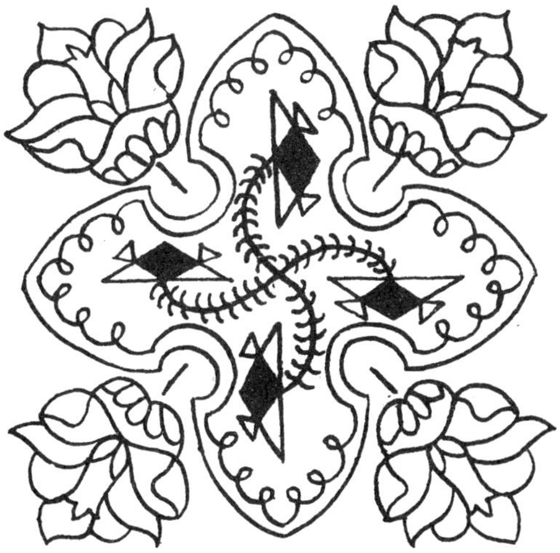

988

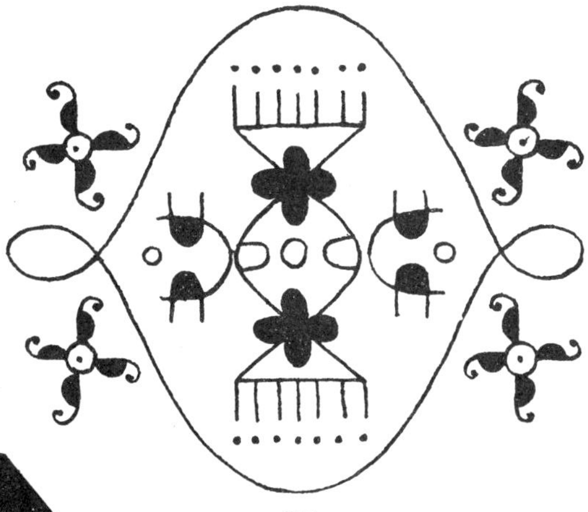

989

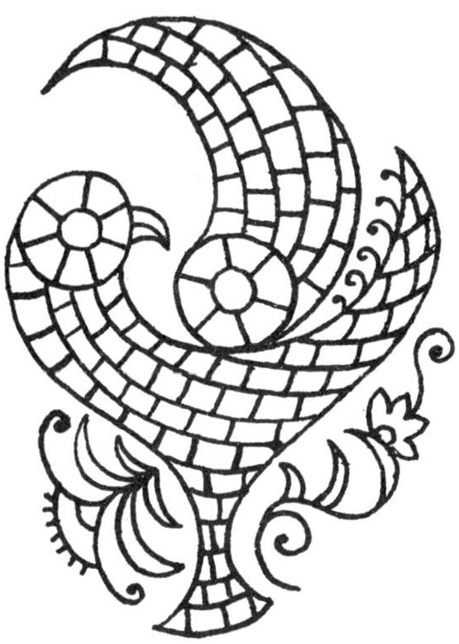

990

991

992

993

994

# Plate 124

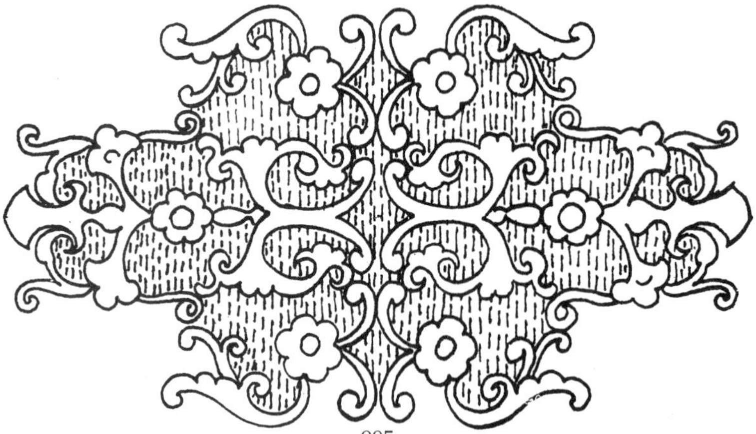

995

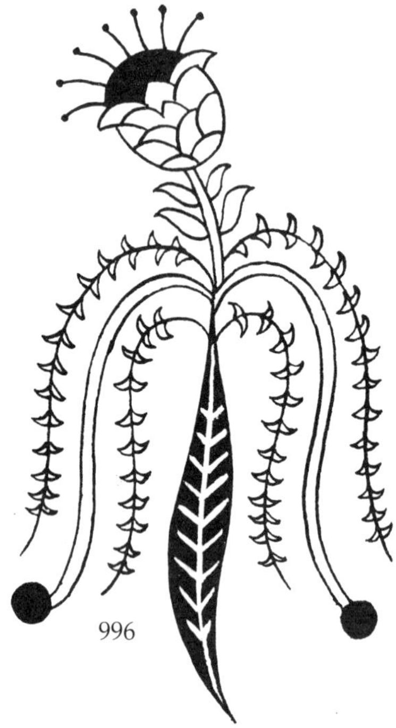

996

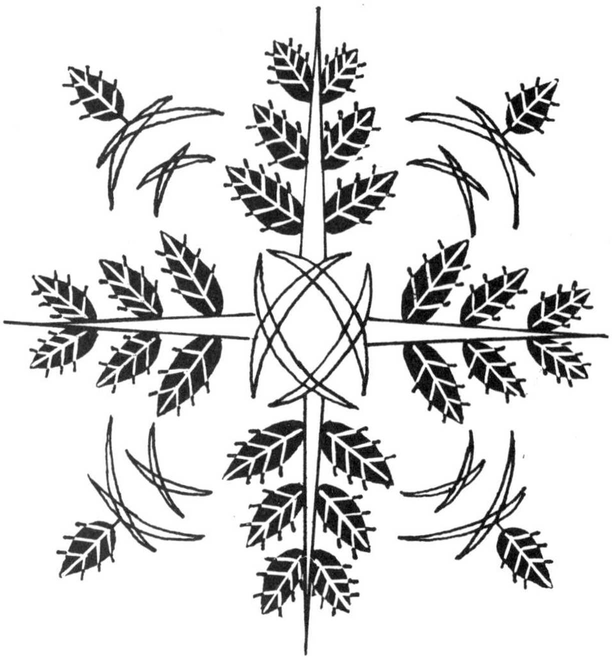

997

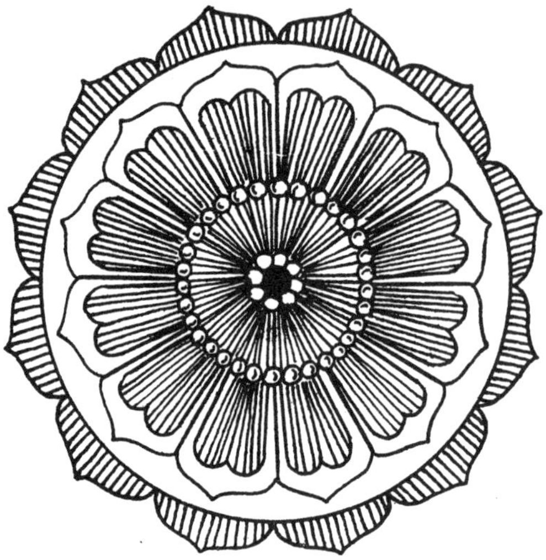

998

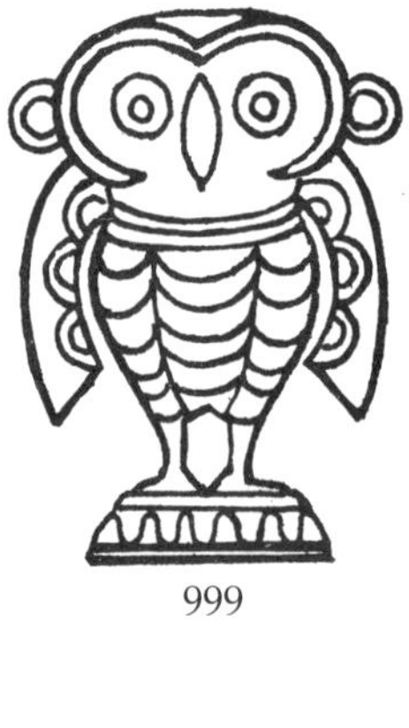

999

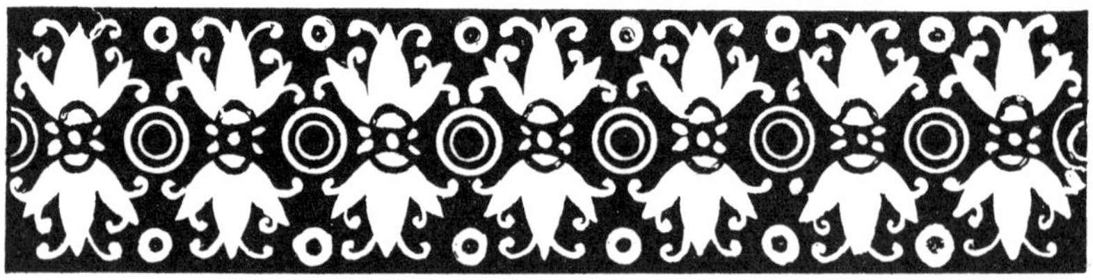

1000